HARPO SPEAKS!

by Harpo Marx

with ROWLAND BARBER

ILLUSTRATED BY SUSAN MARX

LIMELIGHT EDITIONS

Twentieth Printing, December 2017

Published by Limelight Editions (an imprint of Amadeus Press, LLC)
Forbes Boulevard, Suite 200,
Lanham, Maryland 20706, US

Website: www.rowman.com

Originally published by Bernard Geis Associates

Library of Congress Cataloging-in-Publication Data

Marx, Harpo, 1888-1964
  Harpo speaks!
  1. Marx, Harpo, 1888-1964. 2. Comedians--United States--Biogra-
phy. 3. Moving-picture actors and actresses--United States--Biography.
I. Barber, Rowland. II. Title.
PN2287.M54A3 1985   791.43'028'0924 [B]   84-25038
ISBN 0-87910-036-2

*To Bill, Alex, Jimmy, Minnie and Susan
from me with love*

Contents

HARPO SPEAKS!

CHAPTER 1

Confessions of a Non-Lady Harpist

I DON'T KNOW WHETHER my life has been a success or a failure. But not having any anxiety about becoming one instead of the other, and just taking things as they came along, I've had a lot of extra time to enjoy life.

One thing I am not now and never have been is a Celebrity. Strangers never stop me in the street and ask for my autograph. People don't recognize me out of costume. The public has never heard my voice. In this respect I'm a good deal different from my brother Groucho, who is a genuine, fourteen-karat Celebrity.

It wouldn't help to know what I look like; you still wouldn't recognize me. Have you seen the man who answers the following description?

> Little under average height. Slow and easy of movement. Eyes, green. Hair might have been brown once; now too wispy to tell. Complexion, golf-player's tan. No distinguishing features except possibly eyebrows, which are usually raised. Could indicate either bafflement or curiosity. Hard to tell which. Inconspicuous in a social gathering. Apt to sit quietly with hands spread on edge of table, smiling at anybody who passes by. Occasionally says something out of corner of mouth that nobody seems to hear. Age impossible to tell. Could be older than he looks, or prematurely mature.

11

You may think you've seen this man. He might have been the second fellow from the end at the fourth table in the group picture of the Southern Counties Grapefruit Growers Convention. He might have been the fellow you let pass ahead of you in the checkout line at the market because he was only carrying two bananas and a box of Fig Newtons. But it wouldn't have been me. I'm in the grapefruit business, but I don't go to conventions. I like to eat, but my wife Susan does the shopping.

My wife also does the cooking, and she likes to sew, and she paints with oils as a hobby. She was in show business, true, but she left it nearly thirty years ago to marry me. None of our four kids has any notion of ever going onstage. Their respective interests are musical composition, auto mechanics, rocketry and horses. We have three dogs, all mongrels.

We live a quiet country life—or did until my son Alex got his driver's license and did something to the muffler of his old Ford that made it sound like a turbo-jet.

If there is anything distinctive about me, it's the one thing the public knows least about—my voice. I still talk with an East-93rd-Street-New-York accent. The way I pronounce my name it comes out "Hoppo." And when I answer the phone I don't say "Hello," I say "Yah?"—as if I always expect to hear something pretty interesting. Usually I do.

At this point I must make a confession. There is a character who goes by the same name I do who *is* kind of a celebrity. He wears a ratty red wig and a shredded raincoat. He can't talk, but he makes idiotic faces, honks a horn, whistles, blows bubbles, ogles and leaps after blondes and acts out all kinds of hokey charades. I don't begrudge this character his fame and fortune. He worked damn hard for every cent and every curtain call he ever got. I don't begrudge him anything—because he started out with no talent at all.

If you've ever seen a Marx Brothers picture, you know the difference between him and me. When he's chasing a girl across the screen it's Him. When he sits down to play the harp, it's Me. Whenever I touched the strings of the harp, I stopped being an actor.

This Me begins to sound like an unexciting fellow, doesn't he? Maybe I am, but I've been lucky enough, in my time, to do a number of things that most people never get around to doing.

I've played piano in a whorehouse. I've smuggled secret papers out of Russia. I've spent an evening on the divan with Peggy Hopkins Joyce. I've taught a gangster mob how to play Pinchie Winchie. I've played croquet with Herbert Bayard Swope while he kept Governor Al Smith waiting on the phone. I've gambled with Nick the Greek, sat on the floor with Greta Garbo, sparred with Benny Leonard, horsed around with the Prince of Wales, played Ping-pong with George Gershwin. George Bernard Shaw has asked me for advice. Oscar Levant has played private concerts for me at a buck a throw. I have golfed with Ben Hogan and Sam Snead. I've basked on the Riviera with Somerset Maugham and Elsa Maxwell. I've been thrown out of the casino at Monte Carlo.

Flush with triumph at the poker table, I've challenged Alexander Woollcott to anagrams and Alice Duer Miller to a spelling match. I've given lessons to some of the world's greatest musicians. I've been a member of the two most famous Round Tables since the days of King Arthur—sitting with the finest creative minds of the 1920's at the Algonquin in New York, and with Hollywood's sharpest professional wits at the Hillcrest.

(Later in the book, some of these activities don't seem quite so impressive when I tell the full story. Like what I was doing on the divan with Peggy Hopkins Joyce. I was reading the funnies to her.)

The truth is, I had no business doing any of these things. I couldn't read a note of music. I never finished the second grade. But I was having too much fun to recognize myself as an ignorant upstart.

I can't remember ever having a bad meal. I've eaten in William Randolph Hearst's baronial dining room at San Simeon, at Voisin's and the Colony, and the finest restaurants in Paris. But the eating

13

place I remember best, out of the days when I was chronically half starved, is a joint that was called Max's Busy Bee. At the Busy Bee, a salmon sandwich on rye cost three cents per square foot, and for four cents more you could buy a strawberry short-cake smothered with whipped cream and a glass of lemonade. But the absolutely most delicious food I ever ate was prepared by the most inspired chef I ever knew—my father. My father had to be inspired, because he had so little to work with.

I can't remember ever having a poor night's sleep. I've slept in villas at Cannes and Antibes, at Alexander Woollcott's island hideaway in Vermont, at the mansions of the Vanderbilts and Otto H. Kahn and in the Gloversville, New York, jail. I've slept on pool tables, dressing-room tables, piano tops, bathhouse benches, in rag baskets and harp cases, and four abreast in upper berths. I have known the supreme luxury of snoozing in the July sun, on the lawn, while the string of a flying kite tickled the bottom of my feet.

I can't remember ever seeing a bad show. I've seen everything from Coney Island vaudeville to the Art Theatre in Moscow. If I'm trapped in a theatre and a show starts disappointingly, I have a handy way to avoid watching it. I fall asleep.

My only addictions—and I've outgrown them all—have been to pocket billiards, croquet, poker, bridge and black jelly beans. I haven't smoked for twenty years.

The only woman I've ever been in love with is still married to me.

My only Alcohol Problem is that I don't particularly care for the stuff.

So what do I have to confess? I do have one weakness big enough to write a book about. My weakness is people. Since I have never taken the direct route from anywhere to anywhere, I've had time to meet and listen to a lot of people. Back in the twenties, when everybody was talking at the same time, I was one of the few professional *listeners* around.

I've been asked: "When you hung out with people like George S. Kaufman, Marc Connelly, Harold Ross, Sam Behrman, Ben Hecht, Heywood Broun, F.P.A., Dorothy Parker, Ethel Barrymore,

14

Benchley, Swope and Woollcott, what in the world did *you* find to talk about?" The answer is simple. When I was around people like that, there was no use talking. I listened.

For some reason, they all accepted me. I think it was because I accepted them, not as Very Important Persons or geniuses, but as card players, pool sharks, croquet fanatics, parlor-game addicts, storytellers, or practical jokers—whatever they had the most fun doing when they weren't working.

These remarkable people are not the types the average vaudeville comic or self-taught musician is apt to hang out with. Not if he obeys the golden rule for success, that is, and doesn't dawdle or wander off in the wrong direction. Thank God I obeyed my own rules and never went anywhere by the regular route.

If you can follow me from here on out—by way of East Side saloons and hockshops, the Orpheum Circuit, Long Island estates and bordellos, an Ohio River gambling boat, a Russian border guard-post, and Metro-Goldwyn-Mayer—you'll know what I mean. You'll know why I'm thankful.

So. The time has come for me to get my kite flying, stretch out in the sun, kick off my shoes, and speak my piece. "The days of struggle are over," I should be able to say. "I can look back now and tell myself I don't have a single regret."

But I do.

Many years ago a very wise man named Bernard Baruch took me aside and put his arm around my shoulder. "Harpo, my boy," he said, "I'm going to give you three pieces of advice, three things you should always remember."

My heart jumped and I glowed with expectation. I was going to hear the magic password to a rich, full life from the master himself. "Yes, sir?" I said. And he told me the three things.

I regret that I've forgotten what they were.

CHAPTER 2

The Education of Me

A LEGEND HAS BEEN going around to the effect that I never had much schooling. Therefore it might surprise a lot of people to read the following true statement: "Harpo attended lectures at Hamilton College in Clinton, New York, for six years, was given the freedom of the campus, and was celebrated as the youngest student ever to enter a classroom in the history of that hallowed old institution."

Well, I'd better tell the whole truth. The Harpo who went to college was not me. The Harpo who went to college was a dog, a plum-colored poodle. The dog was given to a professor for adoption by Hamilton's best-known alumnus, Alexander Woollcott, who made the statement I quoted above. The legend, I'm afraid, is true. I never had much schooling. The sad fact is, I never even finished the second grade.

Yet somehow I've managed to get myself educated. I'm not the writer or scholar, for example, that Groucho Marx is. I don't pretend to be. But I can read without moving my lips, and I can hold my own in pretty fast literary company without sinking beneath the conversation. I can talk about Monet, American primitives, or Ravel and Debussy without embarrassing anybody—even myself. I like to think I'm up-to-date on politics, world affairs, the struggle for integration, and the problems of teen-agers in America.

I try to be. These things are as exciting to me as cars, clothes and tax gimmicks are to some fellows I know who went to college in person, not by proxy in the shape of a plum-colored poodle.

How I came to be educated, over the years, I don't exactly know. I only know that it didn't happen during my sojourn at New York City Public School No. 86.

When the century turned in 1900, people tried to begin the new century with a clean slate. Some people forgave old debts. Some cleaned their slates by having their names changed. Others did it by giving up rye whiskey, cuss words, or snuff. The New York City Board of Education did it by promoting Adolph Marx to the second grade.

This was a noble gesture, but it didn't work. The year and a half Adolph Marx spent in Grade Two was more of a waste of time and taxpayers' money than the year he spent drifting and dreaming through Grade One.

(Adolph is the name I was given when I was born, in New York City, in 1893. Harpo is the name I was given during a poker game twenty-five years later. During the same game my brother Leonard became "Chico," Julius became "Groucho," Milton "Gummo," and Herbert later became "Zeppo." Those handles stuck from the moment they were fastened on us. Now it's like we'd never had any other names. So we will be known all the way through these pages as Chico, Harpo, Groucho, Gummo and Zeppo.)

Anyway, my formal schooling ended halfway through my second crack at the second grade, at which time I left school the most direct way possible. I was thrown out the window.

There were two causes of this. One was a big Irish kid in my class and the other was a bigger Irish kid. I was a perfect patsy for them, a marked victim. I was small for my age. I had a high, squeaky voice. And I was the only Jewish boy in the room. The teacher, a lady named Miss Flatto, had pretty much given up on teaching me anything. Miss Flatto liked to predict, in front of the class, that I would come to no good end. This was the only matter on which the Irish kids agreed with Miss Flatto, and they saw to it that her prediction came true.

Every once in a while, when Miss Flatto left the room, the

17

Irishers would pick me up and throw me out the window, into the street. Fortunately our room was on the first floor. The drop was about eight feet—high enough for a good jolt but low enough not to break any bones.

I would pick myself up, dust myself off, and return to the class-room as soon as I was sure the teacher was back. I would explain to Miss Flatto that I had been to the toilet. I knew that if I squealed I'd get worse than a heave out the window. She must have believed I didn't have enough sense to control my organs, let alone comprehend the subjects of reading and writing. She began send-ing notes to my mother, all with the same warning: Something had better be done about straightening me out or I would be a disgrace to my family, my community, and my country.

My mother was too busy with other matters at the time to straighten me out with the public school system. For one thing, it seemed more urgent to keep my older brother Chico out of the poolroom than to keep me in the schoolroom.

So my mother appointed a delegate to go confer with Miss Flatto. That was unfortunate. The delegate was the boy friend of my cousin Polly, who was then living with us. He peddled herring in the streets, out of wooden buckets, yelling up and down the neighborhood, "Hey, best here! Best here! Best here in de verld!" Naturally, he stunk from fish; you could smell him a block away.

So one day he turned up in the middle of a class, fish buckets and all. He didn't get very far in his conference with Miss Flatto. She took one look and one smell, began to get sick, and ordered Polly's boy friend to leave the school. All the other kids in the room began to. smirk, holding their noses, and Miss Flatto did nothing to stop them.

I knew I was dead.

The two Irish boys now gave me the heave-ho every chance they got, which was three or four times a day, and Miss Flatto made me stay after school every afternoon for leaving the room so many times without permission. I can still see her finger waggling at the end of my nose, and hear her saying, "Some day you will *realize*, young man, you will *realize!*" I didn't know what she meant, but I never forgot her words.

Partly because he'd made such a fool of himself in front of my class, Polly broke off with her boy friend. I felt pretty bad about this. I also felt pretty bad around the knees and elbows from being dumped out the schoolhouse window with such regularity.

So one sunny day when Miss Flatto left the room and I was promptly heaved into the street, I picked myself up, turned my back on P. S. 86 and walked straight home, and that was the end of my formal education.

There is an interesting sidelight to this episode. On the rebound, my cousin Polly took up with a tailor, whom she soon married, congratulating herself for escaping a life that stunk of fish. Her husband remained a tailor the rest of his life. The herring peddler she jilted became successful in a series of businesses and died a very wealthy man.

I was eight years old when I was thrown out of school the last time. Home at that time was a flat in a tenement at 179 East 93rd Street, in a small Jewish neighborhood squeezed in between the Irish to the north and the Germans to the south in Yorkville.

The tenement at 179 was the first real home I can remember. Until we moved there we had lived like gypsies, never traveling far—in fact never out of the neighborhood—but always moving, haunted and pursued by eviction notices, attachments, and glinty-eyed landlord's agents. The Marxes were poor, very poor. We were always hungry. And we were numerous. But thanks to the amazing spirit of my father and my mother, poverty never made any of us depressed or angry. My memory of my earliest years is vague but pleasant, full of the sound of singing and laughter, and full of people I loved.

The less food we had, it seemed, the more people we had to feed. Nobody grumbled about this. We just worked a little harder and schemed a little harder to hustle up a soup bone or a pail of sauerkraut. There were ten mouths to feed every day at 179: five boys, from Chico down to Zeppo; cousin Polly, who'd been adopted as one of us; my mother and father, and my mother's mother and father. A lot of the time my mother's sister, Aunt Hannah, was around too. And on any given night of the week, any given number of relatives from both sides of the family might turn up, unannounced but never unwelcome.

This put all kinds of burdens on Frenchie, which was what we called my father, Sam Marx. Frenchie was the family housekeeper and cook. He was also the breadwinner. Frenchie was a tailor by trade. He was never able to own his own shop, and during the day his cutting table and sewing bench took up the whole dining room, with lengths and scraps of materials overflowing into the kitchen. At six o'clock he quit whatever he was working on, in the middle of a stitch, and stashed his profession in the hall, materials, tools, tables and all, and turned to the task of making dinner for ten or eleven or sixteen people.

This task would have been hopeless to anybody else in the world, but Frenchie always managed to put a meal on the table. With food he was a true magician. Given a couple of short ribs, a wilting cabbage, a handful of soup greens, a bag of chestnuts and a pinch of spices, he could conjure up miracles. God, how fabulous the tenement smelled when Frenchie, chopping and ladling, sniffing and stirring and tasting, and forever smiling and humming to himself, got the kitchen up to full steam!

Later I found out that Frenchie smiled and hummed not so much over his culinary artistry, but over the prospect of sneaking away to a pinochle game the minute he'd gobbled his share of dinner. Frenchie was terrible at pinochle, but he loved the game and thought he was a crackerjack player.

Unfortunately the same was true of Frenchie as a tailor. Tailoring he also loved and thought he was good at; but he was even a worse tailor than he was a pinochle player.

"Samuel Marx, Custom Tailor to the Men's Trade," he billed himself—bravely and wistfully. Frenchie was a trim and handsome little man, with twinkling brown eyes and a face that was smoothly sculptured around a permanent, thin-lipped smile. He made

20

strangers feel he was holding inside him a secret too wonderful to talk about.

Even in his most threadbare days, he managed to keep an air of elegance. His mustache was always neatly clipped, his fine, dark hair sleekly in place. Given the chance to show it, Frenchie had impeccable taste in clothes and he knew how to wear them. The trouble was, he never doubted that he could make good clothes with the same ease. To give him full credit, he was an excellent judge of color and fabric. He had a genuine feel for material. It was instinctive, like his cooking. But Frenchie also relied on feel to measure a suit (never used a tape measure), to cut a pattern (like a free-hand artist cutting silhouettes), and to sew a suit together (never bothered with a fitting).

So, when Frenchie delivered a finished job to a customer, the family waited for his return with fear and trembling. Would he return with cash or would he return with the suit? More than half the time he returned with the suit.

Periodically, when the unpaid-for suits piled up, Frenchie would pack the rejects along with a bunch of remnants (called "lappas") into two big suitcases and go off, with a shrug and his eternal smile, to peddle them door-to-door in the suburbs. At the same time, with no word of complaint, my mother would hit up her brother Al for a loan and my grandfather would gather up the kit from under his bed and take to the streets of New York to repair umbrellas.

Life had a way of going on, even when Frenchie was out on the road. But the kitchen at 179 was a cold and dreary place until he came home, with his suitcases full of fresh cabbages and ham hocks instead of suits and "lappas."

Throughout all the hungry, rugged days of my childhood, Frenchie never stopped working. He never ducked his responsibility of being the family breadwinner. He tried the best he could, at the job he stubbornly thought he could do the best. Frenchie was a loving, gentle man, who accepted everything that happened—good luck or tragedy—with the same unchangeable, sweet nature. He had no ambition beyond living and accepting life from day to day. He had only two vices: loyalty to everybody he ever knew (he

21

never had an enemy, even amongst the sharpies who fleeced him), and the game of pinochle.

I shouldn't knock Frenchie's loyalty. That's what kept our family together, come right down to it. Frenchie was born in a part of Alsace-Lorraine that had stayed loyal to Germany, even when France ruled the province. So while the official language was French, at home the Marxes spoke "Plattdeutsch," low-country German.

When the family came to America, they naturally gravitated toward immigrants who spoke the same dialect. On the upper East Side of Manhattan (on the border of Yorkville, just as Alsace-Lorraine was on the border of Germany), a sort of Plattdeutsch Society sprang up—unofficial, but tightly knit.

Anybody who spoke Plattdeutsch was okay with Frenchie, had his undying trust. And since Frenchie was one of the few tailors in the city who spoke Plattdeutsch he got a lot of business, out of sheer sentiment, that he never deserved. If it weren't for the mutual loyalty of Frenchie and his *landsmen*, the Marx brothers wouldn't have stayed under the same roof long enough to have become acquainted, let alone go forth together into show business.

The responsibility that was toughest for Frenchie was that of family disciplinarian. A stern father he was not, could not by nature be. But he never gave up trying to play the role.

Whenever I got caught stealing from a neighborhood store, it was a serious offense. (The offense to me, of course, was not stealing but being caught at it.) The guy I robbed would (loyalty again) turn me over to Frenchie instead of the cops for punishment.

Frenchie would suck in his lips like he was trying to swallow his smile, frown at me, shake his head, and say, "Boy, for what you ditt I'm going to give you. I'm going to break every bone in your botty!" Then he would march me into the hallway, so the rest of the family wouldn't have to witness the brutal scene.

There he would whip a whisk broom out of his pocket. "All right, boy," he'd say, "I'm going to *give* you!" He'd shake the whisk broom under my chin and repeat, through clenched teeth, "*I'm going to give you!*"

22

Frenchie, gamely as he tried, could never bring himself to go any farther than shaking the broom beneath my chin. He would sigh and walk back into the flat, brushing his hands together in a gesture of triumph, so the family should see that justice had been done.

I couldn't have hurt more if my father had broken every bone in my body.

Of all the people Frenchie loved and was loyal to, none was more unlike him than Minnie Schoenberg Marx, his wife, my mother. A lot has been written about Minnie Marx. She's become a legend in show business. And just about everything anybody ever said about her is true. Minnie was quite a gal.

She was a lovely woman, but her soft, doelike looks were deceiving. She had the stamina of a brewery horse, the drive of a salmon fighting his way up a waterfall, the cunning of a fox, and a devotion to her brood as fierce as any she-lion's. Minnie loved to whoop it up. She liked to be in the thick of things, whenever there was singing, storytelling, or laughter. But this was in a way deceiving too. Her whole adult life, every minute of it, was dedicated to her Master Plan.

Minnie had the ambition to carry out any plan she might have decided on, with enough left over to carry all the rest of us right along with her. Even in her gayest moments she was working—plotting and scheming all the time she was telling jokes and whooping it up.

Minnie's Plan was simply this: to put her kid brother and her five sons on the stage and make them successful. She went to work down the line starting with Uncle Al (who'd changed his name from Schoenberg to Shean), then took up, in order, Groucho, Gummo, myself, Chico and Zeppo. This was one hell of a job. What made it even tougher was the fact that only Uncle Al and Groucho wanted to be in show business in the first place, and after Groucho got a taste of the stage, he wanted to be a writer. Chico wanted to be a professional gambler. Gummo wanted to be an inventor. Zeppo wanted to be a prize fighter. I wanted to play the piano on a ferryboat.

But nobody could change Minnie's mind. Her Master Plan was carried out, by God, all down the line.

Her relationship with Frenchie, in the days when I was growing up, was more like a business partnership than the usual kind of marriage. Minnie was the Outside Man. Frenchie was the Inside Man. Minnie fought the world to work out her family's destiny. Frenchie stayed home, sewing and cooking. Minnie was the absolute boss. She made all the decisions, but Frenchie never seemed to resent this.

It was impossible for anybody to resent Minnie. She was too much fun. It was Minnie who kept our lives full of laughter, so we seldom noticed how long it was between meals in the days when we were broke.

It never occurred to us that this setup between mother and father was odd, or unnatural. We were like a family of castaways surviving on a desert island. There was no money, no prestige, no background, to help the Marxes make their way in America. It was us against the elements, and each of us found his own way to survive. Frenchie took to tailoring. Chico took to the poolroom. I took to the streets. Minnie held us all together while she plotted our rescue.

The only tradition in our family was our lack of tradition.

Minnie's mother, Fanny Schoenberg, died soon after we moved to East 93rd Street, but Grandpa Schoenberg remained a figure in the household until he finally resigned from living at the age of one century, in 1919. Grandpa was therefore not classified as a Relative. He was Family.

A Relative was anybody who was named Schoenberg or Marx or who spoke Plattdeutsch who turned up in our flat at dinnertime and caused the portions on our plates to diminish. A lot of suspicious-looking strangers became Relatives, but nobody was ever turned away.

Most welcome of all was Uncle Al. A few years back, Uncle Al had been a pants-presser who couldn't hold a job because he kept organizing quartets and singing on company time. Now, thanks to Minnie, his loving sister, personal manager, booking agent and publicist, Al Shean was a headliner in vaudeville. He was our Celebrity, and he played the part to the hilt.

Once a month, Uncle Al came to visit, decked out in expensive flannels and broadcloth, matching fedora and spats, and ten-dollar shoes. He sparkled with rings and stickpins and glowed with the scent of cologne. Frenchie would appraise the materials in Uncle Al's suit and shirt, clucking a bit critically over the tailoring job, while Uncle Al talked with Grandpa in German.

Then Minnie would switch the language to English and the subject to bookings and billings. After a while, Uncle Al would give in to Groucho, who'd been pestering him without letup, and sing for us. This was what Groucho had been waiting a month for. At last, as he got ready to go, Uncle Al would give each of us boys a brand-new dime. This was what Chico had been waiting a month for.

By the time Uncle Al had made his last good-bye, in the hallway, Chico would be two blocks away in the poolroom.

As Al Shean got more famous he raised his monthly bonus to two dimes instead of one, and then went up to an incredible two bits apiece. A whole quarter! Five shows at the nickelodeon! A complete set of second-hand wagon wheels and axles! Twenty-five games of pool!

When I earned or hustled a quarter on my own, I felt guilty if I didn't kick part of it into the family kitty, but not with Uncle Al money. Uncle Al money was pure spending money, whether the soup pot was empty or not.

While the Schoenbergs outnumbered and outtalked the Marxes in the Relative department, Frenchie's side of the family had its share of big shots. Cousin Sam, for example. Sam Marx ran an auction house on 58th Street, in the fashionable area near the Grand Army Plaza, and he was a wheel in Tammany Hall.

Sam's younger brother, Cousin Max, I didn't know so well. He was a theatrical tailor and a good one, so Frenchie was leery of talking shop with him and preferred to remain aloof. I thought "Max Marx" was about the dandiest name a man could have, with the main exception of "James J. Jeffries."

Near the corner of 116th Street and Lenox Avenue, in New York, there is—or was, last I knew—an alleyway called "Marx Place." It's commonly believed to have been named after Socialist Karl. This is not true. It was named after Cousin Sam. Cousin Sam died while Tammany still controlled city government, street-naming, and other such businesses.

The odd-ball relatives on Frenchie's side seemed to come in pairs. My father used to talk with a mysterious kind of reverence about two great-aunts named Fratschie and Frietschie. To me, any two dames named Fratschie and Frietschie had to be a high-wire act or a dancing team. But no. Their act was being the oldest twins in the history of Alsace-Lorraine and dying on the same day at the age of 102.

Oddest of all were two little women, vaguely related to Frenchie, who came to call once or twice a year. They were the only visitors I can remember who never joined us for dinner. They stayed in the kitchen, where they talked to Frenchie in Plattdeutsch, keeping their voices down so nobody else could hear what they were saying. Both of the women wore black skirts down to the floor, and white gloves which they never took off. When the stove wasn't turned on they sat on the stove. When the stove was on, they stood up during their visit. They would leave shaking their heads. Whenever I asked Frenchie who they were, he would only shake his head. I think they came to report who had died that he should know about. I never saw him so desperate to get to a pinochle game as he was after the two little women came to call. Pinochle was liquor and opium to Frenchie, his only way of escape.

So anyhow, at the age of eight, I was through with school and at liberty. I didn't know what to do with myself. One thing was certain: I'd never go near P. S. 86 or come within range of Miss Flatto's wagging finger again. School was okay for Chico, who was in the fifth grade and a whiz at arithmetic, and Groucho, who was knocking off 100's in the first grade, but not for me. I was good only at daydreaming, a subject they didn't give credit for in the New York City school system.

My parents accepted my being at liberty like they accepted every other setback in their lives—no remorse, no regrets. Minnie was too busy engineering Uncle Al's career to have much time for me. She felt she had done her duty anyway, by sending Polly's herring-peddler boy friend around to the school. Frenchie took the news of my quitting with a shrug and a nodding smile. The shrug indicated his disappointment. The smile indicated his pleasure; now I could be his assistant on his next "sales trip" to New Jersey.

I never knew for sure, but I suppose the truant officer must have come around to our flat looking for me. If he did, I know what happened. When he knocked we assumed it was the landlord's agent, come to collect the rent, and we all ran to our hiding places and kept quiet until we heard the footsteps go back down the stairs outside.

As for myself, I never doubted I had done the right thing when I walked away from the open window of P. S. 86, never to return. School was all wrong. It didn't teach anybody how to exist from day to day, which was how the poor had to live. School prepared you for Life—that thing in the far-off future—but not for the World, the thing you had to face today, tonight, and when you woke up in the morning with no idea of what the new day would bring.

When I was a kid there really was no Future. Struggling through one twenty-four-hour span was rough enough without brooding about the next one. You could laugh about the Past, because you'd been lucky enough to survive it. But mainly there was only a Present to worry about.

Another complaint I had was that school taught you about holidays you could never afford to celebrate, like Thanksgiving and Christmas. It didn't teach you about the real holidays like St.

Patrick's Day, when you could watch a parade for free, or Election Day, when you could make a giant bonfire in the middle of the street and the cops wouldn't stop you. School didn't teach you what to do when you were stopped by an enemy gang—when to run, when to stand your ground. School didn't teach you how to collect tennis balls, build a scooter, ride the El trains and trolleys, hitch onto delivery wagons, own a dog, go for a swim, get a chunk of ice or a piece of fruit—all without paying a cent.

School didn't teach you which hockshops would give you dough without asking where you got your merchandise, or how to shoot pool or bet on a poker hand or where to sell junk or how to find sleeping room in a bed with four other brothers.

School simply didn't teach you how to be poor and live from day to day. This I had to learn for myself, the best way I could. In the streets I was, according to present-day standards, a juvenile delinquent. But by the East Side standards of 1902, I was an honor student.

Somehow, between home and out ("out" being any place in the city except our flat), I learned to read. While Groucho sweated over copybook phrases like "This is a Cat—O, See the Cat!" and "A Penny Saved Is a Penny Earned," I was mastering alphabet and vocabulary through phrases like "This water for horses only," "Excelsior Pool Parlor, One Cent a Cue," "Saloon and Free Lunch —No Minors Admitted," "Keep Off the Grass," and words printed on walls and sidewalks by older kids which may not be printed here.

I learned to tell time by the only timepiece available to our family, the clock on the tower of Ehret's Brewery at 93rd Street and Second Avenue, which we could see from the front window, if Grandpa hadn't pulled the shade. Grandpa, who was the last stronghold of orthodox religion in the family, often used the front room to say his prayers and study the Torah. When he did, and the shade was drawn, we had to do without the brewery clock, and time ceased to exist.

I've had, ever since then, the feeling that when the shades are pulled, or the sun goes down, or houselights dim, time stops. Perhaps that's why I've never had any trouble sleeping, and why I've always been an early riser. When the sun is out and the shade is up, the brewery clock is back in business. Time is in again, and something might be going on that I'd hate to miss.

Weekdays, when Minnie was out hustling bookings for Uncle Al, Frenchie was busy over his cutting table, Chico and Groucho were in school, and Gummo and Zeppo were down playing on the stoop, Grandpa and I spent a lot of time together.

Sometimes he'd tell me stories from the Haggadah, lecture me from the Torah, or try to teach me prayers. But his religious instruction, I'm afraid, was too close to schoolwork to interest me, and he didn't accomplish any more with me than Miss Flatto did. Still, without realizing it, I completed a course. From Grandpa I learned to speak German. (I tried to teach Grandpa English, but gave up on it.)

When he was feeling chipper and the shade was up, Grandpa used to perform magic for me. He conjured pennies out of his beard, and out of my nose and ears, and made me practice the trick of palming coins. Then he would stoke up his pipe and tell me about the days when he and Grossmutter Fanny toured the German spas and music halls. Grandpa performed as a ventriloquist and a magician, in the old country, while Grandma played the harp for dancing after he did his act.

I hadn't known Grandma too well before she died, but I felt she was never far away, for Grandma's old harp stood always in a corner of Grandpa's room. It was a half-size harp. Its strings were gone. Its frame was warped. All that remained of its old luster were a few flakes of golden dandruff. But to me it was a thing of beauty. I tried to imagine what it must have sounded like when Grandma played it, but I couldn't. I had never heard anybody play a harp. My head was full of other kinds of music—the patter songs of Uncle Al, the bagpipes of St. Patrick's Day, the drums

29

and bugles of Election Day, the calliope on the Central Park carousel, zithers heard through the swinging doors of Yorkville beer gardens, the concertina the blind man played on the North Beach excursion boat. But I'd never heard a harp.

I could see Grandma with the shining instrument on her lap, but in my daydreams no sound came forth when her hands touched the strings.

I made a resolution, one of the few I can remember making. I was going to get a job and save my money and take the harp to a harp place and have it strung and find out at last what kind of music it made.

When I did earn my first wages, however, I found more urgent ways of spending the dough. It was to be nearly fifteen years before I plucked my first harp string. I was not disappointed. It was a thrill worth saving.

So at any rate, Grandpa, who taught me German and magic, was my first real teacher. My second teacher furthered my education in a much more practical way. This was my brother Chico.

My brother Chico was only a year and a half older than me, but he was advanced far beyond his age in the ways of the world. He had great self-confidence, like Minnie, and like her he rushed in where Frenchie or I would fear to tread.

I was flattered when people said I was the image of Chico. I guess I was. We were both of us shrimps compared to the average galoots in the neighborhood. We were skinny, with peaked faces, big eyes, and mops of wavy, unruly hair. Pop was no better at cutting our hair than he was at cutting material for a suit.

But the resemblance ended with our haircuts. Chico was something of a mathematical genius, with an amazing mind for figures. (Later he developed a mind for nonmathematical figures too. That was how he came to be nicknamed "Chico"—which was meant to be "Chicko," the way we always pronounced it.)

Chico was quick of tongue and he had a flair for mimicking accents. In a tight spot he could pass himself off as Italian, Irish, German, or first-generation Jewish, whichever was most useful in the scrape he happened to be in. I, on the other hand, being painfully conscious of my squeaky voice, was not much of a talker. Not to be totally outdone by Chico, I took to imitating faces and aping the way people walked.

The imitation that gave me the most trouble was Chico himself. He used to walk the streets at a steady trot, head and shoulders thrust ahead, unmistakably a young man who knew where he was going. I practiced walking like Chico for hours. But I never could master his look of total concentration. I just didn't have it under the haircut.

When I quit P. S. 86 I still saw very little of Chico. He never came home directly from school. If he did show up for dinner, he would vanish as soon as he'd eaten. He was conducting some very important research, to extend his knowledge of arithmetic in useful ways. He was learning how to bet on horse races and prize fights and how to play poker, pinochle and klabiash, by kibitzing the action in the back room of a cigar store on Lexington Avenue. He was learning the laws of probability by observing the neighborhood floating crap game as it camped and decamped from cellar to roof and roof to cellar, one roll of the dice ahead of the cops. And he was learning the laws of physics by noting the action and reaction of spherical solids in motion at the Excelsior East Side Billiard Parlor.

When he turned twelve, Chico decided he knew all he had to know about these applied sciences, and he quit school too. He also quit doing research, kibitzing and observing, and got into the action. He has never been without a piece of some kind of action since then and never will for the rest of his days.

Chico was a good teacher, and for him I was a willing student. In a short time he taught me how to handle a pool cue, how to play cards and how to bet on the dice. I memorized the odds against rolling a ten or four the hard way, against filling a flush in pinochle or a straight in poker. I learned basic principles, like "Never go against the odds, at any price," and "Never shoot dice on a blanket." I learned how to spot pool sharks and crooked dealers, and how to detect loaded dice.

Unfortunately, we couldn't raise any action at home. Frenchie was too busy during the day, and his nighttime pinochle game was not open to kids. Grandpa's only game was Skat. We tried to convert Groucho to cards, but we couldn't. Groucho was already turning into a bookworm at the age of eight, and he sniffed at games of chance as being naïve and childish.

There was no place to go but out for the right kind of action. The catch to this was that it took money to get into a game, and more money to stay in a game if your luck was temporarily running slow.

To me there was only one solution. We had to find jobs and earn some money.

Chico thought this was the nuttiest idea he'd ever heard. "You don't *earn* mazuma," he said. "You *hustle* it."

Our first joint promotion, to hustle some scratch for pool and craps, was the Great Cuckoo Clock Bonanza of 1902.

All his life Chico has had an uncanny talent for turning up prospects. It was he who turned up the producer who first put us on Broadway, and made us nationally famous. It was Chico who later turned up the producer—Irving Thalberg—who put us into Grade-A movies. Anyway, the first prospect I can remember Chico turning up was a novelty shop on 86th Street that was having a sale on miniature cuckoo clocks.

These cuckoo clocks had no working cuckoos (the birds were painted on) but they had the genuine Black Forest look, they kept time, and they were on sale for only twenty cents apiece. We had just enough money between us to go into business, since Uncle Al had been to visit the night before, and we still had our Uncle Al dimes.

Chico bought a clock. We got fifty cents for it in a hockshop down at Third and 63rd. Thirty cents profit. We went back and bought two clocks, pawned them for four bits apiece. Chico said business was now too good for me to remain a silent partner. I should start hocking clocks too. So off I went, with my share of the inventory.

I didn't do so well. Turned out that every hockshop I went to Chico had just been to. We looked so much alike that the pawnbrokers thought I was the same kid trying to unload more hot goods, and they wouldn't deal with me.

Chico then said he'd take care of the hockshops, and I should work on people up in the neighborhood. Early the next morning, I took a clock and gathered up my courage and went to the office of the ice works on Third Avenue. The manager there was a friendly guy, who winked whenever the loader chipped off wedges of ice for us kids. He seemed like an ideal customer.

"Cuckoo clock for sale," I said to the manager, trying to sound self-assured, like Chico. "Good bargain. Guaranteed." I don't know why the word "guaranteed" popped out. I must have been carried away by what was, for me, a rare burst of eloquence. So the ice works manager wanted to know how long the clock was guaranteed to run on a winding. Whereupon I heard myself saying, as I began to sweat, "Eight hours."

"All right," he said. "Wind 'er up. If she's still running eight hours from now I'll buy her."

I pulled the chain that wound the clock. I stood in a corner of the office, out of the way, holding the clock, waiting and praying. It was a torturous battle of nerves. Every time the manager turned his back, I gave the chain a little pull to keep the clock wound tight. Along about lunchtime, he suspected what I was doing, and caught me with my hand on the chain with a swift, unexpected look. He took the clock and hung it on the wall, without a word.

At two-thirty, the clock ran down and died. The manager took it off the wall and handed it to me, still without a word. When I ran out of the office, I could hear him behind me, slapping his leg and laughing his head off.

Those were the most grueling six hours I had ever spent and my net profit was, in round figures, zero. I got home to find that Chico's net profit on the clock deal was $11.10. I was ashamed to

33

ask for any more than my original dime back. But Chico insisted I take half the loot—on one condition. He would borrow it and double it for me in a crap game.

And damned if he didn't that same night. By bedtime the total capital of the Marx Cuckoo Clock Corporation was $29.90. Chico counted out my share and gave it to me. I had never touched such a fabulous pile of raw cash before in my life. But I still felt lousy about the ice works fiasco, and I pushed the money back to Chico. "You keep it," I said. "Double it again."

The next day he dropped the whole wad in a pinochle game. Chico said this should be a lesson to me. Trying to redouble my money was going against the odds. Too bad I had to learn the hard way. Next time I would know better.

I never did get my dime back.

There was no hope of having spending-type money in my pocket until Uncle Al's next visit, which would be a long time off, not until after the High Holidays were over and Grandpa lifted the shade and came out of the front room.

Such was my basic education in the Economics of Free Enterprise.

"Today I am a man!" At thirteen I am *bar mitzvah*—graduating not only to manhood but to derbyhood. Not long afterwards I had my first taste of life in the raw, when I went to work for a certain Mrs. Schang (see below).

IDAY, AUGUST 2, 1907 — FOURTEEN PAGES

i Judge Wil—
rt man were
Zeltner, friend
sited Pushcart
rtson, who had
iten over in a
to Whitman.
The first two

ith keeping a
. Twenty-sixth
and ball was
Meyer Eisen-

a Lee Schmidt,
is just "John
rs," began to
the iron rail-
ience from the
bridge.
ded Gen. Bing-
fighting every
put out. He
ever soberer in
ide the Court
brought back
bench its en-
rest deal.
iae. Magistrate
ows," be said
lawy—"

that the Night
ellest opportu-
nt to "soldier"
ghts. They can
points out and
r night getting
t. In one way
policemen, it is

ontinues much
Commissioner
e more men or
go unpoliced as
needed it was
One Hundredth
that seven men

that, and then went up to the room to
find all her jewels, except the three chil-
aren, had disappeared.

INDICTED AS BURGLAR GANG.

27 Charges Against Woman and Three Men Who Robbed Long Island Homes.

Special to The New York Times.

MINEOLA, L. I., Aug. 1.—Fourteen indictments charging burglary and grand
larceny were found by the Nassau County
Grand Jury to-day against August Van
Fehrig, alias Luckner, leader of the gang
of burglars that robbed more than twenty
houses in this neighborhood recently,
cleaning up at least $30,000. Eleven in-
dictments charging the same crimes were
found against Christopher Schang, 19 years
old, a member of the gang, and two indictments for receiving stolen goods were
returned against his aged mother, Mrs.
Alma Schang. Morris Belkowitz, another
member of the gang, was indicted on
three counts for burglary.

When the prisoners were brought into
court before County Judge Jackson for
pleading, Mrs. Schang, who had to be
supported by Sheriff Foster, suddenly
screamed and fell fainting to the floor.
She was carried back to the jail unconscious.

Van Fehrig and young Schang pleaded
not guilty, and will be tried to-morrow.
Belkowitz pleaded guilty, and will be
sentenced Saturday, when Mrs. Schang
will be brought up to plead again.

on. She wa
cian apparel
first time.
sh ly to
him struggl
trying to st
A moment
saw the train
ing Dr. Gal
through the
clothing alre
gasoline whi
broke.
After Mr. C
Van Etten a
scene short
curred, were
tioned conce
money whic
stolen from 1
Their testi
had seen no
the body wa
inquiry at
after the ina
ments that
had been off
cently was
bank official
connected w
to give name

MEND

Newark Su
Foot

With hi
neck as the

Minnie and Frenchie, my mother and father, looking as I remember them best. This was taken outside of Chicago, around the time of World War I. Below: Chico and I were often mistaken for twins when we were young, which led to no end of collusion and confusion.

HARPO

CHICO

Culver Service

The Four Nightingales, shortly after I was shanghaied into show business and made my calamitous debut at Coney Island. Top to bottom: Groucho, me, Gummo, Lou Levy.

Groucho leads the Six Mascots in *"Ist das nicht ein Schnitzelbank?"* I'm at the keyboard. The "girls" are Aunt Hannah (*left*) and Minnie. Below: the *School Days* troupe hits Waukegan. That's "Patsy Brannigan" third from right, first row. With my switch to comedy, Groucho (second from left, standing) was converted to straight man.

The Marx Brothers become men-about-Broadway when *I'll Say She Is* opens in 1924. Seated: Groucho. Standing: me, Zeppo, Chico. If I look a little dazed, it's because I just came from a twenty-hour poker session at a strange hotel called the Algonquin.

"Napoleon scene" from *I'll Say She Is*. Don't ask what the scene was all about—we didn't even know what the title of the show meant. In the role of Josephine is Lotta Miles.

Pancho Marx, in *Cocoanuts*.

Animal Crackers, our third Broadway hit. It was horseplay like this that drove Gummo back to civilian life and into the dress business.

Alexander Woollcott, the Emperor of Neshobe Island. "In a snood mood" was Aleck's own caption for this shot.

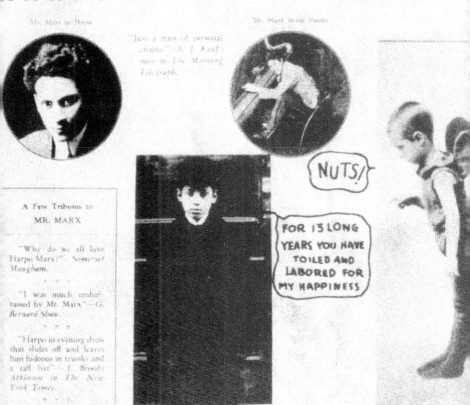

This was the stationery Aleck had made up for me after our summer on the Riviera. Figure at right is Master Alexander Woollcott, age four, in the role of Puck.

Richard Carver Wood

Two croquemaniacs at large, on Neshobe Island. The "blimp at a mooring mast" is Aleck, lining up a shot. The disgusted observer, obviously getting shellacked, is me.

My dancing partner on the Neshobe dock is Irene Castle. In critics'
row are Alfred Lunt, Aleck, and Lynn Fontanne. Below: Basking in
the Vermont sun with (left to right) Aleck, Neysa McMein, Alfred
Lunt and Beatrice Kaufman.

Richard Carver Wood

While Charlie Lederer kib-
itzes, I take on Aleck at
cribbage. Trying to beat
Woollcott at cribbage was
the one lost cause in the life
of Butch Miller (*right*),
more widely known as
"Alice Duer" Miller.

Richard Carver Wood

In the Garden of Allah, Hollywood, flanked by four other refugees from the Algonquin. They are, left to right, Art Samuels, Charlie Mac-Arthur, Dorothy Parker, and Aleck Woollcott.

The Four Imposters. Richard Rodgers, Justine Johnson, George Gershwin (as Groucho) and Jules Glaenzer at a New York costume party.

George S. Kaufman plays a sticky wicket. Character in background obviously suspects he's trying to cheat.

CHAPTER 3

Adrift in Grandpa's Democracy

IN A SHORT TIME, by brother Chico was far out of my class as a sporting blood. I wasn't wise enough or nervy enough to keep up with him. Chico settled into a routine, dividing his working day between cigar store and poolroom, and latching onto floating games in his spare time, and I drifted into the streets.

Life in the streets was a tremendous obstacle course for an undersized kid like me. The toughest obstacles were kids of other nationalities. The upper East Side was subdivided into Jewish blocks (the smallest area), Irish blocks, and German blocks, with a couple of Independent Italian states thrown in for good measure. That is, the cross streets were subdivided. The north-and-south Avenues—First, Second, Third and Lexington—belonged more to the city than the neighborhood. They were neutral zones. But there was open season on strangers in the cross streets.

If you were caught trying to sneak through a foreign block, the first thing the Irishers or Germans would ask was, "Hey, kid! What Streeter?" I learned it saved time and trouble to tell the truth. I was a 93rd Streeter, I would confess.

"Yeah? What block 93rd Streeter?"

"Ninety-third between Third and Lex." That pinned me down. I was a Jew.

The worst thing you could do was run from Other Streeters. But if you didn't have anything to fork over for ransom you were just as dead. I learned never to leave my block without some kind of boodle in my pocket—a dead tennis ball, an empty thread spool, a penny, anything. It didn't cost much to buy your freedom; the gesture was the important thing.

It was all part of the endless fight for recognition of foreigners in the process of becoming Americans. Every Irish kid who made a Jewish kid knuckle under was made to say "Uncle" by an Italian, who got his lumps from a German kid, who got his insides kicked out by his old man for street fighting and then went out and beat up an Irish kid to heal his wounds. "I'll teach *you!*" was the threat they passed along, Irisher to Jew to Italian to German. Everybody was trying to teach everybody else, all down the line. This is still what I think of when I hear the term "progressive education."

There was no such character as "the kindly cop on the beat" in New York in those days. The cops were sworn enemies. By the same token we, the street kids, were the biggest source of trouble for the police. Individually and in gangs we accounted for most of the petty thievery and destruction of property on the upper East Side. And since we couldn't afford to pay off the cops in the proper, respectable Tammany manner, they hounded us, harassed us, chased us, and every chance they got, happily beat the hell out of us.

One way, the only way, that all of us kids stuck together regardless of nationality was in our cop-warning system. Much as I loathed and feared the Mickie gang or the Bohunk gang, I'd never hesitate to give them the highsign if I spotted a copper headed their way. They'd do the same for me and the other 93rd Streeters.

The cops had their system, too. If a patrolman came upon a gang fight or a front-stoop crap game and needed reinforcements in a hurry, he'd bang his nightstick on the curb. This made a sharp *whoinnng* that could be heard by cops on other beats throughout the precinct, and they'd come a-running from all directions, closing in a net around the point the warning came from.

In my time I was grabbed, nabbed, chewed out and shin-whacked by the cops, but never arrested. This may sound miraculous, considering all the kinds of trouble I was able to get into, but it wasn't. My Uncle Sam the auctioneer, don't forget, was a wheel in Tammany Hall. Nephews of men in the Organization did not get arrested.

For another thing, the cops went mostly for the gangs, the most conspicuous targets, and I was not a gang boy. I was a lone wolf. This made me, in turn, more conspicuous to the gangs. Gang boys couldn't tolerate loners. They called me a "queer" and worse. Today, I guess, a kid like me would get all kinds of special attention from the authorities. They'd call me an "antisocial nonconformist"—and worse.

So my pleasures had to be secret ones. I couldn't even fly pigeons from the roof of my own house. Every time I set out a baited cage to catch some birds, the cage would be smashed or stolen. I wanted desperately to have a pet. Once I brought home a stray puppy, and fixed a nest for him in the basement of 179. I had him for exactly a week. As soon as he got used to his new home he felt frisky and began to bark. Some kids heard him and promptly stole him.

The janitor of our tenement, an elderly Bavarian plagued with corns and carbuncles, wouldn't protect my pets. He had a running feud with my family because our garbage pails were full of holes. Every time they went down the dumbwaiter for him to dump, the janitor would mutter and curse and yell up the shaft, "Hey, up dere! Hey! Dem's got *leaks* on!"

I took to spending a lot of time in Central Park, four blocks to the west, the park being a friendly foreign country. It was safe territory for lone wolves, no matter what Streeters we were.

Summers I hung around the tennis courts. I loved to watch the game, and there was always the chance I could hustle myself a tennis ball. In the wintertime the park was not so inviting, unless there'd been a snowfall or a good freeze. When there was snow on the ground I'd hustle a dishpan somewhere ("hustle" being a polite

37

word for steal), and go sliding in the park. This was a risky pleasure. A dishpan in good condition was worth five cents cash from a West Side junk dealer, and I had more than one pan swiped out from under me by bigger kids.

After a freeze they would hoist the Ice Flag in Central Park, which told the city the pond was okay for skating. Nobody was happier to see the flag than I was. I was probably the best single-foot skater in New York City.

Our family's total sports equipment was one ice skate, which had belonged to Grandma, and which Grandpa kept as a memento, like the old harp. And as the harp had no strings, the skate had no straps. I had to improvise with twine, rope, old suspenders, elastic bands, whatever I could find.

I spent many hours on the frozen pond in Central Park, skating gimpily around the edge of the ice on my one left-foot skate. I spent many more hours sitting on the ice, freezing my bottom where my pants weren't patched, tying and splicing and winding, in the endless struggle to keep the skate lashed to my foot.

Oddly enough, winter had fewer hardships for me than summer did. I could always find a warm spot somewhere when it was cold. But when the city was hot, it was hot through and through, and there was no cool spot to be found.

The only relief was temporary, like a chunk of ice from the loading platform of the ice works. That was a blessing to hold and suck on, but it didn't last long. What to do then? Only one thing to do then—go for a swim in the East River. But the way we had to swim, off the docks, was exhausting and we couldn't stay very long in the water.

You can always spot a guy who grew up poor on the East Side by watching him go for a swim. When he gets in a pool he will automatically start off with a shallow kind of breast stroke, as if he were pushing away some invisible, floating object. This was a stroke you had to use when you jumped in the East River. It was the only way you could keep the sewage and garbage out of your face.

One way of keeping your mind off the heat was making horsehair rings. We used to sneak into the brewery stables and cut big hanks of hair from the horses' tails, then braid them into rings. Horsehair

38

rings were not only snazzy accessories to wear, three or four to a finger, but they were also negotiable. They could be swapped for marbles or Grover Cleveland buttons, and they were handy as ransom when you were ambushed by an enemy gang.

Then, suddenly one summer, rings and marbles became kid stuff to me. I found out how to use the city transportation system for free, and I was no longer a prisoner of the neighborhood. My life had new horizons. I, a mere mortal, could now go forth and behold the Gods in Valhalla—which is to say, the New York Giants in the Polo Grounds.

Trolleys were the easiest way to travel without paying. You just hopped on board after a car had started up, and kept dodging the ticket taker. If the ticket taker caught up with you, you got off and hopped on the next trolley to come along. It was more sporting to hang on the outside of the car, but you took a chance of being swatted off by a cop.

It wasn't so easy with elevated trains. You couldn't get on an El train without giving a ticket or transfer to the ticket chopper at the platform gate. To swindle the ticket chopper took a good deal of ingenuity, involving old transfers, chewing-gum cards (which happened to be the same size as tickets), some fancy forgery—and for me, thanks to Grandpa's training—sleight of hand.

Once a year the city would change its system of tickets and transfers, trying to cut down on the number of free riders. But they never came up with a system that couldn't somehow be solved by us kids.

Thus I was now a man-about-town. In my travels I found out, in the summer of 1903, how to watch the Giants play for free. That was the only sure way to beat the heat in New York. When John J. McGraw and his noble warriors took the field in the Polo Grounds, all the pains and complaints of the loyal fan faded away, and he sweltered in blissful contentment.

I was a loyal fan but I could never afford, naturally, the price of admission to the Polo Grounds. Then I discovered a spot on Coogan's Bluff, a high promontory behind the Polo Grounds, from which there was a clear view of the ballpark. Well, a clear view—yes, but clear only of the outside wall of the grandstand, a section of the bleachers, and one narrow, tantalizing wedge of the playing field.

So to tell the truth, I didn't really watch the Giants. I watched *a* Giant—the left fielder.

When the ball came looping or bounding into my corner of the field, I saw real live big-league baseball. The rest of the time—which was most of the time—I watched a tiny man in a white or gray uniform standing motionless on a faraway patch of grass.

Other kids collected pictures of Giants such as McGraw, McGinnity and Matthewson. Not me. I was forever faithful to Sam Mertes, undistinguished left fielder, the only New York Giant I ever saw play baseball.

Eventually I came to forgive Sam for all the hours he stood around, waiting for the action to come his way. It must have been just as frustrating for him down on the field as it was for me up on the bluff. It was easy for pitchers or shortstops to look flashy. They took lots of chances. My heart was with the guy who was given the fewest chances to take, the guy whose hope and patience never dimmed. Sam Mertes, I salute you! In whatever Valhalla you're playing now, I pray that only right-handed pull-hitters come to bat, and the ball comes sailing your way three times in every inning.

Much as I ran away from it every chance I got, the home neighborhood was not altogether a dreary slum. It had its share of giants too, men and women who belonged to the Outside World, who brought glitter and excitement into the lives of the rest of us East Siders.

Such a luminary was Mr. Jergens, who ran the ice-cream parlor around the corner on Third Avenue. Mr. Jergens built and operated the first automobile in the neighborhood, a jaunty little electric runabout. When the runabout came cruising through our street, older kids would jump up and down and throw their caps under the car, yelling, "Get a horse!"

If Mr. Jergens was disturbed by the jeering mobs, he never showed it. He drove straight on, leaning over the tiller, which he held with a death grip, squinting at the horizon of Lexington Avenue like Christopher Columbus sailing for the New World.

I was one of the privileged few in the neighborhood who got to touch the runabout. Mr. Jergens had ordered a suit from Frenchie, and I went along when he delivered it. Mr. Jergens saw me admiring the car, in the alley behind the ice-cream parlor. He grinned at me and promised to take me for a ride. Boy oh boy oh boy! I had heard that the runabout could zoom down the brewery hill at a speed of fifteen miles an hour!

But I never got my ride in the automobile. After making his promise to me, Mr. Jergens went upstairs and tried on his new suit and it was years before he ever spoke to me or my father again.

There were two true aristocrats in our neighborhood, Mr. Ruppert and Mr. Ehret, the owners of the big breweries. Jake Ruppert's mansion was on the corner of 93rd and Park Avenue. This was a fabulous place to me, for the principal reason that Ruppert's garden contained a row of peach trees, which once a year bore lovely, luscious peaches.

Ruppert's garden also contained two huge watchdogs who ranged along the inside of the iron spiked fence, on the alert for peach poachers. It was the theory of Ruppert's caretaker that the dogs would be more vicious if they were kept hungry. This theory backfired. I used to hustle a bag of fat and meat scraps from a butcher, feed the starving dogs through the fence until they got friendly and sleepy, then shinny over the spikes and fill my shirt with ripe peaches.

No fruit ever tasted so sweet as stolen fruit, which was about the only kind I ever had until I became, at the age of eleven, a full-time working man.

There was a spectacular pageant on our street, every weekday of the year. The show went on at nine in the morning, and was repeated at six in the evening. This was the passing of Mr. Ehret through 93rd Street, to and from the Ehret Brewery.

Mr. Ehret rode in a dazzling black carriage, pulled by a team of prize black stallions. A footman and a coachman, in regal uniforms of blue and gold, sat on top of the carriage. The eastern half of our block sloped downhill toward the East River and when the brewer's carriage reached the top of the slope, in the morning, the coachman would stand up and shake the reins and the stallions would charge down the hill in full gallop.

When they passed our house, the stallions were wild-eyed and foaming at their bits, and the cobblestones rang like anvils. When they returned at night, straining against the rise, you could see the sparks fly up from their pounding hooves.

Thunder and lightning. Pomp and circumstance. Glory and magnificence. I wonder how a poor kid who never watched a brewer ride to his brewery, who never shivered with goose bumps when the coachman rose to start the downhill gallop, could ever know that there was another kind of life, the Good Life.

Thanks for the show, Mr. Ehret. Thanks for the peaches, Mr. Ruppert. Sorry I never liked beer.

Then there were the Brownstone People. They weren't as high and mighty as the brewers, but I think they furthered my education about the outside world just as much.

We lived on the tenement side of 93rd Street, the north side. Facing us, on the south, was a row of one-family brownstone town houses. They were not cluttered in front with ugly fire escapes, like the tenements. They were decorated with ivy and window-boxes full of flowers.

What went on inside those elegant houses was something I found impossible to imagine, like the sound of harp music. While other kids wondered about life on Mars or the Moon, I used to wonder about life across the street. For hours at a time, I watched the brownstones and saw the Brownstone People come and go. There were two whom I watched and waited for in particular.

One was a dashing young lady named Marie Wagner, who was a well-known tennis player of the day. I took to following Miss Wagner to Central Park to the courts, where I became her self-appointed ball retriever. The courts had no backstops, and I ran myself ragged chasing down tennis balls. But it was worth it. For an afternoon's work, Miss Wagner would reward me with an old ball.

I couldn't expect to own a tennis ball for longer than a day or two before it got swiped by some older kid, so whenever Miss Wagner paid me off I'd sprint for home and get in as many licks as I could before the bandits turned up. I was conducting a sort of one-man Olympics, competing against myself for new world's records in Tennis Ball Bouncing Against the Stoop of 179 East 93rd Street, New York City.

I kept hoping that one afternoon I'd still be bouncing and catching the ball when Miss Wagner came home. Then she might see me from across the street, and know that I wasn't using the trophy she'd given me in any childish, ungrateful way. I was improving my game.

But she never saw me in action. This was a lingering, cruel disappointment. I had quite a crush on the dashing Miss Wagner.

I regret to confess that the time I set the All-Time Stoop Bouncing World's Record of 341 without a miss, I didn't use a ball of Marie Wagner's. By that time I had become a pretty worldly fellow. I still hung around the tennis courts in the park, but I had turned pro. I retrieved for anybody and everybody, not for love, but strictly for the loot.

My other idol of the brownstones was a gentleman named Mr. Burns, a retired attorney. Mr. Burns was as elegant as his house. When he stepped forth for his daily stroll to Central Park he wore a derby hat, a trim, faintly striped suit, suede gloves, and narrow patent-leather shoes. When the sun shone he carried a walking stick with a silver top. When it looked like rain he swung a long, furled umbrella with a silver handle.

Once I asked Frenchie if Mr. Burns was rich and famous.

Frenchie's answer baffled me. He nodded and said, mysteriously, "British cut."

The most astonishing thing about Mr. Burns, however, was the tipping of his hat. On the street he tipped his hat to everybody. He even tipped his hat to kids! I used to lurk on the corner of 93rd and Lex, waiting for Mr. Burns to start his daily walk. When he came briskly by, headed for the park, he never appeared to see me. But as he passed he never failed to switch his stick or umbrella from right hand to left and tip his derby.

This was a grand and satisfying moment in the life of a lone-wolf, friendless kid.

In my daydreams I knew now what it was going to be like on the absolute pinnacle of worldly success. I would be riding down Third Avenue in my black carriage pulled by four black stallions, munching on ripe, red peaches from the bushel on the seat beside me. As I tipped my derby to people on the streets, right and left, I saw them smile with gratitude, and I could hear the cop saying as he held back the crowd, "Stand back, now! Make way for Mr. Marx, the famous tennis star and left-fielder with the silver handle on his walking stick!" When I passed a peaked-face, shaggy-top kid with horsehair rings on his fingers, I tossed him a peach and a brand-new tennis ball. The kid said, "Bless you, sir!" and a great shout went up from the crowd, and the cop, grinning from ear to car, saluted me with his nightstick.

I tipped my derby again, to the north and to the south, and ordered my coachman to start the gallop.

At Christmastime, the brownstones across the street were even more remote from my tenement world. Wreaths of holly appeared on the doors and in the windows, and at night I could see Christmas trees inside, glowing with the lights of candles.

The one thing I remembered that Miss Flatto had taught me, in P. S. 86, was the legend of Santa Claus. I was entranced by it, but being a young cynic, I told myself it was all a bunch of Irish malarkey. The only time anybody got presents in our family was when Uncle Al came to visit or when Frenchie happened to get paid for two suits at a crack.

Nevertheless, on the night of December 24, a month after my ninth birthday, I decided to give Santa Claus a chance to make good. I hung one of my stockings in the airshaft, pinned under the window. The airshaft, I figured, was the nearest thing to a chimney in our house. Maybe even better. A lot more room for a fat and jolly old guy to shinny down.

On Christmas morning, my stocking was still empty. I didn't tell anybody about it. I was too ashamed of being played for a sucker.

Yet, a year later, when I saw the holly on the brownstones, and the candles flickering on the Christmas trees, I swallowed my pride and hung my stocking again. This time, to bolster my faith, I confessed to Chico that night what I had done. Chico wasn't scornful, or even surprised. He knew all about the Christmas stocking deal. "But," he said, "you got to figure the odds. Figure how many airshafts on 93rd Street, let alone in the rest of the city, Sandy Claus has to shinny down in one night. Then you figure he's got to take care of the Irishers and Bohunks and Eyetalians before he gets around to the Jews. Right? So what kind of odds is that?"

Chico was being sensible and convincing as usual. Still, it was a question of faith versus mathematics. A stubborn glimmer of faith still burned inside me. I left my stocking in the airshaft.

Next morning Chico surprised me. He got to the stocking before I did. When he found it empty, he was disappointed and he was sore. He wadded up the stocking and threw it at me. "When are you going to learn?" he said. "When are you going to learn you can't go against the odds?"

Then he got even madder and called me some pretty unbrotherly names. This was the earliest Chico had ever gotten out of bed, and he had just remembered that the poolroom didn't open until noon on holidays.

The only holidays we shared as a family were the excursions we took, once every summer, to the beach. We couldn't afford to go as far as the ocean, out at Coney Island. We took the cheaper excursion boat from the dock at 96th Street, the one that paddled up through Hell Gate to North Beach, in the Bronx.

At North Beach we had a marvelous time, basking in the sweet air of freedom. We were where no free-loading relatives or rent agents or disgruntled customers of Frenchie's could ever find us. Minnie told jokes and sang songs with Groucho, Frenchie snoozed on the sand, smiling even in his sleep, and Chico would wander off looking for some action. I was supposed to mind Gummo and Zeppo, but I ducked away every chance I got to see if I could hustle a charlotte russe or a hunk of watermelon off some kid smaller than me.

Our feast for the holiday would be a stack of sandwiches, liver-paste and cheese on stiff pumpernickel bread. The cheese was green, and so hard it had to be spread with a paint scraper, but it was delectable.

We would stretch the day to the last possible minute, running—along with the rest of the crowd—to catch the last boat home. By the time the warped old tub chugged back into the East River, all the passengers would be on one side, leaning wearily toward home, and the boat would list until you could reach your hand over the rail and skim the scum off the river. It was a miracle every time it made the dock and got itself hitched to the piles and pulled up level before capsizing.

It was always a melancholy homecoming. For most of us on board, the one-day excursion was the only vacation we would have from a year of hard work and misery. The blind man who played the concertina knew there wasn't another nickel or penny left for his tin cup amongst the whole crowd, but he played on, and sang homesick Italian ballads.

In the boat's saloon there was a piano, bolted with iron straps to the deck. Its keyboard was locked. The piano must have been left over from the boat's palmier days, when the passengers wore white flannels and linens, and there was an orchestra for dancing. Nobody ever played the piano on our excursions, and that was the sad part of the holiday for me.

46

There was one supreme holiday every two years, and there was nothing sad about it. This was not a family affair. It belonged to everybody. The poorest kid in town had as much a share in it as the mayor himself.

This was Election Day.

Months ahead, I started, like every other kid, collecting and stashing fuel for the election bonfire. Having quit school, I could put in a lot of extra hours at it. I had a homemade wagon, a real deluxe job. Most kids greased their axles with suet begged or pinched off a butcher shop, but I was fancier. I scraped genuine axle grease off the hubs of beer wagons, working the brewery circuit from Ehret's to Ruppert's to Ringling's.

I hauled staves, slats, laths, basket-lids, busted carriage spokes, any loose debris that would burn, and piled it all in a corner of our basement. This was one thing the janitor helped me with. The Election Day bonfire was a tradition nobody dared to break. If you were anti-bonfire you were anti-Tammany and life could become pretty grim without handouts from the Organization. Worse than that, the cops could invent all kinds of trouble to get you into. So around election time, there were no complaints up the dumbwaiter shaft about the leaks in our garbage cans.

The great holiday lasted a full thirty hours. On election eve, the Tammany forces marched up and down the avenues by torchlight, with bugles blaring and drums booming. There was free beer for the men, and free firecrackers and punk for the kids, and nobody slept that night.

When the Day itself dawned, the city closed up shop and had itself a big social time—visiting with itself, renewing old acquaintances, kicking up old arguments—and voted.

About noon a hansom cab, courtesy of Tammany Hall, would pull up in front of our house. Frenchie and Grandpa, dressed in their best suits (which they otherwise wore only to weddings, bar mitzvahs or funerals), would get in the cab and go clip-clop, in tip-

47

top style, off to the polls. When the carriage brought them back they sat in the hansom as long as they could without the driver getting sore, savoring every moment of their glory while they puffed on their free Tammany cigars.

At last, reluctantly, they would descend to the curb, and Frenchie would make the grand gesture of handing the cabbie a tip. Kids watching in the streets and neighbors watching from upstairs windows were properly impressed.

About a half-hour later, the hansom cab would reappear, and Frenchie and Grandpa would go off to vote again. If it was a tough year, with a Reform movement threatening the city, they'd be taken to vote a third time.

Nobody was concerned over the fact that Grandpa happened not to be a United States citizen, or that he couldn't read or write English. He knew which side of the ballot to put his "X" on. That was the important thing. Besides, Grandpa's son-in-law's cousin was Sam Marx, a Big Man in the Organization. Cousin Sam had a lot to say about whose name appeared under a black star on the ballot. And it was he who made sure the carriage was sent to 179 at voting time. A man of principle, which Grandpa was, had no choice but to return the courtesy by voting.

Then came the Night. The streets were cleared of horses, buggies and wagons. All crosstown traffic stopped. At seven o'clock firecrackers began to go off, the signal that the polls were closed. Whooping and hollering, a whole generation of kids came tumbling down out of the tenements and got their bonfires going. By a quarter after seven, the East Side was ablaze.

Whenever our 93rd Street fire showed signs of dying down, we'd throw on a fresh load of wood, out of another basement, and the flames would shoot up again. After my stash was piled on the blaze, I ran upstairs to watch from our front window with Grandpa.

It was beautiful. Flames seemed to leap as high as the tenement roof. The row of brownstones across the street, reflecting the fire, was a shimmering red wall. The sky was a great red curtain. And from all over the city, we could hear the clanging of fire engines. Our bonfire never got out of hand but a lot of others did on election night.

Grandpa enjoyed the sight as much as I did, and he was flattered when I left the rest of the boys to come up to share it with him. He pulled his chair closer to the window and lit the butt of his Tammany stogie. "Ah, we are lucky to be in America," he said in German, taking a deep drag on the cigar he got for voting illegally and lifting his head to watch the shooting flames. "Ah, yes! This is true democracy."

I had no idea what Grandpa was talking about, but he was a man of great faith and whatever he said was the truth.

One fine spring day, a revolution occurred in our lives. The Marxes bought a piano.

I hopped with joy when the movers hoisted it up to our flat. It was only a hacked-up, secondhand upright. But to me it was a shining symbol of all the pleasures of the good life, the forbidden pleasures of the outside world.

Very soon I found out that our piano was not intended for pleasure. Minnie had bought it (five dollars down and a dollar a week) strictly for business. It was part of her Master Plan. Uncle Al was now on his way to the top in vaudeville, and the time had come for Minnie to go to work on her own brood and start them on their way. Chico, being the oldest, came first.

Chico would learn the piano. Then he could not only work as a single, but also accompany Groucho, who was developing into quite an accomplished boy soprano. The two nephews would then follow their famous uncle up the ladder of success, bing boom bang.

As for me, I'm afraid I was an afterthought in the Master Plan. It went without saying that I was the untalented member of the family. But so I shouldn't be a total loss, I would take secondhand music lessons. Chico would pass on to me everything he learned from the piano teacher.

The teacher was a hefty Viennese lady with a mustache. She and Chico loathed each other, and Chico hated music, but

Chico did his duty. He never missed a lesson and he practiced every day, even though the piano took eight hours a week out of his pool and pinochle time. He did not, however, take the extra time to pass his lessons on to me, as Minnie had planned. I was never allowed in the living room when the teacher was there, since my presence would have raised the weekly fee from two bits to four. So what piano I learned, I learned by myself.

This, I later realized, was all the better, because Chico's teacher had a certain limitation. She could teach only the right hand. When she played, she faked with the left. Chico kept asking, at first, what he should do with his left hand, and the teacher would say sharply, "Never mind—*that* hand's where the music is"—accenting the statement with a whack of her ruler on her pupil's right knuckles.

So Chico Marx became, at the age of thirteen, the best one-hand piano player in New York City. Well, the best one-hand piano player east of Lexington Avenue and north of 59th Street.

Being entirely self-taught, I was still in the one-finger stage. But I worked over the keyboard like a fiend, driving Frenchie and Grandpa out of their minds, I'm sure. Then came the day I played the chorus of "Waltz Me Around Again, Willie," one-finger version, straight through without a mistake. This was the first accomplishment of my life that I felt really proud of. Flush with triumph, I doubled my repertoire, pecking out "Love Me and the World Is Mine."

My career had begun. As soon as I worked up to using both hands on both songs, I was going to apply for the job of piano player on the North Beach excursion boat. But as it turned out, the next step in my career was something entirely different.

Drifting through the streets, with my head full of beautiful one-finger piano music, I got caught where I never would have been caught in my right mind.

50

By the cellar steps of Goodkind's Bakery, on Third Avenue, was a big stack of stove wood, which the baker sold, three sticks for a nickel. One afternoon I was standing in front of the bakery like a stuffed idiot, and an Irish gang from 96th Street came around the corner and trapped me.

The Irishers said, "Hey, Sheenie! Lookit behind ya!" I turned, without thinking, and they slammed me smack into the stack of wood. In an avalanche of lumber I tumbled into the bakery basement, where the ovens were.

Mr. Goodkind exploded onto the scene in a cloud of flour and fury and hauled me out of the woodpile. He said it was a miracle that no damage had been done to his joint. He asked me if I had a job. I said I didn't. He said I was lying. I did have a job. I was working for him. I was the new Wood Stacker and Pie Sorter for Goodkind's Bakery.

When I finished restacking the stove wood, I was instructed in the duties of Pie Sorter. Fresh-baked pies were slid out of the oven onto a long table, dozens at a time. The crusts were stenciled to indicate their flavor—"A" for Apple, "AP" for Apricot, "C" for Cherry, and so on. I had to sort the pies according to flavor and arrange them on the shelves upstairs.

I went diligently to work, and warm, fragrant work it was. Having a job wasn't so bad after all. For this I would get paid!

My pay, at the end of the nine-hour working day, was one cruller.

I told Mr. Goodkind I was quitting. I had to have a better-paying job than pie sorting. He asked me if I owned a wagon. I told him I certainly did, a wagon with genuine black axle grease. "All right, young man," he said. "I can get a better job for you. My friend Mr. Geiger needs a delivery boy for weekends."

On Saturday morning I reported with my wagon to Geiger's Dairy & Dried Fruits. I was hired on the spot. My hours were all day Saturdays and Sundays until noon. My pay was one dried prune per hour, which was a hell of a raise from one cruller per day.

So at the age of eleven I entered the egg delivery field, having moved up from the pie-sorting profession. My elementary education was over. I was a workingman.

51

CHAPTER 4

Enter: A Character

THE MAN WHO first inspired me to become an actor was a guy called Gookie. Gookie had nothing to do with the theatre. He rolled cigars in the window of a cigar store on Lexington Avenue.

This was the store with card games and bookmaking in the back room, the nearest thing to a social club in our neighborhood. It was Frenchie's home away from home and, along with the poolroom, Chico's too. Since gambling was never the obsession with me that it was with Chico, I didn't spend much time in the back room. Where I had the most fun was on the street, in front of the store.

Gookie worked at a low table, facing the Avenue through the window. He was a lumpy little man with a complexion like the leaves he used for cigar wrappers, as if he'd turned that color from overexposure to tobacco. He always wore a dirty, striped shirt without a collar, and leather cuffs and elastic armbands. Whether he was at his table in the window or running errands for the cardplayers, Gookie was forever grunting and muttering to himself. He never smiled.

Gookie was funny enough to look at when he wasn't working, but when he got up to full speed rolling cigars he was something to see. It was a marvel how fast his stubby fingers could move. And when he got going good he was completely lost in his work, so absorbed that he had no idea what a comic face he was making. His tongue lolled out in a fat roll, his cheeks puffed out, and his eyes popped out and crossed themselves.

I used to stand there and practice imitating Gookie's look for fifteen, twenty minutes at a time, using the window glass as a mirror. He was too hypnotized by his own work to notice me. Then one day I decided I had him down perfect—tongue, cheeks, eyes, the whole bit.

I rapped on the window. When he looked up I yelled, "Gookie! Gookie!" and made the face. It must have been pretty good because he got sore as hell and began shaking his fist and cursing at me. I threw him the face again. I stuck my thumbs in my ears and waggled my fingers, and this really got him. Gookie barreled out of the store and chased me down the Avenue. It wasn't hard to outrun such a pudgy little guy. But I'll give Gookie credit. He never gave up on trying to catch me whenever I did the face through the window.

It got to be a regular show. Sometimes the guy behind the cigar-store counter would tip off the cardplayers that I was giving Gookie the works out front. When they watched the performance from the back-room door and he heard them laughing, Gookie would get madder than ever.

For the first time, at the age of twelve, I had a reputation. Even Chico began to respect me. Chico liked to show me off when somebody new turned up in the poolroom. He would tell the stranger, "Shake hands with my brother here. He's the smartest kid in the neighborhood." When the guy put out his hand I'd throw him a Gookie. It always broke up the poolroom.

I didn't know it, but I was becoming an actor. A character was being born in front of the cigar-store window, the character who was eventually to take me a long ways from the streets of the East Side.

Over the years, in every comedy act or movie I ever worked in, I've "thrown a Gookie" at least once. It wasn't always planned, especially in our early vaudeville days. If we felt the audience slipping away, fidgeting and scraping their feet through our jokes, Groucho or Chico would whisper in panic, "Sssssssssst! Throw me a Gookie!" The fact that it seldom failed to get a laugh is quite a tribute to the original possessor of the face.

The little cigar roller was possibly the best straight man I ever had. He was certainly the straightest straight man. If Gookie had broken up or even smiled just once, my first act would have been a flop and the rest of my life might not have been much to write a book about.

Gookie-baiting was one of the few free pleasures I had left. As I got older, I acquired more expensive tastes.

I spent more time in the poolroom, and the price of pocket billiards had risen from a penny a cue to two for a nickel. That was big money. An evening's pool cost more than I usually managed to bring home from a day's hustling, doing odd jobs and hocking whatever loose merchandise I might chance to find lying around.

What took really big money was the Special Dinner at Fieste's Oyster House. Dining at Fieste's was the supreme luxury of my young life. Not that the food there was any better cooked than the food we had at home—when we had food. No common commercial chef could ever compete with Frenchie. But Fieste's Special included things that Frenchie could only dream of putting on our table: Greenpoint oysters and cherrystone clams on the half shell, deviled crab, grilled smelts, French fried potatoes and onions, a juicy T-bone steak, hot rolls soaked with butter, apple pie with a slab of sharp cheese, and coffee rich with thick, sweet cream.

As I said, a meal like this took really big money. It cost thirty-five cents.

I soon learned what the main pitfall was in saving money. It wasn't temptation, or the lack of will power. It was Chico Marx. Chico could smell money. Hiding my savings at home, anywhere in the flat, was useless. Chico always found it sooner or later.

Once I thought I had him outsmarted. I sold a wagonload of junk over on the West Side, items I had selected off a moving van hitched in front of a house on 90th Street. The junk dealer gave me ten cents cash, the most I ever made on a single wagonload.

I swore that this dime would not wind up in Chico's pocket. For once I was sure it wouldn't, because I had finally found the perfect hiding place. In our bedroom there was a small tear in the wallpaper, near the ceiling. Before Chico came home that night I stood on the dresser and pasted my dime to the wall under the flap of the torn paper. It was a slick job. I went to bed with a feeling of security.

Next morning when I got up there was a bigger rip in the paper than before. My dime was gone and so was Chico. Chico was the only person I ever knew who could smell money through wallpaper. Maybe he didn't have much of an ear for music, but he had a hell of a nose for currency.

So I learned that the only way to protect my money was to spend it as fast as I earned it. I also learned to spend it on something I could eat, or use up, like dinner at Fieste's or a game of pool. My possessions were no safer from Chico's clutches than my money. Chico was a devout believer in the maxim "Share and share alike."

The way he shared my possessions was to hock them as fast as he got his hands on them, and then give the pawn tickets to me as my share.

I was growing up. I wasn't getting much bigger, but I was a lot cockier and wiser. I won my first fight. I beat the hell out of a kid from next door, a detective's son, who was two years older and fifteen pounds heavier than me. Nobody was more surprised than he was—except me. I had never been known as much of a scrapper. I was better known for ducking and running. But now I was a fighting man.

I'd come a long way as a workingman, too. Since the day I was ambushed by the bakery woodpile and got hooked in my first job, I had been hired and fired on the average of once a month. If a job didn't offer any possibilities of fun, graft or petty thievery, I was not apt to take it very seriously. Like the time I spent a whole afternoon making a delivery for a butcher. I was bored delivering meat so I took a shortcut, with stopovers at the poolroom, Gookie's window, the front stoop of my house—where I set my all-time record of 341 tennis-ball bounces—and finally back to the store, where I got fired.

Selling papers was no good. No loot on the side. Shoe-shining was too much of a grind. Junk collecting was all right, but there was always the threat of being highjacked by an enemy gang.

If things got real desperate I could hock a pair of Frenchie's tailoring shears, which was Chico's old racket. As long as I gave him the pawn ticket, Frenchie never seemed to mind and he never asked for the fifty cents the pawnbroker gave me. The worst I could get was a whisk of Frenchie's whiskbroom under my chin.

I was never as blasé as Chico about hustling scratch from my own family. It made me feel guilty, so whenever Frenchie packed to go off on a selling trip, I volunteered to go along as his assistant. I helped carry the bundles of "lappas"—the odd pieces of materials— and when Frenchie made his sales pitch I held up the pieces one by one. This required skillful manipulation, since I had to hold the fabrics so the customer couldn't see the holes or rips. I guess the official designation for my job would be Lappa Displayer and Defect Concealer.

Sometimes, when things got dull and the family was flat broke, I served as Grandpa's assistant. Because the language barrier was too great for him, Grandpa never worked in America as a ventriloquist or magician. For some reason unknown to me, he took to umbrella mending, door-to-door, whenever he needed quick cash.

On his rounds, Grandpa carried a tool kit and a tin can on a wire sling. In the can were coals of charcoal. To get the charcoal white-hot for the soldering iron, the can had to be swung around and around, to fan the fire. My special job with Grandpa was Tin Can Swinger.

Grandpa's umbrella business petered out after a few years. People got wise to the fact they could buy new umbrellas for the prices he charged to mend old ones. I was sorry. Tin Can Swinging was one occupation I could have stuck at permanently. It was fun.

The shortest job I ever had lasted ten minutes. I applied as a helper to an Italian dame who ran a delicatessen near 96th Street, and she hired me as soon as I walked in the store. Then she looked me up and down, with big starey eyes, and asked me to follow her downstairs to the storeroom. When she got me down there she began shaking and breathing hard and making funny wheezy sounds. I was afraid she was having a heart attack.

The dame had another kind of attack in mind. She asked me to hurry up and take my clothes off. I started to unbutton my shirt, thinking maybe she had a uniform for me. She couldn't wait. She grabbed my hand and pressed it to her, all over her body, then under her dress. I couldn't fight loose from her grip. I was never so scared in my life.

Thank God, the bell on the upstairs door rang before the crazy dame could go any farther. She let go of my hand and returned to the store. My hand, I felt, had been tainted. It was nasty, filthy dirty. I had to wash it, immediately. The only facility in the store-room was a big, open pickle barrel. So I washed my hand in the pickle juice and ran upstairs and through the store and never went near the joint again.

My sex education was direct, no punches pulled, and vividly illustrated. I learned a lot more about the subject and its ramifications than most twelve-year-old boys did. But the method had its drawbacks. For years I couldn't eat pickles.

At thirteen I attained manhood, according to the Jewish faith. I was *bar mitzvah*—inducted as an adult member of the synagogue. This didn't mean, however, that I would start going to *shul* every Saturday. The rites were performed out of deference to Grandpa, who would have been bitterly hurt if his grandsons hadn't shown this much respect for their traditional faith. It was the least we could do.

For the occasion, Frenchie made me a black serge knee-breeches suit (pieced together of unsold "lappas") and bought me a derby hat. After the ceremony there was a reception for me at 179 with a spread of sweets, pastries and wine. This, naturally, attracted all the relatives, and it was quite a party. I received four presents. Uncle Al gave me a pair of gloves. Aunt Hannah gave me a pair of gloves. Cousin Sam gave me a pair of gloves. (In my *bar mitzvah* photograph I'm wearing two pairs, one over the other, and holding the third.) Minnie, bless her, gave me a genuine, one-dollar Ingersoll watch.

The inevitable happened. Three days after my *bar mitzvah*, my new watch was missing.

I was pretty damn sore. A present was not the same as something you hustled. I tracked down Chico to a crap game and asked him what about it. He handed me the pawn ticket. I gave the ticket to Minnie and she reclaimed the watch for me. Then a brilliant idea occurred to me. I would show Chico. I would make my watch Chico-proof, so he couldn't possibly hock it again. I removed its hands.

Now the watch was mine forever. I wound it faithfully each morning and carried it with me at all times. When I wanted to know what time it was I looked at the Ehret Brewery clock and held my watch to my ear. It ran like a charm, and its ticking was a constant reminder that I had, for once, outsmarted Chico.

Being a pianist (with a repertoire of two one-finger pieces) and an actor (with a repertoire of one funny face), I began to be more aware of show business.

Sam Muller, the tailor Cousin Polly married, had a shop on Lexington Avenue not far from the Gookie cigar store. For a while, Sam had the job of making the livery for Mr. Ehret's coachmen, and he used to display sample uniforms in the window. Sam's shop became quite a showcase, with the two dummies all dressed up in blue and gold.

58

The Star, a melodrama theatre on 102nd Street, gave Sam Muller two free tickets a week for using his colorful window to hang their posters in. When Sam couldn't use the tickets, he'd give them to Groucho and me. I saw my first stage plays, and I loved them.

Groucho, having been chosen by Minnie to follow in the footsteps of Uncle Al, had already seen Uncle Al on the stage, and he knew his routines and songs by memory. I decided to take Groucho on as a partner (as Chico had once taken me on, in the cuckoo-clock promotion), when I found out that stores in the neighborhood were paying a penny apiece for cats. I've forgotten why they were. There must have been a mouse plague or a cat shortage, or both, that year.

So now I was a promoter. Groucho and I put on a show in our basement. We performed Uncle Al's popular sketch, "Quo Vadis Upside Down." Admission: one cat.

It was my first public performance. As I remember, we grossed seven cats at the boxoffice but made a net profit of only four cents. Three cats got away. Well, that was show business.

An exciting place down on Third Avenue was the Old Homestead Beer Garden. Behind the saloon there was a real garden with an open-air stage, where they put on continuous shows in the summertime—with jugglers, comedy teams, trick musicians, yodelers and German bands.

I used to sneak through the back fence to see the show at the Old Homestead. Sometimes when I got caught I got heaved out. Other times I was put to work, changing the cards on the easel to announce the upcoming acts on the bill. I didn't get paid for this, but I could see the entire program three times from start to finish. My favorite act at the Old Homestead was The Watson Sisters, who did a comedy prize fight act.

Prize fighting itself in those days was not a sport, like baseball. It was show business. A heavyweight title bout was to me the biggest show of any year, greater than the St. Patrick's parade, the election bonfire and The Watson Sisters all rolled into one. This was in spite of the fact that I had never seen a prize fight.

My supreme idol was James J. Jeffries. On the afternoon he

fought Jack Munroe, in San Francisco, I sat on the sidewalk with forty other kids in front of a saloon on 90th Street and Third Avenue. There was a ticker in the saloon. The bartender announced the fight blow-by-blow as it came off the ticker, and some kindly patron was thoughtful enough to relay the vital news to the kids on the street outside.

When Jeffries knocked out Munroe in the second round, a rousing cheer went up inside the saloon, and all forty of us kids jumped to our feet and started dancing on the sidewalk and swinging at each other with roundhouse knockout punches. I came home with a black eye. I couldn't have been happier or prouder if I'd come home with the championship belt itself.

Some of the talk about the Responsibilities of Manhood must have stuck with me after my *bar mitzvah*, because when I was thirteen I landed my first bona fide job, regular wages and hours and everything. And, indirectly, it had to do with show business. I became a bellhop at the Hotel Seville, down on East 28th Street. The Seville was then a high-class theatrical hotel.

I worked alternating shifts of six and twelve hours, with twelve hours off between each shift. I was paid twelve dollars a month, plus two free meals during the twelve-hour shift, and I earned fifty cents a week on the side for walking Cissie Loftus' dog. Cissie Loftus was a famous English music-hall and vaudeville star. Not only that, she was—I thought—almost as beautiful as my mother Minnie.

I have no recollection of why I was fired by the Seville, but of course I was. My next employment was setting pins in the bowling alley at YMHA—Young Men's Hebrew Association—on 92nd and Lex. My salary wasn't half what I made hopping bells, but the hours were better, and I still made enough dough to carry out my present mission in life. My mission was making myself a Neighborhood Character.

Since I had been pretty much a failure as student, fist-fighter, musician and gambler, I decided to follow up on my Gookie success and play it for laughs. I became, therefore, a Character.

The costume I sported upon the streets of the East Side now consisted of pointed shoes, tight-bottomed long pants, red turtle-neck sweater, derby hat, and a sty in my right eye. Other adolescents broke out all over with pimples and boils, but not me. I broke out all in one spot—on my lower right eyelid. I couldn't hide it so I kept the sty as part of the act.

In my new role, I began hanging around older-type fellows, men of seventeen and eighteen. Their talk was mostly about sex. Specifically, they talked about their weekly exploits, every Saturday, down at a place in Chinatown called the Friendly Inn. It was clear to me that I had to go down to the Friendly Inn and "do it." Otherwise I would lose whatever standing I had in the sophisticated crowd I hung around with.

Besides, there were certain masculine urges stirring within me that itched to be assuaged. Besides that, it only cost four bits.

So down I went, one Saturday afternoon, all gotten up in pointed shoes, tight pants, turtle-neck sweater, derby and sty. I took the El train to Chatham Square and strutted over to the corner of Mott and Hester.

The downstairs part of the Friendly Inn was an ordinary saloon. The girls worked upstairs. Business was booming this particular Saturday, and the line of upstairs customers ran all the way through the bar, out the swinging doors, and halfway up the block on Hester Street. I got on the end of the line. I was very conspicuously the smallest and youngest male animal anywhere in sight. In front of me stood a big Polish guy who looked seven feet tall and four feet across the shoulders. I sweated buckets trying to look taller. I sweated so much I had trouble keeping the half dollar from squirting out of my fist.

The line moved with regularity, and not too slowly. Every step forward meant that somebody ahead of me had gotten his money's worth upstairs and had left the Friendly Inn by the back door.

When I made it inside the saloon, into the light, a pimp came along the line sizing up the customers. He spotted me and said, "Get the hell out of here, kid! You want to give this place a

61

bad name?" I ducked out of the saloon—and got back on the end of the line. I had already invested five cents cash in the El ride. I was not giving up.

The next time I got inside, the pimp spotted me and chased me out again. I got back on the end of the line. The third time he saw me he gave up, shrugged, and said what the hell, go on upstairs if I had to have it that bad. I felt I had to have it that bad.

So I shuffled along in line, step by step, past the length of the bar and up the stairs in back. At the top of the stairs, a fat woman smoking a cigarette gave me a towel, took my fifty cents, and told me to go to room number two.

The open doorway of room number two was as close as I ever got to the promised land. Inside, a naked woman lay on an iron bed, her knees raised and her legs spread apart. I never saw her face. She said, "Next? Come *on*, for Christ sake!" I took one look and dropped the towel and ran down the stairs and out the back door of the saloon.

A couple of my pals, who'd already made the trip to the Friendly Inn that day, were waiting for me uptown. It was plain that they regarded me with new respect. "Not bad, huh?" one of them said. I tilted my derby down over my eyes. "No siree," I said. "Not bad at all—for four bits." I walked quickly away, so they wouldn't see I was still trembling from the shock.

My manly urges could itch for a long time before they led me to temptation again.

Groucho got himself a job for after school and weekends as delivery boy for the Hepner Wig Company, down in the theatre district. It was Groucho's wig job that led to my first memorable piece of acting, a performance that I'm still proud of.

One day Groucho brought home a large box from Hepner's, to be delivered early the next morning. We couldn't resist breaking into it. Inside were a dozen ladies' wigs, all shades of blond, red and brunette. Then, of course, we couldn't resist trying them all on in front of the mirror. We primped and postured and giggled and thought we were a couple of prize comics.

Groucho said it was easy for me to impersonate a dame because I already had a woman's voice, which was true. My voice refused to change. This gave me an idea.

"Let me borrow one of the wigs," I said. "I'm going to have some fun with the Baltzers."

The Baltzers were the looniest of all our unrelated Relatives. Old man Baltzer, who was Uncle Al's special friend, was a pinochle fiend, which was normal. He was also a hygiene fiend, which wasn't. Baltzer had such a phobia against germs that he would only use the last sheet on a roll of toilet paper.

The Baltzers had two unmarried daughters. Sister Emmy had resigned herself to being an old maid. She used to give herself parties, sitting in a rocking chair, rocking and talking to herself and eating bananas. Sister Rosie was a better-looking dame, but she never got married either. She had "advanced ideas." She insisted on "trying a man out first" before she would consent to being engaged. No guy she tried out ever asked for her consent.

Mama Baltzer was a flighty woman who felt it was her duty to protect her "little girls" from the perils of the outside world, and neither Emmy nor Rosie—who must have been in their thirties at the time—could leave the house without her permission.

Fortunately Minnie was not home this night, which gave me free access to her wardrobe and cosmetics. I picked out a beautiful blond wig from Groucho's assortment. The hair was curled in bangs in front, and hung to my shoulders in back. Groucho helped me with the powder and rouge, padded me in the right places, hooked me into a dress, and buttoned me into a pair of Minnie's kid shoes.

Groucho followed me uptown to the Baltzers', far enough behind so as not to give me away, but close enough to help if I should get in any trouble. The minute I got on the streetcar the fun began. When I hauled up my skirt to get money for the fare (Minnie always kept her change in a bag pinned to her petticoat), the conductor gave me a big wink. I winked back at him. I saw him say something to the brakeman, at the other end of the car. They both looked at me and winked. When I moved down that way to get off, the brakeman sidled over and without looking at me ran his hand down my backsides. I moved away. He followed me and gave me another feel.

When the car stopped, he said, "How's about it, girlie?" I fluttered my eyelids and pursed my lips—then threw him a Gookie and swung off the platform. I had never seen such a startled look. Now I had complete confidence in my role.

A card game was going on in the Baltzers' living room when I walked in, without knocking. Old man Baltzer was playing with his father, Grandpa Baltzer, Uncle Al, and a friend of Uncle Al's from Chicago. Sister Emmy was kibitzing from her rocking chair.

I swished around a little bit, and said somebody told me there were some fellows up here looking to have a little fun. Mr. Baltzer, Uncle Al and the friend were at a loss for anything to say, but Grandpa was at no loss. He reached out and pinched my knee and told me to come sit on his lap.

Sister Emmy, frozen with horror, started backing away. "Excuse me, excuse me, excuse me," she said in a faint and shaky voice. "I have to get closer to the fire." There was no fire. She edged over to the door, and escaped through it to go warn Mama and Rosie.

I heard the women's voices in the other room, cackling like three seagulls fighting over a dead fish. I was sashaying around, scaring the daylights out of old man Baltzer by threatening to kiss him. He took out his handkerchief and held it to his face. I could imagine what kind of germs he thought I had on me. Uncle Al, who liked to needle his friend about his phobia, kept egging me on.

I was sitting on Grandpa's lap when the three dames burst into the room. When they saw where I was they burst right out again. Then they got hysterical. The three of them, Emmy, Rosie and Mama, ran through the house from room to room—everywhere but the living room—slamming doors and screaming, "Get that prostitute out of this house! *Get her out! Get her out!*"

The screaming and shrieking were too much for old man Baltzer. He stood up and said, talking through his handkerchief,

64

that he was going to call the police if I didn't leave. I stuck out my tongue at him and told him to go ahead and call the cops. He ran out of the apartment—and knocked over Groucho, who was watching the scene through a crack in the door.

At the same time I took off my wig. When they saw it was me, Grandpa Baltzer and Uncle Al started to hoot and howl, and when the womenfolk heard this they screamed and slammed through the house worse than ever.

Old man Baltzer was a good sport, and thought it was a great joke I had pulled. But it took us two hours to get Mama, Emmy and Rosie quieted down, even after they saw me unwigged. And for two weeks afterwards they were too indisposed, with palpitations and nervous attacks, to leave the house.

As I said, it was a performance I was proud of. It made me the family character.

Shortly after my masquerade at the Baltzers', Groucho made his debut on the stage, singing a solo in the olio at the Star Theatre between shows. (The "olio" was a potpourri in which everybody from fire-eaters and bell-ringers to boy sopranos came on for a quick turn.)

So Groucho was now a professional. I, having no exploitable talent, still didn't figure in Minnie's Master Plan. But that was okay with me. I didn't have the least desire to go out on a stage and perform in front of eight hundred people. The thought of it gave me the shivers. I was content to play the character I was inventing, at home and on the streets, and pick up the laughs wherever I could find them.

Minnie's brother Harry was also a no-talent guy, but he was dying to get into vaudeville. Uncle Harry Shean couldn't carry a tune or dance or play any instrument. Minnie and Uncle Al beat their brains out trying to cook up an act for him. Minnie finally got the idea that he should be a ventriloquist like Grandpa had been in the Old Country. Grandpa coached him, but Uncle Harry couldn't learn to talk without moving his lips.

Then Minnie got a second brilliant idea. They would put my kid brother Gummo, who was small for his nine years, inside the shell of Uncle Harry's dummy. When Uncle Harry manipulated the dummy's mouth, Gummo would do the talking. It worked great, in rehearsal. Gummo never forgot a line.

But when they opened the act, Gummo was seized with such stage fright that he couldn't talk, and when Uncle Harry manipulated the dummy's lips, not a sound came forth. He was booed off the stage. That was the end of his fling in show business, and probably the beginning of Gummo's aversion to it.

About this time, Chico became a full-time professional piano player. He was giving the piano the same concentration he had given before to pool and games of chance, and he could play faster and more accurately—with his right hand—than anybody else on our side of Carnegie Hall.

Chico broke into vaudeville as half of the team of "Marx and Shean." His partner was Lou Shean, Polly's brother. Cousin Lou was a plain-looking guy who wore thick glasses, but he could sing along with the best of them. During part of their act, Chico would accompany Lou blindfolded on the piano. This got to be the only part of the act that managers wanted. Soon Cousin Lou dropped out entirely and Chico worked as a single.

The first time I saw Chico onstage was in a theatre on 86th Street and Third Avenue. For a finish he played requests from the audience, blindfolded *and* with a bedsheet spread over the keyboard.

Everybody was getting famous except me. I took to practicing the piano at home like a madman. I got to where I could play "Waltz Me Around Again, Willie" with both hands, then immediately went to work on "Love Me and the World Is Mine." I still wanted that job on the excursion boat.

Once again, the unexpected happened and changed the course of my meandering career. This time the unexpected happened in the person of a strange young man named Seymour Mintz.

66

CHAPTER 5

Enough Black Jelly Beans

ONE OF THE passionate hungers of my early life (I had many others but none so fierce) was for black jelly beans. In the penny assortment they sold in those days there was never more than one of licorice, and eating one black jelly bean at a time only intensified my hunger. Penny assortments were few and far between, for me. Candy counters on the East Side were as thief-proof as bank vaults. Candy was one item I couldn't hustle. No penny in hand, no merchandise.

I told myself I should always save such a delicacy as a black jelly bean for last, like dessert, but I never could. It was like being addicted to peanuts, cigarettes or the opium pipe. One was never enough. The first thing I would do when I got rich, I promised myself, would be to buy all the black jelly beans I could eat.

When I did start making good money, this boyhood hunger had somehow become dormant. I forgot about it. I forgot about it, that is, until one night about fifteen years ago.

My wife Susan and I were going to the movies with Gracie and George Burns in Beverly Hills. On the way to the theatre from the parking lot, we passed a candy shop, the ultra-modern kind that

67

sells old-fashioned candies in glass apothecary jars. I stopped in my tracks. I broke into a cold sweat. I was having a seizure. My old hunger for black jelly beans had suddenly returned, after forty-five years. I excused myself and went into the shop.

I came out with thirty dollars' worth. Susan and the Burnses gave me queer looks but made no comment. They waited to see what the gag was. How could I explain to them that this was no gag, but the satisfaction of a lifetime?

And what a satisfaction! Sweet, aromatic, chewy, delectable black jelly beans—a handful at a time, and always more where the last handful came from! I shall have to let my friend George finish the story, because I fell asleep in the middle of my orgy.

I must warn you that George Burns is not above a little exaggeration now and then for dramatic effect, but here's how he tells it:

"So there's Harpo, in the middle of the picture in a crowded theatre, fast asleep. He's got a smile on his face like a happy drunk and on his lap a bag of jelly beans big as a peck of potatoes which he's passed out already from eating only a couple dozen of. Suddenly he twitches in his sleep. The bag splits. Thirty dollars' worth of black jelly beans explodes—flying all over the joint. Do you know how many jelly beans you can *buy* for thirty dollars? My God, what a scene! The audience doesn't know what's happening, only that it's some kind of disaster. People are yelling and clutching their children and putting up umbrellas. They stampede for the exits and skid on the jelly beans rolling down the aisles and fall into heaps like dead Indians. I tell you, it was worse than the Johnstown flood. Finally they stop the picture and turn on the lights, and the manager gets the panic stopped while the ushers shovel up the debris.

"And Harpo? Harpo slept through it all. Fast asleep with that drunken smile on his face. When the movie is over, Susan wakes him up and when he sees his jelly beans are gone he turns on me and says he ought to slug me one for such a dirty, sneaky trick. Eating all his black jelly beans while he wasn't looking!

"Then he softened up—it being impossible for Harpo to stay sore

68

at anybody, even me—and he patted me on the shoulder. 'That's all right,' he said. 'I'll forgive you, George. I had enough anyway.'

"I try to tell him what happened but he won't believe me, just keeps saying, '*Forget* it, George—I *forgive* you.' To this day he thinks I ate up his whole damn peck of black jelly beans."

I will only say that this much of the story is true: I really had enough, for once in my life. I don't care what happened to the rest of the thirty dollars' worth. That's one old hunger that will never bother me again.

I believe I've finally gained control of myself, but for a long time after I came into the chips, I could only buy things in abundance. I bought stuff by the case and the gross, by job lots and truckloads. Soap, thumb tacks, dehydrated onion soup—everything.

Early in the war, Chico called to give me a hot tip: they were going to ration liquor. I rushed over to a wholesale distributor and ordered enough booze to fill my cellar. When Chico's tip proved to be right, I congratulated myself. Then I got to thinking. I didn't very much care for alcohol, in any form. At the rate I consumed liquor (about three mild social drinks per week), there was enough stock in my cellar to last until the year 2419 A.D., or until I was five hundred and twenty-five years old.

Fortunately, it was a commodity I had no trouble getting rid of.

I suppose my overbuying stemmed, psychologically, from the feeling of insecurity I had as a kid, when I could enjoy so few of the "normal" pleasures of childhood. When I could finally afford them, I couldn't stop making up for all the things I had been deprived of—food and comfort; silly little luxuries; time to play games, and the company of good friends.

By my fourteenth year I was able, on my own, to keep my belly full most of the time. What I hungered most for then was companionship. The error of my lone-wolf days had caught up with me. I wanted to be "in" with somebody. I wanted to like and be liked. I wanted friends. For this reason, I was apt to believe anything anybody told me.

I was about the most gullible mark in New York City, and this was exactly what Mr. Seymour Mintz was looking for.

Seymour Mintz was a pale, thin fellow of about twenty-five who was always in a hurry. He talked fast and he walked fast, with tiny, pitter-pat steps. And he walked on a bias, tilted, as if he didn't have the strength to hold himself straight and might tip over if he didn't keep moving. Anybody else would have been leery of such a strange-looking guy. Not me. I was never so happy to meet anybody in my life.

Mintz had met Groucho and Minnie down in Atlantic City, where Groucho was singing at the time, and he appeared in our flat on 93rd Street one afternoon with a letter of introduction from Minnie. I was flattered to learn that it was me, not Frenchie, he had come to see.

He asked me what I was doing at present. I told him I was at liberty. Then he asked how I'd like to go into business with him as a full partner. He said it might involve an extensive trip on the road, and I'd have to be ready to leave on a moment's notice. That was great with me, just great. It was so great that it didn't occur to me to ask what business I was going to be a partner in.

"Hold tight," said Mintz. "Don't do a thing until you hear from me." And then he was off, skittering down the street on a slant, like a sailboat in a stiff breeze.

Two days later he returned. He'd had business cards printed up. God, they were impressive! MINTZ & MARX. I don't remember what else the cards said. All I could see was my name in print.

"Get your bag packed," said Seymour Mintz. "We're leaving in the morning."

Frenchie worked all night that night, letting out the coat to my bar mitzvah suit and making me a handsome red vest. I borrowed a traveling bag from a neighbor upstairs. Its leather was cracked and its catch was busted and I had to tie it with a hunk of clothesline, but that didn't matter since I had nothing to carry in it anyway except a shirt I swiped from Chico, a pair of sox, a set of Frenchie's long underwear and my turtle-neck sweater.

My partner showed up in the morning, lugging a large suitcase. I had been ready since sunrise, and I must say I looked splendid: new vest, shoes shined, derby brushed, the sty in my eye in full bloom. I still didn't know what I was ready *for*, but it was certainly the beginning of my fame and fortune.

The first thing I found out about my part of the business was that it involved carrying both bags. Mine not to reason why. I staggered with my burden, but I was staggering forth into a dream world. At last I had a real friend, a partner.

We took the streetcar from 93rd Street to 125th Street, where we were to catch the train. When we got to 125th Street, Mintz said we had time to have a bite before the train left. It was always good to take off with a good meal under your belt, he said. Never knew what kind of food you would find in the sticks. So we went to a restaurant on Lenox Avenue.

"Order everything you want and forget about the price," my partner said. "Seymour Mintz is no piker."

I ate the best meal I'd had since my last dinner at Fieste's Oyster House—the Forty-Cent All-White-Meat Chicken Five-Course Special. When the dessert came, Mintz leaned back in his chair and waved the proprietor over and demanded to see a selection of cigars. The proprietor brought four or five boxes to our table, but Mintz didn't like any of them. Too cheap. He waved the proprietor away and said he would go to the cigar store next door and get a decent Havana. Be right back, he said.

Mintz trotted out of the joint and I waited. Five minutes. Fifteen minutes. Half an hour. The waiters were giving me dirty looks. An hour. The proprietor came over and gave me the check. I explained that my partner got detained on a business matter while out buying himself a cigar. Okay, the proprietor said, I could sit there fifteen minutes longer before he started charging me rent.

71

Another hour passed. No sign of my partner. The proprietor took our two bags away. If nothing else, he was going to make sure I wouldn't duck out on him. People came and ate and went. Dinnertime came and passed. I was sick with worry—not about the restaurant bill, but about Seymour Mintz and whatever terrible accident had happened to him.

The waiters started cleaning up the place and stacking chairs on the empty tables. I was the only customer left. The proprietor came over and said, "Well, what about it, kid?" I said I didn't have any money, but my partner would be here any minute now and he'd take care of it. I had faith. I gave the guy one of our business cards. He snorted and threw it on the floor.

Ten minutes later he came back, with a cop. Twenty minutes later I was in the jig. They threw me in a jail cell containing four wooden benches and twelve drunks. I took off my new red vest, rolled it into a pillow, and stretched out on the floor. I didn't know what to think. I just went to sleep.

Early in the morning, the keeper banged his stick on the bars. "Up, up, yez bums!" he said. "Yez're all going before Judge Duffy, so yez'd better comb your hair and look pretty for His Honor."

I had heard about Judge Duffy. "Old Thirty Days Duffy." His reputation had spread throughout the city. Duffy's brand of justice was swift and it was rough. He took a look at the back of your head. If you had a round haircut in back, which was a fad among the tough kids on the East Side, he gave you thirty days. Always thirty days, no matter what the charge or the defense. For years, if you were called in a poker game and you showed three tens, you said you had a "Judge Duffy."

I had insisted that Frenchie give me a round haircut before I left on my business trip.

Sure enough, when they made me stand in front of the bench, the judge read the charge and said, "Turn around, Marx. Let's see what kind of a kid you are."

My heart sank. I turned around. And at that moment, who should burst into the courtroom, running on a bias, but Seymour Mintz. My faith was vindicated. Good old Seymour! He was furious. He started hollering at everybody in sight. The judge had to hammer him quiet. Seymour demanded to know who had rail-roaded his partner into jail and what the charge against me was. When the judge told him, Seymour took out a roll of bills, paid off the restaurant man, and hauled me out of the courtroom.

At the station he bought two tickets to Gloversville, New York, and this time we got straight on the train. When Seymour rescued me from the clutches of Judge Duffy, I was too grateful to ask him where he'd been while I waited all day in the restaurant. I was burning with curiosity, but I trusted my partner now more than ever. Seymour Mintz could do no wrong.

At Gloversville we changed from the New York Central to a trolley line, and rode to a small town about ten miles out in the country. I've forgotten the name of the town. There Seymour checked us into the only hotel, which was a sort of glorified board-inghouse but clean and pleasant.

He told me to wait in the hotel while he attended to some urgent business in the neighborhood. To the innkeeper he said, "Give my partner here anything he wants. Anything. You might hire a horse and buggy for him, so he can travel around if he feels like it. I'll be back in a day or two and settle up."

I thought: If I was a full partner in Mintz & Marx, why didn't I go along on the business calls? But I still asked no questions. Why should I look a gift horse and buggy in the mouth? This was living.

A day passed. Two days. I was eating three whopping meals a day and seeing the sights in style. The hotel man's wife, who'd become very motherly toward me, did my laundry and pressed my wardrobe. I was quite a sight myself, riding through the country-side in a private buggy, sporting my red vest and tipping my derby to the natives, as Mr. Burns would have done. There was a poolroom in town, but I could only kibitz the games since I didn't have a nickel in my pocket. That was too bad. There wasn't a sharpie in sight. I could have cleaned the local shooters with no trouble. What a paradise for Chico!

By the third day there was still no sign of my partner, and I began to get uneasy. By the fourth day the manager's wife was noticeably a lot less motherly. I had to borrow her iron and press my own pants. By the fifth day the manager stopped speaking to me altogether except to ask, with growing suspicion, what had happened to Mr. Mintz. I tried to avoid him. I even gave up eating lunch. The portions I was served had been cut in half anyway.

The livery man came to collect for the horse and buggy, and when I told him I couldn't pay—my partner took care of all financial matters—he had a fight with the hotel man, who'd actually ordered the rig. The carriage rental was added to the Mintz & Marx hotel bill.

One week passed, the longest seven days I ever lived through. The manager gave me the bill and told me to pay up or else. He wasn't going to be taken by any city swindlers. He wasn't impressed by my fancy clothes or big talk about my business partnership. I had to cough up $28.50 cash, then and there.

I told him how sorry I was, but I simply didn't have a nickel. Mr. Mintz, I explained, was often detained on his calls, but he always turned up to pay his bills. The manager was not impressed. He said he'd have to impound my belongings. Then, when he found that my suitcase contained nothing more valuable than a turtleneck sweater and a pair of long-johns, he called the constable.

The constable hauled me off to the nearest jig, in Gloversville. I was baffled and dejected. But I must say this was an improvement over the Harlem jail I had slept in the week before. My new cell was spotless, had a cot with a soft mattress, and I was the only tenant.

The next morning I'm awakened by an awful noise in the jailer's office. My first thought was, "Oh my God, the village mob has come to lynch me!" Then I recognized the voice making most of the noise. It was Seymour Mintz, yelling all over the joint about the outrageous, blankety-blank way they had treated his innocent partner.

Seymour took out his roll of bills and bailed me out of the jig. I was free again. This time I asked questions, plenty of questions, but Seymour wouldn't give me any answers. He was still too sore at the hotel man and the constable, and kept muttering and cursing about the scandal of backwoods justice.

We took the train thirty or forty miles to another town. Seymour signed us into the hotel. "Have yourself a good time here, partner," he said. "I'll be back tomorrow morning." Before I could protest, he skittered down the street and out of sight, lugging his suitcase and tilting over at a perilous angle.

It was all too familiar. It was all too clear that I was not going to have myself a very good time in this town either.

This was a more expensive hotel. I was stuck in the biggest room, the only one with its own bathroom, and by the end of three days— no sign of Mintz, of course—the bill had already reached the fifteen-dollar mark.

I made the first move, and copped a plea with the manager. I told him my partner had run out on me a couple of times before, staying away longer than he intended—but begged him not to worry because Mr. Mintz always came back to settle accounts. My frank approach didn't do much good, however. "This kind of monkey business don't go with me," the manager said. "You pay up for your three days here or I'll call the sheriff."

When the sheriff arrived, I put on my derby, picked up my bag and went obediently along to the local jig.

The sheriff let me telephone New York City—reversing the charges, which was unusual in those days. I called the neighborhood drugstore at 93rd and Lex, and they got Minnie—who was back from Atlantic City—to come to the phone. When I told her what had happened she hit the roof. The idea of Frenchie letting me go off on the road with a crook like Seymour Mintz! Why, you could tell from the way he walked he wasn't on the level. Minnie had forgotten that Mintz had first latched on to me through her introduction.

75

Anyway, she borrowed the money for the hotel bill and my return fare from Uncle Al. Three days later I was home again. The firm of Mintz & Marx was dissolved. My collection of business cards went down the dumbwaiter with the garbage. It would be a long time before I saw my name in print again.

It was a long time, too, before I found out the truth about Seymour Mintz, why he had taken me on, and what he did every time he disappeared. Actually it was Frenchie who found out—from Seymour's father, who came around to announce that he was no longer responsible for his son's debts. If anybody could get this word to Seymour he would appreciate it. Mr. Mintz thought Frenchie might know who his son's current partner was. Apparently there'd been two or three new ones since my retirement.

Seymour's racket was this: In his suitcase he carried samples of trousers and haberdashery—elegant, expensive-looking goods. He'd show these to merchants and take orders at ridiculously low prices. The prices he quoted were hard to resist, and he had no trouble getting big orders and big cash advances. These advances were the rolls of bills he flashed when he swooped to my rescue—in Judge Duffy's court and in the upstate clink.

None of his orders was ever delivered, of course. That's why Mintz had to keep on the move and move fast.

My job on the road, unbeknownst to me, was that of decoy. After Seymour dumped me in a hotel, he worked all the small towns in the area, taking orders and collecting money against them. When he figured he had the territory milked dry, he came running back, hollering with phony outrage, to bail me out. Then we jumped to the second town, where he signed me into the hotel and took off to fleece a new batch of suckers.

He always assured his prospects that his partner, Mr. Marx, was staying in the Hotel So-and-so, working on deliveries. If they wanted, they could call the hotel at Mr. Mintz's expense and verify this. Fortunately, nobody ever inquired any further while I was involved. If anybody had raised a stink, Mr. Mintz would have taken it on the lam and Mr. Marx would have taken the rap.

Seymour had been caught up with more than once, and each time his father had had to pay off the merchants who'd been swindled. Finally old man Mintz got fed up and refused to shell out another cent. As a result, Seymour's last partnership was his biggest one—with the state of New York. He served two years in Dannemora State Prison.

I was deeply hurt by it all—but not by being arrested three times or by having to pay back the twenty bucks Minnie borrowed from Uncle Al. I was hurt because I had lost a friend, Seymour Mintz. The experience should have given me pause for reflection and made me a keener judge of people, their character and motives. But I'm afraid the only lesson I learned was simply, "Never trust a guy who walks on a bias."

In the next five months I was hired and fired twelve times. I hadn't learned any business lessons during my upstate trip either.

My first job was as cigarette boy at the Freundschaft Club, a German joint down on 79th Street. This was a big private club with poolroom, beer hall, dining rooms and cardrooms, on three floors. It was run by a red-faced, mustachioed guy who looked like Kaiser Wilhelm, which was what we called him behind his back.

I worked alternating shifts of eight and twelve hours, for a salary of twenty-five cents a day plus meals. I did all right between meals, too. I would put away nine, ten, twelve hamburgers at a sitting. The chef was stunned by my capacity. He used to win bets with other guys on the staff on how much I could eat without stopping. If I had a piece of the action I could put away fourteen hamburgers, no trouble at all.

As cigarette boy, I didn't actually sell cigarettes. I gave them out for club tickets, or chits. No money was supposed to change hands. That was a depressing thought, so I soon remedied the situation. I got a nice little side line going, selling cigarettes for less per pack than the members paid for the chits. My racket was doomed, however. I found out that at the end of every month the Kaiser took careful inventory of the stock and checked it against the sale of chits. Well, I would worry about that when the time came. But when the time came I had nothing to worry about, since I no longer worked there.

Coming off my shift one night I was starved, as usual, so I sneaked down to the kitchen and swiped a roast chicken. As luck would have it, Kaiser Wilhelm stepped into the elevator I was riding back upstairs. I shifted the chicken quickly behind me, stuffing it under my shirt. But my look must have given me away. The Kaiser grabbed me by the shoulder and spun me around. The roast chicken fell to the elevator floor, and that was the end of my employment at the Freundschaft Club.

My next two positions were in the cloak-and-suit industry, farther south in Manhattan. I was hired first as a ragpicker. My job was to sweep up all the rags from the cutting-room floor and stuff them in huge bags, to be weighed out at the end of the day. At the end of one day, a bag of rags weighed suspiciously high. That was because I was asleep in it. I was fired.

I was then hired down the street as a delivery boy for Edwards, Engel & Lefkowitz, another cloak-and-suit house. I lasted much longer there—a week and a half. For once, I wasn't fired. I resigned. I was ordered to deliver a monstrous bundle of suits to Wanamaker's Department Store. By the time I made it down to Astor Place, I was so exhausted I decided to stay there and apply for a job at Wanamaker's.

I was sorry to leave the garment district. I had just worked out a dodge for getting a full-course meal for five cents. This required that I eat in a long, narrow restaurant at rush hour, when the joint was jammed like a six-o'clock subway car. I would order a full-course meal at a table in the rear, then take the check and fight my way to a table in the front, where I'd order a sweet roll and coffee. The check for this—for five cents—was the one I'd pay, having torn up the check for the de luxe luncheon.

I had to watch my pennies that year. I was still paying off the money Minnie had borrowed from Uncle Al, and I kicked in most of the rest of my salary to the family. This left me barely enough for carfare, plus a nickel a day for dinner, plus an occasional two cents to treat myself to a Horton's ice-cream cone.

Once I lost my carfare home and went into a cigar store to borrow a nickel. I offered the counterman my vest as security. Without a word he went to the back of the store. He returned holding a vest exactly like mine. "I been stuck with this one you gave me for six months now," he said. "No soap." It was the same old story. The other vest was Chico's. He'd been there before me.

So anyway I gave the department stores a whirl. I was fired from Wanamaker's when I was caught in a crap game. I worked for Stern's for a few days, and also for Gimbel's. Forgotten why Stern's and Gimbel's fired me, which is probably just as well.

Next in my steady rise to becoming a failure in business, I was a cash-boy at Siegel & Cooper's, a store to which I was attracted by reason of its having an escalator. I had ridden only once on an escalator. I thought it would be fun to ride one up and down all day and get paid for it.

When I got the job, one of the first things they told me was that the escalators were for customers only. All employees had to use the back stairs.

Not discouraged, I struck up a friendship with the escalator guard, who seemed like a sympathetic fellow. He was. When he found out what I had in mind, he made a deal. He'd turn his back whenever I took a ride if I did him a favor and swiped a sheet of trading stamps for him the next time I went to the cashier's office.

I pinched a sheet of five hundred stamps and slipped them to the escalator guard. But still no ride. There was more to the deal. Now the guard wanted me to go cash the stamps for him.

This sounded pretty risky, but the guard said, "They won't recognize you through the window, kid. You're too new here."

Well, they recognized me. My sty gave me away. Fired.

After this I was at liberty much too long for comfort. I was getting mighty hungry, so hungry that I even went to Edwards, Engel & Lefkowitz to ask for my old job back. The foreman was still sore at me for having quit without notice and gone over to Wanamaker's, but the bookkeeper felt sorry for me. He gave me a note to a friend of his named Haverhill, a shipping broker who had an office way downtown near the Battery.

The following Monday I went to work for Mr. Haverhill. This

turned out to be the first job I ever took seriously and showed signs of making good at. Yet it was, ironically, the only job I was ever unjustly fired from.

The function of F. M. Haverhill's office was to obtain customs permits for firms to ship goods abroad. I remember two of the clients well: the Pfauder Tank Company and the Ansonia Clock Company. I remember them well because, after my first day in the office, I did all the work. I took the calls, listed specifications of shipments, went to the steamship companies to get the export permits, and delivered the permits to the clients' offices.

I was happy to be this busy, and carry this much responsibility. If I say so myself, there was no more efficient shipping brokerage clerk in New York City.

If any problems came up, I took them over to a saloon on West Street, which was where Mr. Haverhill spent his working day. My boss was a tolerant, aristocratic gentleman of the old school. He forgave me my mistakes, and was a patient teacher. He had only one failing. He was a lush.

Although my boss was seldom there, I was never lonely on the job. Haverhill shared office space with a trucking firm. Two cheerful men, a Mr. Wicks and a Mr. Thornton, ran the trucking business, and they treated me as an equal since I ran the brokerage business.

This was a new part of town for me, down by the harbor, and I very soon came to love it. On the Battery, at the very tip of Manhattan, was the Aquarium, a fascinating place, and there was a public swimming pool nearby. Also nearby was a Max's Busy Bee, one of a chain of marvelous cut-rate diners. Max of the Busy Bees, whatever else he might have been, was the office boy's best friend. He provided exactly the kind of food we liked the best, at prices we could afford to pay.

At the Busy Bee, smoked salmon on rye sold for three cents per square foot. Lemonade to wash it down cost a penny per pint glass. A jumbo piece of strawberry shortcake, oozing with fresh berries and smothered with whipped cream, was three cents. And while you were eating, countermen would yell out the day's specials, to keep your appetite whetted: "Take a fresh-baked blueberry pie home to Mother! Nine cents apiece!" "Give the family a treat tonight! Whaddaya say? Today only—chocolate walnut layer cake, double size eleven cents!"

With the boss holed up cozily in his saloon, I could take an hour and a half or two hours for lunch. All I could eat at Max's Busy Bee. A swim in the pool. A nap in the sun. A stroll through the Aquarium looking at exotic fish. Then back to my desk and my official documents, to take care of my important clients.

This was a job I could work at forever. Could there be a catch to it? There was. There was a duty I hadn't been told about when I was hired.

While Mr. Haverhill and the trucking firm shared our office space, half and half, they didn't split the rent half and half. On the first of every month Haverhill played a game with either Thornton or Wicks, and the loser had to pay the entire month's rent. The game was Who Can Kick the Highest, Keeping One Foot on the Floor? If Haverhill kicked higher than Thornton or Wicks (who tossed to see which of them would compete), the trucking outfit paid the rent. If Haverhill was outkicked, he picked up the tab for the month.

On the first working day of June, the 3rd, I reported to the saloon for my weekly instructions, and that was when Mr. Haverhill explained the rent-kicking arrangement to me. He wasn't in very good shape, looking as if he'd spent the whole weekend in the saloon. So I offered to help him over to the office for his monthly kick.

Mr. Haverhill was touched by my concern, but he said it wouldn't be necessary. He simply wasn't up to anything so strenuous. He wasn't well, not well at all—the old liver, didn't I know. He couldn't win, and he couldn't afford to lose. Therefore he designated me to take his place.

At that age my height was a full five-foot-two. Thornton was six foot even and Wicks was six-foot-three. I told the boss I couldn't possibly kick against either of them. "Nonsense," said Mr. Haver-hill. "Think big, m'boy, and you'll be big. Think tall, be tall. If I didn't have faith in you I wouldn't let you handle the permits. Now go—show me you have faith in me."

I went. I kicked. I lost. My opponent was Wicks. Even with cheating, my left foot three inches off the floor, I couldn't get my right toe any higher than Wicks's chin. I returned to the saloon with the rent notice. I wasn't too upset because I was sure now it was all a practical joke.

It was no joke. Mr. Haverhill stared morosely into his shot of whiskey and said he would have to let me go at the end of the week. He regretted this deeply. I had been a good, diligent em-ployee, he said, and I had a great future ahead of me—in any capacity except as rent kicker. When I collected my final salary he gave me an unexpected bonus: a package of matzohs, to take home for the next Jewish holidays. I had never known a nicer man. I felt he was a true friend, and therefore I felt sorry for him when he had to fire me.

I didn't feel sorry for myself because I never had and didn't know how to.

Wicks, the trucking man, who was the immediate cause of my leaving the brokerage business, was also the indirect cause of my becoming a professional musician. Through him one of his clients, a Mr. Wentworth, hired me for a special job delivering some flowers to an address in Brooklyn. He promised to pay me for this with a ride on a horse, any Sunday I wanted.

When I got to the house in Brooklyn there was an Irish wake in progress. It had been in progress for some time, and the mourners were no longer very mournful. They insisted I join the shindig. I was afraid not to. Somebody poured me a tumbler full of rotgut booze. Even the smell of it made me dizzy. The crowd yelled for me to drink 'er down. I looked around desperately for a means of escape. I would have been happy to change places with the corpse in the coffin. Then I spotted a piano. How about if I played a tune for them? Everybody whooped and drank to the idea. What this wake needed was a little music to liven it up.

I parked my derby on the piano, upside down, and banged out "Waltz Me Around Again, Willie." I wanted to switch to "Love Me and the World Is Mine" but they wouldn't hear of it. They only wanted to hear "Waltz Me Around," again and again, faster and louder. The faster and louder I played, the drunker the mourners got and the more they cried and the more dimes they dropped in my derby.

I came home with a hatful of silver. I now perceived what Chico saw in the piano, much as he detested it and much as he would rather be playing pinochle. There was money in it.

Being at liberty again, I gave this serious consideration. I asked Chico what he could do to break me into his field. I couldn't have asked him at a better time. He was then working at a beer garden in Yorkville but he had just been asked to play in a nickelodeon across the street, where the piano player, a kid named George Gershwin, had been fired because customers complained his music hurt their ears.

It was a natural setup. Chico and I looked more like twins at that time than we ever had. So one night I slid onto the piano stool in the *brauhaus* and Chico played in the nickelodeon, and nobody knew the difference. Nobody knew the difference, that is, until I had played my repertoire of two numbers in the same key six times over, ignoring all requests for other tunes. Then a dame who felt like singing "Love Me and the World Is Mine" asked if I could please play it just a little higher, to fit her register. The only way I could play it higher, of course, was to play it an octave higher—still in my one and only key, the key of C.

That did it. The manager paid me off and asked me to leave the premises. He couldn't figure out how I had degenerated to such a lousy piano player overnight.

I appealed to Chico again. The trouble, he said, was that the beer

83

garden patrons were used to his style, and it was unfair that I had to follow him. He had a new proposition. He would make the rounds and audition. Any job he was hired for I could take over, fresh.

This worked fine, up to a point—the point where managers and paying customers found out that I could play only two tunes in one key. Chico got the jobs. I turned up to play. I got fired.

It was discouraging. I was making a few bucks one night here, one night there, but the turnover was killing. It couldn't go on forever. In a year's time, I figured, Chico would have conned me into every joint in town and I would have been canned out of every one of them and that would be the absolute end of my career at the keyboard.

Then a momentous thing occurred. I answered a PIANO PLAYER WANTED ad. I auditioned on my own, and on my own I got hired.

Exactly how momentous this was destined to be I didn't know, bless my simple, trusting soul.

CHAPTER 6

Love Me and
the World Is Mine

T‌HE ADDRESS in the ad I answered for a piano player was on the Bowery. It turned out to be a saloon. When I told the bartender why I was there he jerked a thumb toward the back room and said, "Mrs. Schang."

In the back room stood the biggest woman I had ever seen. She was about six-foot-two and none of it fat, but all bone and muscle, a Powerful Katinka in the flesh. She was leaning on a piano, smoking a cigarette and drinking straight gin.

"Mrs. Schang?" I said. I was so struck by the sight of her that my voice came out even squeakier than usual. "Mrs. Schang? You advertised for a piano player?"

She looked at me through narrow eyes, hard. She slammed her shot glass on the piano top. "You little Jew son-of-a-bitch," she said, in a voice at least an octave lower than mine. "Get out of here!"

I started to walk out. "Hey, wait a minute!" she called. I stopped. "What's your name, kid?" she said.

I told her my name was Marx. "Marx? *What* Marx?" she roared.

"Adolph Marx," I said.

Mrs. Schang poured herself some gin and sipped it while she studied me carefully, up and down and sideways. I was wearing my usual outfit, derby, turtle-neck sweater and sty, with a new pair of shoes that had high heels and extra lifts to make me look taller. In the towering presence of Mrs. Schang, my new shoes didn't do much good. I felt about two feet tall.

Finally she said, "All right, let me hear you play."

I launched into "Waltz Me Around Again, Willie." She stopped me halfway through. "If you want the job, okay," she said. "When will you be ready to go? The job ain't here. It's in my place."

I said I was ready right now and asked what street her place was on. Street, hell, she said. Her place was on Merrick Road, out in Freeport, Long Island. Did I still want the job? I said I sure did. "Okay," said Mrs. Schang. "Eight dollars a month plus room and board."

I had passed my first solo audition.

My new boss and I rode the train to Freeport. She didn't talk to me, not a word, during the trip. We were met out on the island by a tall, skinny kid about five years older than me, who drove us by horse and buggy to a joint on Merrick Road. Mrs. Schang didn't speak to him, either. It was a week before I found out he was her son.

My new place of employment was a joint called "The Happy Times Tavern." There was a bar in front, and a dance floor in back with an upright piano, where four girls solicited prospects. The girls made their money upstairs, where they took their customers. Half of what they made, I learned, they had to fork over to "the Madam," as they called Mrs. Schang. The Happy Times Tavern was a road-show version of the Friendly Inn, back in Chinatown.

My job as Mrs. Schang outlined it was simple. "When I tell you to start playing the piano, you play," she said. "If a fight starts you get behind the piano and stay there—understand?—until I tell you it's safe to come out. I take care of all the fights around here."

In spite of her ominous briefing, the joint seemed pretty quiet my first day there. Mostly I sat around the back room talking with the girls and playing for them. We got along great. Two of them I liked especially. They couldn't hear enough of "Love Me and the World Is Mine," and sat with tears in their eyes while I played it again and again.

Then, about six-thirty, Mrs. Schang yelled, "Here they come! Start playing! Good and loud!"

The girls braced themselves, as if they were getting ready to face a firing squad. I started playing, good and loud. And in they came— about twenty of the dirtiest, meanest-looking men I had ever seen. A canal was being dug near Freeport at the time and this was the crew, thirsting for liquor, women and roughhouse.

There wasn't any serious trouble with the canal diggers until Saturday night, the only night they stayed late. They were paid on Saturdays. A free-for-all broke out after two customers came to blows over whose turn it was with one of the girls. Following orders gladly, I ducked behind the piano. The brawl didn't last long. Mrs. Schang waded into the thick of it swinging a bung-starter. By the time she'd heaved six guys out the back door, two at a time, the rest of the crew got the idea and quieted down.

The seventh guy she grabbed was me. She hoisted me out from behind the piano and dropped me onto the stool. "I'm paying you to play, you son-of-a-bitch," she said. "Play!" I obeyed. I had never played worse, but I had never played louder, either.

I soon settled down into a routine at the roadhouse. It wasn't so bad, really. In some ways I'd never had it so good. I could make eight bucks a month and keep eight bucks, since my living expenses were taken care of. In a few months I could resign and go home independently wealthy.

Besides the girls, there were three others on Mrs. Schang's staff, and they were friendly toward me too. Mr. Schang, the Madam's husband, a silent fellow with stooped shoulders and sunken eyes, was the handyman around the joint. Their son, Christopher, took care of the horse and did all the driving. A German guy named Max, who was about my size but a good deal older than me, was the bartender. Both Mr. Schang and Christopher took orders from the Madam the same as Max and all the rest of us. And like any of us, they would pass the warning along if the Madam started hitting the gin. When Mrs. Schang went on a binge, she would roar around the joint like a wounded bull. It was wise to stay out of her path on such occasions.

While things were never exactly quiet in the Happy Times, I felt it was a good, secure place to work. Then I began to sense that something fishy was going on. There was more to this operation than met the eye.

One night during my second week there, the Madam called me into the bar after the diggers had left. She said she had some business to attend to on the outside, along with Christopher and Max.

"I want you to mind the saloon until we get back," she said. "Don't forget—gin ten cents, whiskey fifteen, beer a nickel. Don't try to get away with anything, because I've marked the bottles and checked the register."

Now I was a part-time bartender, which in the saloon business was a hell of a step up from being a full-time piano player. The three of them returned in an hour or so. Max took over again, and I went back to my stool in the back room, and it was business as usual.

But not everything was as usual. An odd change had come over the Madam, her son, and Max, between the time they left and the time they returned. The Madam was strangely silent. She stood by the bar slugging down the gin, saying nothing. Max's hand shook when he poured her drinks. Christopher wandered around like a lost soul. I'd never seen such a quick change in a guy. He seemed to have aged fifteen years in the hour he was gone.

Next week the same thing happened. The Madam told me to take over the bar. If anybody wanted to dance, she said, they could go to hell. I was not to leave the saloon. The three of them were gone longer this time. When they got back, it was worse than before, the change that had come over them.

The mysterious nighttime "business trips" got to be part of the routine. I tried to find out from Max what was going on. The more I pumped him, the more he shook and the more he tightened up. I asked the girls if they knew. They didn't know and didn't care. It was plain that Mrs. Schang didn't want me to know any more than I did. When she caught me hanging around Max, pestering him, she cursed me out and told me never to set foot in the saloon unless she gave the order.

The next day Max didn't show up for work. Christopher took over behind the bar. I never saw Max again, never again heard mention of his name. After Max's disappearance Christopher stewed in a perpetual state of the jitters and the Madam got roaring drunk and stayed drunk. The mysterious business trips stopped.

A week later Mrs. Schang finally sobered up. She had absorbed so much gin it stopped having any effect, and this seemed to make her madder than ever before. She came in the back room and grabbed me off the piano stool. "Get in the buggy, out front," she said. "You're driving tonight."

By the time I got my derby and got in the buggy she was already there, waiting for me. Then she told me to run to the kitchen and get a meat knife. When I did, she slit her pocketbook and stuck a pistol and a pint of gin between the cover and the lining. She said to get going, and fast.

I asked where we were going. Mrs. Schang said, "Keep driving east until we get to the Pot O' Gold. I'm going to kill Louie Neidorf."

I didn't know who Louie Neidorf was, and I didn't care. I had never seen anybody fire a gun before. The prospect was so thrilling I could hardly hold the reins. We pulled up in front of the Pot O' Gold—a roadhouse on the other side of town, about five or six miles away.

"Don't tie up the horse," said Mrs. Schang. "We're going to have to leave here in a hurry. Come on inside."

We went inside. We sat at a table facing the door. Mrs. Schang plunked down her pocketbook in front of her. She narrowed her eyes, and waited. Every time a guy walked in the door, I said, "Hey! Is that him? Is that him?" and she gave me a swift kick in the shins under the table and growled, "Shut up, you."

We sat there for over half an hour. A lot of guys came in, but Mrs. Schang's hand never came out of her pocketbook. I was getting desperate. I was pleading with her now whenever anybody walked through the door. "Isn't *that* him?" I was saying. "That *must* be him!" Oh, how I wanted to see that gun go off!

Finally she spat on the floor and said, "Somebody, God damn it, has tipped him off. He's not coming. Let's go home."

The Madam charged out of the Pot O' Gold cursing a blue streak, with me running to keep up with her. Her eyes were wild and her hair was flying all over the place. She plotzed herself in the carriage and took out her gin bottle and took a long swig. I never saw anybody get so drunk so fast. All of a sudden she got the idea she had fired at Louie Neidorf and missed him.

"You little son-of-a-bitch!" she screamed. "I missed!" Now it was all my fault.

We tore back toward home. I was standing up, shaking the reins, and I was scared now, shuddering with hot and cold flashes. The horse clopped down Merrick Road in full gallop, but still not fast enough to suit Mrs. Schang. She was swilling gin and getting fiery boiled, and between gulps she screamed at me to drive faster. I was in a daze. My head was spinning in crazy circles. It was a horrible, hideous nightmare.

When she drained the gin bottle she let out a curse I'd never heard from a woman's lips before and flung the empty bottle— smashing the one remaining carriage light into oblivion. She tore the reins out of my grip and began to whip the horse's rump unmercifully. Thank God the horse knew the way. We were careening through inky blackness.

When we got to the Happy Times Tavern the Madam pulled to a stop. She jumped out and ran for the saloon, desperate for a refill. Over her shoulder she yelled at me to put the horse away.

The poor beast was lathered with sweat and foam and wheezing like a leaky steam engine. I managed to get him out of harness and into his stall before I started heaving up. I was too sick to move. I went to sleep on a pile of straw.

When I woke up in the morning Christopher Schang was there in the stables crying. The horse was dead. Christopher started wailing at me that this was the best friend he ever had, and I had killed him. How should I know from a horse, that you had to cool him out after a gallop and put him to bed with a blanket on?

I felt sicker than ever when the Madam learned the news, late the next afternoon. She was still drunk, and she looked at me with mean, unadulterated murder in her eyes. I began to play the piano with such force that my fingers stung. For once, I hoped there would be a big, rough crowd in the Happy Times. Anything to keep the Madam's hands diverted from my throat.

A big crowd came that night. Just as the diggers swarmed into the joint I felt suddenly dizzy, like I had during the wild ride the night before. The back room started lifting and sinking and turning around in a circle. I lost all control. I fell off the piano stool. One of the girls helped me up. I fell off again. This time Mrs. Schang saw me. She bellowed at me to get the hell back on the stool and start playing. I staggered to my feet and fell against the keyboard. The Madam grabbed me and sat me straight, so hard that the butt of my spine felt like it was cracked.

The third time I dropped to the floor she was back in the saloon. Two of the girls picked me up and dragged me upstairs and laid me on the bed, while another girl went to call a doctor. The doctor came. He felt my forehead. He opened my shirt and looked at me closely.

"Measles," the doctor said.

When word of my condition was passed downstairs, I could hear Mrs. Schang roar, clean through the floor, "I don't want no sick Jews in my place! *Get him out of here!*"

The next thing I remember I was waiting on the platform of the Freeport railroad station. The back-room girls had chipped in to buy me a ticket to the city, and two of them—my special friends—had brought me to the train.

The train came. They helped me on board. One of the girls said, "You don't know how lucky you are, kid, to come down with the measles." The other girl was about to cry. "I'm going to miss you, honey," she said. "I'm going to miss that song you play so beautiful."

The four whores of the Happy Times were the first fans I ever had, and I shall always be grateful to them.

The story had three endings. First, I got over the measles in short order, thanks to Grandpa's care and Frenchie's chicken soup. Second, a story in a New York paper was brought to my attention a month or so after I came home from Freeport.

INDICTED AS BURGLAR GANG

MINEOLA, L.I., Aug. 1—Fourteen indictments charging burglary and grand larceny were found by the Nassau County Grand Jury today against August Van Fehrig, alias Luckner, leader of the gang of burglars that robbed more than twenty houses in this neighborhood recently, cleaning up $50,000. Eleven indictments charging the same crimes were found against Christopher Schang, 19 years old, a member of the gang, and two indictments for receiving stolen goods were returned against his aged mother, Mrs. Alma Schang.

When the prisoners were brought into court before County Judge Jackson for pleading, Mrs. Schang, who had to be supported by Sheriff Foster, suddenly screamed and fell fainting to the floor. She was carried back to the jail unconscious. . . .

It was obvious to me who had ratted on the Schangs—Louie Neidorf, the guy who never showed up that night at the Pot O' Gold. Little Max, the missing bartender, was never found. The Long Island police were pretty certain the Schang gang had done him in, but they didn't have enough evidence to make a murder rap stick.

The third ending to the Freeport episode came years later. That was when I finally found out why the Madam had given me such a funny look when she first saw me, in the Bowery saloon, and why she kept making such nasty references to my religion and ancestry.

One night, in the middle of a crap game in a Pullman car, while we were traveling the Pantages Circuit, Chico confessed that he had been the Happy Times piano player before me, while I was upstate with Seymour Mintz. When I turned up to audition, Mrs. Schang thought I was Chico. Then, when I played, she knew I wasn't, and took a chance and hired me.

Chico also confessed that he had been fired by Mrs. Schang for a far less innocent reason than coming down with the measles. He'd become a little too friendly with one of the girls in the back room.

I now regarded myself, after the events of the summer, as more of a man than a boy. With this new confidence I sailed forth from my sickbed and got myself a job playing for a nickelodeon.

I had learned a whole set of fancy variations on my two tunes, enough so I could accompany any kind of movie without the audience realizing that I was repeating myself. For comedies: "Waltz Me Around Again, Willie," played two octaves high and fast. Dramatic scenes: "Love Me and the World Is Mine," with a tremolo in the bass. Love scenes: a trill in the right hand. For the chase: either song, played too fast to be recognized.

The nickelodeon was down on 34th Street in Manhattan, and it was mainly patronized by people traveling through that district. The joint was stuffy and smelly. People talked, ate and snored through the pictures. Kids yelled and chased each other up and down the aisles. But after the Happy Times Tavern, it was like a rest home.

For some reason, mothers with nursing babies liked to sit down front near the piano. Maybe they thought that music was a nice, soothing accompaniment to breast feeding. Anyway, I used to have fun with them. In the middle of a quiet scene I'd suddenly whack

93

the hell out of a chord, just to watch the nipples snap out of the babies' mouths.

It was while I was working at the nickelodeon that Gummo joined Groucho onstage in vaudeville. With a kid named Lou Levy they opened at Henderson's, a Coney Island beer garden, as a singing trio.

One afternoon, in the middle of the movie, my mother marched down the aisle of the theatre to the piano. She ordered me to leave at once and come with her. Minnie's face was set with desperation and determination. She was in some kind of a jam, and from the look of her, it could be serious trouble. Minnie had never come to me for help in a crisis before. Without question, I got up from the piano stool and followed her out of the nickelodeon.

I don't think the audience knew the difference when the music stopped. They went right on talking, stuffing themselves, sleeping, and nursing their babies.

It was not until Minnie got me on the El train that the awful truth of her mission struck me, like a bolt of lightning out of a clear sky. We were headed for Coney Island. I was being shanghaied. I was being shanghaied to join Groucho, Gummo, and Lou Levy. On a stage. Singing. In front of people.

On the train, Minnie screened me with a newspaper while I changed into a white duck suit, my costume. At the same time she tried to teach me the words to "Darling Nelly Gray." I was too weak with dread to protest. My mind went blank. I couldn't possibly learn the song before we got to Coney Island.

Didn't matter anyway, Minnie said. As long as I opened my mouth in the right places—by keeping an eye on Groucho—I didn't have to make a peep. It would be best I didn't try to sing, in fact. I was supposed to be the bass, and my squeaky voice could ruin the whole effect. The only important thing was that Minnie get a quartet onstage. In the first place, she had bought four white duck suits in order to get a decent price on costumes (there was a mark-down only in sets of four) and it was idiotic to let the fourth white duck suit go to waste.

In the second place, the featured act on the bill was "That

Quartet," a famous singing group of the day. It would look pretty cheap if Minnie could only put a trio of boys on instead of a quartet.

When I arrived backstage at Henderson's Gummo greeted me with a soulful, brotherly look of commiseration. He didn't need to speak. His eyes said all he had to say: *So she hooked you too, huh?*

We came into the wings to wait for our cue. A comedy juggler was finishing up his act on the stage. I could hear Them, out there, the Audience. Some of Them were laughing, some hooting, the rest of Them rumbling with insolent, impolite indifference. I wanted to run away, but I couldn't move.

We were supposed to march onstage military fashion—Groucho in the lead, followed by Lou, myself and Gummo. Our cue came. Groucho marched. Lou marched. And Gummo marched—practically up my back, because I still couldn't move. I was rooted to the spot.

Minnie hissed at me. I just stood there. Minnie pushed me. She pushed me harder, a real hefty shove in the small of my back. I went stumbling out of the wings and onto the stage. As I caught my balance, the thought sizzled in my mind: *You're not a boy any more. You're a man. Don't let on you're scared.*

I came to a halt beside Lou Levy. I turned. And there They were. A sea of hostile, mocking faces across the footlights. And here I was, with nothing to hold onto, absolutely nothing. With my first look at my first audience I reverted to being a boy again. My reaction was instantaneous and overwhelming. I wet my pants.

It was probably the most wretched debut in the history of show business.

Every turning point in my life seems to have been a low point, a time of terrible disappointment or disaster. I never planned any changes in the course of my career. The changes just happened. The only ambitions I ever nourished were to be left fielder for the New York Giants, a full-time tin-can swinger for an umbrella mender, or a piano player on an excursion boat. I never achieved any of these ambitions. What I actually became was what I was driven to be in a time of disaster.

The rock-bottom low point of my early life was that time I went onstage and disgraced myself in the company of my brothers and in front of the public, at Coney Island. I became, therefore, an entertainer. Nothing that I could have done could have frightened me more.

Nobody heard me sing in the quartet that night at Henderson's. It was all I could do to open my mouth at approximately the same time that Groucho, Lou and Gummo opened their mouths. But I sang, a voiceless swan song. I sang farewell to the streets of the East Side, to hustling and hopping trolleys and swindling ticket-choppers, farewell to happy-go-lucky, hired-today-and-fired-tomorrow wandering from job to job, farewell to "Waltz Me Around Again, Willie" and Max's Busy Bee. Like it or not, I was in show business for the rest of my days.

At the age of fourteen, I didn't like it a bit.

CHAPTER 7

"Greenbaum, You Crazy Kids!"

My mother decided one night in the year 1910, after a brutal, fruitless day of battle with New York booking agents, that we should live in the central part of the country. New York was not right for us. Too much big-time competition. Where we should be was in the hub of the small-time vaudeville circuits and wheels, where an act like ours would have a fighting chance.

So the next day we packed up our things and on to Chicago we moved, lock, stock and Grandpa.

By juggling her accounts, signing notes, and putting the touch on Uncle Al, Minnie was able to make a down payment on a three-story, brownstone house in a fairly respectable Chicago neighborhood. The Marxes had, at last, a place to call their own. And a fabulous place it was, to us. It had no grimy stoop, but a genuine front porch—which Grandpa immediately took over as the equivalent of the front room on 93rd Street. For Frenchie, there was the luxury of a huge kitchen, where he could cook with gas. He no longer had to depend on his sons to swipe wood or coal before he could get a meal on the stove. Best of all, the house had a basement big enough for a pool table.

The house also had a mortgage big enough to plug a storm-drain, but that was nothing to worry about, we told ourselves. We were now bona fide property owners, shareholders in America. We had risen in class far beyond our wildest dreams. Who should worry about Mr. Greenbaum, who held the mortgage, coming around for the monthly payment? Hadn't we ducked, dodged and outfoxed the rent agent back on 93rd Street for eleven years? None of us had the foresight to realize that there was no place for a family to hide in a one-family dwelling.

Besides, we did all right in Chicago—at first. Minnie had been right, apparently, in hauling us out of New York. Here she could get us theatres to play. Not the best theatres, or even in the best neighborhoods, but bookings that paid good, green money none the less.

But before long we ran out of offbeat, small-time theatres to get booked into. There was no place for us to go except on the road.

The vaudeville circuits that guaranteed an act thirty weeks of work for a season wanted no part of us. We put up with whatever we could find for ourselves: one-night stands, conventions, picnics, benefits, anything that guaranteed a minimum of dinner and train fare. Looking back, I simply don't know how we survived it. Those early days on the road were sheer, unmitigated hell. They made my earlier days on the streets of the East Side seem like one long recess period.

We had to brazen our way into strange towns in the Midwest and down South, where we knew we had three strikes against us. One: we were stage folks, in a class with gypsies and other vagrants. Two: we were Jewish. Three: we had New York accents. And, well—strike four: the Four Nightingales weren't very good.

We had no itinerary. We took the train until we came to a town. We got off the train, walked to the local theatre or "air-dome," made a deal for a percentage of the box-office take, plastered the town with posters announcing our show, opened, and prayed for the best. If we made more than train fare money, we stayed the night in the cheapest hotel or boardinghouse we could find and took the morning train out of town. If we couldn't afford this, we slept on the night-train coach. If we couldn't afford even the train, we walked.

If an audience didn't like us we had no trouble finding it out. We were pelted with sticks, bricks, spitballs, cigar butts, peach pits and chewed-out stalks of sugar cane. We took all this without flinching —until Minnie gave us the high-sign that she'd collected our share of the receipts. Then we started throwing the stuff back at the audience, and ran like hell for the railroad station the second the curtain came down.

When we went to a hotel, we never asked to see the accommodations first. We only asked what the rates were, paid up if they were low enough, and went straight upstairs and to sleep. We knew what the accommodations would be like anyway—gritty, smelly, either stifling hot or freezing cold, and infested with vermin. But a bed was a bed, even with four adolescent boys fighting for the spaces between lumps and broken springs, and it was a luxury.

In our first three years on the road, we must have walked the equivalent of the length and breadth of the state of Texas, lugging two bags apiece, crammed with posters, props and costumes. We walked through heat waves and blizzards, through dust storms, rainstorms and hailstorms. We were bitten bloody by horseflies and mosquitoes.

The bugs were even worse indoors. Cheap hotels in the South and Southwest were apparently set up as bug sanctuaries by some Audubon Society for Insects. Fleas, ticks, bedbugs, cockroaches, beetles, scorpions and ants, having no enemies, attacked with fearless abandon. They had the run of the house and they knew it. After awhile you just let them bite. Fighting back was useless. For every bug you squashed, a whole fresh, bloodthirsty platoon would march out of the woodwork. In one hotel the ants were so bad that each bed was set on four pots of oxalic acid. This kept the ants off. It also kept them from competing with the fleas and the bedbugs, who had the human banquet all to themselves.

Dressing-room windows never had screens. If the windows were shut, you could suffocate. If they were open you could be bitten to a red pulp by mosquitoes before you got changed and made up. We kept our health and sanity by improvising smudge-pots,

99

burning green grass in tin cans. Of course we couldn't see through the smoke and had to put our make-up on by braille, and sometimes we didn't stop coughing until halfway through the show, but we survived.

We survived the food we had to eat, too. Our standard fare was boardinghouse spaghetti, chili and beans. Even when we had extra dough, we could seldom get anything better. By the time we finished a show, restaurants and cafés would be locked up for the night. We'd be lucky to find a guy selling tamales from a pushcart, by the station. Once we had the nerve to complain that our hot tamales were not only cold but were caked with dust and crawling with what looked like lice. The pushcart vendor said we could go to hell. If his stuff was good enough for white folks, he said, it was good enough for us New York Jews.

We put on our act in ball parks, amusement parks, schoolhouses, now and then in a real theatre, but mainly in air-domes —shedlike outdoor theatres. Top admission for our shows was usually ten cents indoors, and five cents outdoors. With only nickels and dimes coming into the box office, our percentage of the take would be pretty damn small. Even so, we had to fight for it most of the time. We were completely at the mercy of local managers and booking agents. If they ran off with the share of the receipts they had promised us, we had nobody to appeal to. There was nothing we could do except pick up our bags and start walking to the next town, before we got thrown in the jig as vagrants.

So that was the Road of One-Night Stands, our life from 1910 to 1915. It was a miracle that we stuck it out. A lot of very brave and determined show people fell by the wayside doing what we were doing. It wasn't that my brothers and I had any more guts or determination than the guys who gave up. But we had Minnie, and Minnie did. She was our miracle.

If you should ever hear an old-time vaudevillian talk about "the wonderful, golden days of one-night stands," buy him another drink, but don't believe a word he's saying. He's lying through his teeth. If a movie producer or a Broadway director should tell you he made it the Hard Way by struggling through the Borscht

Circuit in the Catskill Mountains, humor him along. He's not lying. He's just too young. His memory doesn't go back far enough to know what the Hard Way really was.

My own memory, of my own days of struggle, is a crazy jumble of time and places. I never kept track of time, never believed in calendars. I never had much of a sense of geography either. I probably traveled twenty-five thousand miles and played in three hundred different cities and towns in the twelve years the Marx Brothers worked out of Chicago. From the sound of that, I ought to be a walking atlas. Not so. About cities and towns I remember very little. What I remember are railroad-station waiting rooms, boardinghouse dining rooms, one-dollar hotel rooms, dressing rooms, poolrooms and men's rooms—all of which look pretty much alike in any city or town in any part of the country.

About the history of our act, what we did onstage and when, I'm not a very reliable authority. I never saved programs or clippings, or kept a diary of any kind. If I want to check on some historical fact about the Marx Brothers, I look it up in the book Kyle Crichton wrote about us or I consult the family historian, Groucho. (Chico, with his photographic memory, should be the historian, but his memory is selective as well as photographic, and what he has selected to remember are things like the poker hand he held at 1:35 A.M. on the night of January 15, 1917, while riding in a Pullman car called "The Winnetaska Rapids," or the name of a girl I once met in Altoona, Pennsylvania, whose name I would prefer not to have remembered.)

At any rate, to keep the record straight, I have checked with Mr. Crichton's book and with Groucho, and I find that these were the steps in the evolution of our act in show business:

1. Groucho Marx as a single: boy soprano and actor.
2. Unnamed duo: Groucho and Gummo.
3. The Three Nightingales: Groucho, Gummo and Lou Levy.
4. The Four Nightingales: Groucho, Gummo, Lou Levy and Harpo.

101

5. The Six Mascots: Groucho, Gummo, Harpo, plus bass singer and two girl singers (Minnie and Aunt Hannah if none others available).
6. The Marx Brothers in *School Days:* same personnel as (5), with later addition of Chico, who finally joined the act.
7. The Marx Brothers in *School Days* and *Mr. Green's Reception:* same personnel as (6).
8. The Marx Brothers in *Home Again:* same as (7), with Zeppo replacing Gummo when Gummo got drafted in World War One.
9. The Marx Brothers in *On the Mezzanine:* same as (8), plus chorus girls, dancers, actors who got paid for falling down, getting squirted at, etc.
10. *The Marx Brothers' Shubert Revue:* same as (9) but with fewer girls, dancers and actors and plus Minnie, who got briefly back into the act.
11. The Four Marx Brothers in *I'll Say She Is, The Cocoanuts* and *Animal Crackers,* on Broadway: same as (9) only more of them, plus blondes who got paid for being chased by Harpo.
12. The Four Marx Brothers in Paramount Pictures: more of everybody and everything.
13. The Three Marx Brothers in M-G-M Pictures: same as (12) but minus Zeppo, who returned to civilian life, and plus half the population of Culver City, California.
14. Unnamed duo: Chico and Harpo (available for night clubs, benefits, state fairs, stock shows, etc.).
15. Groucho Marx as a single: quizmaster, author, singer (Gilbert & Sullivan).

That's the straight dope, our grand tour down through the ages, from Groucho the soprano to Groucho the baritone. Frankly, I wouldn't believe a word of it if I hadn't read it in a book and my kid brother with the mustache hadn't confirmed it. My memory, as I said before, is a crazy jumble.

Some important things happened to me during steps (4) through (8) of our evolution. I became a pantomime comedy actor. I became a harpist. I acquired enough self-confidence to enjoy having people laugh at my goofy sight-gags and listen to the music I played seriously but all wrong.

What I remember today, I suppose, are mainly the events that had to do with these three developments. What follows is what I remember. The itinerary is therefore mixed up regarding chronology, places, and names of persons living or dead. But it's Harpo's itinerary, not History's.

Coney Island, New York. Made my debut at Henderson's and peed in my pants. I felt shamed and disgraced, but Minnie wouldn't let me quit the act on any such flimsy pretext. She hung my trousers out to dry in the sea breeze between shows. By the second show I was much less scared, so enthusiastic in fact that everybody was afraid I might sing. But I didn't. I just opened my mouth when Groucho did.

Asbury Park, New Jersey. Two years later, I was still the fourth Nightingale. I reassured myself it was only a temporary thing, as a favor for Minnie. I was now an active member of the quartet—I sang, which was doing nobody a favor. Minnie added class to our quartet by buying us red paper carnations to wear in our lapels when we opened in Asbury Park. It became an eternal challenge to Minnie to add more class to our act.

Boston. I got my first laugh onstage, at the Old Howard Theatre in Boston, the famous burlesque house. We, the Nightingales in the white duck suits with the fake carnations, did a turn in the olio, between burlesque shows. With hands on each other's shoulders and swaying in tempo, we sang "Mandy Lane." We were scarcely noticed during our number (even by the piano player, who

103

concentrated on watching the clock for his dinner hour to start) until our last night there.

At the Old Howard the loges came all the way around the house, like a giant horseshoe, and the end boxes hung over the stage. On Saturday night, between burlesque shows, there were three drunks in the end box at stage right. They were loud and restless during the olio, and especially during our rendition of "Mandy Lane." In the middle of the song, I heard one of the drunks say to his pals, "Hey, lookit! Watch me get the second kid from the end!"

The second kid from the end was me. He got me—with a jetstream of tobacco juice, smack down the front of my white duck jacket.

"Watch this!" said the drunk. "I'll get him again!" Before he could get me again I backed up two paces and marched to the lee side of Groucho, without losing a beat or diverting my eyes from the audience. The audience howled. They'd never seen anything funny in the olio before, and probably never did again. But it wasn't funny to me—or to Minnie, who spent most of the night scrubbing the tobacco-juice stain out of my costume.

Tuscaloosa, Alabama. Working out of Chicago now, on one-night stands, I would have loved to get a laugh any way I could. Anything to break the boring routine of being a squeaky, white duck Nightingale. Groucho had the only authorized comedy in the act, when he came out as a butcher's delivery boy, carrying a basket with a string of frankfurters hanging out. This, which was supposed to be hilarious, led to our closing number—a song called "Peasie Weasie." "Peasie Weasie" had endless verses, enough for all the curtain calls we'd ever get. It should have been endless. It cost Minnie fifty dollars, which was in those days an infinite amount of money.

Like any other litter of undisciplined, high-spirited kids, we were apt to bust loose at any time with horseplay, in a kind of spontaneous combustion. But where other kids expended their energy in pillow fights, Kick the Can, or King of the Mountain, to the consternation of their parents, we often did it by knocking to pieces an act we were being paid to perform, to the consternation of our parents *and* the manager who hired us *and* the public who had paid to watch us.

This night in Alabama we were so bored that we stopped singing in the middle of "Mandy Lane," when we spotted a large bug walking across the stage. The four of us got down on hands and knees and began to follow the bug, making bets whether it was a beetle, a cockroach, or a bedbug.

This kind of nonsense, on company time, was of course a valid excuse for the manager to bring the curtain down and cut us off without a cent. Frenchie, who was sitting in the middle of the house, working as our Laugh Starter (after having spent the whole day selling yard goods and lappas from door to door) was helpless to do anything about us. But Minnie wasn't. She was in the wings, watching our every move, craning her neck like a suspicious mother goose.

When we started crawling after the bug, Minnie got us back in line before we went far enough to get ourselves canned. She hissed to get our attention. Then she uttered, in a stage whisper, an all-powerful, magic word:

"*Greenbaum!*"

Greenbaum, you will recall, was the banker who held the mortgage on our house back in Chicago. Missing a monthly payment to Mr. Greenbaum could mean the loss of our new home and our membership in the aristocracy of property owners. Worse than that, it could mean the loss of a basement big enough for a pool table.

A single utterance of the magic word rarely failed. When it did, Minnie didn't care what the audience might think. She'd belt it out loud and clear: "Greenbaum, you crazy kids!"

Hammond, Louisiana. Our white duck suits were weather-beaten, threadbare and woebegone. The Nightingales' class was fading fast. We couldn't afford new costumes, so Minnie dressed up the act by buying (for a block of free tickets and two dollars cash)

105

two used mandolins for Gummo and myself to play during the finish, and she renamed our act "The Six Mascots."

Groucho already had a guitar, and all the spoken lines in the act. Gummo and I had nothing to do but sing in the quartet and strum our mandolins between verses of "Peasie Weasie." Gummo didn't care, but I did. I wanted a specialty of my own. I practiced the piano every chance I got.

Somewhere in Mississippi. I made my debut as a piano soloist, playing "The Holy City" in the seven variations I had taught myself, from waltz to ragtime. It was not a very well attended debut. I had to compete with a lynching on the other side of town, and the theatre was only a quarter filled. Still and all it was a success. Minnie said I could keep my specialty in the act.

Somewhere in Arkansas. I found out that comedy work was not all laughs. After the show, while we sat around swatting flies and counting to see if we had enough dough to sleep in beds that night, a native character rode up to the stage door on horseback. "Which one of you's the comical feller that carries the basket of sausage meat?" he wanted to know.

Groucho, thinking he had a new admirer, stepped forth and identified himself. The native looked down from his saddle with glinty, hostile eyes. "That's mah sister who plays the pi-anna in this yere the-ayter," he said. "Ah don't want to hear you makin' that kind of talk to her agin, or I'll blow your Yankee brains out. You hear?"

Groucho heard. He thought he'd added a subtle touch earlier that night by winking at the pianist in the pit when he entered as the butcher boy, and saying, "I love my wife, but oh, you kid!"

Somewhere in Texas. We lost Jenny, our girl singer. Jenny had a beautiful soprano voice, except that she always sang off key. She was good-looking, too, except that her left eye was cockeyed and used

106

to wander all over the place, and Minnie had to make up a special peekaboo wig for her that covered it. Otherwise Jenny was a grand gal, except that she was a nymphomaniac.

She prowled hotly after everything in long pants—theatre managers, hotel clerks, local idiots and local dignitaries alike. Fortunately, we were still a boys' act and wore knee pants and she didn't consider us fair game. Finally, Jenny became too much of a problem. By mutual agreement of the Marxes and whatever town we were in, she was asked to leave—leave the state of Texas altogether, preferably.

Still we felt sad when the sheriff escorted Jenny down to the station and the northbound train pulled in, sad and a little guilty too. But when the train pulled out we didn't feel so bad. Jenny waved us a cheerful farewell—from the cab of the engine, where she was sitting on the engineer's lap.

There were no girl-singer replacements to be found in those parts, so Minnie wired Aunt Hannah, in New York, to borrow the fare from Uncle Al and hurry down to join us. Aunt Hannah could only sing three notes, but she wasn't the problem the grand gal she replaced had been, either. She had her own wig.

Denison, Texas. This was a time and a place I shall never forget. The year was 1913, or maybe 1915. Come to think of it, the place might have been Bonham or Sherman instead of Denison. But it was Texas. That is a fact. A far more important fact is that, in this town, the Marx Brothers were reborn, professionally. We became a comedy act.

The audience loved the Six Mascots in Denison. So much so that the local manager asked us to play a second night, but on one condition: that we didn't repeat the same show. If we did something new, he could get the same audience to come back again. Minnie, without a second thought, agreed. We hadn't had a chance to make this kind of loot since our first weeks in the virgin territory of Chicago.

Then Minnie had a second thought. We didn't *have* anything new to do. We had one show, period. After the bass solo,

Groucho's solo and butcher-boy routine, my "Holy City," the mandolin trio, the sextet medley, and "Peasie Weasie," our repertoire was exhausted. The only other thing we knew how to do was take bows, and if we felt the audience wasn't paying enough attention, lead a group-sing of "Dixie."

Minnie called a family conference, around the boardinghouse dinner table. What could we possibly put on tomorrow night? New scenery might help disguise our old act. But there was no new scenery to be had. In fact, there was no scenery at all, since we performed not in a theatre but in a school assembly room. Groucho, the veteran trouper of the family, had an inspiration.

"Why not put on *School Days?*" he said. "I had to follow the act clear across Montana and I know it by heart."

School Days we had all seen, at least once. It was an old Gus Edwards routine, a tried-and-true chestnut. Minnie took mental stock of our costumes and props. We had everything we needed. As for the stage set—the school assembly room was perfect.

Groucho gave us the rundown on the scene, and Minnie did the casting. Herr Teacher—Groucho. Hebrew Boy—Gummo. Patsy Brannigan, the Teacher's Despair—Harpo. Mama's Boy (always "the Nance," in the trade)—the Bass. Bright Little Girl—Aunt Hannah. Not-So-Bright Little Girl—Minnie.

My Patsy Brannigan costume was a delight. Minnie got out the wig she'd made up for Jenny, our ex-girl singer, cut off the piece that used to cover Jenny's cockeye, and dyed the wig red for me. She sewed bright patches onto my traveling pants, which were pretty well shot anyway, and I used a piece of rope for a suspender. The rest of the costume was my beloved turtle-neck sweater and a decrepit beaver hat that Minnie scrounged out of the boardinghouse attic.

For a final touch before going onstage, I reddened my ears, painted on some freckles and blacked out three of my front teeth. I couldn't wait to get on. I hadn't felt so eager about playing a part since the time I dressed up like a two-bit whore and scared the bustles off the Baltzer sisters.

Waiting for my entrance, I sat by the mirror admiring my new get-up. I threw myself a big, fat beauty of a Gookie, and just then

Minnie came by. She didn't think I was being very funny. She rapped her fist on my shoulder. "Greenbaum," she said quietly, shaking her head. I got her message. No hokum. No horseplay. Stick to *School Days*.

We stuck to the scene and we were a great success. The audience liked us better the second night, as comedians, than they had the first night, as singers and mandolin-pickers. My big scene in the new act was the alphabet bit, with Groucho. It went something like this:

TEACHER (whacking his slapstick—a pair of barrel staves): Patsy Brannigan, no more shenanigans! You will stand up and give the alphabet.

PATSY (scratching his head, thinking hard): The alphabet—the alphabet— Gimme a start, teacher.

TEACHER (glares at Patsy, nose-to-nose): All right, *dumkopf*, I'll give you a start. "Ah—ah—ah—"

PATSY: Ah!

TEACHER: Not "Ah"—"A!"

PATSY (heading for his seat): That's the alphabet—"A."

TEACHER: That's not the alphabet. Come back here.

PATSY: There's more?

TEACHER: There's more. Please continue.

PATSY: Gimme another start.

TEACHER: "Buh—buh—buh—"

PATSY: "Buh?"

TEACHER: "Buh."

PATSY: "Buh?"

TEACHER: "Buh."

PATSY: "Buh?"

(During this exchange they have sunk, nose-to-nose, nearly to the floor)

TEACHER: Not "Buh," *dumkopf!*

PATSY: Give me a hint.

TEACHER: What is it buzzes around the flowers? Bzzzzz?

PATSY: (starts waving and slapping at invisible bug).

TEACHER: "Bee!"

109

PATSY: "Bee!" That's the alphabet—"A, B." (heads for his seat)

TEACHER: Come back here, young man. That's not the alphabet.

PATSY: There's more? Gimme a hint what comes after B.

TEACHER: I'll give you a hint. What's the first thing you do when you wake up in the morning? Sssssssssss—

PATSY: (gives teacher a shocked, pop-eyed look).

TEACHER: "C," *dumkopf!* The first thing you do in the morning when you wake up is "see."

PATSY: That's not the first thing I *do* in the morning.

TEACHER: (ends the hopeless lesson with a crack of the slapstick).

Say what you will, it was a hell of a lot better than being a Nightingale or a Mascot in a white duck suit and singing "Mandy Lane." The audience thought so too. They loved it in Denison (or Bonham or Sherman) in 1913 (or 1915).

CHAPTER 8

The Silencing of Patsy Brannigan

THE MARX BROTHERS in *School Days* was the featured part of our show now. It went over great all through the South and Southwest, and we spent more than half our nights in hotels. In big towns (big for small-time vaudeville) like Alexandria, Louisiana, or Lubbock, Texas, we were held over two and even three nights. Frenchie went back to Chicago with the overdue mortgage money, and with vague ideas of going into business for himself, opening the Midwest's first Alsatian restaurant. In Commerce, Oklahoma, Minnie hired an Indian girl as prima donna, not so much because of her voice but because she wore her hair in long braids. The Bright Little Girl in *School Days* had to have pigtails, and Aunt Hannah, increasingly prone to heartburn and gall-bladder attacks from a steady diet of cold hot tamales, spaghetti and fried beans, had fled home to New York, taking her pigtail wig back with her.

Minnie notwithstanding, we began to work some variations and bits of new business into the school scene. We got a big laugh one night when the Teacher made me take my hat off and an orange fell out. I gave the orange to the Teacher, and he told me to put my hat back on because he'd like another one for later. We got a bigger laugh later on when Teacher said, "Can't you get noddings through your thick head?" and Gummo stuck a stiletto through my hat and I answered Herr Teacher with an enthusiastic nod.

Ada, Oklahoma. We were still straining at the bit to tear loose and rough it up onstage, but Minnie was too vigilant for us. Then, this night in Ada, we got a golden opportunity to pull out all the stops. In the middle of *School Days*, while Teacher was giving the Hebrew Boy a "lesson in der Englisher langvidge," the audience suddenly got up and ran out of the theatre.

Minnie got up from her school desk, left the stage, and ran after them to see what had happened. With the audience gone, and Minnie too, we went to town. The Bass and the Prima Donna backed off in panic, while Groucho, Gummo and I grappled, swung, ducked, tripped, tumbled, tore our costumes to shreds and knocked the scenery to pieces, mugging like three demented apes. When Minnie came back we were still at it.

"Stop!" she said. "They're coming back! It was a runaway mule and they caught him."

The audience came back but we didn't stop. We'd gotten up too much steam. Minnie was hopping and hissing and Greenbauming all over the joint, but she had no effect. This time we knew we were doing the right thing. The audience hooted and hollered right along with us. How else would you follow a runaway mule, except with horseplay?

The manager agreed that it was a good, lively show. He also agreed to make fair and square deductions from our percentage for the cost of broken sets and fixtures. It was a long time before we took liberties with the act again. With the deductions, our net profit was minus seven dollars, which we were requested to pay before we left town. We were stranded, and summer was coming on like a blast furnace. Minnie had to swallow her pride and wire Uncle Al for getaway money.

112

Springfield, Missouri. En route home we took a chance on a stop-over, and played a one-night stand. When we finished our act, the manager asked if one of us would like to make a little extra dough. His illustrated-song singer hadn't shown up, and he'd be happy to pay five dollars to whoever would volunteer to take his place. I'll never know why, but I volunteered to sing. My voice was still undecided whether to change to a man's register or give up and stay falsetto. Maybe I felt guilty for being the ringleader in the Oklahoma horseplay.

So I sang for the song slides. A worse performance was never given the hook on amateur night. When I came off the manager was furious. Instead of paying me five dollars, he said he was going to fine me five dollars. I was furious, too. "Yeah?" I said. "Try and collect your lousy fine." Groucho, Gummo and the bass singer loyally closed ranks beside me.

He did try to collect, with the help of a stagehand. They came after the four of us with blackjacks. We surprised them. We produced our own blackjacks. (This surprised Minnie, too, who didn't know how well prepared we were.) There was a bit of a scuffle, but we made it to the train with only minor cuts and bruises. It was a moral victory. I did not pay the five-dollar fine. But neither were the Marx Brothers paid for their night's work.

And so, back to Chicago. Home again after six months on the road, we licked our wounds, scrubbed the alkali dust out of our pores and the lice out of our hair, and had a Roman orgy on Frenchie's cooking.

I went forth into the city to see what had happened in the world of pool, pinochle and poker during our absence. Groucho got a stack of books from the Public Library and curled up to read his way through the summer. Gummo went to hang out with Zeppo in a neighborhood garage, tinkering and learning the mysteries of the motor car. Chico was back in New York, working as a single.

Our holiday didn't last very long, however. We soon scraped the bottom of the savings Minnie had been squirreling away, and Mr.

Greenbaum showed no signs of becoming suddenly friendly and forgiving toward the Marx family.

There was only one thing to do: back to work. We couldn't wait for the new season to begin. Minnie, fortified with programs and clippings from our triumphal tour with *School Days*, went downtown to make the rounds of booking agents. We spent the rest of the summer in and out of the city, making short hops to outlying precincts on one- and two-night stands.

Frenchie, having given up his idea of opening a restaurant, pitched right in. He became our Business Manager and Advance Man, as well as Laugh Starter. As Business Manager he arranged for our train trips, and for boardinghouse accommodations, if we should have to stay over where we played. The standard price was, in those days, $1.60 over the coach fare for a Pullman upper berth. Frenchie would dicker with the ticket seller as he would with a customer over a ravelly lappa. He would hold out for a price of one dollar for an upper. The ticket man would not give in. By company rules, he couldn't shave the price. "So all right," Frenchie would announce, "everybody into the coach!"

We would march dutifully on board the coach. We knew that Frenchie could never win a haggle with the Pullman ticket office, but we always gave him the respect of letting him try. Once we got under way, Groucho would scout through the train. If he found an empty upper berth, he'd offer the conductor a dollar for it. The conductor would be glad to pick up an easy buck on the side, and he would turn his back when all four of us climbed in, whooping and hollering. If the porter saw us and made a stink, Groucho would give him a quarter. The most we had to spend would be $1.25—a saving of thirty-five cents over the full price. Thirty-five cents was not to be sneezed at. It was worth a movie show and a game of pool for the four of us.

Sometimes Grandpa went along on our short hops, so that he might see more of the country he had naturalized as his own. On these occasions Frenchie insisted, gallantly, on buying a lower berth for Grandpa, who was then in his nineties. But after the train started Grandpa would insist on climbing into the upper berth and giving us kids the lower. This made him feel he was making a contribution to our success. To be truthful he was. There was a hell of a lot more rest to be had in a lower berth, if shared by four active Marx Brothers.

Most of the time that summer Frenchie traveled ahead of us, as our advance man. It was his job to get the theatre lined up, the posters put out all around town, and to find a nice, clean boarding-house that was in our price range. If a place was clean enough but not so hot in the kitchen department, Frenchie would move in and do the cooking. Naturally, nobody had ever tasted food like Frenchie's in Cedar Rapids, Kalamazoo or Urbana, and that was why he was always being asked to stay in town and open up a restaurant.

When Frenchie wasn't there to do the cooking, we ate leftovers. Boardinghouse leftovers were the same from Seattle to Sandusky: cold macaroni and cheese with all the cheese picked out, stiff, cold dabs of mashed potatoes turning yellow at the edges, a lonely pickle floating amongst seeds in a bowl of pickle juice, moldering masses of stale bread pudding, and coffee three times warmed over with milk in it, turned a sickening mauve in color and covered with a pucker of scum. I didn't complain. I was too hungry. Everything tasted all right to me—but boy, how we missed Frenchie!

It wasn't always easy to get Frenchie launched out of the city as advance man. The move to the Midwest and the rise of his sons in show business hadn't changed my father much at all. He was as accepting, as trusting, as sweet-natured and absent-minded as ever.

One night we all went out to the 63rd Street Station to see Frenchie leave Chicago. It was a tearful farewell, full of soggy sentiments and kisses. You'd think he was departing to be our advance man for a tour around the world. As the train pulled away, he waved and waved, dabbing a tear from his eyes, and we dabbed and waved back.

Twenty minutes later, Frenchie was in downtown Chicago. He'd boarded the train on the inbound instead of the outbound track.

So the next night he set out alone, full of advice about which side of the station to stand on. Frenchie wanted no silly, sentimental farewells this time. He was so determined to be businesslike, in fact, that he forgot to take his ticket. As we pieced it together later, he had just as much trouble getting out of Chicago the second time.

Frenchie's English had not improved greatly since the day he arrived in the States from Alsace-Lorraine. He had special trouble with his d's and t's. To the railroad ticket man he said: "One fare please for Derradaw." This the ticket man could not comprehend. Frenchie tried again. He still couldn't get through. Finally he said, "Whod the hell, you know, id's a place doo-ninedy from here."

He was sold a ticket for $2.90 and he got on a train, an outbound train.

Early the next morning Minnie got a long-distance telephone call from Frenchie. Minnie said, "Hello, Sam?" Frenchie said plaintively, "Minnie, where am I?"

Luck was with him. It turned out he was in Terre Haute, Indiana, which was where he was supposed to be. "Dod's ride," said Frenchie. "Derradaw!"

We made enough money that summer to buy ourselves a second-hand pool table for the basement. But before we could hustle up cue sticks and balls to play with, the fall season was upon us and it was time to hit the road again.

Waukegan, Illinois. In the middle of my first bit in *School Days,* the business with the orange in my hat, I happened to look into the orchestra pit. I couldn't believe my eyes. Instead of giving the orange to Teacher, I let out a whoop, wound up like a baseball pitcher and heaved the orange at the piano player in the pit. The piano player caught it and threw it back. When Groucho and Gummo saw what was going on they started whooping too. We heaved everything we could get our hands on into the orchestra pit—hats, books, chalk, erasers, stilettos.

The piano player surrendered. He climbed up onto the stage, sat at one of the school desks, and joined the act. It was Chico.

I don't remember much about the rest of the performance that night, except that Chico ad libbed a hilarious part as an Italian boy, and the fiddle player in the orchestra was so broken up he nearly stopped the show. The fiddle player was a local kid named Benny Kubelsky. Until this day—when, as Jack Benny, he's known as Waukegan's First Citizen—he still can't look at the Marx Brothers without breaking up.

Ann Arbor, Michigan. We now had Chico and a full two-act show. Act One was *School Days* and Act Two, *Musical Varieties.* "Always leave 'em with a song," Minnie said. "If they go away whistling, you've got a hit." We didn't agree. We thought it would be better to leave 'em with a laugh. The comedy act should close the show, not open it. "Greenbaum to that," said Minnie.

The season's first crisis arose when we hit the college town of Ann Arbor. Our tenor, whom we had hired for $25 a week, quit us flat for an act that payed $27.50 a week. His part as the Nance in *School Days* wouldn't be missed, but his operatic solo was one of the highlights of the musical half of the show. Also, he owned the only tuxedo in the company, and this had added a lot of class.

Groucho told Minnie not to worry. He'd sing "La Donna E Mobile." That was fine, said Minnie—but what about the tuxedo? Chico had it all figured out. "Fire the piano player in the pit," he said. "I'll play the opera number on the stage piano, and with the dough we save we can rent a tux."

Minnie blessed us all and took off for Chicago, to go shopping for a new twenty-five-dollar tenor.

So Groucho did the tenor's aria. Well, he *started* the aria. After about twelve measures, a hysterical, compulsive urge for horseplay crept over him (we all felt it coming on, what with Minnie gone) and he stopped singing.

"I don't like your key, Giuseppe," he said to Chico.

"How about this key, boss?" said Chico, transposing to C-minor.

"Worse," said Groucho.

I was standing in the wings. But not for long. This was too much fun to miss out on. I ran onstage and bumped Chico off the stool and began to play "The Holy City," the quickstep-march variation.

117

Groucho knocked me off. Chico knocked Groucho off. I knocked Chico off. Through the whole wacky round-robin the piano kept being played and Groucho kept singing "La Donna E Mobile"—in double-talk Italian.

Well, it brought the house down. We kept on clowning all the way to the finish, when we played a six-hand, three-key version of "Waltz Me Around Again, Willie"—Chico on the stool, me sitting on Chico's shoulders, and Groucho crouching behind us, reaching his arms around Chico like tentacles, and all of us singing.

We collapsed like a house of cards, jumped up, grabbed our mandolins, and sailed into "Peasie Weasie." We had never had such fun or such an ovation before. We took seven bows, and there was no need for anybody to sing "Dixie."

For the first time, our act was reviewed in the paper. The local critic was very flattering. "The frolicsome Marx Brothers, with their operatic antics," he wrote, "were a welcome and refreshing change from the usual tired vaudeville act we've been seeing on Main Street." The manager asked if we could play there the rest of the week. Groucho, our spokesman in Minnie's absence, said we might consider it if the price was right. The manager made an offer that was hard to resist. He said he would pay the whole week's rental on the tenor tuxedo. It was a deal.

Minnie was terribly depressed when she got off the Michigan Central milk train the next day. She had beaten all the bushes in Chicago and hadn't flushed a tenor who would leave town for less than thirty bucks a week. We showed her our review, and she took heart.

Then she said, with a delayed take, "*What* operatic antics? In the *second act?*"

We told her the whole story, truthfully. Minnie had strong opinions and she was stubborn, but she was neither a diehard nor a fool. She thought for a minute, vaguely and wistfully whistling "La Donna E Mobile."

Then she said, "I told you boys we should never try to be anything but a comedy act. Like I've said time and time again, 'Always leave 'em with a laugh.' " She reconsidered briefly, and added, "As long as you send 'em home whistling."

Kalamazoo, Michigan. We worked out a compromise with Minnie. The second part of our show would be half clowning and half musical varieties. We patched together an afterpiece, a routine we entitled *School Days Twenty Years Later*, or, *Mr. Green's Reception*. Mr. Green was the new name we gave to the Teacher.

In the afterpiece, Mr. Green (Groucho) has retired. On the anniversary of his retirement, he invites his old pupils to a reception at his vine-covered cottage in the country. Patsy, Giuseppe, Izzy and Mama's Boy are grown men now. They have become, it so happens, singers of songs, players of the piano, pluckers of the mandolin, and fun-loving comedians. They give their old teacher a gala entertainment.

I think the real reason Minnie capitulated to our doing *Mr. Green's Reception* was that she saw a spot in the act to pin class on. The spot was Mr. Green's cottage. The class she pinned on it was a gross of red paper carnations (one buck a gross, wholesale).

To be more precise, it was I who pinned the fake flowers on the stage set. I had become very close to Minnie. I was her confidant and her Chief Assistant in the Special Effects (class) Department. I spent more time onstage patching flats, touching up the paint job and wiring on carnations than I did acting or making music.

Mr. Green's Reception went over just as big as *School Days*. The only trouble we had with it was in Kalamazoo, where we were hired to play a whole week.

The Kalamazoo trouble occurred at my entrance. I came on as Patsy (twenty years older, with the same ratty red wig, turtle-neck sweater and blacked-out teeth, but with long pants on), carrying a trash can.

> MR. GREEN (who has miraculously lost his German accent somewhere during the intermission): And who might you be, my good fellow?
> PATSY: Why, Patsy Brannigan, the Garbage Man.
> MR. GREEN: Sorry, we don't need any.

In Kalamazoo, like every place else, this got a laugh. But because of it, we got fired off the bill. The owner of the theatre came back and uttered those fearful words of doom: "You're shut!"

It was hardly our fault. We didn't know the current scandal in Kalamazoo—which was that the theatre owner's wife had just run off to Escanaba with a city garbage collector.

We were shut, but we still got a good review in the local paper. Minnie read it six or seven times. She closed her eyes and whistled and thought for a while, then said: "Boys, we're ready for a circuit. We've got to go where the big agents can see us."

And so, back to Chicago. Minnie pasted our Michigan clippings in a scrapbook, tucked the scrapbook under her arm, and took the streetcar downtown where the booking offices were. Right off the bat she got us booked into a theatre called the Thalia, in a Polish neighborhood.

We played *School Days* and *Mr. Green's Reception* at the Thalia for one week. We got one review. It said: "The so-called Marx Brothers do well, but in the worst kind of act in vaudeville. In other words, they are so good they stink." I don't think any big agents bothered to show up.

Minnie's faith was undiminished. The day after we opened she sent a telegram to Uncle Al—not for money, but for help in the shape of new material.

Uncle Al took the train from New York, and caught the last night of our stand. He agreed with the reviewer. We were good and our material stunk. Uncle Al sat up all night in the kitchen, sketching out a new second act. He kept a few of our old bits of business, but what he concocted was ninety percent new, including the title. *Home Again,* he called it.

In *Home Again,* Mr. Green had not only retired to his carnation-covered cottage but he had somehow gotten rich enough to take a trip abroad, with his "swell" wife (Minnie) and his "fresh" son (Gummo). The scene opened with the Greens arriving from Europe. The air was full of streamers, confetti, and Groucho's bilious jokes about seasickness. On the dock to greet the boat were Chico, a waterfront loafer, and me, a waterfront rough-neck. I started a fight with Chico. A cop came on to break it up. Chico and I turned on the cop and broke *him* up. Mr. Green then

120

invites everybody to a reception at his country estate. The curtains parted to reveal the full set—the old carnation-covered cottage and, upstage, a huge prop boat.

At the finish there was to be a spectacular Special Effect. It would be the greatest thing witnessed on a stage, Minnie told Uncle Al with admiration, since Ada Isaacs Menken last made an entrance on a live white horse, back in 1879. Everybody would pile onto the boat, and the boat, which was mounted on rollers, would glide across the stage while we all sang and all the lights went out except the lights on the deck. It was a far cry from "Peasie Weasie."

It all sounded great to me except for one thing: Uncle Al didn't write a single line for me. I protested. Uncle Al said I could add wonderful contrast to the act if I played in pantomime. The hell with that. I would ad lib all the lines I wanted to, I said.

"Okay, okay," said Uncle Al. "Go right ahead."

Kankakee, Illinois. On our shakedown cruise of *Home Again* we found that Uncle Al was not exactly infallible. Some of his New York jokes were not funny at all to Midwest audiences. For example:

MR. GREEN: This must be the Far Rockaway boat.
MRS. GREEN: How do you know?
MR. GREEN (twitching his nostrils): I can smell the herring.

It did not go over very big in Kankakee, Illinois, about the herring.

Champaign, Illinois. The critic in the Champaign-Urbana paper wrote something like: "The Marx Brother who plays 'Patsy Brannigan' is made up and costumed to a fare-thee-well and he takes off on an Irish immigrant most amusingly in pantomime. Unfortunately the effect is spoiled when he speaks." Then he went on to discuss minor points, like the climax of *Home Again* being the most thrilling scene ever witnessed in Champaign, etc.

121

When I read the review I knew Uncle Al had been right. I simply couldn't outtalk Groucho or Chico, and it was ridiculous of me to try. It was a cruel blow to my pride nevertheless. When I announced to Minnie that I would never speak another word onstage, she knew I had been hurt, and she looked at me with sorrow and sympathy. But she didn't say, "Forget it—what does *he* know?" She said nothing.

I went silent. I never uttered another word, onstage or in front of a camera, as a Marx Brother.

Belleville, Illinois. Being a full-time pantomimist now, I worked hard thinking up stage business that didn't require spoken lines. I swiped a bulb-type horn off a taxicab and stuck it under my belt before going on in *Home Again.* When Chico and I started our fight and the cop clomped on and yanked me off Chico, the horn went *whonk!* and we got a hell of a big new laugh.

East St. Louis, Illinois. I created my own, personal afterpiece. At the finish of the act the boat pulled away and sailed across the stage with everybody on board except me. I came following after, swimming—honking my horn like crazy and spitting out a stream of water with each stroke. Hell of a big new laugh.

And so, back to Chicago. After delivering me a serious lecture, the gist of which was Greenbaum, Minnie went downtown once again with the scrapbook. She got us hired to play the Pantages Circuit. We had made it—a thirty-week tour. No more one-night stands. No more haggle for box-office percentages. A hotel room every night! The Marx Brothers were on their way.

Aurora, Illinois. (And here I jump backwards in my itinerary, by a couple or three years.) The Six Mascots were not doing so hot. Minnie, pondering this, went into Chicago to do something about our depressing condition. The act needed more class, badly. But what?

In Chicago Minnie found the answer. It had to do with me. I received a cryptic telegram in Aurora, Illinois:

DON'T LEAVE TOWN UNTIL YOUR SHIPMENT ARRIVES BY FREIGHT. PAYMENTS ON IT ONE DOLLAR PER WEEK. DON'T GET IT WET. MINNIE.

I didn't know what to expect. Something for me to put in the act? A new costume? A trained dog? A unicycle?

What arrived on the freight car was a monstrous, odd-shaped black box. Inside the monstrous box was the biggest musical instrument I had ever seen.

A harp.

CHAPTER 9

Poom-Pooms, Pedals and Poker

AFTER I HAD HAD the harp for two weeks, it was in the act. Before, when we played the *oom-poom-pooms* to accompany a song, the mandolins whanged out the *oom's* while Groucho did the *poom-pooms* on his guitar. Now I did the *poom-pooms* on the harp. The harp poom-poomed and echoed with re-poom-pooms all around the joint.

I found out that the price of my harp was forty-five dollars (ten bucks of Minnie's money down and one buck of my money per week). This gave me new respect for the instrument. Groucho got new respect for it, too. Groucho I could now drown out—his voice, his guitar or his mandolin—any time I wanted to, with a lusty swipe on the harp strings.

Gadsden, Alabama. After a year of hunt and pick, ponder and pluck, and trial and error, I played my first solo on the harp— "Annie Laurie." I got a big hand and a demand for an encore. The

124

only encore I could think of was doing "Annie Laurie" over again, with fancy long swoops on the strings (I didn't know yet that these were called glissandos) between phrases of the melody.

The presence of the harp (the harp alone, and not the harpist) had raised our average monthly income by five dollars. Once again Minnie had gambled and hit a winner. The odds were right, by Chico's Law. Four bucks a month for payments, five bucks a month return.

Little Rock, Arkansas. For the first time I played solid chords as well as a line of melody and swooping glissandos, in my exclusive new harp arrangement of the Sextet from *Lucia.* From the audience I got respectful applause. From Groucho I got dirty looks.

St. Joseph, Missouri. On the way from the theatre to the poolroom I stopped in my tracks when I saw a display in a ten-cent-store window. In the middle of the display was a framed picture of an angel, sitting on a cloud and playing a harp. What stopped me was the fact that the angel in the picture had the harp leaning against her *right,* not her left shoulder. Since nobody had ever told me otherwise, I had been playing with mine against the wrong shoulder.

That was my first harp lesson. I switched the instrument to the other side, the right side, and felt a lot more professional. Belated thanks, F. W. Woolworth, for the tip.

Muskogee, Oklahoma. A harpist, I was beginning to learn, had problems that nobody else had, not even a tuba player or a string-bass player. A tuba had no strings. A string-bass you could carry with you on a trolley car.

The harp, when plucked politely, has a soft tone that doesn't carry very far. A harpist has to have total silence when he plays a

125

serious piece, or he won't be heard at all. I found that audiences were usually aware of this, and very cooperative. This wasn't always true, however, of other performers on the bill.

Sharing the bill with us in Muskogee (or maybe it was someplace in Kansas) was an "escape artist," a limp little Hungarian, who let his wife, a husky Cherokee Indian, tie him up in knots. His act was to wiggle free of the ropes—which had been tied, of course, in deceptive, breakaway knots—in time to a chorus of "The Prisoner's Song."

Well, the theatre here was so small that in the wings at stage left there was only room for a toilet, nothing more. In the *pianissimo* part of my Sextet from *Lucia* I heard a funny noise that didn't come from the harp. I looked offstage. The Hungarian escape artist was sitting on the can, facing me, with the toilet door open.

I was so stunned by this sight I stopped playing. In that moment of silence, the guy flushed the can. It was a sound heard round the theatre, all the way back to the top of the balcony. The audience, not knowing but what it was a special effect on the harp, burst into applause.

I got even. On Saturday night the escape artist asked if I wouldn't please take his wife's place, so she could get their baby ready to make the train. I was very happy to oblige him. I went onstage during his act and tied him up with *my* kind of knots. When they finally brought the curtain down he was still grunting and writhing on the floor. He couldn't get free from knot number one. They had to drag him offstage by his feet and cut him loose with a jackknife.

This was a kind of aggravation that angel harpists never had to put up with.

Laredo, Texas. In Laredo we shared the bill with one of the saddest vaudeville acts I ever saw—"The Musical Cow Milkers." It was a team. The guy led a live cow onstage and while his wife, in sunbonnet and pinafore, squatted on a stool and milked the cow, they sang duets.

126

After opening night the manager fired them. They would be replaced on the bill, he said, with a second solo by the "Marx boy who wears the wig and plays the big zither or whatever you call it."

The male half of the Musical Cow Milkers was very bitter about being fired. He walked across the border to Mexico and got drunk and mailed a dead rabbit to the Laredo theatre manager.

Minnie came down with a sudden attack of loyalty and motherly love. Mr. and Mrs. Musical Cow Milker had three small children. Minnie went to bat for them. She yelled and wept and begged for the couple to be rehired. At length, her eloquence swayed the theatre manager.

"All right, all right," he said. "I'll take 'em back. I'll put 'em on. I'll put 'em on in place of the Marx Brothers. You're closed."

Youngstown, Ohio. By now my harp had racked up a lot of mileage and taken a lot of mauling, in and out of baggage cars, delivery wagons, hotels and theatres. It was aging prematurely. The post was getting wobbly and warps and cracks were setting in. What happened to it on my retreat from Youngstown, Ohio, didn't help a bit.

Youngstown is one city I remember clearly. Something unexpected happened every time I played there.

Between shows during our first date in Youngstown, I went to an auction at a jewelry store. The jeweler happened to be a friend of a friend of Chico's, and he knocked me down a ring I took a fancy to, for two bucks. I just happened to feel it was a good-luck piece. It had better be, I thought, because when I put it on I couldn't get it off.

When we finished the show on Saturday night, the manager came back and said it was the mayor's birthday and we were all invited to his birthday party. We didn't feel like partying. We wanted a good night's sleep before the jump to Indianapolis, so we politely declined. But the mayor was insistent. He had the police chief back a paddy wagon up to the stage door and herd us in. Like it or not, we were going to the mayor's birthday party.

My memory of that night is not clear. I had two drinks, the first

127

two drinks of my life, and I got very drunk. I remember Chico getting a crap game going. I remember dodging the mayor's wife, who took quite a shine to me. When she got me trapped in the pantry, the police chief came to my rescue. The next thing I remember is being driven home by two cops, along with a dame I had never seen before. This dame was a lot more predatory than the mayor's wife. But it was not my virile charm she was after. She was after my two-dollar ring.

The dame must have grappled for half the night, trying to get it off. In the morning the ring was still on my finger, and she was gone. The rest of the troupe were also gone, on the train to Indianapolis.

I got a great idea. Why not drive to Indianapolis, instead of taking the train? I bought a secondhand Model-T touring car, loaded the harp onto the back seat, cranked up, and chugged off into the sunset. It was a rugged journey, to put it mildly. The old Ford struggled on the best it could, straining through axle-deep ruts, crunching over rocky creek bottoms, slogging through mud-holes and pounding over potholes. Everything that could go wrong with a Model T went wrong with mine. I pushed it and cranked it and kicked it. I coaxed it and I cursed it. And somehow I nursed it, before it gasped its last, dying chug, into Indianapolis.

It was a feat I would have been proud of, except that my harp had taken the worst beating of its life, on the back seat of the Ford. For the dough I squandered on the car (had to sell it for junk), I could have bought a brand-new harp.

Somewhere north of Mobile, Alabama. We were making the Saturday night Pullman jump from Montgomery to Mobile. About four o'clock in the morning I woke up with a hell of a jolt. We had stopped moving. The train had jumped the tracks.

When we piled out of our car, we saw that the wreck was a pretty bad one. The Pullman was intact, but the baggage car and the forward coach, for colored passengers, had been badly bashed, and people were screaming with pain up ahead. We pitched in to give whatever first aid we could.

Within an hour, two insurance-company "adjusters" appeared on the scene. They went down the line of the injured, getting them to sign releases by making spot-cash settlements—bad bruise one dollar, gashed face two dollars, broken arm five bucks, broken leg ten bucks, and so on. Once anybody signed, naturally, he no longer had the right to sue the railroad and get a fair settlement for his injury.

I suddenly remembered my harp. I got to the baggage car before the adjusters did. The case was smashed to splinters, but the harp itself didn't show a bit of new damage, which was a miracle. But nobody paid off on miracles. So I heaved the harp off the car onto the tracks. There was now no doubt it had been through a disastrous wreck. The harp was a wreck itself.

The insurance man came along, inspected it, and asked me what the replacement value was. Forty-five dollars, I told him. He handed me a release to sign. "The rule is fifty percent," he said. "But you look like a nice young fellow. I'll pay you twenty-five dollars."

Minnie caught me on the point of signing the release. She grabbed the pen from my hand and gave it back to the adjuster. "You don't pull that on us," she said. "We're getting a lawyer to handle this matter."

The insurance man said, "Damn Yankees."

Mobile, Alabama. Minnie went shopping for a local lawyer to sue the railroad. She found one. He examined the harp and the case and said he'd handle the lawsuit on a contingency basis. The railroad settled right away. After giving the lawyer his cut, our share of the settlement was two hundred dollars.

And that is how I came to get a new harp, my first really good harp, with pedals and everything. I resolved to treat it better than I had my old forty-five-dollar model. I would play it on the right shoulder from the start. I would learn to tune it right (all I knew about tuning the harp was that I was tuning it wrong). I would learn to use the pedals and play it in other keys besides E-flat. And I would never take it for a ride in a Model-T Ford.

Rockford, Illinois. We were on the Pantages circuit, playing a couple of local spots before making the great swing to the West Coast and back through Canada. In Rockford, the four of us and a monologist named Art Fisher started up a game of five-card stud, between shows.

At that time there was a very popular comic strip called "Knocko the Monk," and as a result there was a rash of stage names that ended in "o." On every bill there would be at least one Bingo, Zingo, Socko, Jumpo or Bumpo.

There must have been a couple of them on the bill with us in Rockford and we must have been making cracks about them, because when Art Fisher started dealing a poker hand he said, "A hole card for—'Harpo.' A card for—'Chicko.' One for—" Now that he'd committed himself, he had to pass "o-names" all around the table.

The first two had been simple. I played the harp and my older brother chased the chicks. For a moment Art was stuck. Then he continued the deal. A card for "Groucho" (he carried his dough in a grouch-bag), and finally a card for "Gummo" (he had a gumshoe way of prowling around backstage and sneaking up on people).

We stuck with the gag handles for the rest of the game and that, we thought, was that. It wasn't. We couldn't get rid of them. We were Chicko, Harpo, Groucho and Gummo for the rest of the week, the rest of the season, and the rest of our lives.

Later, when we decided to make it official, and have our Art-Fisher names put on the program, the typesetter made a mistake, and left the "k" out of Chicko. The power of the printed word being what it is, "Chico" is the way it has been spelled ever since.

Still later, Gummo left the act and was replaced by Herbie, the baby of the family. Herbie, since he was always chinning himself and practicing acrobatics, we named "Zippo." "Mr. Zippo" was the star of a famous trained chimpanzee act. Our Zippo, understandably, felt that we were being very unflattering, and he insisted on spelling his stage name "Zeppo."

You never could tell what you might be dealt in a poker game in those days.

130

Through darkest Kansas, on the Rock Island Line. It was while touring the Pantages-time that I became a full-fledged gambling man. With the rest of the company, we traveled the whole season in a private railroad car. This was not a Pullman, but a "tourist" car with hard, woven-straw seats. There was nothing deluxe about it. Still, it was a happy home between stands for thirty-some people. In the car we ate, read, wrote letters, made love, argued, fought, rehearsed, and sometimes slept but most of the time played cards. The air was forever full of smoke and the jingle of money.

Our car was treated with very little respect by the railroads. It was bumped and jerked and shuttled around and often left forgotten on sidings miles from anywhere. We never deboarded at a station, like civilians. We would wind up in freight yards, along with pig iron, sheep, and cattle, where there was nobody to tote trunks and baggage except the owners.

Poker was the big game in the car, and we had some mighty wild, sleepless jumps on the Pantages-time.

One season there was a guy named Mons Herbert in the company. Mons used to set a dinner table on the stage, and play "The Anvil Chorus" by blowing knives and forks against each other. For a finish he would blow up a prop roast turkey and deflate it in such a way that it played "Oh, Dry Those Tears" out of its rump.

It wasn't his lung power we admired Mons Herbert for, however, as much as his gold teeth. He had a dazzling mouthful of gold. Because of this he was our favorite poker player. He never knew it, but he flashed signals every time he picked up a hand. If he showed two gold teeth we knew he held three of a kind, or maybe two pairs. Three gold teeth: a straight. Four: a flush. When he didn't open his mouth, and no teeth showed, you knew he held nothing, and any pair could beat him.

On the Pantages we were paid off each week by the local manager, and we all had cash in our pockets during the jump to the next date. Still, I never bet for very high stakes. Like Groucho, I continued to send most of my dough home to Minnie. Chico was just as loyal and well-meaning as Groucho and I, but he apparently

131

didn't trust the United States mails, because what he sent home to Minnie were mainly IOU's.

Butte, Montana. On Monday nights in Butte, Montana, a special section of the house was reserved for the local prostitutes and madams. You could always be sure of a wonderful audience on Monday nights in Butte. With them, you could do nothing wrong. If anybody blew up or missed a cue or pulled a boner, they loved that too. I never did, but my dog once did.

He was a big Airedale, named "Denver" after the town I'd picked him up in. Denver was very devoted to me. I had to shut him in my dressing room during our act or else he'd follow me onstage. I could never convince Denver that the Marx Brothers were not a dog act.

Once, this time in Butte, Denver got loose while I was watching the "class act" on the bill (a ballet troupe) from the wings. Looking for me, he wandered onstage. One of the dancers tried to shoo him off, but Denver was in no hurry. He had some important business to take care of first. He ambled over to the easel that stood next to the proscenium arch. In the rosy glow of the easel spotlight he lifted his leg and did his business, all over the card reading "Danse Orientale." From the way the chippies hollered and screamed, it was the greatest finish any ballet ever had.

The manager didn't agree with the audience. He fined me five bucks and made me keep Denver tied up outside the stage door at all times.

Elko, Nevada. It was along about here that I first worked out my "going under the carpet" bit. In the scene I was being chased by a cop. I couldn't find any place to hide. Desperate, I lifted up the edge of the rug and (as the audience saw it) slid under it feet first, on my back, and vanished completely, as if I'd turned into a sheet of cardboard. Not the slightest bulge showed in the carpet.

The stunt never failed to rock an audience (especially if—when I could get away with it, in some of the rougher towns out west— I poked a finger through a hole in the carpet).

The trick, of course, was in the way the stage had been prepared before the act. The floor the carpet was spread on was not the real floor, but was built up by using parallels, or platform boxes. Under the middle of the carpet, there was a gap between parallels, covered with a canvas set-piece. It was into this slot that I slid to make my astounding disappearance.

San Francisco. As we hit San Francisco, so did the rain. My God, how it rained. I got soaked going to the theatre, so after the matinee I went out to buy a raincoat at the first place I could find.

The first place I could find was a hockshop. I bought a dapper-looking, secondhand trench coat for three dollars. It may have looked dapper on the rack but on me, I found out after I bought it, it hung like a tent. What the hell, at that price I didn't care what it looked like so long as it kept the rain off. I ran back to the theatre and hung it in the backstage john to dry.

When I put it on after the evening show, the coat fell apart at the seams. I was sore as hell. I sloshed over to the hockshop, in the tattered, flapping trench coat, to get my three bucks back.

By the time I got there I wasn't sore any longer. I always have trouble staying angry for more than five minutes at anybody, over anything. So I left the hockshop not with my three bucks back, but with my unstitched trench coat, *and* a clarinet I had just bought for six-fifty.

So that it wouldn't be a total loss, I wore the coat in the act the next day. It was a natural. I couldn't have come up with a better comedy coat if I'd had one custom-made. It was perfect with my battered plug hat, ratty wig, and underslung pants with the clothesline belt. I lined the trench coat with huge panels and pockets—enough room to stash half a trunk's worth of props in. I was highly pleased with my purchase, and with the foresight I had shown by selecting it out of all the raincoats in San Francisco.

133

Seattle. A violin player named Solly Soloshky joined the company. He was a hell of a fiddler but he had one shortcoming. He could only play naturals, no accidentals. He tried to teach himself but he had some kind of a block against sharps and flats and simply couldn't master them. This cut down his repertoire, and therefore his billing, considerably, and made him very unhappy.

I showed Solly how it was done on the harp, with pedals, and he was almost sick with envy. I felt sorry for him. There wasn't much I could do for Solly then, but I swore that when I got back to Chicago I would case the music stores for a violin with pedals, and if I found one I would buy it and send it to him.

For all I know, Solly is still hopefully waiting for the fiddle with pedals on it.

Fargo, North Dakota. As the season neared the end, we all got bored with ourselves, our act, and the rest of the company. Thirty weeks was a long time. It was Groucho who cracked under the strain first. Groucho was filling in for the m.c., who'd been fired off the bill. He introduced "The Creole Fashion Plate"—a female impersonator—as "The Queer Old Fashion Plate," whereupon Groucho was fired off the bill.

(The most fascinating performer I knew in those days was a dame named Metcalfe who was a *female* female impersonator. To maintain the illusion and keep her job, she had to be a male impersonator when she wasn't on. Onstage she wore a wig, which she would remove at the finish, revealing her mannish haircut. "Fooled you!" she would boom at the audience in her husky baritone. Then she would stride off to her dressing room and change back to men's clothes. She fooled every audience she played to, and most of the managers she worked for, but her secret was hard to keep from the rest of the company. Every time she went to the men's room, half the guys on the bill would pile in after her.)

And so, back to Chicago. Home was the weary, footsore trouper, home from the distant provinces. Summer was a-coming, and all was well with the world. Minnie was in the living room, pasting up her scrapbook. Frenchie was in the kitchen, cooking sauerkraut and ribs. And Grandpa was on the porch, rocking in his chair, watching the automobiles go by and calling out the makes aloud: "Fort . . . Moxfell . . . Fort . . . Dotsch . . . Shtoots . . . Pockart . . . Moxfell . . . Fort . . ."

This was the second summer of the First World War. Gummo was the only one of us to be called up in the draft, and he was serving with the army at a camp near Chicago. I was serving with Chico, in a card room in the back of a cigar store on 45th Street. Actually, there were two cigar stores at that location, with two card rooms, back to back. This proved to be a most fortunate arrangement.

There was a city law that all games had to cease at one o'clock in the morning. Late this night, I was playing pinochle in one card room and Chico was playing in the adjoining place. At five minutes to one, Chico's game broke up, and he came over to kibitz me. I had just been dealt a fabulous hand in spades, and I had the bid, four hundred points. The curfew was creeping up on me and I began to sweat. If I lost this hand I'd be broke for the rest of the summer.

Chico gave my cards a quick look over my shoulder. He signaled me to stall, then moseyed around the table and out of the room, by the back way. I stalled. Half a minute later I was wanted on the telephone. It was Chico, calling from next door. "Blank your ace of diamonds," he said, "and lead the jack of trump. . . ."

In his brief amble around the card table Chico had memorized all the opposing hands. He told me exactly how to play. I rushed back and followed his instructions and on the stroke of one o'clock I hauled in the stakes and the kitty.

The only guy who was a match for Chico at pinochle was a Chicago character named Pete Penovitch. Pete had wonderful looks—a natural disguise for a gambler. He was a big six-footer, but baby-faced, with sleepy eyes, and a shock of prematurely white hair. He looked like an overgrown, lazy kid. But he was far from lazy. He had the busiest mind I ever encountered, and a photographic memory to go with it. When he played he demanded total

135

concentration and never tolerated so much as an ash tray on the table to distract him.

Pete won at gambling any way he could, fair means or foul, and managed to make more than a few enemies over the years. Even when I first knew him, when he was in his early twenties, he would never sit with his back to a door. I remember the first time I ate out with Pete. When his stack of wheat cakes came, he lifted the one on top and ate the second flapjack first. By force of habit, he was unable to deal even wheat cakes from the top of the deck.

Later on, when Pete was one of Al Capone's bodyguards, he got in a bad jam. His mouthpiece advised him to get out of town— way out of town—until the heat was off. "Okay," said Penovitch, "I'll go on a hunting trip." "Great," said the lawyer. "Where'll you go?"

"Milwaukee."

"*Milwaukee?* What the hell are you going to hunt in Milwaukee?"

"Oh," said Pete, "cats, dogs, whatever they got around there."

For a while he ran a gambling casino in Chicago. When he first opened he showed me his layout. He was really proud of the joint. His roulette wheel alone, he said, could pay the nut. It was rigged so the house couldn't lose—even if the players had every number covered. "If that ever happened," he said, "the pill would jump off the wheel, hop out the door, and roll down Michigan Avenue."

Pete used to come around to the house and shoot pool with us, sometimes with his friend Nick the Greek. Our basement was in a continuous uproar. Everybody shot pool in those days, even Grandpa, who was nearly a hundred years old. Grandpa never had to wear glasses, and he continued to smoke his pipe, roll his own cigars, call out the cars, and shoot pool, right up to the end.

The only one of us who couldn't tolerate the mad life day in and day out was Groucho. Groucho had to have privacy, to read. For hours at a time he would read in his Elgin roadster, parked on 33rd Street. Once he finished a book sitting in his car in a garage, while it was hoisted up on chains, being repaired.

136

To be truthful, life was not all pool and pinochle for the rest of us either. We played for a lot of army camps that summer. And long before the summer was over, Minnie got the bug again. It was time for a better circuit. It was time for her boys' next rise in class.

Once again, Minnie did it. She got us a week's booking into one of the best showcases in town, the Wilson Avenue Theatre. The Wilson was under Albee management, and it paid the same scale as the Chicago Palace. (E. F. Albee was the all-powerful Emperor of big-time vaudeville, who ruled from a throne room above the New York Palace—*the* Palace.)

After our run at the Wilson, we were signed for thirty weeks on the Orpheum circuit. This was it! We had risen in class as far as we could go, short of playing the Palace itself. The Marx Brothers were on the Big Time.

CHAPTER 10

But Can You Carry It on the Chief?

WE HEADED WEST for our first swing on the Orpheum-time aboard the Santa Fe Chief. Being greenhorns, we listened to the veterans on the train. One thing you should always remember, they told us, no matter how rich you got. The cardinal rule on the Orpheum was: "Never buy anything you can't put on the Chief."

I already knew about this. When we were signing for the tour, the guy in the front office said to me, "But what about the harp?" "What do you mean, what about the harp?" I said. "I mean," he said, "can you carry it on the Chief?" I told the guy where I had hauled a harp, through all kinds of weather, through wrecks and washouts, on all kinds of freight cars and baggage cars. I never made a jump without it, and never lost it. "I knew a guy on the Pantages-time," I said, "who lost a coffin, with his wife's body in it, but I never lost my harp."

Another greenhorn on the Chief was the fiddle player from Waukegan whom we had broken up so badly the night Chico first joined the act. He now called himself "Ben Benny," and was half of the musical act, "Benny and Woods." Benny didn't know what kind of a living hell he was headed for. For thirty solid weeks he had to follow the Marx Brothers on the bill.

Hollywood, California. While I was playing the Orpheum in Los Angeles, the boys convinced me I should try for a job in the movies. I was a natural for silent pictures, they said. I didn't talk anyway, and I was pretty good at stunts and pratfalls. I was given a screen test, by some assistant director at M-G-M. I flunked it. The guy didn't even say, "Wait until you hear from us." He said, "Get outta here and don't come back."

Like any rubberneck tourists, we tried to get into the Douglas Fairbanks studio to watch the leaping, dashing, swashbuckling Fairbanks shoot a picture. We couldn't get past the gate. There was a high stucco wall around the studio—no chance of sneaking in. But Groucho wouldn't give up. He plunked himself down on the sidewalk, facing the studio wall. "Let's sit here for a while," he said. "Maybe he'll jump this way." We sat for a long time, but Doug never jumped our way.

Lately, on the road, I had been seeing lots of movies. But Fairbanks I only saw if I couldn't find a Chaplin picture playing anywhere. Charlie Chaplin was my idea of comic genius. I would watch a Chaplin picture four, five or six times over. What an artist!

I had a chance now to see some of the great acts in vaudeville, too. I think my all-time favorite was Blossom Seeley. Now, there was a gal with class. She was one of the first to carry her own lighting with her. She was said to have been the first artist to use the dramatic effect of an overhead baby spotlight. Once when a dancer on the bill heard this he sniffed and said, "Why, Leonardo da Vinci used an overhead baby four hundred years ago in 'The Last Supper'!"

I also saw some pretty unusual artists while traveling on the Orpheum. I think the most original were "Collins and Hart," who featured a cat that blew a whistle. On this point, George Burns, that erudite historian of vaudeville, agrees wholeheartedly. "Nobody ever stole *that* act," he said.

Montreal, Quebec. Here I ran into the inimitable Wingy Tuttle, part-time jewelry salesman and full-time character. "You don't want to stay in a hotel," Wingy told me. "Come over and stay with me. I'm living with some friends here. They won't mind if you move in the apartment too."

I thanked him, and after the show I went to the address he had given me. Right away, Wingy and his friends invited me to join them for a late dinner. It was a good, home-cooked dinner. Then, after dinner, half a dozen girls came trooping in. Staying here, I said to myself, was going to be a lot better than two weeks in a hotel.

Then a Chinese kid came in the apartment, and the next thing I knew, all the guests—Wingy and his friends and the girls and all —were sitting in a circle on the floor. The Chinese kid started cooking something over a little alcohol burner. He put the stuff he cooked into a pipe and started passing the pipe around the circle.

I had taken lodgings in an opium den.

I stayed there nevertheless until our show closed, and it *was* a lot better than any hotel. No wild chases in the corridor, no fights or noisy poker games. All night, every night, everybody but me sat on the floor smoking the pipe and talking in low voices. It was the most peaceful place I ever stayed in.

When it came time to leave Montreal, Wingy said he'd like to buy me a going-away present. I told him he'd done enough for me already—forget it. I knew that he had to live by his wits, and that sometimes his supply ran low. But Wingy insisted. He had to send me off in style.

Before train time he took me into Jaeger's, a shop that sold expensive Scotch woolens. He had the clerks in Jaeger's going crazy, filling the order for my going-away assortment: a cashmere overcoat, two cashmere suits, two dozen argyle socks, sweaters, trousers, neckties and shirts, all the best, the very best.

Wingy paused to ask me, casually, when my train pulled out. I told him, in twelve minutes. He turned to the manager and said: "I want everything altered and pressed and packed and de-livered to Mr. Marx's Pullman car in eleven minutes."

When the manager said that this would be quite impossible, Wingy blew his top. He rose up to his full height and pounded on the counter and shouted, "Do you know what this means, my good man? This means I am forced to cancel the whole order! That ain't all! I and Mr. Marx will never again so help us put on another stitch of Scotch-type goods!"

He hauled me out of the shop and hailed a taxi to rush us to the station. At the station he insisted he should at least pay the cab fare. But then he found he had left home without a nickel on him. I slipped him a five-spot. Wingy said he was ashamed to take it. But he took it—only, he said, because he knew I would understand, being such a good pal, the embarrassing spot in which he found himself in.

It was the most beautiful touch I was ever a victim of. Yet I regarded—and still regard—Wingy Tuttle's show in Jaeger's as a gesture of true friendship. It was the only way he knew how to express his affection, and it took real guts to carry it off. I never had a nicer sendoff from anywhere.

New York City. One of our great contemporary heroes was Benny Leonard, the lightweight champion of the world. Show people and fighters always seemed to have a great affinity for each other. With Benny Leonard we felt a special bond. He was also from the East Side of New York, and he was no bigger than we were.

When we were on the Orpheum-time, we often crossed paths with Leonard, who was making a tour doing exhibition bouts. We caught each other's shows and spent all our free time horsing around together. He let us take turns sparring with him, and we taught Benny some of our stage routines.

Benny's manager and constant companion was Billy Gibson, the hustler and operator who later handled Gene Tunney. Gibson, one story was, had been set up in business and given a percentage of Benny Leonard by the notorious Arnold Rothstein. There were a lot of stories about Billy Gibson, who was an irrepressible little butterball. Once he was having a drink with some friends in a speakeasy. Another patron, beefy and drunk, came over and asked if he was Benny Leonard's manager. Gibson said, proudly, that he was. The drunk said it was nothing to be proud of—*he* could lick that Jew-boy with one punch. Gibson put down his drink. He challenged the stranger to say that again. The stranger said it again. Gibson hauled back and cut loose a roundhouse right smack on the other guy's jaw. It was like hitting a rock. The drunk just stood there and gave him a wink. "Well," said Billy, "maybe you could," and went back to his drink, nursing his sore hand.

It was Billy who came up with the proposal that the Marx Brothers and Benny Leonard go on tour together. Right away we agreed.

So now we were in New York again, getting ready to go on the road in the Benny Leonard troupe. Benny had commissioned Herman Timberg to write a new act for us. The result was *On the Mezzanine*, an act which lasted an hour, and was practically a show in itself.

It was in *On the Mezzanine* that I first did a piece of business that was to be my favorite for many years. The scene was a hotel suite. A good-looking girl is on the phone. "But how will I know you?" she asks, then says, "Oh—you'll be wearing a brown suit with a white carnation." Enter Groucho, Chico and me, all in brown suits with white carnations. We have overheard the conversation at the other end of the phone. On our heels the hotel dick comes in. The hotel's silver has been stolen, he says, and a witness reported that a guy in a brown suit with a white carnation pulled the job. He grills Groucho and Chico, gets nothing but gags. He turns to me and says, "You've got an honest face. You don't want to be a crook, do you?" I nod my head yes. "You just stay away from these other two guys," he says. "They'll only get you into trouble." I make a contrite face, stick out my lower lip, and shake my head.

Impressed by sparing me from a life of crime, the detective shakes my hand. A knife falls out of my sleeve and bounces on the floor. The detective shakes harder. Three more knives fall out. Intrigued, he shakes my other hand. Half a dozen knives clatter to the stage. He shakes both hands, and still more silver comes spilling out.

When I first did the bit, I had twenty pieces up my sleeves. I eventually worked up to dropping three hundred knives, with a silver coffeepot tumbling out of my coat for a finish.

We tried out *On the Mezzanine* in a neighborhood theatre on 14th Street, and knew we had a winner. Benny Leonard packed up his gloves and I packed up my knives and on the road we went.

St. Paul, Minnesota. I worked out a new refinement on the knife-dropping gag. I would single out a dame in the audience, sitting down front. All the time the detective was shaking the cutlery out of my sleeves I would give this dame a frozen stare, kind of a modified Gookie.

The dame I singled out this night in St. Paul fainted dead away when I began to stare at her. We had to stop the show. I felt terrible. I jumped down into the orchestra pit, where the ushers had carried the lady. When she came to and opened her eyes and saw me leaning over her, she fainted again.

Cedar Rapids, Iowa. The only complaint we ever got from the public over our material was while we were on the road with Benny Leonard. At one point in *On the Mezzanine* Groucho, Chico and I—I can't remember what it had to do with the scene —limped across the stage in a parody of "The Spirit of '76." A committee of professional patriots complained to the theatre manager that this was disrespectful to Old Glory and the great traditions of the U.S.A. and should be cut from the show. So far as I know, it was the only time we ever offended anybody. We never worked "dirty." We never used any Jewish expressions on-stage. Our comedy may have been broad, and pretty hokey at times, but it was clean. We never resorted to a bedroom or bathroom *double-entendre*, as a lot of comics did, to get a laugh out of a tough audience.

And so, back to New York. With the Benny Leonard troupe disbanded, we thought we'd try our luck working out of New York City. I had been having attacks of tonsillitis off and on for months now (it was a good thing I didn't have to use my voice onstage, be-

143

cause half the time I didn't have any voice), and I decided now was a good time to have my tonsils removed.

Chico said he knew just the doctor for me. This guy was good and the price was right—$32.50 and ask no questions. Chico could dig up a bargain in any line you wanted to name, from wholesale haberdashery to cut-rate tonsillectomies.

I called the number he gave me and the doctor made an immediate appointment for the operation. The office was up in Harlem, in the basement of a private house. When I got inside I heard the doctor's voice but I couldn't see him. He was standing behind his desk. He was a dwarf.

He sat me in a Morris chair and told me to open my mouth and relax. He put on a kitchen apron, got a wooden box, stood on the box, took some instruments out of his apron pocket, and went to work. When he clipped the first tonsil he slipped and fell off the box. He picked up his instrument from under the Morris chair, wiped it off on the apron, climbed back on the box, and clipped the other tonsil.

He told me I'd better lie down on the bed for a while before I went home. He put away his operating-room equipment—the bloody apron and the wooden box—then returned carrying a big portfolio. "Now, I have here something you might be interested in," he said. "You don't have to talk—just nod or shake your head."

As he opened the portfolio he said, "I do etchings, very fine etchings." He held up a picture of a naked guy chasing a naked broad across the Central Park Mall. "Like this one?" he said. I shrugged. "Tell you what I'll do," said the little doctor. "This beautiful etching is worth ten dollars at least. But it's yours for two-fifty. Thirty-five dollars pays for the operation *and* the ten-dollar etching."

I don't remember if I bought the etching or not. I only remember that I got out of there as fast as I could, as soon as I stopped bleeding.

It was, to say the least, a startling piece of surgery. The most startling thing about it is that ever since that afternoon in the Harlem basement, no doctor has ever looked at my throat without

144

admiring the job that had been done on my tonsils. Once a specialist in Beverly Hills said, "There's only one surgeon who could have done such beautiful work." He was right, but he was also wrong. The surgeon he was thinking of was not a dwarf who had to stand on a box to operate.

Minnie came east to get her boys rolling again. The time had come to push the Marx Brothers up to the absolute pinnacle—the Palace. We were famous in Albuquerque, Butte, and Kankakee, and even in Chicago and L.A. Now we had to become famous in New York City.

Minnie stormed the citadel. But the best she could get for us, with all her clippings and fast talk, was third on the bill at the Albee Theatre up in Boston. We decided to take it.

Boston. We were a much bigger hit than the last time we played Boston—as the Four Nightingales, the night the guy spit tobacco juice on me in the Old Howard. In fact, we were such a hit that the Boston manager telephoned E. F. Albee, the emperor himself, to report on us. Albee gave him an order: Make the Marx Brothers the headliners on the bill. When the manager came to tell us the good news, he said, "Where the hell have you fellows been?" We could have told him, but it would have taken all night and half the next day.

Saturday night we got a wire from the Albee office, telling us we were booked for two weeks in New York City—one week at the Royal and one week at the Palace. The Palace! We were zooming now and nothing could stop us.

And so, back to New York. We were taken in tow by a guy named Murdock, Albee's chief-of-staff. Murdock had a passion for honey. He had pots of honey on his desk and he carried a jar of honey in his pocket. But no matter how much he ate, it didn't seem to affect his disposition. He was paid to be tough to actors.

Murdock told us we were a very lucky act, before we went onstage at the Royal. Mr. Albee had great confidence in us, to

145

have booked us into the Palace sight unseen. So now, he said, we'd better go out there and give 'em hell, and prove the boss's judgment was right.

Well, we went out there, on the stage of the Royal, and we were a dismal flop.

The audience was predominantly Jewish. They had come thinking we were a Jewish act. From the moment Groucho came on and made jokes in English instead of Yiddish, they sat on their hands. All of our relatives turned out to see us, too. When not one of them was mentioned once in our act they all got sore, and when we came out for bows they sat on their hands.

Murdock didn't bother to come backstage after the show. He and the rest of the front-office boys had left the theatre by the front door. Before we had gotten out of costume, we got the fatal call: we were canceled out of the Palace.

Minnie wouldn't give up. She flew over to headquarters and bearded Murdock in his den. She cited the record, she quoted reviews, she explained and she apologized. She pleaded and begged and wheedled and fussed and fumed and ranted and raved. Murdock fled into the inner office for an emergency transfusion of honey. When he came out, Minnie started in on him all over again.

He had met his match. He gave in. It was the only way he could get Minnie out of his office. The Marx Brothers could play a week at the Palace, he said—*but*, they would have to open the bill. The opening act was the floor-mat of vaudeville. If you opened the bill, your status was only slightly higher than that of the ushers. For an established act, this could be suicide.

Minnie said we'd do it. The Palace was the Palace. We'd show them.

The Palace, New York. We opened the bill at the Palace. For the first six or seven minutes our act was a total waste, while the audience—notorious latecomers at the Palace—got seated. Then the laughs began to come. We finished in a riot.

Murdock had been watching from the back of the house, like

146

a vulture. When we went off, he came back to our dressing room. "Maybe," he said begrudgingly, "you aren't as bad as you looked at the Royal."

We were moved up to third on the bill. We got such a reception that the next act raised a stink with the management. It was unfair to follow the Marx Brothers, the way we got the audience all riled up. We were moved to the first spot after the intermission. Then we got complaints from the next two acts that came on after us.

Before the week was over we were closing the show, where nobody had to follow us.

We were held over for a second week. In the middle of the week Frenchie arrived from Chicago, in a style befitting the father of the newest stars of New York vaudeville—on the Twentieth Century Limited, with a lower berth all to himself.

Frenchie had come, as it turned out, not only to bask in our new glory, but to resume his old job as Laugh Starter. He thought he was doing us a favor. We tried to explain that while it had been helpful for somebody to start the audience laughing back in Fargo or Muskogee, we really didn't need a Laugh Starter at the Palace.

Nevertheless, Frenchie watched all our performances from the middle of the house. He didn't have to start any laughs, but he did meet some interesting people.

One matinee he sat next to a guy who kept shaking his head during the act. Frenchie asked him what his trouble was. The guy said he was feeling sorry for the boy on the stage, the one with the red curly hair who played on the harp.

Why did he feel sorry for him?

Why, because the poor boy couldn't talk. He was a mute. And it was a crime and a shame to make a kid with an affliction like that work in vaudeville and make a fool of himself in front of the public.

Frenchie reassured him that it was all part of the act. Off the stage, Harpo could talk. He was perfectly normal. The stranger knew better. That kid up there was a mute. You could tell from the way he behaved.

Frenchie was getting hot under the collar. He was about to reveal who he was, when the guy said, "You wouldn't like to make a little bet on it, would you, Mac?"

Indeed Frenchie would. "A dollar—even money?" the guy wanted to know. Frenchie considered this carefully. He was a wild pinochle player, but he was a very timid bettor. A dollar was a lot to gamble at even money. Frenchie shook his head. "I'll give you two to one," the guy said. Frenchie thought: What would Chico say? Chico would say the price wasn't right. Frenchie shook his head. The guy was pretty sure of himself now. He raised the odds again, and again. Finally Frenchie agreed they had a bet, at five to one. For a price like that he could take a chance.

"How are we going to prove it so you'll know I'm right?" the guy asked, and Frenchie said they would go backstage after the show and talk to Harpo. "They won't let us go backstage at the Palace," the guy said, and Frenchie said, "Sure, why nod?"

The two of them came into the dressing room after the show. "Hoppo," said Frenchie, "I wand you to meed a frent of mine." I shook hands with the stranger and said that any friend of my father's was a friend of mine. The stranger laughed. He handed Frenchie a five-spot and said it was a dirty trick but it was worth it if I'd give him my autograph. Frenchie couldn't understand why the fellow called it "a dirty trick." It was a legal bet, they had shook hands on it, and he had won it fair and square.

Chico, when he heard the full story, was never prouder of his father.

We decided that since we were successes now, we would pension off Minnie and send her back to Chicago with Frenchie. If anybody ever had, Minnie had earned herself a permanent vacation.

The Emperor's Throne Room, New York. The first Marx brother to get in trouble after Minnie's retirement was me.

Frank Fay, the famous monologist and m.c., was staging a series of shows he called "Sunday Concerts," in out-and-out defiance of Albee's monopoly. Fay wasn't the most popular guy in vaudeville, but we all admired him for this. It took a lot of guts to buck the Empire. One day during our run at the Palace, Fay called me up and asked if I would appear on one of his Concerts—as a single, since he knew that any act working for Albee was forbidden to play for him.

I told him I'd be glad to. I didn't see any harm in it. What difference would it make? I was on the program as "Arthur" Marx, not "Harpo." I didn't even play the harp. I did a piano number and a brief pantomime bit.

Apparently it did make a difference. On Monday morning I got a call from the front office. I was summoned to appear before Mr. Albee promptly at twelve o'clock noon. I was prompt, and I was scared. To me, E. F. Albee was more powerful than the President of the United States. I was passed through three barricades of secretaries and into the inner sanctum, the throne room of the Emperor, where very few common subjects had ever set foot.

He was sitting at his desk, eating lunch. He asked me if I'd like to join him for a bite. I politely refused. In my condition, I couldn't have kept down a teaspoonful of chicken broth. He told me to sit down, and apologized for eating in front of me. He ate. I sat. When he finished his lunch he offered me a cigar, and lit one for himself.

We smoked our cigars. Albee talked about this and that, show-business small talk. I said nothing. I waited for the ax to fall.

Finally the boss stood up. I stood up. Now it comes, I said to myself. But Albee just smiled, shook my hand, and said, "Well, it was nice of you to come and chat with me, Harpo. I hope you'll do it again."

That was the end of my audience with the Emperor. He had never come to the point of why I had been summoned, but the point was clear enough. Everything I did was watched and re- ported on. I had better keep my nose clean. The next time I was called to the throne there would be no cigars or small talk.

Albee ruled in mysterious ways, but he was all-powerful. I kept my nose clean.

Cleveland, Ohio. On our last night at the Albee Theatre in Cleveland, Groucho, Zeppo and I were sitting around the backstage lounge while the movie part of the show was on. Chico rushed in with startling news. "Our next date is all set," he said. "We're going to play London, England."

Who said so? we wanted to know. Abe Lastfogel, said Chico. He'd just talked to him on the phone. Lastfogel handled our bookings out of the William Morris office, our new agents. And where did Abe get the idea of sending us to London? From Chico, it turned out. Chico had called him that morning and said we were ready for a change of scene, like maybe England or someplace.

It took a little time, but we managed to find out exactly why Chico was so hot for a change of scene.

It seems that Chico had been cleaning up on the Cleveland locals at pool, until two nights ago, when a sharpie turned up and clipped him for twenty bucks. This hurt. Chico swore revenge.

By a fortunate coincidence, the great billiard artist Willie Hoppe—who was, naturally, an old friend of Chico's—was then in town on an exhibition tour. He agreed to do Chico a favor. Chico got some dark glasses and a checkered cap for Willie, had him turn up his coat collar, then took him over to the poolroom where the sharpie hung out. There he introduced him as a "friend from the show," who'd enjoy a friendly game or two.

Hoppe played strictly according to Chico's script, and shot a serious, awkward game. But bad as he was the sharpie let Hoppe beat him. Thereupon a bet of twenty-five bucks was made on the next game. On his first shot, Chico's "friend from the show" ran two hundred and twenty balls.

Before the sharpie paid him off, wondering where the hell *he'd* come from, an old guy walked in the poolroom and recognized Chico's ringer clean through the disguise.

"Why, you know who you're playing with?" said the old guy. "That's Willie Hoppe!"

And that was why Chico was eager to put as much space as he could between himself and Cleveland, Ohio. Still, regardless of how the booking came about, a trip to London sounded mighty good to all of us.

150

London, England. Everybody said the Marx Brothers would be an instant sensation in London. Music-hall slapstick was the English audiences' special cup of tea. Us they would eat up like kippers and crumpets.

So what happened? We opened at the London Coliseum and we were razzed off the stage.

It was a worse fiasco than the Royal, much worse. People began to hoot and whistle and throw pennies at us. Groucho went to the footlights and said, "We came all the way from America to entertain you, so you might at least throw shillings." We had never been so humiliated in public in all our professional years.

The manager was fit to be tied. But he wasn't disappointed in us. He thought we were great. He explained what had happened. The Marx Brothers, being headliners, were billed over the Premiere Danseuse, a dame who had never been demoted to second billing at the Coliseum. The Danseuse was hopping mad. So she organized a claque to give us our come-uppance, and supplied them with coins to throw at us.

The dancer won. She got back her top billing at the Coliseum and we were switched to another theatre, the Alhambra. At the Alhambra we were a smash. London couldn't get enough of us. We couldn't get enough of the Londoners, either. We'd never known such doting, unrestrained audiences. Not only that, we found that the English everywhere gave actors and vaudevillians special treatment. In hotels and cafés, on ships and buses and trains, we got top priority and so did our baggage. It was a far cry from the days of one-night stands at home, the days of stale bread pudding, bug-ridden hotels, crooked managers, and trudging from town to town like unwanted gypsies.

Here there was genuine kindness and dignity in show business —even between the most eminent impresarios and the seediest performers. One scene I will never forget. We were presented in England by a famous promoter and sportsman named Cochran. When Cochran called for auditions to round out our show at the Alhambra, a mob turned up. Every act in the British Isles—except the Coliseum Danseuse—wanted to share the bill with the

151

balmy Marxes. Cochran, who hated to say no to anybody, had the painful duty of turning down ninety-eight percent of the hopefuls.

One of these was an aged hoofer—he must have been damn near eighty—who'd obviously spent his last copper getting his costume out of mothballs and into immaculate condition. He came out in gray suit, gray derby, gray spats, gray shoes, and swinging a gray cane—straight out of a Victorian music hall—and went into his song and dance. He put up a courageous, dapper front. But his bones creaked, and his voice had rusted to a croak. It was an embarrassing moment.

Cochran, down in the orchestra, raised a hand to stop him. "I thank you very much," he said unhappily. "I shall let you know."

Then, instead of retreating in defeat and humiliation, to make room for the next act, the ancient hoofer stepped grandly down to the footlights. He leaned over and pointed his cane at the conductor.

"Maestro," he said, "would you please play four bars for me to go off with?"

The conductor complied. The old gentleman danced offstage to the music, waving his derby, as if it were his fourth curtain call. Everybody in the house, including the impresario, broke into applause.

The only disagreeable thing about England, that trip, was the climate. It was chilly and damp when we got there and it kept getting chillier and damper. I never once got really warm, outdoors or in. Chico and I shared an apartment near the theatre, where the only heat came from an open coal grate. Our last night there was the coldest yet. As the last of our scuttle of coal was burning out, we decided the only way we could keep from freezing was to bundle up in all the clothes we had with us and stay up and play pinochle, instead of going to bed. But the chill came creeping through every layer of every shirt, sweater, suit, raincoat and overcoat we had on.

"What the hell," said Chico. "We can't die of pneumonia our last night here. That would be ungrateful, after all they've done for us." So saying, he pulled a drawer out of the dresser, stomped on it and smashed it and threw the sticks in the fire. We played two hands of pinochle, then it got cold again.

We burned up the rest of the drawers, one by one. Then the bureau itself had to go. Next we threw on the chairs and played cards standing up. Before dawn the fire began to die again. We broke up the table and piled it on the fire and had to finish the pinochle game sitting on the floor.

We took off for the boat-train first thing in the morning, too early to wake up the landlord to tell him good-bye and thank him for a pleasant stay. But we left him a note, and enough dough to replace all the extra firewood we had burned. We left the note on the mantelpiece—which we hadn't been able to rip from the wall, although, God knows, we tried.

So in spite of the climate, my last memory of England was a warm one.

Aboard the S.S. Homeric. We had risen so high in class that now the rule was: "Don't buy anything you can't put on the Cunard Line." I brought back a lot of things I couldn't have carried on the Chief, including an English sheep dog named "Hokum." I expected complications getting him into the States, but Hokum came straight off the boat, with no bother whatsoever about quarantine.

The truth was, the authorities were so intent on nabbing Harry Kabikoff that they didn't bother to impound my dog, or even check his papers.

Harry Kabikoff was a fighter, a lightweight, who once made the mistake of trying to clobber Benny Leonard in an exhibition back in St. Paul, and had gotten himself decked by the champ. Kabikoff became quite a pal of Leonard's after that performance, and of ours too. The day we sailed for England, Harry came to the boat to see us off. When the boat sailed he was still in our stateroom. He had a notion he'd like to try his luck in the English ring. We had to put up bond for him and pay for his fare across. Harry's luck in the English ring was no better than his luck in the Minnesota ring. He came to see us off at Southampton, and somehow tarried too long in our stateroom again, and we had to pay his fare back home. The Cunard Line was satisfied, but the U.S. State Department was not. So when we landed, all the officials were too busy hunting for the tiger we had smuggled in to bother about the illegal entry of any sheep dog.

By the time Harry got off the hook, with our help, Hokum was home free, to all intents and purposes a bona fide Yankee Fido.

New York. Among the other things we brought back from abroad was an inflated opinion of how good we were. The conquest of London had gone to our heads. We got on our high horses and refused to kowtow to the Emperor of the Palace. What the hell, we were now royalty ourselves. The next thing we knew we were in a fight to the finish with E. F. Albee, over a minor issue. It didn't take long for the finish to come.

When we worked an Albee theatre out of town, our act lasted forty minutes. It was a sort of afterpiece to the movie on the program. There would be as many as twenty people besides ourselves in the company, including extras, musicians and stagehands. We were on a fixed budget, and this involved a detailed, cent-by-cent accounting. If we ran over budget on production costs, the deficit was made up out of our salaries. Whenever this happened we howled all the way to New York, but it never did us any good. The accounting department was mighty, and it prevailed.

On returning from England, we were booked to take a company on a swing through upstate New York and over to Cleveland. The itinerary was okay with us, but we told Murdock we didn't approve of the budget. Specifically, we felt that the allocation for stagehands was $19.50 too high.

Who the hell were we to question an item on the budget? Murdock wanted to know. We were the Marx Brothers, International Artistes, that's who the hell we were. We wouldn't give in. Murdock said we were crazy. The budget had been drawn up by Mr. Albee himself, and it couldn't be changed. We told him what Mr. Albee could do with his budget.

The next day Mr. Albee told us what we could do. We could look for work elsewhere. Furthermore, we were never to set foot again in an Albee theatre. Good, said we. Now we were free to go on to bigger things.

Too late, the sobering import of what we had done sank in. We had kicked ourselves smack off the pinnacle of vaudeville. Too late, we learned that Albee's power ranged far beyond his own empire. When you were on his blacklist, doors were closed in your face all over town. Still, we were a headline act. What to do? The first thing we did was to send for Minnie. She came charging out of retirement on the next train east.

Minnie turned the city upside down and at last she found an open door, the door of the Shubert brothers' office. Nobody warned us, unfortunately, that it was a trap door.

The Shuberts had come up with the scheme of sending revue companies out on the road, in cut-rate, cutthroat competition with Albee and the Orpheum. These companies were known as "Shubert Units," and they were headlined by outcasts and exiles from the big-time circuits. This qualified us. We were welcomed with open arms, and papers were signed for the creation of the Marx Brothers Shubert Unit.

Our new bosses were famous in the theatre, but not for their liberal treatment of performers. A Shubert Unit had to pay its own way. Each unit had an advance man to put out posters and arrange for theatres (which had to be off the beaten track, since all the big houses were controlled by the moguls the Shuberts were fighting). But there was no budget for advance publicity. There was no advance money for the company, or expense money, or even a guarantee. The unit paid itself from week to week out of box-office receipts, on a fixed percentage.

Under these conditions, we had to stage a full two-hour show, not just a forty-minute act, as we had for Albee. We had to hire variety acts and musicians, and cook up an afterpiece that required a minimum of props and scenery. The more the Shuberts had to lay out in production costs, the more they whittled down the company's box-office percentage.

For all this, the Marx Brothers were the Marx Brothers. We'd done it the hard way before and we'd do it the hard way again. We hit the road.

Buffalo, New York. We landed in Buffalo to find no posters up, no theatre lined up for the unit to play in. Our advance man was running a week behind the show. Business was lousy.

Milwaukee, Wisconsin. Business got worse. We had to cut our people from half salary down to one-third salary. Acts were pulling out right and left, and replacing them wasn't easy. The Shuberts declined to accept our collect calls, or reply to our telegrams for help.

In Milwaukee, Minnie announced that she had the answer to our troubles. "All this show needs," she said, "is a little more class, like some new special effects. That'll pack 'em in."

When Minnie spoke these words, I was hearing a voice out of a past that I hoped I had forgotten, a past of hockshop mandolins and fake carnations. I couldn't believe we had fallen all the way back to this. Just four months ago we had been the guests of honor at the London town house of the Duke of Gloucester.

But Minnie lived only for the present, and the job at hand. Her present job, in Milwaukee, was to make a breath-taking spectacle out of the Chinese number in the first act. She lit on this number for the simple reason that one of the girls in the unit was stuck on a local boy whose father owned a Chinese restaurant and who agreed to give Minnie all the Chinese props and decorations she wanted, if we would plug the restaurant during the show.

Minnie had an inspiration. It would be a rain scene. For the special effect, two stagehands would shower rice down from the flies, while lights played through the falling rice for atmosphere. It would be the most thrilling thing ever seen in Milwaukee, Minnie proclaimed.

It was not, however. That night it was raining hard outside, real rain. The theatre roof leaked. The special-effects rice, sitting high

156

above the stage in two big cans, got pretty wet by the middle of the first act. It came time for Minnie's new number. When the stagehands got the cue to start the shower, two fat globs of soggy rice plummeted to the stage. The kids onstage didn't know what hit them. They got the hell off before they could find out.

Death in Milwaukee, or, China Strikes Back.

Indianapolis, Indiana. By now our advance man was two weeks behind the show. Bills were piling up. Our credit was exhausted. We were served with a lawsuit. A lawyer had notified us that all our assets—costumes, props and sets—would be attached the minute we arrived in Indianapolis. Sure enough, when we arrived the lawyer was there to greet us, with a deputy sheriff.

But they were stymied. They couldn't lay a finger on us, because our assets had already been attached. We had the papers to prove it. Minnie had arranged this, through a friendly lawyer, on our way through Chicago.

The only place we could find to play in Indianapolis was an amphitheatre that seated like four thousand people, miles from the center of town. When we complained about the size of the joint, the manager told us not to worry. He had a wide, portable screen that could be set up across the middle of the auditorium, giving it a false back, and giving the effect that a half-empty house was really a full house.

The Indianapolis opening of the Marx Brothers' Shubert Revue was attended by 128 paying customers. The manager obligingly moved the screen down eight more rows, to the one-quarter mark. Attendance at the second performance was 34.

After the second show I saw Minnie pacing the stage, whistling vaguely, squinting at the light borders, and rubbing her hands. I knew what was coming. A new special effect. Ah, but this one was different! No fancy scenery, nothing as tricky as raining rice. This one would be done with lights alone. But what a lighting effect! When word of Minnie's new spectacle had buzzed around Indianapolis, the house would be jammed to the rafters!

157

Minnie worked out her scheme with the spotlight operator. It was simple, she said. While the company sang "Moonlight Bay," the spotlight man would project the moon and a galaxy of stars on the ceiling and the proscenium, and rippling water on the floor of the stage and the apron. So simple it was genius, true theatrical genius.

To give Minnie credit, it might indeed have been a brilliant effect. We never had a chance to find out. That night the spotlight operator turned up drunk. He got confused about Nature's laws, let alone Minnie's cues. He had the moon and the stars shining on the floor and water rippling all over the ceiling.

Well, word buzzed around Indianapolis, all right. The total attendance for our fourth show was a nice, round figure. Ten people. Even with the screen behind the second row, it still looked like ten people.

Now even Minnie had to face reality. We were washed up. We were stranded. We didn't have enough dough to pay our way out of the hotel. We could sneak out of the hotel, but we still didn't have train fare to any point beyond Kokomo. We didn't have enough dough to pay the kids in the company the price of dinner. It was the end of the line for the Shubert unit and it looked like the end of the Marx Brothers, headliners on the Orpheum, the hit of the Palace, and the toast of London. I had seven cents in my pocket.

Her sons were afraid to say it, but Minnie said it: "We'll have to wire Al for a loan."

We knew that Uncle Al was financially good for our getaway money. He now had a new partner, a guy named Gallagher, and owned half-interest in the most popular song in the country, "Mr. Gallagher and Mr. Shean." But Minnie was not exactly sure if she had sent the telegram to her brother's right address. She wouldn't admit it, but she was also afraid that even if Uncle Al received the wire, he might decide that this was the last straw, and refuse to bail us out.

"Boys," she said, "we can only wait and hope."

While waiting and hoping, I went for an aimless walk in the

outskirts of Indianapolis. I was depressed, and confused, and I had to be alone. I kept telling myself that something good always happened every time I hit bottom. But I didn't believe it. What could happen? What could I do? Groucho could go back in vaudeville as a single. Zeppo could go back to Chicago with Minnie, where he'd have no trouble finding a job. He was the only high-school graduate in the family. Chico could land a job as a piano player, on his own terms, anywhere.

But me? What was I trained to do besides being a Marx Brother? Well, I could play the harp on a New York City ferryboat, for nickels and dimes. Beyond that, nothing.

As I walked, a long-forgotten voice came out of the past. Miss Flatto. Miss Flatto, waggling her finger at my nose and saying, *Some day you'll realize, young man. Some day you'll realize!* Okay, so now I realized. I had come to no good end, exactly as she had predicted. I was a man of nearly thirty years and here I was stranded in a strange city with seven cents in my pocket and no way of earning cent number eight. *Okay, Miss Flatto,* I said to the voice in my memory, *you've had your revenge.*

It was the only time I ever felt sorry for myself.

I came out of my daze. I was startled to find I was standing watching an auction sale. The inventory of a little general store in the suburbs—groceries, notions and dry goods—was being auctioned off. There were about twenty people there. They must have been jobbers, mostly, because the auctioneer was knocking down the stock in big lots. I was careful to keep my hands in my pockets, so I could resist any crazy impulse to make a bid, and blow my entire capital of seven cents.

The shelves were nearly emptied out and most of the crowd had left, but I still hung around, having nothing better to do with myself. Finally everything was gone except one scrub brush, the former owner, hovering in the background, the auctioneer, myself, and an elderly Italian couple. The elderly couple had been there all the time. Either they had no money or they were too timid to make a bid on anything. Whichever it was, they exchanged sad looks now that the auction was winding up.

The auctioneer was tired. "All right," he said. "Let's get it over with and not horse around. I have left here one last desirable item. One cleansing brush in A-number-one, brand-new condition, guaranteed to give you floors so clean you can eat off them. What am I offered?"

The old Italian guy and his wife looked at each other, searching for the key to the right thing to say. The auctioneer glared at them. "All right!" he yelled. "It's only a goddam *scrub* brush!" They held on to each other like they had done something wrong.

I said, quickly, "One cent."

The auctioneer whacked his gavel. He sighed and said, "Sold-thank-God-to-the-young-American-gentleman-for-one-cent."

I picked up my brush and handed it to the old lady. She was as touched as if I had given her the entire contents of the store. The old man grabbed my hand and pumped it. They both grinned at me and poured out a river of Italian that I couldn't understand. "Think nothing of it," I said, and added, "*Ciao, eh?*"—which was the only Italian I could remember from 93rd Street.

They thought this was pretty funny, the way I said it, and they walked away laughing. I walked away laughing too. A day that had started out like a nothing day, going nowhere except down, had turned into a something day, with a climax and a laugh for a finish. I couldn't explain it, but I hadn't felt so good in years. A lousy penny scrub brush had changed the whole complexion of life.

When I got back to the hotel the money had arrived from Uncle Al. Just as I anticipated, it had been decided that Groucho should audition as a single, Zeppo return to Chicago with Minnie, and Chico hire out as a piano player.

To all of these decisions I said: "Nuts."

This was the longest serious speech I had ever made in front of the family, and everybody listened. Then everybody started talking. We talked ourselves out, until all our self-pity was gone. What had happened to us was our fault, not the Shuberts' or anybody else's. And what was going to happen to us would also be our own doing, not the Shuberts' or anybody else's.

Aboard the east-bound Pennsy. The other passengers on the coach kept complaining, so we bribed the porter a quarter and spent the night in the men's room of the nearest Pullman car. I tootled on the clarinet and played pinochle with Chico. Groucho smoked his pipe and read a book. Zeppo did deep knee-bends. At the same time we were all working, throwing ideas into the kitty and putting together a show we could do back in New York. None of us stopped to think how idiotic and deluded we were. *What* show? For *whom?* We were not only exiled by the moguls, but now even the scavengers wouldn't touch us.

Absolutely idiotic. And thank God we were. The train ride from Indianapolis to New York, clacking through the blackness from the end of the line to what looked like the beginning of nothing, was the most momentous jump we ever made. For me, it was the prologue to a new kind of life in a new kind of world.

CHAPTER 11

The Name Is Woollcott

IT WASN'T MUCH OF A SHOW, but it kept Chico in pinochle money and the rest of us in eating money. It was a three-day tabloid, or "tab show," in which everybody doubled in brass. Groucho was master of ceremonies, tenor, and straight man in the afterpiece. Chico doubled as piano player and monologist, besides doing comedy in the afterpiece. I played harp and clarinet, spelled Chico at the piano, and dropped knives. Zeppo was the juvenile and the baritone, and also the prop man and the stage manager. Minnie was leading lady, character woman, producer, company manager, and wardrobe mistress.

Since we had been thrown to the lions by the lords of the vaudeville jungle, we had to hack out our own circuit. The Marx Brothers Circuit, justly unsung and unfabled in the annals of show business, was made up of the least known side-street theatres in Brooklyn and the Bronx, with a western swing to Hoboken, New Jersey. Oh, how the mighty had fallen!

We were surviving, but that was all. The future was a bleak, blank zero. Nobody of importance came to see us because we didn't let anybody know where we were playing. We were even too ashamed to let our relatives know. Indianapolis looked better all the time. We were broke back there, but at least we still had stature as big-time headliners.

"Hang on, hang on!" was Minnie's rallying cry. "I'll find a way!"

It was not Minnie, for once, who led us into greener pastures. It was Chico who found the way. He found it—where else?—in a pinochle game, one Sunday night. He found a live one. A guy with dough. A guy with enough dough to put a legitimate show together.

The "live one" was a producer named Joseph Gates. He was better known around Broadway as "Minimum" Gates, because of the quaint way he auditioned an actor. A Gates audition consisted of his turning his back on an actor and saying, "So what's your minimum salary?"

Actually, Gates's bank roll was not his own. He had found an angel, a pretzel manufacturer from Hackensack, New Jersey—Herman Broody by name. Broody had promised his girl friend he'd put her on the stage. He had the stage for his girl, but no show. He came to Gates and gave him the dough to build a production.

So now Gates was looking for a star to build the production around. He had about decided to sign a black-face comedian named Wilson, who had worked as a single on all the big circuits and whose minimum salary was six hundred dollars a week. Chico went to work on Gates. Why not sign the Four Marx Brothers for the show? By sheer coincidence, said Chico, the Marx Brothers' minimum was also six hundred dollars a week. Gates couldn't see it. Too many guys in the act. They'd clutter up the stage.

Chico wouldn't let go. He kept after him like a dog with a bone. He even let Gates beat him in three straight hands of pinochle. That may have been what did it. Anyway, Gates reported to Broody that he was undecided whether to sign Wilson or the Marx Brothers for the lead.

Broody was surprised at Gates's indecision. Why, there was no choice at all! What the hell—if you could get one ton of pretzel salt for six hundred bucks at one place and four tons for six hundred at another, you went to the second place. Didn't Gates see the simple, practical, hard-headed logic of that? If he could get four actors for the price of one, then grab 'em before they got away.

We were hired.

163

Our new show, for reasons unknown even to the writers, was called "I'll Say She Is." Since it had full-stage production numbers like "Perfumes from Hindustan" (followed by a team of gilded toe-dancers who were eternally griping about "the goddam beads on the floor left over from the Hinderstand bit"), and since our own big scene lasted over forty-five minutes, the show was billed as a musical comedy, not as a common revue.

I'll Say She Is had an out-of-town tryout in Allentown, Pennsylvania, then opened in Philadelphia. At the end of summer we were still playing to capacity. Business was too good to close. So the show continued to run until the day after Thanksgiving, when Broody decided Gates should take it on the road.

The tour lasted a year and a half. We were in the legitimate theatre now. We looked down our noses at acts that toiled away at the two-a-day and three-a-day grind of vaudeville. We only had to do matinees on Wednesdays and Saturdays.

Consequently, we had more time off than we'd ever had before. During the Philly run, I had time to learn the game of golf. I also had more time for music. I learned half a dozen new tunes for the harp. My old clarinet had fallen apart, and I replaced it with an eight-dollar job I found in a Philly pawnshop.

My dog Hokum also kept me busy. On the golf course one Sunday he flushed a skunk out of the rough. He had to be confined to the theatre basement and I had to hire a kid to help me keep poor Hokum doused with toilet water around the clock. When I took him out for his first airing, in my open runabout, a sudden thunderstorm came up. Hokum panicked, jumped out of the car, and I never saw him again.

During our Chicago run we had a long, happy reunion with Pete Penovitch and with our mutual friend Nick the Greek. They went with us to the ball park at least twice a week, when the

White Sox were in town. We were in good company. The Greek always bet a big bundle—sometimes as much as ten G's—on a ball game, and he would make "good-luck bets" with us, riding the other way. He'd give us four-to-one when the bookies' odds were even money.

During this same stand, I first met a man who was to become a lifetime friend, Mr. Ben Hecht. Groucho and I had read Hecht's 1001 *Nights in Chicago* and, being fans of the author, we wanted to meet him. We found out where he lived through Covici's Bookstore (which was like the local poolroom for Chicago writers and painters at the time), and the four of us went around to his apartment.

Groucho said: "You Ben Hecht the fiddle player?" Hecht said he was, and asked us in. We stayed all night. Hecht played the violin, I played the piano, and Ben and Groucho sang, improvising dirty parodies on popular songs. We saw a lot of Hecht and got to know his buddy Charlie MacArthur who was also loony enough to be to our liking.

In one of his memoirs, Hecht recalls this particular summer in Chicago and mentions being haunted by "a perpetual Halloween called the Marx Brothers." He should talk! He played the spookiest fiddle I had heard since Solly Soloshky. I must admit, however, that he was a fair writer and a better than fair poker player.

Except for these bright interludes, the road was the road, grueling and tiresome. A hotel was a hotel and a train was a train. When you'd been in one you'd been in them all, and we'd been in them all for fourteen years too many. We threatened to quit the show. They raised our salary. We said we would still quit—unless they took *I'll Say She Is* off the road and opened it in New York City.

Ever since we first opened in Philadelphia, we had been promised that the show would go to Broadway. The management kept stalling, saying the show still needed more testing out of town. Now we held them to their promise. A year and a half was enough of an out-of-town tryout for any show. Either *I'll Say She Is* went to New York or the Marx Brothers took a walk. We were the mother-lode of a gold mine, and we knew it. Without us the whole thing would turn to a pile of slag. Our threat worked. We went to New York.

The Casino Theatre on 39th Street was leased and May 19 set for the opening. Apparently, the plot was this: open at the Casino, get crucified (it simply wasn't a production of Broadway caliber), run a couple of weeks to appease the Marx Brothers, then head back out on the road. We were warned not to put our trunks in storage.

On the afternoon before the opening I was sitting in Lindy's restaurant. It was sad to think that a month from now I'd be in Albany or Columbus or Baltimore. During rehearsals I'd been staying at the Princeton, a theatrical hotel, with the rest of the cast. Tonight, after the show, I was going to move in with Minnie and Frenchie, who had taken a house on Long Island. I had a home again, and during the day a choice of two homes-away-from-home, Lindy's or Reuben's. I was back with my own people, who spoke my language, with my accent—cardplayers, horseplayers, bookies, song-pluggers, agents, actors out of work and actors playing the Palace, Al Jolson with his mob of fans, and Arnold Rothstein with his mob of runners and flunkies. The cheesecake was ambrosia. The talk was old, familiar music. A lot of yucks. A lot of action. Home Sweet Home.

I got up to go to work, with absolutely no enthusiasm, and told the boys to save my seat. I took a cab down to the Casino. The marquee lights had just been turned on. THE FOUR MARX BROTHERS IN "I'LL SAY SHE IS." I was not impressed. I was a realist. I kept hearing the words: *Sorry, boys—you're shut.* But what the hell, I thought, remembering the empty seat in Lindy's, it was going to be fun while it lasted.

The story of the Marx Brothers' Broadway debut, on the night of May 19, 1924, has been told many times. It has been rehashed in columns, articles and books, and on the radio. How Minnie fell off a chair while being fitted for her opening-night gown and broke her leg, and had to be carried into her box at the Casino. How one famous critic was furious at his paper for making him cover "some damn acrobats." How the Marx Brothers stood the audience on its ear. How the disgruntled critic laughed so hard he cried.

There is very little that I can add to the story, I'm sorry to say. All I can remember, in all honesty, is doing the show, getting some good laughs, taking a few bows, then going home alone to Long Island and straight to bed. Minnie, because of her busted leg, decided to spend the night in a hotel.

At eight o'clock in the morning the phone rang. It was Groucho. He was excited. "Hey, Harp, wake up!" he said. "Have you read the reviews?"

"What reviews?" I said. "*Variety* doesn't come out until tomorrow."

"No, the *newspaper* critics," said Groucho. "The *Sun*, the *Times*, the *Trib*, the *World*—the big critics."

"Yah? They liked us?"

"They *loved* us. We're a hit! Listen—" I interrupted Groucho to say I'd rather go back to bed than listen to any reviews. I didn't know anything about Broadway critics, only about the mugs who wrote for *Variety*. All I ever read in the papers were the sports pages, and once in a while a column like S. Jay Kaufman's or F. P. A.'s "Conning Tower." If the "big critics" liked our show that was nice, but it was nothing to wake up a guy at eight in the morning about.

Groucho wouldn't get off the phone. "Let me read you how it starts out in the *Sun*," he said. "This you gotta hear."

"All right, all right, all *right*," I said. "Go ahead—it's your nickel."

Groucho then read, to my growing embarrassment:

> Harpo Marx and Some Brothers. Hilarious Antics Spread Good Cheer at the Casino. By Alexander Woollcott.
>
> As one of the many who laughed immoderately throughout the greater part of the first New York performance given by a new musical show, entitled, if memory serves, "I'll Say She

Is," it behooves your correspondent to report at once that that harlequinade has some of the most comical moments vouchsafed to the first-nighters in a month of Mondays. It is a bright colored and vehement setting for the goings on of those talented cutups, the Four Marx Brothers. In particular, it is a splendacious and reasonably tuneful excuse for going to see that silent brother, that sly, unexpected, magnificent comic among the Marxes, who is recorded somewhere on a birth certificate as Adolph, but who is known to the adoring two-a-day as Harpo Marx.

Surely there should be dancing in the streets when a great clown comes to town, and this man is a great clown. He is officially billed as a member of the Marx family, but truly he belongs to that greater family which includes Joe Jackson and Bert Melrose and the Fratillini brothers. Harpo Marx, so styled, oddly enough, because he plays the harp, says never a word from first to last, but when by merely leaning against one's brother one can seem richly and irresistibly amusing, why should one speak?

Groucho paused.

"Is that all?" I said. "Didn't the son-of-a-bitch say anything about you or Chico or Zeppo? What did he think—I was doing a single? Is he blind or something?"

Oh, there was more, Groucho said, plenty about all the rest of them. He just thought I'd like to hear the part about me. "Like me to read it again, old clown?" he said.

I hung up on him and went back to sleep.

At ten o'clock the phone rang again. A voice I had never heard before said, "Have I the pleasure of addressing Mr. Harpo Marx?" From the way he spoke, I couldn't tell if he was a con artist or a ham actor Groucho had hired to pull a gag on me. I was very suspicious. "I'm Harpo Marx," I said. "Who's this?"

"The name is Woollcott," he said. "Alexander Woollcott." The name didn't ring any bells. I didn't connect it with what Groucho had read over the phone. I'd been too sleepy at the time.

"Sorry," I said. "Don't think I know you." I was still suspicious.

"I do a little chore now and then for the New York *Sun*," the guy said. "I did a little chore last night, as a matter of fact. I reviewed your new show. And now I would like very much to meet you."

I didn't know what to say. Woollcott went on. "Forgive me for being so presumptuous and calling you out of the blue," he said. "I got your number from Charlie MacArthur, who seemed to think you wouldn't mind."

Oh, well, so he was a friend of Ben Hecht's friend Charlie. He was all right, then. I told him so, and he laughed and said, "Now that we've exchanged references, can we meet? Will you receive me if I barge into your dressing room after the show tonight?"

"Sure, why not?" I said, and he seemed very pleased.

Before he hung up, he said, "By the bye, Mr. Marx, how did you like my little piece in this morning's *Sun?*" I said I thought it was the lousiest review I had ever read, and he laughed so hard I had to hold the receiver a foot away.

When he hung up, I reflected that a guy who laughed like that couldn't be all bad. I'd give him a little time after the show. It wouldn't hurt. Then I'd go over to Lindy's and relax, where nobody ever used words like "behooves" and "splendacious" and "presumptuous."

Alexander Woollcott "barged" into my dressing room—literally. I had no idea what a "big New York critic" ought to look like, but I didn't expect this. He looked like something that had gotten loose from Macy's Thanksgiving Day Parade.

I couldn't help thinking of Mons Herbert's old vaudeville act in which he blew up the rubber turkey. If Mons had blown up a plucked owl, put thick glasses and a mustache on it, and dressed it in an opera cape and a wide black hat, this is what it would have looked like.

"The name is Woollcott," he said, and his voice didn't change my first impression. It was a voice that could have been reproduced

169

by letting the air out of a balloon, a downbeat inflection with a whiny edge to it. Coming from him it sounded hoity-toity and supercilious, and I didn't like it a bit.

We shook hands. Woollcott sighed and settled his bulk onto a rickety dressing-room chair with surprising ease. He rested his hands on the head of his cane, blinked, twitched his mustache, then broke into a grin that wasn't supercilious at all. If anything, he was being shy. He had come to see me not as a critic, but as a starry-eyed fan.

"Well, Marx," he said. "So you didn't approve of my piece in the morning's paper."

Nope, I sure didn't, I told him. At least I didn't approve of the part I could understand. He laughed and said, "Might I ask what you disapproved of specifically?"

I had read the whole review by now. "You got us all mixed up, Mr. Woollcott," I said. "Groucho's not the oldest—Chico is. Zeppo's not the stage manager—he's the juvenile."

"And what about Harpo? Did I get him right?"

"Tell you the truth," I said, "I couldn't tell from the things you wrote whether you were giving me the raspberry or trying to give me a build-up, because I didn't know what half the words meant. If you're looking to give me a build-up, forget it. I don't work as a single. I work with my brothers or not at all."

He stopped smiling, and took off his hat. "My dear Marx," he said, "I was neither flattering your performance nor making light of it. I meant every word I wrote. You are the funniest man I have ever seen upon the stage."

I didn't know how to return a compliment like that, so I said, "What about my harp solo? How did you like that?"

"I still think you're the funniest man I have ever seen upon the stage," said Woollcott. "Consider yourself fortunate, Marx," he added, "that I am not a music critic."

So he was one of those characters. He made you a compliment, then jabbed the needle in. I had known guys like that, who couldn't help needling any more than a wasp could help stinging. It was a type of guy I loved to have around. They were the world's greatest patsies for practical jokes. I began to like this Woollcott.

170

He said he was sorry if he'd offended me, but he had an unfortunate social disease. He always spoke whatever came to his mind. "My friends will tell you," he said, "that Woollcott is a nasty old snipe. Don't believe them. Woollcott's friends are a pack of simps who move their lips when they read.

"Nevertheless," he continued, hoisting himself up off the chair, "I should like them to meet you, tonight. I should like to show them a true artist. You might bring some light into their grubby little lives. I take it you're free for what's left of the evening?"

I had to get out of this fast. If his "friends" talked the way he did I would have absolutely nothing to say to them. I didn't know the language. "Sorry," I said. "I've got a date I'm already late for."

Woollcott did not intend that I should refuse his invitation. He squinted down his nose at me and said, huffily, "A young lady, I presume?" I shook my head.

"Some business matter of great urgency?" he asked, with heavy sarcasm.

I nodded my head yes. "Poker game," I said.

His grin returned. "Bravo!" he said. "Precisely what my friends and I have in mind! Are you a good poker player, Marx?"

I told him I played a pretty fair country game.

He clapped his hands. "So be it!" he said. "The minute you're out of grease paint, come buckety-buckety over to the Hotel Algonquin. Shall we say eleven-thirty?"

I was trapped. "Okay, eleven-thirty," I said. "But first, would you mind showing me your teeth?" He bared his teeth. "Too bad," I said. "No gold. Well, I'll keep looking."

"No gold?" said Woollcott, waiting for the gag.

I told him I was still looking for another guy as nice to play poker with as Mons Herbert, who used to tip his hand by the number of gold teeth he flashed. This delighted Woollcott. "And what did this walking bonanza do upon the stage?" he asked.

"He played the 'Anvil Chorus' by blowing on knives and forks," I said, "and for a finish he blew up a turkey until music came out of its ass."

Woollcott laughed so hard he had to sit down again. He wiped tears from his eyes and said, "Dear God, why can't I have friends

171

like that!" I refrained from telling Woollcott why I had been reminded of Mons's act in the first place, when he had entered the dressing room.

He put on his black impresario's hat, adjusted his cape, and stuck out his hand. "A rare pleasure, sir," he said. Instead of giving him my hand I gave him my leg, the old switch gag I had used since *On the Mezzanine*. He pushed my knee away in disgust. "See here, Marx," he said, with the full hoity-toity treatment. "Kindly confine your baboonery to the stage. Off it, you are a most unfunny fellow."

I liked him more and more.

The Algonquin was an oddball kind of a joint. I couldn't figure it out. It obviously wasn't a theatrical hotel, because nobody was sitting around the lobby playing two-handed pinochle or reading *Billboard*. It didn't have the smell of a commercial travelers' hotel, and it didn't have the phony trimmings of a tourist trap. Being none of these things, it had to be a blind, a front. But what the Algonquin was a front for, I couldn't figure out either.

When I inquired for Mr. Woollcott's room, the guy at the desk gave me a funny look. I thought: Oh-oh, now he's going to ask me for the password. But he must have decided I was all right. He gave me the number of a second-floor suite.

When I got to the suite I felt a lot better. It was just eight guys playing cards in a room filled with smoke and littered with ash trays, coffee cups, cast-off jackets and ties, and stacks of poker chips.

Woollcott, now in shirt-sleeves like all the rest of them, put down his cards, jumped up, and took my arm. "Harpo," he said, "meet the Thanatopsis Inside Straight and Literary Club. Harpo, Thanatopsis. Thanatopsis, Harpo."

Thanatopsis? What was this? A mob of Greek revolutionaries?

The guys at the table seemed friendly enough. They smiled and said polite things. I said, "Finish your hand, for God's sake," and then they seemed even friendlier.

When the hand was over, Woollcott introduced me around. Only one name meant anything to me—Frank Adams, "F. P. A.," the famous columnist of the "Conning Tower." Groucho and I had been mailing in contributions to the "Conning Tower" for years, and had succeeded in having a few of them printed. I never thought I'd be shaking hands one day with the Keeper of the Tower himself. As for the rest of the cardplayers, I could only remember them as a bunch of guys named "Benson," which was what one of the names sounded like. I had a lousy memory for names.

I met a plump Mr. Benson with a toothbrush mustache and a surprised look; a huge shaggy one who looked like he was wearing last week's dirty laundry; a tall one with a booming voice and a handsome ruddy face; a tall, sad-faced one who kept twisting an arm around his head and massaging an ear the hard way; a bald Mr. Benson with glasses, and a Benson with uncombed hair who looked like a cowhand who'd lost his horse.

Weeks later, when I finally got them all straight, I realized that I had been introduced to, respectively, the writers Robert Benchley and Heywood Broun, Herbert Bayard Swope, the editor of the New York World, the playwrights George S. Kaufman and Marc Connelly, and Harold Ross, the editor of Judge who was then cooking up an idea for a new magazine to be called The New Yorker.

If I had known that night in May who these characters really were and that I'd been lured into a den of intellectuals, I would have scrammed out of the joint and run all the way to Lindy's, where my empty seat was still waiting for me. But not knowing any better, I stayed and played poker. My luck was lousy, but it was otherwise a surprisingly pleasant evening.

The most popular sport between hands was baiting Aleck Woollcott. That was how I learned how hard Woollcott had tried to get out of reviewing I'll Say She Is. F. P. A. had him squirming while he retold the whole story. Seems Woollcott had come to the Algonquin before the opening, cursing about having to cover "some damned acrobats called 'The Marx Brothers,'" and looking for somebody to take his place and write the review for him. He tried threats, cajolery and bribery, but had no takers. In last-ditch desperation he latched onto Adams. Adams said sorry, but he had a date for the evening. He was taking a lady English professor to the theatre. When Woollcott finally gave up and dragged himself into the Casino, muttering with self-pity, he discovered Adams and his date already sitting in the theatre. He was so furious he swore he'd never speak to F. P. A. again.

"Now look at the old fraud," said Adams. "He wants the world to think he invented the Marx Brothers, and he brings one of the acrobats in here like he was presenting his favorite son at court."

"I hope you fry in hell," said Woollcott.

The game broke up early. The big weekly game would start Saturday afternoon at five o'clock, they told me, and they expected me to be there. It was easy to see why: they wanted more of my dough. I'd dropped a hundred dollars. I said good-bye to Woollcott, Adams, Benson, Benson, Benson, Benson, Benson, and Benson, and said I'd see them Saturday.

I had passed the initiation. I was now a member of the Thanatopsis Inside Straight and Literary Club. I've often wondered if I ever would have made it if I'd been a winner that night.

Downstairs at the Algonquin was where the conversation flowed, often at a round table in a corner of the dining room. Years later, when everybody was getting nostalgic about the twenties, this became known as *the* Round Table, and people were written up as being "Members" of the Algonquin Round Table.

The Thanatopsis Club did have official members, but the downstairs gathering never did. It was nothing more than one long shmooze, with people drifting in and out, eating, arguing, gossiping, telling jokes, talking shop and having brainstorms. Along with the other upstairs cardplayers—Woollcott, Adams, Benchley,

Broun, Swope, Kaufman, Connelly and Ross—I spent a lot of time at the Round Table. There was no telling who else might turn up—regulars like Deems Taylor, Donald Ogden Stewart, Peggy Wood, Jane Grant and Dorothy Parker, or strays like Helen Hayes, Charlie MacArthur, Edna Ferber, Bernard Baruch, Ring Lardner, Otto H. Kahn and Will Rogers.

Woollcott had lunch at the Algonquin every day. Through him I met four extraordinary women, who were to be very close to me for the rest of the decade: the actress Ruth Gordon, Neysa McMein, the painter and illustrator, Alice Duer Miller, the novelist, and George S. Kaufman's brilliant wife, Beatrice.

Alice Duer Miller was the most dignified and cultivated lady I had ever met. I thought it would be impossible for me to ever get to know her. Then one day I found out that the greatest single passion in Alice Miller's life was not writing or literature, but the New York Giants. I told her how I used to watch my one Giant— Sam Mertes—from Coogan's Bluff. She was enchanted. Alice said she had felt there was something rare about me that she liked, and now she knew what it was. From that moment on we were very special friends. We shared the faith, a bond that could only exist between Giant fans.

Aside from my brief exchange with Alice Miller, I had nothing, absolutely nothing, to contribute to the Round Table. Yet I was accepted immediately as somebody who belonged there. They didn't really expect me to talk. It wasn't only that I played a goofy mute onstage, and sometimes offstage, too. It was mainly because I brought to the table another kind of talent—the one talent it lacked—the ability to sit and listen.

The Algonquin was a refuge for the brightest authors, editors, critics, columnists, artists, financiers, composers, directors, producers and actors of the times. The dining-room corner was a hotbed of raconteurs and conversationalists. But until I came along, there wasn't a full-time listener in the crowd. I couldn't have been more welcome if I had had the power to repeal Prohibition.

Bernard Baruch and Herbert Bayard Swope got me cornered one Sunday and wouldn't let me go. For eight straight hours, they took turns talking to me while I gave the cues like an orchestra leader —for Baruch to shut up and Swope to talk, and Swope to shut up and Baruch to talk.

Miss Flatto, I said to myself, should see me now.

I took an apartment in town, on East 57th Street, but only slept there. I spent the rest of the time on the West Side—at the theatre, at the Algonquin, and at Aleck Woollcott's joint. Aleck shared a cooperative town house over on West 47th Street with Harold Ross and his wife, Jane Grant, and an old college friend named Hawley Truax. When Aleck wasn't holding court at the Algonquin he held court at home, slopping around all day—no matter who was there—in his pajama bottoms and an untied kimono. At night, however, he liked to put on the dog. Everything had to be just right, the cocktails and the dinner, and everybody had to be dressed up and on time.

The first time he asked me to his place for an evening, he said he'd be delighted if I could bring my brothers along too—provided, he added, that they behaved like gentlemen. That was all I needed to hear.

As Ross told me later, Woollcott was annoyed as hell when everybody had showed up at the appointed hour except the Marx Brothers. Punctuality was an obsession with him. Then he got even more annoyed when an unearthly, screeching racket started up outside the house, drowning out the story he was telling. He flew into a rage and threw open the front door.

The racket was being made by Groucho, Chico, Zeppo and me, riding on a street carousel and yelling like four wild urchins.

When Aleck saw who it was he laughed and clapped his hands like a kid at his first look at a circus. Then he got sore again—not because we'd lugged a merry-go-round up to his doorstep but because we were late, which was unforgivable.

Woollcott considered that Woollcott was the hub the world

revolved around. If he wasn't the center of attraction he was miserable, and when he was miserable, somebody caught hell. He was a diabolical master of the insult. He could slay a victim with one stab of a phrase or a word. Some of his victims became undying enemies. Others, like me, became undying friends.

I first caught the brunt of Woollcott's wrath in a lecture on punctuality, the day of the carousel. He didn't stay sore very long, however. I wouldn't let him. I didn't understand half the names he called me, like "arrested adolescent." When he finished his tirade, I gave him the innocent-eye bit and said, "*Arrested adolescent.* How did you know about that? I never told you I was thrown in the jig when I was the partner of Seymour Mintz."

That got him. The red went out of his face. His eyes lit up and his mouth hung open at the prospect of hearing a juicy new story. This I had already learned about Aleck. He couldn't resist hearing a story.

He was a marvelous audience once you had him. He could have given lessons to Frenchie in laugh starting. For all his sniffy airs, I never knew a guy so easy to break up—as long as he wasn't the butt of the joke, as long as the story wasn't on him.

Aleck could never hear enough about my early days. He loved to hear me tell about Miss Flatto, the herring peddler, and the window in P. S. 86. He loved to hear my recital of the jobs I had had, from lappa displaying and tin-can swinging to ragpicking and rent kicking. When he felt blue, instead of asking the piano player to play "Melancholy Baby," he would ask me to tell about the Friendly Inn, Madam Schang, my debut at Coney Island, the Mississippi train wreck, Pete Penovitch, or the Musical Cow Milker who mailed the dead rabbit to the theatre manager in Laredo, Texas.

He felt it was his responsibility to keep me out of mischief. He was like a stern old bachelor uncle, although he was actually only six years my senior. At the same time, he was more generous and more patient than anybody I had ever known.

I think he liked me because I never tried to hide the things that I should have been ashamed of according to conventional rules— my lack of education, my colossal ignorance, my lack of ambition.

177

Basically, the only way I had changed in twenty years was to move down the East Side from 93rd Street to 57th Street. I still lived from day to day, and had fun wherever I could find it. I made no bones about the fact that I'd rather play games than work. Now, at last, I had enough time to play, and enough money. I had begun to pay myself back with interest for everything I'd missed out on when I was a kid.

I wasn't having a second childhood. It was my first real childhood. The crazy part of it was, I was spending it as a member of the Woollcott gang, hanging out with the brightest and most famous delinquents of the 1920's.

Perhaps the one thing Woollcott had in common with me was his ability to stay young and enjoy childish pleasures, no matter how old he became. He was a fanatic on games. There was always some kind of game going on wherever Aleck was. Cribbage, poker, parcheesi, bridge, backgammon, craps, casino, anagrams and charades indoors, croquet and badminton outdoors, and word games and guessing games anywhere and everywhere he went.

Whether he was taking Harold Ross on at cribbage at a hundred bucks a game or trying to top George S. Kaufman's outrageous puns over lunch at the Algonquin, Aleck went all out. He played to win. He was a sore loser. He was even more insufferable when he won, because he couldn't resist rubbing salt in the wounds. Woollcott never welshed on a gambling debt. He kept meticulous records of his wins and losses, and expected everybody he played with to be just as efficient.

Aleck went all out in everything he did. The better I knew him the more I was amazed by his capacities—for games, food, talk, friendships, feuds, causes, and long hours of concentrated hard work. His curiosity was endless. So was his enthusiasm, whenever he discovered something that moved him, or tickled him. And when Woollcott enthused, everybody else, by God, had to enthuse too. "Everybody else" could mean his inner circle (as when he "discovered" croquet), New York City (as when he "discovered" the Marx Brothers), or the world at large (as when he "discovered" Japan, the Hall-Mills murder case, the plays of Thornton Wilder,

178

Goodbye Mr. Chips, Seeing-Eye dogs, and Walt Disney's *Three Little Pigs*). Woollcott was no hidden persuader. For nearly twenty years he was the most conspicuous persuader in America.

Because of his sharp tongue, his lack of modesty, and his peculiar looks, Woollcott was a sitting duck—or a squatting owl—for anybody to mimic or lampoon. There was nobody in public life easier to caricature until Adolf Hitler came along, with the possible exception of George Bernard Shaw.

Woollcott was caricatured aplenty, mostly in words. Ben Hecht described him as "a persnickety fellow with more fizz than brain." Harold Ross once said he was "a fat duchess with the emotions of a fish." James Thurber called him "Old Vitriol and Violets."

Another editor on *The New Yorker* said Woollcott was "one of the most dreadful writers who ever existed." I think this guy and everybody else who stuck pins in Aleck took him too seriously, much more seriously than he took himself. Aleck's first love was the theatre, anything theatrical, whether it was the Broadway stage, the movies, the circus, an animated cartoon, a sunset, or a murder trial. To me, Woollcott was a ham actor—not a deep thinker or a serious writer, but a great, big, wonderful ham. Anybody who knew him and didn't realize this took *himself* too seriously.

Once I told Aleck how stupid I felt, tagging along in his shadow, sitting beside him at the Round Table, and never opening my trap. "My dear Harpo," he said, chuckling, his fat round belly jiggling out of his kimono, "you're a smarter fellow than I am. I am the best writer in America and I have nothing to say either. But I'm not smart enough to keep my mouth shut."

Ninety percent of the time he was "on." The other ten percent of the time, when he was "off," he was his own severest critic. He used to characterize himself as an overgrown boy-child, and refer to himself by sickening baby names like "Acky" and "Wookie."

Most people, of course, saw him when he was on. Very few of us had the privilege of being with him when he wasn't ham acting. I was, I believe, one of the five people who, over the years, knew and loved Alexander Woollcott the best. The other four were Alice Duer Miller, Beatrice Kaufman, Ruth Gordon, and a man named Joe Hennessey, who did the dirty work for Aleck—seeing his steak was cooked rare enough, driving his car, keeping him on schedule, and trying to pacify the people he insulted.

I could never figure Aleck out completely, nor he me. He was too complicated and I was too simple. Our friendship was a life-long game of "Who Am I?" It was frustrating, exasperating, and sometimes downright silly, but it was a good, rewarding game. Woollcott was what I had believed, in the innocence of my youth, that Seymour Mintz was going to be. He was a true friend. Moreover, it was physically impossible for him to walk on a bias.

I'll Say She Is ran for over a year, and it made us the richest we'd ever been. I recognized now the power and importance of the New York critics—particularly the man on the *Sun*, who was behooved to write something about the Marx Brothers at least once a month.

Chico had all the action he could handle. He was in Pinochle Paradise. Groucho could buy all the books he wanted, instead of going to the public library. I had joined the Algonquin mob and lived in a happy new world. Minnie and Frenchie bought a new house farther out on Long Island. They bought a new four-door Chevy, hired a chauffeur, and began to live it up.

Minnie organized a ladies' poker club, which met four times a week. Minnie's furs and jewels kept shuttling back and forth from the local pawnbroker, since she still made a religion of trying to fill a straight in poker. Hang the odds, said Minnie. She had borne five sons all in a row and it was therefore her destiny to hold five cards all in a row. But the odds, not destiny, prevailed. And so, back to the old hockshop.

Frenchie could at last be the Beau Brummel he'd always fancied himself to be. He was now a walking fashion plate that made Mr.

Burns, the hat-tipper of 93rd Street, seem in retrospect a walking ad for secondhand fumigated clothing.

Beau Brummel he might have become, but otherwise Frenchie had changed very little. The first day the new chauffeur came to work, Frenchie had himself driven to the grocery store to do the marketing. He came out of the market laden with bundles, got into the shiny new Chevy, and had the chauffeur drive on. He made two more stops, then directed the way back to the Marx residence.

The driver didn't make a move to get out of the car when they got home, and Frenchie asked if he wouldn't like some lunch. He said thanks, but it wasn't his lunchtime. The least he could do, said Frenchie, was help carry in the bundles. That he was willing enough to do. In the kitchen, after dumping the bundles, he just stood around waiting, so Frenchie suggested he might go clean the car, if he didn't want lunch.

"Look, Mac," said the driver, "I don't want no lunch and I'll clean my car when I damn well feel like it. All I want is my money."

Frenchie called for Minnie. He didn't have the heart to fire a servant. Minnie came and immediately got the situation cleared up. The man in the kitchen was not the chauffeur they had hired. When Frenchie had come out of the grocery store, he had gotten into the wrong new Chevy, driven by the wrong guy in a leather cap. He had taken a taxi.

In some ways Frenchie was getting surer of himself. He now had the strength of his convictions, on important issues. Late in the summer of '24, he invited a friend to be his guest for a drive up to the mountains and a weekend in a hotel. At a certain point on Route 17, south of Middletown, Frenchie and his friend got into such an argument as to whether they were then traveling uphill or downhill that they nearly came to blows in the car, and Frenchie ordered the chauffeur to turn around and drive straight back to New York.

I had become quite a dude myself, after our show settled down for a run. I was not the fashion plate that Frenchie was, however. I was more the hot-sport type. I favored golf caps or straw skimmers, blazers, and white linen knickerbockers. Alexander Woollcott said that nothing in the world made him sicker than the outfits I wore on the street, with the exceptions of Maxfield Parrish's painting and the poetry of Edgar A. Guest.

Aleck was constantly trying to change the style of my headgear from Broadway to Continental. He himself favored berets, and the kind of hats that spies and opera impresarios wore in movies. One hot day in July he and I, both wearing berets, were walking east on 42nd Street. Near the corner of Fifth Avenue, I noticed a shop advertising straw hats for sale at two bucks apiece. I ducked into the store. Woollcott kept on walking and talking. In the store I grabbed a hat off the counter and plunked down two dollars. I ran out wearing the new skimmer and caught up with Woollcott, who hadn't broken stride or stopped talking. It wasn't until we were waiting for the light at Fifth Avenue that he did a double-take, noted the switch in my headgear, and made a face like he was about to throw up.

There were few dull moments while *I'll Say She Is* was running. The boredom that used to come toward the end of a season on the road never crept into the Casino. All that crept in was madness. We kept the joint a bedlam six nights and two afternoons per week, from the marquee to the dressing rooms.

One day at lunch, Woollcott told me he was bringing Minnie Maddern Fiske, the Grand Lady of the American Theatre and one of his great idols, to see our show on Thursday night. "Kindly see to it, Harpo," he said, "that you live up to all the extravagant lies I've told Mrs. Fiske about you."

Through somebody, probably Harold Ross, I got hold of a photograph of Aleck in his academic robes, taken at Hamilton College. I had the picture retouched and blown up, and on Thursday I pasted it onto the display in the lobby of the Casino, so that Alexander Woollcott, in cap and gown, was in the middle of the chorus line of *I'll Say She Is,* kicking in unison with the gals to the left and right of him.

I knew Aleck must have seen the doctored poster in the lobby and I knew he was sore, because he didn't bring Mrs. Fiske backstage after the performance. The next day he gave me the silent treatment at the Round Table. He didn't speak to me until one night a week later. The occasion was the opening of a show called *Izzat So* down the street from the Casino. Groucho, Chico, Zeppo and I got in costume early that night and stood under the marquee of our theatre, playing mandolins and singing sad songs as the first-nighters and critics walked past to the opening.

When Woollcott came by he didn't look at me, but he nearly knocked me down in passing, and said, under his breath, "Jew son-of-a-bitch."

This struck me as being very funny, although it wasn't one of Woollcott's best. It wasn't even original. It was the punch line from my story about Mrs. Schang and the Happy Times Tavern, Aleck's favorite tale of true-life adventure.

The next day he was his old, yakkity self again, as if nothing had happened.

I was now a harpist with eight years' professional experience. I decided it was time I should learn to read music and to play the harp correctly, but I was a little shy about going out to look for a teacher.

As it happened, a teacher came to me. A guy came back after a matinee to say how much he'd enjoyed the show, and how "terribly original" he thought my playing was. I didn't know whether this was a dig or a compliment, until he told me he was a harpist with the Metropolitan Opera Company. I asked him if he might give me lessons and he said he'd be flattered to, at twenty bucks a throw. We made a date.

183

When I arrived at the studio for my first lesson, the maestro told me to start playing immediately, anything. I led off with the Sextet from *Lucia*, the nearest thing to a classical piece in my repertoire. He watched me so closely his nose was practically sticking through the strings, and he kept talking to himself: "*Ah, yes!* . . . *Ah, so!* . . . *Extraordinary!* . . ."

When I finished the sextet he fluttered a hand and told me to keep playing, anything, anything at all. "But don't you think we ought to start with how to read notes?" I said. He shook his head and made impatient noises with his tongue and said to play.

I played. Every eight bars I stopped to ask what about the notes, and he kept saying I didn't need notes—just keep playing.

Then he began to stop me, to ask me questions. Could he see again how I did that glissando? Could I do that trill again? If I brought up the subject of reading music, or pedal work, or fingering, he promptly shut me up.

By the time the hour was up, I had taught the maestro my whole lousy technique. When he took my twenty bucks, he said he couldn't tell me how much he looked forward to our next session. I told him he didn't have to, since there wouldn't be any next session.

That was the end of my formal study of the harp.

In the thirty-five years since then, I have had many legitimate harpists, including great virtuosos like Salzedo and Grandjany, ask me to demonstrate my technique. They were utterly fascinated that I could get any sound at all out of the instrument, the way I played it, let alone some pretty good sounds. I was always willing to demonstrate, but damned if I would ever again pay twenty bucks to give any teacher a lesson.

The nearest I've had to a regular teacher has been a lady named Mildred Dilling. I first met her in a music store where she was trying out a new harp. She was playing a piece called "The Music Box." I introduced myself and confessed that I couldn't read notes, and asked her if she would please teach me to play "The Music Box." She was delighted to. We soon became good friends. It was she who introduced me to the world of Bach and Mozart, Debussy and Ravel. Thanks to this fine and generous artist I came to realize that the Sextet from *Lucia* was not, after all, the greatest piece of classical music ever written.

Like all the others, Miss Dilling never tried to change my screwball technique. But she was glad to help me in any other way. Many a time I've telephoned her (sometimes from across the country, waking her up in the middle of the night) when I've gotten stuck on a tricky chord. Night or day, she wouldn't fail me. She'd hitch her harp close to the phone in her studio and play the chord over and over until I got it, at the other end of the wire.

What you might call an Extension Course.

The night of the closing of *I'll Say She Is*, quite a gang was waiting in the Algonquin to congratulate me on our successful run. When I shook hands with F. P. A. he said nothing, but a hotel knife dropped out of his sleeve and clattered onto the lobby floor. I think that was the exact moment I knew, without any reservations, that I belonged to the world of Woollcott and his friends— and to no other.

I never did get back to Lindy's.

The night after we closed, Aleck invited me to go along with him to cover the opening of a new play. He had a hunch that he might need company for the ordeal, and he was right. It was a play in two acts about a pioneer airmail pilot. The story, as I remember, went something like this: Pilot crashes. Drags himself to an Indian wigwam. Indian family, mother, father, daughter, dressed in skins, take him in. Daughter goes for pilot, pilot goes for daughter. Mother discovers them in smooch. Mother exclaims to father, "Our little girl has become a lady!" Father misconstrues, swears to avenge his daughter's honor. First act curtain. Act two: Pilot still limping around wigwam, still sneaking off with daughter. Father, wrathful, confronts daughter. Daughter swears pilot has done nothing to her except vouch true love. Old man confronts pilot. Pilot makes tragic confession, proving nothing could have

185

happened between him and daughter. Reveals vital part of his anatomy had been severed in plane crash. Curtain.

Woollcott's summary of the play, in the next morning's paper, I shall never forget. It was two sentences long: "In the first act, she becomes a lady. In the second act, he becomes a lady."

Nearly every producer on Broadway wanted to sign us up for our second show, including Ziegfeld, Dillingham, and even (shades of Indianapolis!) the Shuberts. The one guy who didn't go after us was the one guy we wanted to work for—Sam Harris.

Irving Berlin, who had become quite a fan of ours, went to bat for us. Strictly as a favor to Berlin, Harris agreed to look over some of our acts, in his office. He looked us over. He said he'd let us know.

To take up the slack, we signed for a couple of out-of-town stands in *I'll Say She Is*. We were playing in Syracuse when a call came from Sam Harris. He said he wanted us to star in his next production. So that a minute wouldn't be wasted, a writer was already on his way to Syracuse to talk to us and knock out some new blackout sketches for us.

The last thing we wanted was a blackout writer hanging around, knocking out new sketches. We had plenty of sketches of our own. What we wanted to do was a real show, not a corny revue. But we didn't want to trouble Mr. Harris. We decided we'd take care of the writer ourselves.

He turned up backstage that night, a small fellow with a cocky manner, and introduced himself. We just stared at him. Zeppo did all the talking. "Take off your coat," he said, and the guy took off his coat. Zeppo pulled up the guy's shirt sleeves and said, "So you want to write us a new show, huh?" He felt the muscle on the guy's right arm and shook his head. He felt his left arm and shook his head again. The guy started to squawk and Zeppo said, "Didn't Sam tell you how we do business with writers?"

186

The guy looked puzzled, then apprehensive. Zeppo rolled up his own sleeves. In those days Zeppo had biceps like Charles Atlas. "Okay, writer, let's go," he said. "Rassle you to a fall. You write us two shows or nothing."

The blackout man grabbed his coat and ran. We never saw him again.

When he reported back, Sam was not perturbed, as we found out later. He paid the guy off, then called up George S. Kaufman, and said, "I need a big writer who can wrestle, George. How tall are you?"

When George learned what Sam needed a big writer for, he said, "Are you crazy? *Write* a show for the *Marx* Brothers? I'd rather write a show for the Barbary apes!" But Sam was not perturbed.

Our second Broadway hit was *The Cocoanuts*—music by Irving Berlin, and book by George S. Kaufman and Morrie Ryskind, staged by George S. Kaufman.

CHAPTER 12

No Use Talking

The Cocoanuts got off to a roaring start at the first rehearsal. George Kaufman sat on the empty stage, under a worklight, and began to read the script. Halfway through the first scene, Chico fell asleep. Somewhere in the second scene, I fell asleep. It wasn't that I was bored. I felt comfortable, and confident. There would be no need for Zep to rassle Kaufman and Ryskind, two shows or nothing. I had heard enough to know that they'd written no string of blackouts, but a real musical play—whatever the hell it was about.

By the time we opened in Boston, Kaufman didn't know what it was about either, we were ad libbing so much. Whenever a new bit occurred to Chico or me, we did it. Whenever a gag popped into Groucho's mind, he delivered it. The first performance ran forty minutes too long. All the critics and most of the audience had left long before the curtain finally came down.

Berlin, Kaufman and Ryskind stayed up all night trying to hack the show down to size. They cut a chorus here, a chorus there, and a couple of dance numbers. The next day we obediently rehearsed the new version. The next performance ran even longer. There was scarcely enough dough in the box office to pay the stagehands' overtime.

188

Berlin, Kaufman and Ryskind held an emergency meeting. Only thing to do, said Kaufman morosely, was to cut another production number, two more choruses, and two songs altogether. Irving Berlin yelped like he'd been stabbed in the back. "My God!" he said. "Any more cuts and this will be a musical without any music!"

Kaufman had a long, lugubrious brood, twisting an arm around his head and massaging an ear, and rubbing his collarbone with his chin. "Tell you what, Irving," he said. "You waive the songs and I'll waive the story."

The only song Berlin was willing to take out was a ballad that he admitted was "no good even as a show tune." The ballad was "Always," which wasn't heard in *Cocoanuts*, but which had a life of its own long afterwards. Irving bled over the other cuts like a doting but helpless father watching his babies go to the guillotine.

The crisis came to a head when the stagehands' union gave Sam Harris an ultimatum: the crew had to be out of the theatre by eleven o'clock at night or they'd walk off the production. Sam came to our dressing room immediately after the Saturday matinee. George and Irving were already there. Sam asked them, in his gentle, unruffled way, to please step outside. This, he explained, was a matter between him and the boys.

Chico, Groucho, Zep and I knew exactly what to do, without any premeditation. We grabbed Sam, stripped off his clothes and threw them out the dressing-room door. Sam, shaking his head but otherwise unperturbed, stepped outside, bare-naked, commenced to pick up his clothes, and said to Kaufman and Berlin, "Perhaps you fellows had better deal with them directly."

The unfunny part of it all was that the audiences didn't think we were worth laughing at. None of us came out and said it, but the Marx Brothers were running scared. What we were doing was playing to each other, not to the people out front. We were in bad shape and we knew it.

But the minute the curtain went up in the Lyric Theatre for the New York opening, all the tribulations of Boston were forgotten. Aleck was out front with the other Algonquin regulars, and so was Minnie—all daring us to outdo *I'll Say She Is*. I felt great, and I

189

felt like having some fun. During the tryout I was never in on the script conferences, since I had no lines to be changed. While the others conferred, I would retreat to my hotel room, where I worked out some ideas of my own. Now we could put them into action.

Our first scene had been tried a dozen different ways, but never seemed to come off. Opening night, in New York, it came off. This is how it went:

Groucho is behind the desk of a Florida hotel (the story had to do vaguely with the Florida real-estate boom). Chico and I come in looking for rooms. A bellhop tries to take my bag. I won't let him have it. We grapple and the bag falls open. Its total contents are three telephone directories. We go to sign in. I lean on the desk and do takes while Chico and Groucho do all the talking. The phone rings. Groucho says, "You want ice water in room 202? I'll send up an onion. That'll make your ice water."

I'm bored. A Western Union boy (tired of waiting for his cue) comes in with a stack of telegrams. I grab the telegrams and start tearing them up. This is such wonderful sport that I don't want to stop. I jump over the desk and grab mail out of the pigeon-holes and tear it up too. My enjoyment is so infectious that Groucho pitches in and helps me tear up the letters. When the last pieces flutter to the floor, I'm dejected. "Sorry the afternoon mail hasn't come in yet," Groucho says apologetically. Now what to do? I clap my hands, grab the pen out of Groucho's hand and throw it like a dart at a plaque on the wall. A bell rings. Groucho hands me a cigar.

We had the joint in a riot and we didn't let it simmer down for the rest of the night. We were a hit. Now George Kaufman could smile again. But we still didn't know George well enough. He came backstage with his chin on his chest and said that Act One seemed to be all right, but Act Two needed another cut. Somewhere in the middle of Act Two—he wasn't exactly sure where—he could have sworn he heard one of his original lines.

Cocoanuts ran a full season on Broadway, and played on the road for two years.

We never did stop ad libbing. No two performances were ever quite the same. One matinee, during the second month in New

York, I cooked up a little surprise for Groucho. During one of his quieter scenes, while I was offstage, I selected a blond cutie from the chorus, and asked her if she'd like a bigger part in the show. She was willing and eager. I told her all she had to do was run screaming across the stage. She did, and I tore after her in full pursuit, leaping and bounding and honking my horn. It broke up Groucho's scene, but when the laugh subsided, Groucho was ready to top it. "First time I ever saw a taxi hail a passenger," he said. So I chased the chorus girl back across the stage the other way, trying to catch Groucho flat-footed. I didn't. "The nine-twenty's right on time," he said. "You can always set your clocks by the Lehigh Valley."

Luckily for me, my blonde's boy friend was not in the audience that afternoon. After the show, I found out I had picked the hottest girl in the company. Her boy friend was Jack Legs Diamond, and Legs wanted his bimbo stashed securely in the chorus, where she wouldn't "get mixed up in no monkey business with them loony actors." I made a quick switch of blondes before the evening show.

The chase became a running gag in *Cocoanuts*—it was fun if only to see what Groucho's topper would be—and then became part of my permanent repertoire. My stature as an actor was growing, you might say, by leaps and bounds.

I was having a most prosperous year all around, largely at the expense of the other members of the Thanatopsis Club. The big weekly game began at five o'clock on Saturday afternoon, and usually lasted into the gray light of Sunday morning. I was allowed to drop out at eight o'clock, to do the show. I would run to the theatre, get the nuisance over with, then run back to the Algonquin to get on with the important business of the evening—all without bothering to get out of costume.

Kaufman was the only garrulous member of the Thanatopsis

—when he was dealing. Otherwise he never spoke a word. Whenever he got the deal, he started telling stories to throw the rest of us off our game, with the usual result that his game wasn't so steady either.

Over the years, I was the most consistent winner, Heywood Broun the hardest-pressing player, and Aleck Woollcott the worst. Swope was probably the best player there, but he only played at the Algonquin for fun. He did his serious gambling elsewhere.

Woollcott the poker player and Woollcott the cribbage player were not the same person. They weren't even related. At cribbage, Aleck was absolutely unbeatable. Harold Ross spent a good part of his life and tore out a good part of his hair (fortunately he had acres of it to spare) trying to beat his old war buddy at cribbage. Once after a game in which he was smartly lurched by Woollcott, Ross slammed down his cards and howled to the heavens, "This goddam Woollcott knows something about this goddam game that the guy who invented it didn't know!"

Yet at the poker table Woollcott was hamstrung, like Minnie, by a superstition. Where Minnie's weakness was filling inside straights in draw poker, Woollcott had a thing about the king of clubs showing in stud. Whenever the king of clubs was his first or second face-up card he would raise. If anybody else got it, he would fold. It was a ritual with him. As a consequence, he was sometimes eminently beatable at poker.

Shaggy big Heywood Broun hulked over his cards in a constant sweat. If he came out winners on a Sunday morning, he was in even more of a sweat. The rest of us accepted personal checks when we settled up after a game, but Broun had to have cash. He'd rather settle in cash for a percentage of what was due him, as little as fifty cents on a dollar, than take a check for the full amount— even from somebody as solvent as Herbert Bayard Swope, his boss on the New York *World*.

One Saturday night Chico sat in with the Thanatopsis. He played his usual reckless game and dropped twelve hundred dollars. Broun was the winner. When Chico offered Broun a check for twelve hundred, Broun said he'd take one thousand in cash, instead. Chico said he didn't have a thousand on him. Broun offered to settle for seven-fifty. Chico didn't have seven-fifty.

"How much *have* you got on you?" Broun asked, and Chico emptied his pockets and counted his money. Eighteen dollars. Broun pondered whether he should take the eighteen bucks, cash in hand, or take a chance on Chico's check for twelve hundred. For once he decided to take a chance, even though Chico's reputation had preceded him to the Algonquin.

Broun was at the bank when it opened Monday morning to deposit Chico's check. It was no good. He came roaring after Chico like a wounded bear. Chico grinned and told him not to worry. A mere small oversight. "Put the check through again tomorrow," he said—then added, "but not before noon."

The check bounced the second time. Broun came charging back to Chico. "Look," said Chico, "I told you not to put it through until twelve o'clock, didn't I?"

"What the hell!" Broun roared. "I didn't get to the bank until five minutes *after* twelve!"

"I'm sorry," said Chico. "That was too late."

Like Woollcott, Broun was a great talker and a great laugher. When he laughed, the whole two hundred fifty pounds of him shook, and the dishes must have rattled on the shelves of the Algonquin kitchen. Unlike Woollcott, Broun didn't worry about literary style when he talked. He wanted to like everybody he met, which made him one of the best-liked guys in New York City. The only grudges he ever held were political, never personal. When he resigned from the *World* in 1928 because he disagreed so violently with the paper's policy on the Sacco-Vanzetti case, his friendship with Swope continued as warm as ever.

One day Broun called me up and asked me if I'd like to come over to his place and meet Mabel Normand, the Hollywood star. I'd never met a real, live movie queen, and I was so delighted at the prospect that I put on a suit and a tie, something I hadn't done since Zeppo's wedding.

I met the beauteous Miss Normand in Broun's bedroom. Broun didn't rise to introduce us. He continued sitting in his rumpled

193

bed, in rumpled pajamas (everything that touched him instantly
—magically—lost its press), swatting at a punching bag that hung
from the ceiling. He was conscientiously following his doctor's
orders to get plenty of rest and exercise every day.

That winter, the winter of *Cocoanuts*, we took to bringing in
snacks from home and the delicatessen for our poker sessions and
ordering less food at the Algonquin. Apparently, the room-service
waiter complained to the management, because one Saturday night
there was a large, hand-painted sign tacked to the inside of the door
of our suite:

<blockquote>
Basket Parties Not Welcome
—Frank Case, Proprietor
</blockquote>

The Thanatopsis Inside Straight and Literary Club, we felt, was
the victim of unjust, ungrateful and cavalier treatment. We voted
to take our business elsewhere. We gathered up our cards and chips
and trekked across town in a convoy of taxis to the Colony restaurant, where we were graciously received and given a private room
to play in. Case called immediately to apologize. We decided to
give him two months of Saturdays to reflect on his dastardly deed
before we moved back to his joint.

Leaving the Colony late one freezing night in January, I shared
a cab with Woollcott and Broun. The two of them were at each
other's throats, tooth and nail, slur and insult, in some ridiculous
literary argument. I couldn't get a word in sideways. My place was
the first stop. When I got out of the cab, Aleck muttered, "Tell
the driver where to drop us off, like a good boy, Harpo," then
launched back into his tirade against Broun.

I did not like his condescending attitude, so I said to the driver:
"The other two parties want to go to Werba's Theatre, Brooklyn."
Werba's was a burlesque house in the far-off, frozen reaches of
Flatbush.

Two hours later, I was awakened out of a deep sleep by the
telephone. I still couldn't get a word in sideways. The person at
the other end of the wire delivered one sentence—"*You Jew son-*

of-a-bitch!"—then hung up. Woollcott and Broun had argued all the way over the Brooklyn Bridge before they realized what kind of a ride they were being taken for, and coming back the cab had slid on the ice and stalled. By the time they got home they were in the early stages of frostbite.

When guys like Aleck and Heywood held the floor, there was no use my talking. But I had my own, illiterate way of making my presence felt, as I demonstrated that night.

As for Aleck's standard crack at me whenever I took him for a ride, the epithet he borrowed from Madam Schang, I must point out that it was uttered in anger, all right, but it never had the slightest tinge of malice or defamation to it. Once a reader sent Aleck a letter accusing him of being anti-Semitic. Aleck was deeply hurt by the accusation, yet he didn't want to stir up a fuss over the matter. "Miss Dorothy Parker," he wrote back, "has seen fit to name my apartment 'Wit's End.' In the light of the faith of most of my good friends who share with me its modest delights, I should see fit to rename it 'Jew Drop Inn.' "

The Thanatopsis returned to the Algonquin, where Frank Case greeted us with a lovely WELCOME HOME floral wreath, and all was well with the world.

F. P. A. was never in better form. Once, between games, he said he had seen an incredible sight earlier in the day—Harold Ross tobogganing. (Ross wasn't with the club that night.)

"For God's sake—Ross tobogganing!" said Kaufman. "Did he look funny?"

"Well," Adams said, "you know how he looks *not* tobogganing."

Robert Benchley, about this time, was paying a lot of attention to a protégée of his, a young actress named Helen Walker. One Saturday he arrived late at the poker game. Somebody asked where he'd been, and Benchley said, "Cuing Helen Walker."

"Please," said Adams, without looking up from his cards, "no baby talk at this table."

When Swope retired from the New York *World*, we kidded him unmercifully about being unemployed. He continued to live like an emperor. He was chauffeured about in a limousine. He gave

195

fabulous parties at his estate on Long Island, and he maintained a town house on Fifth Avenue. He gambled for astronomical stakes outside the Algonquin. But we made out he was more to be pitied than envied. He had no job, and no visible means of support.

Once he was playing bridge with Broun, Adams and myself. Broun, reviewing the bidding, said, "Who the hell bid six no-trump?"

"I did," said Swope.

"And who the hell are you?" said Broun.

"I," he replied grandiosely, "am Herbert Bayard Swope. Age—48. Address—1165 Fifth Avenue, New York City."

"Occupation—housewife," said F. P. A.

One night I brought around a copy of *Shouts and Murmurs* for Aleck to autograph. Aleck signed the book, handling it with loving tenderness, then sighed and said, "Ah, what is so rare as a Woollcott first edition!"

"A Woollcott second edition," said F. P. A.

Nobody was more delighted by this crack than Harold Ross, who was in an on-again phase of his famous off-again on-again feud with Woollcott. Ross squeezed his eyes, clutched his hair and was seized with a violent trembling. This meant he was laughing. Ross was so easy to break up that he could never tell a story straight through without breaking himself up. His favorite was a true story about a Chinaman in San Francisco who had two whangs. But nobody ever heard the end of it. Every time he tried to tell it, he'd have such a seizure of eye-squeezing, hair-clutching and trembling that he'd be too weak to finish.

Benchley happened to arrive one Saturday night—late again—between deals, when nobody was talking. As a matter of fact, we had just talked ourselves out on a most depressing subject: Prohibition. The New York papers had been yelling for open war on the sale of hooch, and a record number of speakeasies had been pad-locked that week.

"Why so quiet?" Benchley asked.

F. P. A. gave him a reproving look, put a finger to his lips, and said, "Moment of silence, for the Unknown Bootlegger."

196

A moment of silence was a phenomenon that never occurred downstairs, at the Round Table. I kept my trap shut, but the joint was so thick with talk that I seldom had a chance to hear myself not talking.

A lot of what was said was way over my head. A lot of it was shop-talk, inside jokes from out of the *World*, *The New Yorker* and *Vanity Fair*. Books I had never read, plays I had never seen and people I had never heard of were torn apart with great hilarity. All this was lost on me. But I never ceased to be fascinated. I never stopped listening. Once I fell asleep in the dentist's chair while I was having a molar drilled, but I never fell asleep at the Algonquin.

Crazy bits and fragments of Round Table talk come back to me still, over the years, like isolated lines from an old show whose title and plot I've long forgotten. I can hear the voices clearly, voices of some of the most brilliant people who ever lived, but what I hear them saying is not always brilliant, and never very profound.

KAUFMAN: Want to hear me give a sentence using the word "punctilious"?

WOOLLCOTT: Give a sentence using the word "punctilious."

KAUFMAN: I know a man who has two daughters, Lizzie and Tillie. Lizzie is all right, but you have no idea how punctilious.

F. P. A.: Guess whose birthday it is today!

BEATRICE KAUFMAN: Yours?

F. P. A.: No, but you're getting warm—it's Shakespeare's.

BROUN (*who'd taken up oil painting*): You have no idea how hard it is to sell a painting.

F. P. A.: If it's so hard, why don't you try just selling the canvas? I'll give you a note to some tent-makers I know.

197

BROUN: No more griping. Today I shall be bold, resolute and gay!

KAUFMAN: I hear they've just taken in a new partner and now the firm is Bold, Resolute, Gay and Berkowitz.

CHARLIE CHAPLIN (*in a conversation about blood pressure*): Mine is down to 108.

KAUFMAN: Common or preferred?

DOROTHY PARKER: I met a strange fellow up in Canada, the tallest man I ever saw, with a scar on his forehead. I asked him how he got the scar, and he said he must have hit himself. I asked him how he could reach so high. He said he guessed he must have stood on a chair.

FAMOUS ACTRESS (*bragging about her husband*): Look at him! Isn't he beautiful? And do you know, I've kept him for seven years now!

DOROTHY PARKER: Don't worry—he'll come back in style.

HERMAN MANKIEWICZ: You know, it's hard to hear what a bearded man is saying. He can't speak above a whisker.

ALICE MILLER (*to Woollcott, on settling up a loss at cards*): You sir, are the lowest form of life, a cribbage pimp.

BERNARD BARUCH (*to Swope*): You, sir, are a foul-weather friend.

BENCHLEY: Have you heard the one about the little boy on the train?

KAUFMAN (*who's heard it twenty times; for some strange reason it's Benchley's favorite joke*): No.

198

BENCHLEY: A man gets on the train with his little boy, and gives the conductor only one ticket. "How old's your kid?" the conductor says, and the father says he's four years old. "He looks at least twelve to me," says the conductor, and the father says, "Can I help it if he worries?"

ROSS: This looks like a nice day for discoveries. Let's discover something. Maybe we could get a key and a kite and go discover electricity.

F. P. A.: I think Benjamin Franklin already did an experiment like that. Wasn't he the guy who flew a kite and discovered the air-cooled car?

ROSS: Well, I could go out and lie in an orchard and let an apple hit me on the head and discover Newton's Law of Gravity. This could lead to the invention of the elevator and nobody would have to walk upstairs any more.

KAUFMAN: A funny thing—I happened to be lying in an orchard this very morning. Only it was a fig orchard, and a fig hit me on the head, and that made me think of the Law of Gravity, and I said to myself, "This will lead to the invention of Fig Newtons, and maybe I could sell the idea to some big biscuit company and make myself a fortune."

WOOLLCOTT: Well, it's buckety-buckety back to work for little Acky. (Exits, singing)

> *I hope you fry in hell,*
> *I hope you fry in hell,*
> *Heigh-ho the merry-o,*
> *I hope you fry in hell!* . . .

One day I complained to Swope, as we left the Algonquin, about the chicken-feed stakes in the Thanatopsis games. We had a summer lay-off from *Cocoanuts*, and I had a hankering to play some real cards, for real money.

The next day I was en route to Florida with Swope. We were riding in the private railroad car of Harry F. Sinclair, the oil magnate, along with the producer Florenz Ziegfeld and six or seven

199

financiers named Benson. For the whole trip south I sat quietly eating my words. I never touched a card. Those guys' stakes made me feel I was a kid back on 93rd Street, hustling for pennies. When the train pulled into West Palm Beach, they were still playing. The car was switched onto a siding. They sat there playing all the rest of the day and far into the night. Before I got dizzy from counting, I saw a million dollars change hands.

At Palm Beach, I was the guest of the guy who financed the Ford Motor Company, but I was invited to have my dinners at the Vanderbilt mansion, along with Swope, Sinclair and the others. All I had known about Florida was what I had learned in *Cocoanuts*, and it certainly wasn't like this.

For the first time in my life, I felt completely out of place. I simply didn't belong here—or so I thought until Mr. Emerson, the husband of Alfred Vanderbilt's widow, came down for dinner. He was made up as Abraham Lincoln, whiskers, wart, stovepipe hat, the whole works—and nobody paid him any special attention. The next night he made his entrance as Ulysses S. Grant. On the third night he was Teddy Roosevelt in Rough Rider uniform, complete to a set of prop teeth. He expected no comments or compliments. It was simply a thing he got a kick out of, dressing up like historical figures he admired.

Who'd ever think I'd find the sixth Marx Brother married to a billionairess and living in the ritziest house in the ritziest resort in America?

I felt better after seeing Mr. Emerson. I felt better yet when I discovered that Colonel E. R. Bradley operated a gambling casino in town. But my pleasure was short-lived. I began losing heavily at *chemin de fer*.

Joseph P. Kennedy, the Boston financier, came to my rescue. He took me aside and told me it hurt him to watch me throw my money away. The action in Bradley's casino was too fast for me, he said, and I was obviously losing more than I could afford to. "I've got a better kind of action for you," he said. "I'll give you the names of two stocks. Buy either one of these and you'll get your money back."

As soon as I got to New York I bought the cheaper of the two stocks. I did recoup my losses from *chemin de fer*, barely. The other stock—which was Coca-Cola—went up a thousand points and split three times. It would have made me rich,

Shortly after we got home, Swope took me to the races at Belmont Park. Swope was not only a shrewd horseplayer but a State Racing Commissioner as well. So when he gave me a horse in the feature race I made a bet of two thousand bucks—four times what I had sunk in the market on Kennedy's tip. Swope's horse came in dead last. It was the last time I ever bet on the horses.

I was very happy to rejoin the fun-loving Thanatopsians and play for chicken-feed.

Herbert Bayard Swope was like the times he lived in—expansive, vigorous, colorful, unsnobbish, outspoken, and always ready for a game or a gamble. His estate at Sands Point, Long Island, had the same honest magnificence about it. The first time I was invited to Sands Point, Swope said, "How about coming out to the Island for a weekend, Harpo? Bring some things in case you stay over—but, you know, travel light."

It was the first time I had ever heard the expression "come for a weekend," and I wasn't sure what it meant. I stuck a toothbrush and a pair of pajama pants in the pocket of my raincoat and took off. When I got to Sands Point, the Swopes were serving cocktails to thirty people, dressed in flannels and tea frocks. Half an hour later an uninvited contingent of ten more guests arrived. Pearl Swope sent for her housekeeper and told her there'd be forty instead of thirty for dinner. The housekeeper nodded and smiled, and an hour later forty people sat down to a superb feast. I was the only guy without a dinner jacket. When Swope saw I was uncomfortable, he suggested that everybody remove their jackets, since it was such a hot evening.

Twenty more guests showed up after we ate, and all the men had to remove their jackets as soon as they got there. When the party got in full swing, I got restless. Then I spotted a fat guy whose wallet was sticking halfway out of his hip pocket. I tailed him, snatched the wallet, counted the dough inside, and slipped it back in his pocket. Then I ducked around the wing of the house and met the guy coming the other way and bet him ten bucks I could tell by looking at his face how much money he was carrying on him. The guy said sure, he'd take the bet. When I told him the exact amount—($950 and some change)—he was so amazed he damn near dropped his drink.

I handed him back his ten bucks and told him what the gag was. He was so delighted that he begged me to come to all of his parties for the rest of the season, out in Southampton, and pick his guests' pockets.

I was a social success.

That was the era of the Long Island Estate. I toured the big-time circuit, from the Swopes' to the Talbots' to the Whitneys' to the Guggenheims' to the Otto Kahns' to the Pulitzers'. One I didn't get to was Marcus Loew's, which Woollcott alone of the Algonquin mob had the opportunity of seeing.

Aleck was commissioned to write a magazine piece about Marcus Loew, the movie-theatre tycoon. He agreed to write it because he happened to like Loew. That was a condition of Aleck's. He never did an article about anybody he didn't like. An interview was arranged, with more protocol involved than in a meeting of two heads of state. Aleck would visit Loew at home, on Long Island, at ten o'clock sharp in the morning. Loew himself would answer the door, no monkey-doodle with servants. Then he and Woollcott would sit down in a quiet place, and talk for two hours. At the end of two hours, Aleck would get up, walk out, and return to New York City.

At ten o'clock sharp on the appointed morning, Woollcott rang the bell at the main entrance to the Marcus Loew mansion. Loew was right on schedule. He opened the door. He was alone, no butlers or maids in sight. Loew was nervous, but obliging. He said, "Let me hang your hat and cloak in the closet here."

Loew opened the "closet" door—and was amazed to discover it led to five rooms of his mansion he had never seen before.

Housing was not much of a problem in the 1920's.

The biggest love affair in New York City was between me—along with two dozen other guys—and Neysa McMein. Like me, Neysa was an unliterary, semi-illiterate gate-crasher at the Algonquin. But unlike me, she was beautiful and bursting with talk and talent. A lot of us agreed she was the sexiest gal in town. Everybody agreed she was the best portrait and cover artist of the times.

Her studio was our third most favorite hangout, after the Algonquin and Woollcott's apartment. We had some wonderful parties in Neysa's place, and I was always the last to leave. Neysa had undertaken to teach me about art. She was an entrancing teacher, and I was a dedicated pupil. Perhaps because I was a pantomimist by trade and didn't have much use for words, I fell in love with the fine arts.

One of my proudest moments occurred when I reported to Neysa that I had spent an afternoon with Aleck and the Averell Harrimans at an auction on 57th Street and had purchased my first painting, a small, original Degas. Neysa kissed me, oh boy oh boy!

She kept telling me I should paint too. "You'll never be lonesome, Harpo," she said, "as long as you have some paint, a brush, and some canvas." This idea I laughed at. I told her I could only possibly do two paintings—one called "Waltz Me Around Again, Willie," and the other, "Love Me and the World Is Mine."

Neysa had one failing as an art instructor. It was, as far as I knew, her only failing, period. That was her passion for fires. If a siren or bell should sound during one of our late-night seminars, that was the end of the seminar. Neysa was such a fire buff that she once dashed to Penn Station and jumped on a train when she heard there was a four-alarm fire burning in Philadelphia.

We went on tour with *Cocoanuts*. When we settled down for our run in Chicago, I was surprised to find that Chicago had become a dull place. Ben Hecht was in New York. Pete Penovitch was away, probably visiting friends in Joliet. What to do with myself? Damn it all to hell, Neysa was right. I should paint.

I rented a studio. I spent $350 on oils, brushes, props, smock, beret, and a couple of acres of canvas. I asked the guy in the artists' supply store where I could get a model, and he gave me a number to call. A model came to my studio, a well-stacked brunette. I asked her how much she charged, and she said, "How do you want me—nude?"

I said, "Of course." Ten seconds later she was out of her clothes and in the nude.

Remembering how Neysa posed her models, this way and that, to catch certain highlights and shadows, I posed my girl this way and that. After each new pose I went back to the easel. But I didn't have the courage to bring brush to canvas. I was scared. For the first time since the night I made my debut on the stage on Coney Island, I had stage fright.

Half an hour passed. I meditated. I inspected my brushes. I uncapped tubes of paint and studied them and smelled them and recapped them. I fiddled with the skylight. I put a scarf in the crook of the model's arm—so. I put a rose in her teeth—so. I went back to the easel and stared at the canvas. What would Neysa do next? Now I remembered. She would sketch in the model with some crayon. That was my trouble: I had to sketch before I could paint. I picked up a piece of black crayon. I held up my thumb and squinted to get the model in perspective. All I saw was my thumb. It was shaking. I didn't have the courage to make a mark on the canvas. I began to sweat.

Finally the girl said, "Do you mind if I have a smoke, Mr. Marx?"

On the way to her coat to get a cigarette, she sneaked a glance at my easel and saw that the canvas was a total blank. She said, "Don't you even know how to *draw*, Mr. Marx?"

"No," I said, "I don't. But I want to start. I want to start with you."

"Well," she said, forgetting about having a smoke, "let me show you a few pointers. I'll sketch you in. You sit over there."

"How do you want me—nude?" I asked. She said it didn't matter. I didn't bother to undress. Cheaper that way.

So it came about that the model, undraped, painted the artist, fully draped. The two of us worked together, taking turns posing and painting, for several weeks. She showed me how to mix colors and how to use brushes and how to adjust the lighting. I didn't show her much in return, but she didn't seem unsatisfied.

My model had to leave Chicago before I did. She left me with a challenge "Mr. Marx," she said, "what you should do next is a self-portrait of yourself. It might be kind of hard but you must do it, for your own personal good."

Using the bathroom mirror, I painted a self-portrait. When it was finished it looked exactly like my Aunt Hannah.

I never used a live model again. I've been painting, off and on, ever since. I've done a few pretty nice things—but only because I know that any resemblance I get is not going to be to anything I'm looking at.

Before I left Chicago I sold my first oil. I had kept one of my cockeyed nudes because it was painted on the biggest piece of canvas I owned and I'd had it put in a pretty lavender frame. I decided to use the canvas for a landscape. So I painted trees over the nude—purple trees, to match the frame.

When *Cocoanuts* was about to leave town, I took my landscape to an art dealer and offered it for sale. The dealer looked at the painting and said, "Why?" I held it up to the light and showed him how the original nude still came through, through all the layers of purple. "Well," said the dealer, "it *is* sort of a novelty," and he gave me five bucks.

When I left the gallery, I made a recount and realized that the canvas and frame alone were worth twenty-seven fifty. But what the hell, I'd sold a painting! From what Neysa had told me, it had taken a lot longer for Rembrandt, Cézanne or Van Gogh to make their first sale.

When the show moved to Boston, I set up shop, with easel, model, smock and beret, in my suite in the Parker House. Early in the run, my old friend Eddie Cantor came to town, playing in *Kid Boots*. I arranged the scene, then called Eddie and asked him to drop by my place for tea. Eddie, who was as proper as any Bostonian, said he'd be delighted to have tea with me.

I carefully refrained from telling him about my new career as an artist. What he saw when he came to the hotel was totally unexpected. I had left all the doors open. When I heard his soft, falsetto "Hoppo?" I yelled at him to come on in—I was busy.

He walked through one open door, then another door, and I yelled at him to keep coming. He came through the last door and stopped cold. The first thing he saw was my model, a gorgeous young blonde, nude upon a chaise longue with a rose between her teeth. Then he saw me behind the easel, squinting at the model and painting with great concentration.

Eddie, flustered by the presence of the naked girl, rushed over to the easel to make some kind of polite, face-saving comment about my painting. What he saw me doing on the canvas was filling in the colors on a big drawing of Mutt and Jeff.

He made a queer little croak, then turned and paddled out of the suite without saying a word.

I thought maybe I'd gone a bit too far with the gag, so after the show that night I took my harp to Eddie's hotel and played a serenade by the door of his room. Unfortunately, before Eddie could come out and tell me how thrilled he was, a house dick came along and kicked me out of the hotel.

My dalliance with the fine arts didn't go to my head, I'm happy to say. When I got back to New York I found I hadn't lost the old touch. The first day in town, Chico and I took a stroll through Times Square and, having nothing better to do, decided to sell money to a policeman.

We stopped a friendly looking cop in front of Lindy's and asked if he'd like to buy some used cash, cheap. He gave us a tolerant smile, winked, and walked on. We stopped him again. Chico flashed a dollar bill and said our special introductory offer was one buck for ninety cents. He gave the cop the dollar. The cop thought for a minute, rubbed the bill, then gave Chico ninety cents. Next we offered him a two-dollar bill for one-seventy. He bought the two-dollar bill.

It was obvious he was humoring us along until he could decide whether we were a couple of nuts or a team of con artists. It was also obvious that he liked the bargains he was getting. But by the time we offered him a five-spot for four-fifty, he was convinced that something fishy was going on. He said he was going to haul us both in, unless we told him what our racket was.

Chico shrugged and gave him a cheerful grin. "No racket, officer," he said. "We just like to sell money, that's all."

The cop muttered that he was right in the first place—a couple of nuts. He got away from us as fast as he could.

Not long after this, I felt in the mood for another good deed. The beneficiary this time was Tiffany's, the famous jewelry store on Fifth Avenue. Tiffany's, I told myself, was too stuffy for its own good, and something had to be done about it.

I bought a bag full of fake emeralds, rubies and diamonds, at Woolworth's, then went to Tiffany's. I asked to look at some diamonds. The clerk pulled out a tray of stones, and while I looked at them I turned over the bag from Woolworth's, behind my back. Jewels went spilling and bouncing all over the joint. Bells rang. Buzzers buzzed. Store detectives appeared out of the woodwork, hustled out all the other customers and locked the doors. Meanwhile the whole sales staff, including the manager, in cutaway coat and striped trousers, were down on their hands and knees retrieving my sparkling gems.

When they were all collected and put in my hat, the manager saw they were phony, every one of them. The attitude of Tiffany's changed abruptly. The store dicks hustled me out the door, with the recommendation that I never return to the premises. On the way out, for a final touch, I tipped the doorman a giant ruby.

Tiffany's, I found out, had a long memory. Five years later I went back there to make a legitimate purchase, some silver for a wedding present. The minute I stepped into the store, two detectives recognized me and grabbed me. I convinced them I was carrying no fake jewels. Nevertheless, they stood close by while I bought the gift, and followed me to the door with visible signs of relief.

On the way out, I tipped the doorman a giant ruby.

One Saturday night the Thanatopsis convened without playing poker. A well-known female impersonator named Bert Savoy had drowned off Coney Island after being struck by lightning, and the next day a New York columnist had written an obituary for him in the form of a love letter. (Also on the following day, so the legend goes, all the pansies at Coney Island were wearing lightning rods.) Anyhow, the letter to the departed Savoy was one of the most revolting and mawkish things we had ever read. So we spent the evening sitting around the poker table composing telegrams to the columnist. I remember three of them:

"WHERE WERE YOU WITH THE WATER WINGS? WORRIED."
"I'M FOREVER BLOWING BUBBLES. WORRIED."
"LETTER RECEIVED. NO CHECK. WORRIED."

George Kaufman, one of the collaborators on the telegrams, was shocked when he saw that we really meant to send them. For all his flair for the theatre and his biting, irreverent wit, George was a very conservative guy and something of a timid soul in public. I never knew a man so easy to embarrass.

In fact, embarrassing George Kaufman became a rewarding

hobby for me. When he was embarrassed, he would blush and stammer and twist himself into knots. When he was acutely discomfited, he would try to wind his right arm twice around his head and reach back to his right ear.

Kaufman especially hated arguing over who should pay the fare when he took a cab with somebody else. Such scenes were unbearable to him. Paying cab fares became an obsession with George. He used to keep a supply of neatly folded bills in his breast pocket—fives, tens and singles—so he could make a quick draw and pay the driver before anybody started making a scene.

Ordinarily I let George pay, without protest, but one day I resolved to cure him of his obsession. I cut a small hole in my pants pocket and stuffed the pocket with bills. George and I shared a taxi from Woollcott's house to the Algonquin. When we got to the hotel I jumped out of the cab, opened my fly, reached in, pulled out a five-spot and handed it to the driver. There was quite a crowd around the hotel entrance, and I had a good audience. George was too mortified to speak. He slunk out of the cab, red-faced and twisted in knots, praying that nobody would recognize him.

One time I was traveling with Beatrice and George to their country home in Bucks County, Pennsylvania. We decided to have lunch on the train. The diner was crowded, and an old lady asked if we minded her taking the fourth chair at our table. That was okay with us. It was only mildly embarrassing to George. He was apprehensive, I could tell, that I might somehow get involved with the old lady and make a scene. But I said nothing to her. I didn't even look at her.

She finished eating first. The waiter brought her check on a saucer. Still not looking up from my plate, I reached for the saucer, salted and peppered the lady's check, and ate it. Kaufman twisted in such agony that I was afraid he was going to screw himself through the bottom of the car.

That weekend, at the Kaufmans', we got into a hot session of croquet. During a game one of the servants came to the court to announce that two ladies from the Society of Friends were in the

209

house, keeping their appointment with Mrs. Kaufman. Beatrice excused herself—she'd forgotten the date, something to do with local charities—and said she'd only be gone a few minutes.

Half an hour passed. George was getting edgy. It would be his shot as soon as the game resumed, and he was in a good position to win. He couldn't wait any longer. He went inside to rescue Beatrice from the Quakers. Twenty minutes passed. No Beatrice. No George either. Now I was getting edgy. I looked in the window. There sat both the Kaufmans, cozily sipping tea with the ladies from the Society of Friends. I went to the kitchen and dumped a bottle of ketchup down the front of my shirt and pants. I went to the doorway of the living room, where I stood, dripping ketchup.

"Excuse me, Ma'am," I said, addressing Beatrice. "I've killed the one cat and he'll be ready for dinner, but I still haven't caught the other one. Will one be enough?"

The visitors departed in haste, and our game resumed. Beatrice couldn't stop laughing over the Quakers' retreat, but George was practically reduced to ashes. He couldn't get his ball through another wicket, and never did make it to the stake.

The pursuit of happiness by me and my pals was seldom interrupted. We lived in a world of our own. Only once in a great while did anything occur to remind us that the bigger world beyond our own was not eternally full of fun and games.

Poverty I had never forgotten, and never could. But meanness and stupidity I had been spared for a long time—until I had an unhappy reminder in the early summer of 1927. I made a fishing date with Paul Bonner, a book-collector friend of Woollcott's, and Pie Traynor, the third baseman of the Pittsburgh Pirates. I said I'd take care of the accommodations. I wired a hotel out in Montauk, Long Island, for reservations.

The hotel wired back: "RESERVATIONS CONFIRMED. TRUST YOU ARE GENTILE."

I was sore as hell, but I didn't bother to wire back. Why should I stir up a fuss and embarrass Bonner and Traynor and ruin the weekend? Better to turn the whole thing into a joke.

So when I entered the Montauk hotel I had my pants rolled above the knees, wore a tam o' shanter, smoked a pipe, walked with a crooked cane, and signed in as "Harpo MacMarx." The place was deserted. At dinner we were the only diners. Twenty waitresses stood around watching us eat. I began to feel depressed, and I finally told Bonner and Traynor what the "joke" was. They got sore and insisted we should move to a hotel where nobody cared what anybody's name was.

That made me feel a lot better. While we were checking out the manager came over to us. I said to him, "Lad, could ye dir-r-rect me to the near-r-rest Jewish temple?" and threw him a Gookie and we blew the joint.

I rented myself a bachelor-size summer estate on Long Island Sound, near Great Neck, and retired there with my current dog, a retriever who was disguised as a black poodle. I looked forward to a summer of nothing to do, with nobody to listen to. I bought me a kite and fixed up a special rigging so the string could tickle the bottoms of my feet while the kite flew and I stretched out and snoozed on the grass. This has always been a Marx family weakness, the passion for having our feet tickled. To me it was the ultimate luxury, the absolute end-all of gracious living.

My life of ease didn't last very long, however, thanks to my dog and my friend Woollcott. Every time I drifted off to sleep, massaged by the kite string, the poodle would fetch a big wet pebble from the shore and drop it in my hand, a command for me to throw it so he could retrieve it.

211

Then I got a wet pebble from Aleck—a letter inviting me to come spend the rest of the summer on his island up in Vermont. Being from Woollcott this, too, was a command. I reeled in the kite, closed up the house, put the poodle in a kennel, stuck a toothbrush and a pair of pajama pants in my raincoat pocket, and took off for Neshobe Island, Vermont.

CHAPTER 13

Buckety-Buckety into the Lake

Neshobe Island was in the middle of Lake Bomoseen, in west-central Vermont, not many hills away from the southern arm of Lake Champlain. Although Champlain was a hundred times bigger than Bomoseen, Aleck regarded it as a minor body of water, simply a convenience for his friend Theodore Roosevelt, Jr., to land his seaplane on when he flew up from New York for a visit.

Aleck's island was only seven acres in size, but it held a wonderful variety of terrain and vegetation—miniature meadows, hills and cliffs, quarries and beaches, wild flowers, flowering vines and bushes, maples and evergreens. The water surrounding the island was forever changing. It could be smooth as glass one minute, then suddenly churning with whitecaps, from updrafts and downdrafts of mountain winds.

Neshobe was to Aleck the most beautiful spot on earth. It was the only place where he ever lived happily alone, without an audience. Here he was the audience. Neshobe Island was in fact a kind of theatre to Aleck, with a continuous show. Each dawn raised the curtain on a new scene, each season was a new act, and each year a new drama. The last act was autumn and its climax was October, when the turning maples ringed the lake with red and orange fire, unbroken except for the white stems of the birches and the blue-green spires of the pines.

When Aleck bought the island it was with the idea of making it a personal, solitary retreat. But he found himself loving it so much that he had to have somebody to share it with, so he turned the island into a private club for his innermost circle of friends. Charter members of the club included Alice Duer Miller, Neysa McMein, Beatrice Kaufman, Ruth Gordon, the Raymond Iveses (he was an accountant and insurance man), Raoul Fleischmann (co-founder with Ross of *The New Yorker*), Howard Dietz (a songwriter), George Backer (a newspaper publisher), and Harold Guinzberg (a book publisher, founder of The Viking Press).

For an outsider, an invitation to Bomoseen was more than a feather in the social cap. It meant you had been nominated for the Alexander Woollcott Roster of Who's Who. If you were invited a second time, it meant you had been elected. There was only one honor higher than this, and that was being asked to join the island club as a full-fledged member.

I was invited up for a weekend. I was invited again, which put me in a class with Alfred Lunt and Lynn Fontanne, S. N. Behrman, Charles Brackett, Lilly Bonner, Irene Castle, Ethel Barrymore, Katharine Cornell, Noel Coward and Theodore Roosevelt, Jr. Then I was awarded the final honor. I became a member. The only other guy who made it in my time was Charles Lederer, the present-day screenwriter and producer, who was then a literary protégé of Aleck's. Damned if I know why I qualified. Maybe Aleck considered me his cribbage protégé.

The thing we cherished most about the island, along with its natural beauty, was its isolation. Whenever we stepped onto Neshobe, we left Western Civilization behind and entered our own primitive society. Aleck would have been content to keep the island in the Stone Age. The most modern appliances he would tolerate, at first, were kerosene lamps, a hand pump for water, and an outboard motor for the launch. Bit by bit, for the sake of his guests' comfort, he softened. He had a new clubhouse built, with plumbing and electricity. But he still kept the ancient, original farmhouse for his personal quarters. (Eventually Aleck built a rambling stone house on a ridge overlooking the lake on all sides, and this became his permanent home for the last seven years of his life.)

Our privacy we fought for and protected at all costs. The mainland was only a quarter of a mile away, and near the dock was a large resort hotel which we could see from the island. The natives, in true Vermont fashion, didn't bother anybody who didn't bother them, but the tourists were a pretty nosy bunch.

The rumor got around that there were "famous people living on that dinky island," and that there were "a lot of crazy goings-on out there." One day while I was waiting on the mainland for the launch to pick me up, two dames were sitting on the dock gazing at the island. One of them was looking through a pair of binoculars. I sidled over behind them, and heard the dame with the binoculars say, "Will you look who's there, in a bathing suit! It's Marie Dressler!"

"Marie Dressler" was of course Alexander Woollcott, taking his daily dip.

One day Alice Miller went for a walk and rushed back to report a harrowing thing. A group of tourists, she said, had rowed over to the island and were down on the beach having a picnic. I volunteered to deal with the interlopers. I stripped off all my clothes, put on my red wig, smeared myself with mud, and went whooping and war-dancing down to the shore, making Gookies and brandishing an ax. The tourists snatched up their things, threw them into the boat, and rowed away fast enough to have won the Poughkeepsie Regatta. That put an end to the snooping that season. It also, I'm sure, started some juicy new rumors about our crazy goings-on.

Three natives were allowed on Neshobe: the guy who brought over mail and supplies, and the couple who worked as cook and handyman. I remember the handyman because he had made himself a clamp for his hernia out of a length of wire and a wooden peg. Whenever his rupture gave him trouble, he just gave the peg a few turns and tightened 'er up. He didn't set much store by such foolishness as doctorin'.

Joe Hennessey actually ran the club. Joe, besides being Woollcott's private secretary, did the ordering, kept the books, kept the handyman busy on the grounds, saw that guests were met on the mainland and were assigned places to sleep, and made sure that Aleck's steaks were properly broiled. Beefsteak was Aleck's staple food. When he ordered dinner in a restaurant he put on quite a scene. He would keep the waiter bringing out steaks until he found the exact cut that suited him. Then he would tell him, with elaborate gestures, exactly how the chef should prepare it: "Passed slowly over the flame—so—then turned and passed over the flame once again—so." God forbid if it should arrive any other way except charred on the outside and cold, bloody raw on the inside.

Dinner, on the island, was only part of the evening ritual. The first ceremony at day's end, for which everybody gathered in the clubhouse, was Cocktails. From Cocktails until the last good night, Woollcott presided over the evening like a combination Social Director, Schoolmaster and Queen Mother. He called the turns in the conversation, snuffed out arguments that didn't involve him, and decided which games should be played.

If Aleck felt ornery, he'd challenge somebody to cribbage or anagrams, and the rest of us could fend for ourselves. If he felt mellow, he'd propose we play a "family" game—poker, Murder, a guessing game, or some game he'd just invented.

It seemed to me that Aleck invented games as a way of probing deeper into the character of people he loved. His curiosity about his friends was endless. He asked me so many questions about details in my life that I thought he must be writing a book about me. He once spent the better part of a week tracking down a newspaper report of the Schang trial and presented me, as a birthday present, a photostat copy of the story in the *Times*. He spent years hunting for Miss Flatto, my old nemesis from P. S. 86, and by God he eventually located her.

That's how intensely he would poke into our lives—not out of any hidden, abnormal motives, but out of genuine curiosity. Aleck was impressed that a human being could be put together in the first place. He was absolutely astonished that one could be put together in such a way as to give Alexander Woollcott pleasure.

His people-probing quizzes went like this: "Which person—aside from a friend or a relative—would you bring back to life, if you had the power?" Or, "Name the greatest single song ever written." I remember that the person most frequently named in the first was Abraham Lincoln. In the second (and this was by secret ballot, after long thought), the replies were unanimous: "Silent Night."

We played "Categories" and "Ghosts" and our own variation of an old guessing game, "Famous Persons." In this, you gave the famous person's last initial and stated what he was famous for, and the others had to guess the person. I stumped the club once (but only once, I must add), when I announced I was thinking of a person beginning with a "C" who was famous for making people fall on their fannies. Nobody got it. I was thinking of Chippendale, the guy who designed the chairs with the spindly legs.

That was when I learned I was not supposed to win at such games. Aleck got huffy and said my statement of Chippendale's claim to fame was farfetched and not in the spirit of the game. Then he changed the subject, to put himself back in the limelight.

"Do you want to hear me give a sentence using the word 'Demosthenes'?" he asked. Of course we all said yes, and Aleck said, "Demosthenes can do is bend, and hold the legs together."

Another time I got my ears pinned back was when success at poker went to my head, and I challenged Woollcott to a game of anagrams. He snorted, saying I would be a lamb leading myself to slaughter. Well then, I said, give me odds of a hundred to one. "My dear Harpo," he said, "I shall bet a hundred dollars to your one that you don't make a single word you can keep." We played. I wound up without a single word in front of me.

Nevertheless, I still felt lucky that night. So I challenged Alice Duer Miller to a twenty-five-word spelling match. "How many words should I spot you?" said Alice. I said I figured I had about a twenty-word handicap. Alice thought I wasn't being fair to myself. "Tell you what," she said, "I'll let Neysa spell for me, even money, best out of twenty-five. Let Aleck decide on the words."

I figured Neysa and I would be just about evenly matched. But she did a hundred per cent better than me. She spelled one word right. The word was "thrifty," which I would have given ten to one had two f's in it.

That was my last fling at intellectual jousting.

Our favorite indoor sport was the game of Murder. A session of Murder would begin at cocktail time and sometimes last all the way through dinner. It goes like this:

We start by drawing lots to pick the District Attorney. Then we draw to see who will be—known only to himself—the Murderer. This done, the D.A. retreats and the rest of us go on with cocktails and small talk, wandering around the clubhouse, warming ourselves by the fireplace, reading, or strolling outside to admire the sunset. As soon as the Murderer manages to be alone with somebody else, he points to him and says: "You are dead." The Victim slumps down, forbidden by the rules of the game to leave the spot of the crime or make any sound until he is discovered.

When the Victim is discovered—usually along about dinnertime —the D.A. is called in to begin the investigation. Everybody is a suspect. Every suspect, except the Murderer, has to answer truthfully, to his best recollection, where he was at any given time prior to the discovery of the crime, what he was doing, and with whom. The D.A.'s job is to deduce from the pattern of answers and alibis who is lying, and is therefore the Murderer. It's a marvelous game.

One night Aleck drew the D.A. slip. "Oh ho!" he said, giving us a smug, owlish look, one by one. "You'd better be crafty, Evil One, whoever you are! Little Acky has never lost a case!" The Evil One was me. I had drawn the Murderer slip. It was true that Aleck had never failed to solve a murder. So I decided I should take him for a ride on this one.

It was the longest game we ever played, by far. By the time Joe announced that dinner was ready, everybody had scoured the joint and no Victim had been found. We sat down to eat. Only then was it suspected that there'd been foul play. There was an empty chair. Alice Miller was missing. Aleck, who'd been waiting at the table all this time for the crime to be discovered, refused to let anybody eat until he had a crime to work on. We were starved, but Aleck would not relent. He didn't care if his steak came out as spongy as a steamed frankfurter. The dirty work had to be uncovered first.

It wasn't until eleven o'clock that Neysa found Alice, through a keyhole. She had locked herself in a toilet in the rear wing of the clubhouse, and by the rules of the game she was not permitted to get up and let herself out.

What had happened was this: I had remembered that the gals occasionally sneaked back to use the rear-wing toilet when the main bathroom was occupied, and soon after becoming the Murderer I had sneaked back there myself. I unrolled the toilet paper a ways, wrote a fatal message in lipstick, then rolled the paper back up.

It was Alice who got the message. Being such a good sport, she remained at the scene of the crime, slumped and quiet, for five hours.

Aleck put the finger on me without having to ask a single question. I had outsmarted myself. I had tipped my hand without knowing it. What I had written in lipstick on the roll of toilet paper was:

YOU ARE DED.

Little Acky had a terrible tantrum and went to bed without his supper. He refused to play with anybody who didn't obey the rules. The Murderer had to confront the Victim face to face or else there was no crime committed. The idea of making poor, gallant Alice sit on the john for five hours! Alice herself, on the other hand, couldn't have been more delighted. A stroke of genius, she called my plot. Too bad it had to be an illiterate stroke of genius, she added.

Besides, she had been able to compose, in her mind, a whole

chapter in the novel she was currently writing while cooped up in the can.

Alice Miller was the only club member who did any serious work on the island. She kept a daily schedule at her desk, turning out the poetry and fiction so much admired by millions of readers. Aleck worked with Joe Hennessey on his correspondence an hour or so each morning, but did no other writing. Neysa did a little sketching now and then, but no commercial painting.

Otherwise nobody worked at all. Daylight hours were for us hours of pure relaxation—except for the Morning Dip. The Morning Dip was one of Aleck's rules: Everybody in the water before breakfast, no matter how freezing cold the lake might be. Aleck, with all his rolls and layers of protective suet, was impervious to cold water. While the rest of us shook and turned blue, he would float around serene as an empty scow, wearing his glasses and reading a book propped on the dome of his belly, and wondering why the rest of us were such sissies. Woollcott was the only guy I ever knew who could float vertically as well as he could horizontally. From a distance, you could never tell whether his top or front was up.

After the swim, Aleck and Alice always retreated to their studies, and the rest of us were free to read, snooze, talk, play, ramble or gamble.

For a guy whose life had been confined to tenements, trains, hotel rooms and dressing rooms, there was always something new and exciting to do at Neshobe. I used to spend hours tooling around the lake in a sailing canoe. Sometimes I got stuck in the middle of the lake in a flat calm and had to paddle home. Other times I'd be out when a sudden storm swooped down off the mountains, and I'd wind up pinned to the rocks on the mainland shores.

Fishing was fine in Lake Bomoseen. My luck was fine too, but I had to give up fishing for sentimental reasons. One day I caught a nice, big bass. For the hell of it I marked him with a clip and threw him back in. Next time I fished, I caught the same big bass. Again I threw him back in. A week later I caught the guy a third time. By now we had become good friends. He never bothered me, being a good Vermonter, so why should I bother him? I stopped fishing.

Besides swimming, sailing and fishing, the club offered badminton, and the island itself offered Indian relics, to be had for the digging up. But the greatest sport of all was the game of croquet.

For five years of my life croquet was my hobby, avocation, recreation and dedication. I lavished more time, dough and passion on the game of croquet than the average sugar-daddy did on his baby-doll. The whole madness began on Neshobe Island.

On the first day of my first visit up there, Aleck asked me if I'd like him to teach me The Game. "*Teach* me?" I said. "Just tell me the rules and I'll take you on, any price you want to name." He gave me a funny look and said all right, if I insisted on learning the hard way, we'd play for ten bucks a game, loser's option to double the bet for the next game.

Croquet I knew vaguely as a pastime for kids and elderly couples, something to do with tapping balls along the grass with long wooden hammers. Hardly anything for a virtuoso of the pool cue or the golf club to take seriously. I began to wonder about Aleck. He was a rough-and-ready gambler, indoors. But outdoors—*croquet?*

I didn't wonder very long. The croquet that Aleck played was no pastime for kids or elderly couples. He played for keeps. He was a crack, accurate shot and he was a cunning strategist.

I didn't know the game *had* a strategy. I soon learned. You had to know when to go for position and when to go for the wicket, when to go for the stake instead of turning Rover, where to send your opponent's ball when you hit him, and which of a dozen different ways to send it. If you were playing partners, you had to remember at all times who was dead on who, and you had to know how to use your partner's ball without leaving him out of position or vulnerable to an opponent.

221

The course on the island was rugged and tricky. The wickets were laid out on a hard, fast surface, on what was once a badminton court. Beyond this there were no bounds or limits. A ball had to be played from wherever it lay. On one side, the court was bordered by a stand of tall maples, thick with underbrush. Beyond the trees a cliff dropped sharply to the narrow beach at the edge of the lake. The only ground rule was that if your ball landed in the water, you had the choice of playing it out or placing it on the beach and losing a turn.

After five days of steady croquet, I began to get the hang of the game—but too late. By Saturday night, when the club's bets for the week were settled, I owed Aleck nine hundred dollars in croquet money. I had been taken but good—not cheated or swindled, but skunked in an honest, out-in-the-open game.

Aleck made a generous show of mercy. Since I was a rank beginner, he offered me a chance to recoup some of my dough at Russian Bank, a form of two-handed solitaire. I didn't even need to touch a card. He said he would deal and play both hands, his and mine.

Well, Aleck got on a losing streak. He lost, while the hands he dealt for me kept winning. He refused to quit until his luck changed. It didn't change. By settling-up time the following Saturday, I was an eleven-hundred-buck winner at Russian Bank. My net profit, after losing at croquet, was two hundred bucks.

Before very long I had played enough and practiced enough to hold my own on the court. By the end of summer, we were all pretty much on a par—Aleck, Neysa, Beatrice, Fleischmann, Dietz, Lederer, Alice and myself.

Croquet became a hopeless addiction. It combined the best elements of golf, billiards and poker. Fresh air and sunshine were added benefits—except that we also played through rains and fogs, aiming by ear, and in wild storms where we argued almost to the point of fist fights over whether knocking a hailstone out of the way counted as a turn.

Nobody ever "choked up" or went off his game under pressure. We were always on our game and we always had supreme confidence. Some of the damnedest shots were made on Neshobe Island. Balls were sent sailing down through the trees to the lake like they had wings. The same balls came sailing back up the cliff, over the brush and through the tree trunks and onto the court, like they had eyes as well.

When I got the feel of the game, I began to fool around with innovations. Drawing on my vast experience in poolrooms, from Lexington Avenue to San Francisco, I was the first to introduce the three-shot, or double carom, to croquet, and I also invented a new way of getting a Rover out of the game.

Unless you've played the game as we did, you've never known the thrill that erupts inside you when you hit an opponent's ball from twenty yards out, when you skim through a wicket from a difficult angle, or when you hit two balls so they neatly spread-eagle a wicket.

I knew Alexander Woollcott for eighteen years and eight months. I shared with him many moments of jubilation. I was beside him when he received awards and commendations, and when he got letters of tribute that brought warm tears to his eyes. Nothing, however, ever gave Woollcott a greater joy of pride and fulfillment than a good shot in croquet.

When Aleck sent an opponent's ball crashing down through the maples of Neshobe Island, he would swing his mallet around his head like David's slingshot and whoop, "Buckety-buckety! Buckety-buckety! Buck-ket-ty-buck-ket-ty-in-to-the-*lake!*"

When Aleck pulled off an exceptionally tricky shot—hovering over his mallet like a blimp at its mooring mast, while he aimed with profound concentration, then hitting his ball so it sidled through a wicket from a seemingly impossible angle or thumped an opponent after curving with the terrain in a great, sweeping arc—he was in his own special heaven.

He would dance around the court on his toes, kicking his heels together (unaware that his shorts were falling down), and singing in the exuberant soprano of a cherub in a Sunday-school play:

> *I'm des a 'itto wabbit in de sunshine!*
> *I'm des a 'itto bunny in de wain!*

This was a sight to behold, both the crackerjack shot and the ballet of the blimp that followed it. I never saw a man, or a kid, even, happier than Alexander Woollcott upon the croquet court at Neshobe Island after he had pulled off some delicate, deft maneuver, or dealt an opponent a nasty whack.

It's sad to realize that today, three decades later, when there's supposed to be more of everything, there are no more wabbits in de sunshine or bunnies in de wain. Famous Persons, anagrams, Murder, and croquet are lost in the TV shuffle, and that's an awful shame. My God, those games were fun!

I must take credit for the most celebrated croquet shot ever made on Neshobe Island. Well—half credit, since Charlie Lederer was my partner in the game and in this particular gambit.

It was my turn. I was dead on Charlie and couldn't use him to get in position for my next wicket. I didn't have a very good shot at Charlie anyway. In fact, the only ball within twenty yards of mine was Aleck's. Aleck's ball was only fourteen inches away, but it was smack against the opposite side of a big maple tree. It was an impossible play. There was nothing nearby I could use to carom my ball off of and get it to Aleck's side of the tree.

Charlie and I puzzled over the situation for half an hour. (There was no time limit for "impossible" shots.) Then we got an idea. While Lederer stayed on the court as a decoy, taking sights and lining up trajectories for me, I got a saw from the tool shed, then went down to the dock and untied one of the automobile tires that were used for boat bumpers. I sawed the tire diametrically in half, and carried one of the halves up to the court.

I laid the half-circle of tire around the maple tree. It was a dandy banked tunnel, leading from my ball to Woollcott's. I shot. The ball rolled around the tire, out the other end, and *smacko*— a direct hit.

There was no toe-dancing or kicking of heels. Woollcott smashed his mallet deep into the turf of his beloved island and stomped off toward his quarters, muttering that he conceded the game and would never again play with such a _____-_____ing horse's ass as Harpo Marx.

"Correction!" he snapped, turning back to stick his head around the corner of the clubhouse. "Not 'horse's'—*faun's*—ass!"

I didn't know what that meant, but I was certainly flattered to be called it by Alexander Woollcott.

The next morning Aleck was gone from the island when the rest of us got up, and so was Joe Hennessey. This meant that Aleck had taken a cooling-off trip, to recover from the incident of the tire. Most likely he'd gone on a cemetery hunt, in which case he'd be back at the end of the week to recite through cocktails and dinner and half the rest of the night all the "sweet, fantastic names" he'd copied off old tombstones—like "Felicity Calm De-Witt," "Happy Ivy Wentworth," "Deuteronomy Newton," "Lucy Fur Thomas," "Honesty Policy Dredge," "Onward Christian Purdy," or his favorite four sisters, "First Cora Hooker," "Second Cora Hooker," "Last Cora Hooker" and "Immaculate C. Hooker."

Later, I made some of these trips with Aleck. He couldn't pass a cemetery without having Joe stop the car so he could explore the boneyard—grave by grave, stooping to read out loud the inscription on each and every one. What started out to be a viewing of the autumn colors or a back-road tour of the mountains invariably wound up as an excursion to a graveyard.

In the fall of 1934 he took me along on a pilgrimage to a cemetery in the little town of Plymouth, Vermont. There he led me quickly past all the other gravestones and over to a simple headstone in a family plot. The only decoration on the grave was a tiny American flag, the kind that kids buy in a dime store. On the headstone was carved, simply, "John Calvin Coolidge, 1872–1933." Aleck inspected the grave in silence, from every aspect.

I can think of nobody who ever lived who was more unlike Woollcott than Calvin Coolidge, politically, physically and emotionally. Yet Aleck had a half-secret, perverse fondness for the tight-lipped Yankee President.

Lest I should think he was being a mushy old fool, when he finished his study of the grave he did a little tippytoe jig, then ordered Joe to drive us straight back to Bomoseen for a game of Murder.

A strange man, Woollcott was. He seemed to love the idea of death in all its aspects. But while his mind carried on a morbid flirtation with death, his heart was stuck on life. He loved the pure existence part of living, the yapping, scrapping, laughing, eating, romping, exploring-the-world part of it—but never, sad to say, the intimate, sexual part of it.

I didn't know until after Aleck's final flirtation with death that he had been ravaged by a near-fatal case of the mumps when he was twenty-two years old. Its cruel aftermath may have been one of the reasons he felt compelled to live three times harder than anybody else ever had the right or the capacity to live.

On the train back to New York, I dozed among my memories of the island summer: Alice Duer Miller standing stately and alone among the pines when she should have been at work inside, waiting for the sound of the launch from the mainland, waiting for news of how the New York Giants had made out the day before. . . . Charlie Lederer calling her "Butch," which pleased her more than if she'd been knighted and addressed as Lady Alice. . . . The sound of Neysa's laughter, as carefree as any little girl's on a holiday from school, or as any song of a meadow lark. . . . The bewitchery of Beatrice Kaufman, Aleck's "Lamb Girl," lighting up a dark room with her presence, igniting a dying conversation with the spark of her wit. . . . The sound of music coming across the water on Saturday nights from the open-air dance on the mainland, tinny and gay, like a crazy, woodland honky-tonk (the only times we ever felt tolerant toward the tourists). . . . The reading of plays around the fireplace, the wonderful voices of the Lunts, Ethel Barrymore, Ruth Gordon and her husband Gregory Kelly, the familiar voices of the islanders reading the minor parts, and the audience of one: me. . . . Aleck, during his last two days on Neshobe, sailing around and around the island in a dinghy, going buckety-buckety over the chopping waves for hours on end, savoring the scenery of his personal paradise like it was vintage champagne. . . . The first signs of autumn, when you could almost see the maples turning, leaf by leaf, from green to gold and orange. . . . The sad look of the closed-up clubhouse, the nakedness of the court with the wickets and stakes taken up and put away, and the weird silence, with no *whack* or *tonk* of mallet on ball or ball on ball. . . . And the last boat ride to the mainland dock, with Aleck playing cribbage all the way and never once glancing up from the cards or the pegboard for a last look at the lake and the island; he'd said his good-bye from the dinghy the day before and, being a critic, he hated anticlimaxes and never had to stick around for encores or curtain calls.

CHAPTER 14

Croquemaniacs of the World, Unite!

THE CROQUET MANIA was upon us like a plague. Croquet became the most serious thing in the lives of a lot of people who should have been concerned with far more important matters. The most hopeless cases in New York, besides Aleck, Beatrice, Neysa and myself, were Kaufman, Swope, Dietz, Fleischmann, F.P.A. and a group of financiers—among them, Harold Schwartz, Harold Talbot and Averell Harriman.

We got a special permit from the city to play in Central Park. Weekends we usually played at Swope's joint on Long Island, where the course was even bigger. It was so vast and hilly you sometimes had to yodel to let your partner know where you were.

Once during a hot game at Sands Point (they were all hot games there), Swope's butler came to the court to announce that Governor Al Smith was calling from Albany. "Tell him to hold the phone," said Swope. "It's my shot." The Governor held the phone and the affairs of the state of New York were halted for twenty minutes, while Swope made three wickets. During another game I remember, Swope gave his partner the worst bawling-out I had heard since P. S. 86, for making a "stupid shot, worthy only of a moron with ten thumbs." His partner was a two-star general.

Neysa, Aleck, Charlie MacArthur and I once spent a wild and wonderful weekend at Otto H. Kahn's estate. The minute we arrived there we started to play croquet, without bothering first to pay respects to our host. Kahn's course was as flat and smooth as a billiard table. It was more like a golf green than a croquet court, which gave me an idea. I started experimenting with a golf-type swing, using the mallet like a mashie. The other three gleefully joined in the experiment, and the croquet balls went zooming all over the place. Garden furniture got knocked over. Greenhouse windows were smashed. Servants ran the gauntlet from main house to guesthouse with arms clutched over their heads. Kahn himself fled to his yacht, which was anchored in the Sound at the foot of the lawn, and hoisted a white flag. He didn't emerge from the yacht until nightfall, when the world was once again safe from croquemaniacs.

Once, at Harold Talbot's estate, not even nightfall stopped us from playing. When it got dark, we drove our cars through the shrubbery and around the house, lined them up by the court, and turned the lights on. There were seven dead batteries the next morning, but it was worth it. The night game was good and close, and I won it with a lucky triple carom.

The mob was invited up to Averell Harriman's preserve in the Adirondack Mountains for Thanksgiving. There we played through a heavy snowstorm, while a crew of eight men stood by with snowplows, shovels and tractors, and scraped off the court between games.

Croquet was the cause of jealousies, feuds and fights. When we weren't playing we sat around for hours rehashing games, arguing over tactics, analyzing shots and second-guessing each other's mistakes. The two worst offenders were Swope and Woollcott. They were eternally backbiting and bickering on the court. Off the court they yammered and yelled at each other over minor rules and obscure points of strategy. They were deadly serious, and we were continually fearful there might be bloodshed.

We called them the Katzenjammer Kids.

When the Katzenjammer Kids' vendetta reached the boiling point, the rest of us prevailed upon them to settle the whole business with a croquet match, each to put up five hundred dollars, the stakes to go to the winner of the best two out of three games.

The great grudge match began at Sands Point, Woollcott's red and blue versus Swope's yellow and black. Aleck's partner was Neysa McMein. Swope's was Charley Schwartz. Aleck won the first game. When Swope won the next one, Woollcott insisted the rubber game should be played on a neutral court. The tournament moved to the Bonners' estate for the play-off.

The crucial game got under way in deathly silence. Then, halfway along, when it was his turn to shoot, Swope asked Woollcott to refresh his memory on who was dead on who. He'd forgotten. (Once you've hit, say, the yellow ball, you're dead on yellow and can't hit him again until you've gone through a wicket.) What annoyed Swope more than anything else was Woollcott's fantastic memory. Woollcott could recall every shot made in a game, and he knew at any given point who was dead on who. It was his single greatest advantage in croquet.

Aleck sniffed. He chose to ignore Swope's request.

Swope repeated the request. Aleck turned his back on him and said to Neysa, "Would you kindly inform that gangling, red-faced Yahoo that it is against the rules to review the play. If he wants to know whom he's dead on he should remember to remember."

"There's no such rule, Woollcott, and you know it," said Swope.

Aleck couldn't resist a rip-roaring face-to-face argument. He turned to Swope and said, "More important than rules, by far, are the ethics of fair play."

"Who writes 'the ethics of fair play'—Alexander H. Woollcott?"

"They are not written, dear Herbert. They are established by precedent."

Swope snorted. "So what's the precedent for not telling me who I'm dead on in this game?" he said.

"I'll give you a precedent, dear boy," said Aleck. "In a bridge game you wouldn't ask your partner in the middle of a hand how many trumps had been played, would you?"

230

"God damn it, Woollcott!" Swope thundered. "That's *indoors!*"

Indoors or out, Aleck was adamant. Swope played a ruthless, smashing game, but he wasted two shots on dead balls and Aleck won the match. The Katzenjammer Kids went on feuding, worse than ever.

The only partners who never lost were Abercrombie and Fitch, who must have sold us fifty thousand bucks' worth of imported croquet equipment during the middle and late twenties. We used nothing except hand-turned English mallets and balls. The wickets, which were scarcely wider than the width of a ball, were made of English steel.

We guarded our mallets and pampered them as if they were rare, sensitive pets. I turned the spare bedroom in my apartment into a "cold room" (no steam heat, constant low temperature) for my mallets, so they wouldn't split or warp during the winter.

My cold room, it turned out, had unexpected benefits. One night after a show I picked up two good-looking gals in a café near the theatre. I couldn't make any time with either one of them in the café, so I asked them to come on over to my place for cake and coffee and a couple of laughs. It was a mistake. I was dead tired. The broads wanted to do nothing but talk all night. They wouldn't take any hints, so I tried a more direct method of getting them out of my hair.

"By the way," I said, "I don't want to scare you, but if I should start acting peculiar, don't pay any attention. I get these fits, see, late at night sometimes. But I'm not violent every time, only once in a while."

This had no effect except to start them off on a giggling binge. So then I asked if they'd care to see my collection in the cold room. *Oooh!* They'd *love* to! I guess they figured I was going to show them dirty pictures.

I made them put their coats on, then took them in the spare

room and closed the door. I opened the closet where I kept my mallets and said, "Look! There they are!" The girls seemed very puzzled.

I picked up a mallet and fondled the shaft and the head, making soft, loving sounds. "Isn't it beautiful?" I said. "Would you like to feel one?" They shook their heads, speechless for the first time since I had picked them up. They were beginning to get scared. I moved in for the kill.

I lit a cigarette, bugged my eyes, then exhaled a bubble instead of smoke. That did it. The two broads scrambled out of the cold room and ran all the way out of the joint, screaming, *"He's having a fit! He's having a fit!"*

While they waited for the elevator to come, one of them happened to turn, and saw me standing in the open doorway, making a Gookie. They started screaming again. When the elevator man arrived he was ready for trouble. Then he saw it was only me. We exchanged winks, and I went peacefully to bed.

Otherwise life was pretty depressing, after winter set in. Central Park wouldn't be ready to play in again until April, and that seemed like an eternity away. But shortly after the first of the year I made a happy discovery. Across the street from my apartment house was a single-story garage with a large, flat roof. It was a perfect layout for a court!

I talked to one of the two partners who ran the garage and told him I'd like to rent his roof for a croquet court. I'd have some matting put down. I'd keep the snow cleared off and the roof in good condition, and our playing wouldn't bother anybody in the garage below. The guy didn't say a word until I finished my spiel. Then he said, "What croquet? What kind of a racket is that? Don't bother me—get outta here!"

The next day I buttonholed the other partner and gave him the pitch. He said, "Never heard of no such game as 'croquet.' You're full of crap. Get lost, Mac."

I wasn't discouraged. That night I had a salesman bring samples of matting around to my dressing room, so I could test them. I picked out one that was just right—gave the ball good speed and an accurate roll. The salesman estimated the cost of covering the roof would be five hundred bucks. Fine, I said. I'd call him and give him the order as soon as I'd taken care of the details of renting the space.

And so, back to the garage. Both partners were there and they saw me coming. I heard one of them say to the other, "Here comes the nut about the roof."

We haggled for an hour or so—the partners trying to worm out of me what my racket was, me trying to get out of them how much rent they wanted per month. When I said I already had an estimate on the matting and a crew lined up to lay it down, they got tired of kidding me along.

"Out, out!" said the senior partner. "Off the premises and stay off, crackpot!"

I changed my tactics. I asked them if they'd like four tickets to see a Broadway show that night. So that was the racket, they said—peddling tickets! I assured them there were no strings attached. I only wanted them to know I wasn't a phony and that I had a regular job. One of the partners said, "For Christ sake let's take 'em and get rid of this screwball." He got on the phone and checked with the theatre. He found out the tickets were for real. He also found out they were for a Marx Brothers show. "No kidding?" he said. "Are you one of them?" I modestly admitted I was. They accepted the tickets.

Next morning I showed up at the garage ready to do business. The senior partner met me at the door. "Well," I said, "did you see the show?" Yes, they saw it. They took their wives and saw it. And now they knew I was nuts. I was jerkier on the stage than I was in real life, if that was possible. Too dumb to even say anything.

He whistled for his partner. "This crazy son-of-a-bitch," he said, "has the nerve to come here after we seen him in his stupid show last night!"

Would I remove myself from their place of business for the last time, or would they have to call the cops? For the last time I explained, as patiently as I could, what I was after and the kind of money I was willing to lay out. I even tried to explain the game of croquet.

233

Now they were really suspicious. "You look to spend five hundred bucks so you can hit a frigging ball around on our roof?" said one of them. And the other said, "There has to be an angle to this —watch it, Fred."

"Absolutely no angle," I said. "All I've got up my sleeve is this." I hauled out a certified check for one hundred dollars, payment in advance for one month's rent. They looked at me with disbelief. Then they examined the check. They took it.

I rushed to break the news to the Katzenjammer Kids. (I hadn't wanted to tell anybody about my fantastic discovery until the deal was closed.) They were delighted. "Let's go play!" said Woollcott. "Wait!" said Swope. "Let's do it right. We've got to form a club. The first thing we do is schedule a meeting." Herbert Bayard Swope was a big man who could only do things in a big way.

We decided that six others should be invited to be charter members: Neysa McMein, the Kaufmans, the Schwartz brothers, and Averell Harriman. Now, I said, I could call the matting people and get the crew to work on the surface. Not so fast, said Swope. The club must first approve of all contracts, bids and expenditures by majority vote. We would take this up in a meeting.

A whole month of meetings was devoted solely to choosing a name for the organization. We could only agree upon a temporary name—"The New York Croquet Club." "What about the matting?" I kept asking, and Swope kept saying, "First things first, Harpo. First we have to draft the bylaws."

One day, two months after I had discovered the roof, one of the garage men whistled at me from across the street. "Hey, crackpot!" he called. "A guy here wants to talk to you."

The third man on the premises was a city fire inspector. He said, "I hear you got it in mind to use the top of this garage for some kind of ath-a-letic contest which requires the use of inflammable matting. Sorry, fellow. Against the Code."

What had happened was that Swope, in Doing the Thing Right, had talked to Mayor Walker, and Mayor Walker had talked to the Fire Commissioner, and the Fire Commissioner had looked it up and found it was against the city regulations.

Spring was late that year. But what the hell, it was bound to come. If the first robin showed up, could the first *tonk* of croquet ball be far behind? And then it would be back to Central Park, and Hurrah for the Red, Blue, Yellow and Black!

On the second Sunday in May I got a call from Woollcott. He was very excited. "Harpo," he said, "I've rented a villa on the French Riviera for the summer."

"Hey, that's great," I said. "You'll love it there." I didn't think it was great at all, because I was beginning to dream of Neshobe Island, the only place in the world where I wanted to go. I had no idea whether Aleck would love it on the French Riviera or not, either, because I'd never been there. As a matter of fact I didn't know it from the Italian or the Hungarian Riviera or Loew's Riviera in Brooklyn.

"Something else, me bucko," said Aleck, with the purr in his voice that meant I was being conned. "I think it would be elegant if you came along with me."

"Oh, no," I said. "I can think of forty better places to spend the summer, all of them on Long Island in a hammock. Thanks a lot, but have a nice time, give my love to the folks over there and send me a postcard home."

On Saturday, May 19, 1928, we sailed for Europe on the S.S. *Roma:* Aleck, Beatrice Kaufman, Alice Miller and myself.

CHAPTER 15

The Bam-Bang-Sock-
and-Pow Part

THE LIVING WAS EASY IN 1928. Life was mostly fun and games
and the world was our private, million-dollar playground. All of
us had, somehow, the means to do anything we wanted to do.
Income tax was a nuisance—like getting yearly license plates for
your car—but hardly a burden.

We weren't mercenary, or dollar-mad. Dough was simply a
commodity we liked to have and therefore had, the same as air
to breathe, coffee for breakfast, and a fourth for croquet. F.P.A.
summarized our attitude when he said, "Money isn't everything,
but the lack of money isn't anything."

When Aleck took over the Villa Galanon, on the Mediterranean coast of France near Cap d'Antibes, he lived and played the
host in the grand manner. Hang the expense. He was out to make
his mark on the international set. He made it, but it wasn't easy—
thanks to me. I didn't exactly care for the type of dog Aleck put on,
on the Riviera. It brought out the worst of the Patsy Brannigan in
me.

For a week before the villa was ready, the four of us—Beatrice,
Alice, Aleck and myself—stayed in a small hotel, the Antibes.

Woollcott favored this hotel because it was very French and very quiet. It was, as he put it, "off the 'rout' of the red-neck, rubberneck tourists."

I didn't favor this hotel at all. The only action in the joint was a one-franc slot machine in the lobby, by the foot of the stairs. Every time I passed the one-armed bandit I dropped in a coin, pulled the lever and walked on through the hostile glares of the Frenchmen in the lobby, while behind me the machine turned and clanked to a stop. You'd think I'd set off a firecracker in the reading room of a public library. Woollcott refused to walk downstairs with me, on account of my vulgar exhibitionism.

One evening I came down for dinner, dropped a coin in the slot, pulled the lever and walked on. When I reached the dining-room door, all hell broke loose. The machine hit a jackpot. The lobby burst into a riot. The quiet nontourists stomped and cheered and applauded. They did everything except dance the can-can and sing the "Marseillaise" to celebrate my stroke of luck.

When we checked out of the hotel, two days later, the manager said, "I hope we have the pleasure of your company soon again, *monsieur*"—not to Woollcott, but to me. Literary figures came and went by the dozen in the Hotel Antibes, but the slot machine hadn't been hit for three and a half years.

Aleck was very happy to be set up at last in the Villa Galanon, where I would be under his vigilant, owlish eye.

Woollcott was in his element on the Riviera that summer. Soon after we got there, he wrote to Edna Ferber: "I am here leading the life of a rosy, middle-aged dolphin." There were times, however, when he was oddly—for him—placid. He would stand for long moments of silence gazing from the top of the cliff at the deep, cold-blue sea and the shallow, hot-blue sky. I think he was secretly wishing he was a fresh-water wabbit in Vermont again, instead of a Mediterranean dolphin.

237

These placid moments, which became less frequent as the season got under way, were usually interrupted by Guy, the major domo, chauffeur and chef of Galanon. Guy would march up to Aleck on the double and out of breath, like an aide reporting to Napoleon in the midst of battle. There was a running battle going on, the battle for dinner. Each night's dinner had to be a victory, a triumph of Guy and the *haute cuisine* over the peasant forces of common food.

Guy never lost a battle. He never won without a fight, however. He skirmished from dawn to the dinner hour. He attacked the village market, ambushing the butcher, the wine merchant and the greengrocer. He sparred with the dairyman. Back at the villa he exchanged volleys with the pastry cook, the housekeeper, and the gardener. He fought off sneaky, rear-guard attacks by balky stoves and stopped-up plumbing. He rallied sauces and soufflés with rousing battle cries, urging them on to blend and to rise.

It was between these skirmishes that Guy threw on his alpaca jacket, wetted down his wild thatch of hair—which kept struggling to stand, like a field of wheat after a cloudburst—and marched off to find his commander-in-chief, M. Woollcott, to report on how the battle was going and ask for any change of orders on the wine. After a mumbled exchange in French (not loud enough for the enemy to overhear), Guy would rush back to the front, rip off his jacket, and leap into the fray. Just when shattering defeat seemed certain, and the villa seemed doomed to fall into a pile of smoldering rubble, the battleground would become suddenly silent.

Guy, in a spotless white jacket, his hair glistening smooth, would appear through the kitchen door. He would incline his head toward Aleck, closing his eyes in a moment of sublime reflection, and announce quietly, *"Monsieur est servi."*

Whether it was dinner for ten, fifteen, or just the four of us, it would be magnificent. We got the full treatment every night, from hors d'oeuvre to soup to fish to roast to salad to dessert to cheese, with wines between and cognac following after (except for me; I didn't dare drink anything stronger than Vichy water). As a chef, Guy rated my highest compliment: he was almost as good as Frenchie.

All due respect to him, I don't think Guy could ever have won a dinner battle if he hadn't been motorized. If he'd been a foot soldier he could never have pulled off his lightning raids on the village market. Even a horse-cavalryman couldn't have made such breath-taking dashes back through the lines for emergency supplies —a bottle of Marsala, when there'd been a change in sauces, or an extra liter of cream, if the menu had been changed from hot soup to cold. Guy made it because he had a car. His vehicle was an ancient jalopy—a touring car, ancient of vintage but stout of heart. It never failed in line of duty.

The jalopy had two speeds, the way Guy drove it—full speed ahead and dead stop, with nothing in between. Yet, he never had an accident. This was not because he was safety-conscious, but because pedestrians and other drivers were. When they heard him coming they got out of the way. They were able to hear him coming because Guy had the notion that the horn was an extra gas pedal. The accelerator by itself wasn't enough. To maintain full speed ahead, he pushed the gas to the floor and kept squeezing the horn bulb, even down an empty country road. Cattle, goats and donkeys for miles around took to the hills when they heard the whonk-a-whonk-a-whonk of the rampant jalopy.

Guy offered to let me drive his car any time I wanted to. At first I was flattered. Then I realized this was his way of letting me know I was slightly lower in class than the three other Americans at the villa. Ladies and gentlemen did not drive. They were driven. Beatrice and Alice were ladies. Aleck, le patron, was a gentleman. Me, I could drive the car.

Guy never could quite figure me out. The language barrier didn't help much. The day we moved into the villa and Guy came to my room to help me unpack, I tried to get across the idea that I'd prefer being called "Harpo" instead of "Monsieur Marx."

He got hung up on "Harpo." He pronounced it a dozen different ways, none of which sounded vaguely like my name. I did a pantomime of playing the harp. "Ah!" he said. "Monsieur est harpiste?" I nodded my head yes. Then he looked around for the harp. "No," I said, "no harp here. Harp in America."

I could not be, according to Guy, a harpiste if I didn't have a harp. We were back where we started. Finally he seemed to get it. "*Harpon? Harpon?*" he said. He laughed, then made a motion like he was throwing a spear. "*Comme ci? Comme ci?*" he said. Now it was my turn to be puzzled. Guy saw from my look that spear-throwing had nothing to do with it. He shrugged, thought for a moment, then got another idea.

"*Appeau?*" he said, hopefully.

That was more like it. That was almost how I pronounced it myself, East Side style—"Hoppo." To illustrate that now he understood, he began to whistle through his teeth. Somehow he must have known that onstage I whistled instead of talking. I nodded and whistled back at him. We nodded and smiled and whistled at each other for a while, and Guy said, "*Ah oui! Monsieur l'Appeau.*"

I shook my head. He'd lost it again. He went back to *Harpon.* I said "*Oui!*" He tried *Appeau* again. I said "*Oui*" to that too. Guy raised his eyebrows, shrugged, and held up the palms of his hands. He went back to work and back to calling me "monsieur."

Just then Aleck came by. Aleck and Guy had a long jabber in French. I didn't like the tone of their conversation, not at all. First Aleck, then Guy, then both of them, would look at me and laugh. "What's so damn funny?" I wanted to know, and Aleck explained. The word *harpon* meant "harpoon" in French, and *appeau* meant "bird call."

"I've instructed Guy," he said, trying hard to keep a straight face, "that you have no preference, and like to be called by either name."

So, depending on his mood, I was either *Appeau* (friendly mood) or *Harpon* (unfriendly) to Guy for the rest of the summer. Whenever I told him his grenadine of beef or his cucumber soup was delicious, I was a bird call. But when I put a hand over my wine glass, refusing a rare Chateauneuf-du-Pape in favor of seltzer water, I was a plain old harpoon.

There wasn't room for a croquet layout at Galanon, but one terrace overhanging the sea was big enough for badminton. Because of the fierce wind, the mistral, we had to use special, heavily weighted birds. Once we got the hang of it, our games were as fierce as the wind and hot as the Mediterranean sun. Aleck, who played against his doctor's orders, was amazing at badminton. He was quick on his feet. He was a placement artist and he had a deadly, slashing backhand. On the court he was indeed a "rosy, middle-aged dolphin"—if you could imagine a dolphin in sagging shorts and flapping bathrobe.

Alice Duer Miller was even rosier. Badminton was the one game at which she could always beat Aleck.

Sports on the Riviera were much more strenuous than on Neshobe Island. One day the wind changed, and the sea came booming at the shore in long, smooth breakers and everybody started riding the surf. This looked like something I should try. I was fearless in those days. I'd try anything, once. So I climbed down the cliff to the water and asked somebody to show me how to use a surfboard. Five minutes later I took my first solo ride on the waves, stunting around on one leg like a hot-shot daredevil. An hour later I was being towed behind a high-speed launch, out to an island that was famous for its bouillabaisse made with octopus.

(When Guy heard about this, he went into a sulk and called me nothing but a harpoon for a week. My eating a vulgar fisherman's stew like *bouillabaise de poulpe* was a slur on his *haute cuisine*.)

Somebody told me that the only way to get a true picture of the Riviera was to see it from the air. A bird's-eye view of the coast, they said, was a thing of unforgettable beauty. So one Sunday I drove over to the Cannes airport, where they advertised plane rides for fifty francs a spin.

The plane was a survivor from World War One, an open-cockpit Salmson biplane held together with splints and patches. Since I was so short, the pilot put a wooden box on the seat for me, so I could see over the rim of my cockpit all right. I saw over it, all right. I stuck out of the cockpit like an Eskimo in a kayak, more out than in, and I spent the whole flight hanging on for dear life to a wire strut. My bird's-eye view of the Riviera was a close-up of

241

the knuckles of my right fist, beyond which I didn't have the nerve to look, and the beauty of which was quite forgettable.

That was one thing I tried only once.

The Riviera was pretty strong on indoor sports, too. Besides the usual kind, it offered roulette, baccarat and *chemin de fer*, in some lovely, enticing casinos.

The first casino I sampled was in Juan-les-Pins. I wandered in there one quiet afternoon. I was the only American in the place but I figured, what the hell, the spots on a deck of cards were a universal language, and I got into a small game of *chemin-de-fer*.

I was wrong about the language. Right away the dame next to me began to heckle me, in French. She resented the fact that I could only talk by making faces and signs. She was even more annoyed by the fact that I was chewing gum. She started mocking my gum chewing and this made me good and sore.

The next time I made the high bet and got to play a hand against the bank, I was dealt a seven-count. By the rules I should have just stood, but being sore I signaled the banker to deal me a third card. I got a four face-up, which put my count back down to one. The banker won the hand on a two.

The French dame, who had a hundred francs riding on me against the bank, hit the ceiling when she saw the cards I'd been dealt. She started to jab her finger at me and howl like a siren. The next thing I knew, a platoon of casino officials, all of them with beards, appeared out of nowhere and started a loud argument with the dame.

While they yammered away I went quietly off to a corner of the casino and stood on my head.

When the dame spotted me upside down in the corner she pointed my way and screamed louder than ever. Two officials rushed over to me. They hesitated. They weren't sure whether to address my feet or bend down and yell at me face-to-face. They

242

compromised and yelled at each other. I didn't like the sound of their voices. I swore I heard words like *police* and *sûreté*. But I was damned if I'd stop standing on my head until they calmed down.

Thank goodness an Englishman who could speak French came into the casino. He got the story from the guys with the beards, then knelt down on the floor like he was looking under the bed for a lost collar button, and said to me, "Old boy, it seems you've broken a rule of the game, and you're being asked to pay this lady a hundred francs."

I came down off my head, gave the dame her hundred francs, tipped everybody in sight—including the dame—a stick of Juicy Fruit and blew the joint.

Now that the international incident was settled and war clouds no longer hovered over Juan-les-Pins, I decided to switch casinos and try my luck at Monte Carlo.

When I told Aleck this, he clapped his hands and said, "Marvelous idea! We shall all go to Monte Carlo—and it's my treat, bunnies. Dinner at the Café de Paris is on me. Good King Alexander is full of *noblesse oblige* and feels like bestowing *largesse* upon the poor."

"You'd save a lot of scratch, King, if you bestowed your *largesse* upon a chair and stayed home," I said. Aleck was feeling so good that he laughed and refrained from calling me the name I expected.

Guy, who was the head of protocol at Galanon, told us what to order at the Café de Paris and what we should wear to the casino —evening dresses for the ladies, simple and not too much jewelry, and black tie and dinner jackets for the gentlemen. When he saw me about to leave in polo shirt, blazer and white ducks, he was horrified. He had a frenzied consultation with Aleck. Aleck shrugged. He turned to me and said, "How can I explain you to Guy? There's no French word for 'boob.' "

I went as I was, which was the only way I was ever comfortable anywhere I went.

Dinner was great. Guy had touted us onto the best food on the Riviera. When we got to Monte Carlo, about eleven o'clock, I was feeling well-fed and lucky. I couldn't wait to get into the

243

action. But I couldn't get past the outside entrance. A guy as big as Jess Willard and dressed like an ambassador blocked my way.

"I'm sorry, monsieur," he said, pointing to his throat. "You will not be allowed in the casino without a tie."

"He's quite right, you know," said Aleck. He'd been waiting all night for this. He gloated and swept grandly into the casino, with Beatrice on one arm and Alice on the other.

Fortunately I was wearing black socks. I went outside into the shadows. I took off my socks, tied one of them into a bow beneath my shirt collar, stuffed the other one in a shoe, stuck my shoes inside my belt, and went back to the entrance. The same guard was there. This time he smiled and said, "Forgive the inconvenience, monsieur, but you know—the regulations. Please go in. Your friends will be expecting you."

It was the first time I ever gambled with a tie on, but I made out very nicely. I was, in fact, too lucky at roulette. In the "Little Casino," where I played, if you got on a streak and hit like five numbers in a row they'd declare the bank closed. In this part of the joint they saw to it a guy never made over a thousand bucks. So when my winnings reached the five-hundred mark, I took to slipping stacks of chips to other guys to bet for me, on a commission.

That fattened my bankroll but killed my fun. Whenever you hit a number in this casino you had to tip the four croupiers. I'd been making them work for it. Before they got a tip from me the croupiers had to line up and sing "Merci beaucoup, monsieur!" in harmony. By God, at that they sounded better than the Four Nightingales ever did.

Later, when I kibitzed the action in the "Big Casino," I felt like a piker. The center of attraction at the roulette wheel was a retired carpet-sweeper manufacturer, a doddering old coot of eighty-five who played in a wheel chair, with a male nurse in attendance. He was betting a thousand American bucks on red, on every turn, and he was winning consistently.

At one in the morning the nurse said it was past his patient's bedtime, and insisted on wheeling him home. Before they left, the old guy handed over a wad and told the dealer to bet a thousand for him on red, once every half hour for the rest of the night.

The next morning I checked back and found out how much the old guy had collected. While he'd been sleeping, the dealer had won him a net of twenty-two thousand dollars.

Not long afterward another American, this one a cotton-fabric king, didn't do so well in the Big Casino. He lost more than ten times the amount the carpet-sweeper king had won, also in the space of one night. The cotton-fabric man came unraveled. He went out on the terrace at dawn and blew his brains out.

On the following night I went to Monte Carlo on the hunch that this would change the tide of luck. My hunch was wrong. I lost every cent I came with, inside of two hours. Instead of slinking home, like a good sport, I went around the Little Casino asking everybody in sight, in a loud voice, "Where's that cliff you're supposed to throw yourself off of when you lose?"

The management was very sensitive about this, after what had happened on the terrace eighteen hours earlier. They cornered me and asked me how much I had lost. A thousand francs, I said. So they counted out a thousand francs and paid me off, whereupon I was politely heaved out of the joint, black-sock necktie and all, with a strong hint that I never return.

Pete Penovitch, I said to myself, simply wouldn't believe it, the way they operated this joint. They put down the red carpet for an eighty-nine-thousand-dollar winner, then turned around and kicked a loser out.

The hell with Monte Carlo. I set up my own casino, at the Villa Galanon. I ran the operation my way, and I never had a customer squawk. That was more than the boss of Monte Carlo could ever say.

I had gone to the flea market in Nice, where I bought the nuttiest thing I could find. This was a thing called a Chinese fly-trap. It was a fantastic construction of bamboo, wire and string, which flies could fly into but couldn't fly out of. The Chinese fly-trap was designed to be humane, which was why it was so complicated. When the flies were trapped they weren't killed, or even injured. As long as the bottom door was shut they couldn't get out, but they could live inside in style until they died of old age, or whatever unswatted flies die of.

I was a gambling man as well as a humanitarian, however, being equal parts Pete Penovitch and Albert Schweitzer, so I turned the flytrap into a casino.

After a lot of serious thinking (I missed Chico, who could have figured the whole thing out in a minute on the back of a pawn ticket), I arrived at what the odds should be on a fly surviving the trap. Two to one. This would give the fly a sporting chance and give the house a chance to win its rightful share as well.

What I did was to catch only a few flies at a time, then block the entrance. When I trapped a batch of customers I marked them, one by one, by dabbing a broom straw in red ink and poking it through a slit in the trap. Then I opened the door and gave them all their freedom.

Here's where the odds came in: when a marked fly came back and was trapped a second time, I did him in with the blunt end of a chopstick. First-time suckers got painted red and let loose. Second-time losers got squashed. (I used to give the same kind of odds to mosquitoes who pestered me when I practiced the harp. I would only swat the ones who sang higher than the A-flat above middle C. The rest went free.)

I was amazed at how few flies came back to the trap. I'd never dreamed so many flies would be smart enough to know they had a good thing going at 2-1 and would stay away.

Beatrice and Alice were very impressed by what the Chinese flytrap revealed, to wit: your average housefly was a much better gambler than your average person gave him credit for. Aleck was more alarmed than impressed. He said I was dooming the human race by developing a super-intelligent race of flies. But that didn't stop him from betting on the flies against the trap. When he ran his winnings up to fifteen francs I declared the bank closed and went out of business. Now I knew what it was like to be on the side of management. I couldn't cover the nut for red ink.

Our summer seemed to divide itself into three phases—the Gambling Period, the Literary Period, and the Society Period.

Woollcott broke me into the Literary Period by easy stages. Step number one was to introduce me to Somerset Maugham. Aleck knew I was already an admirer of Maugham's. Without knowing who he was, I had singled him out as the best aquaplaner on the coast. When Aleck told me he was an eminent author and perhaps the most famous resident on the whole Riviera, I was doubly eager to meet him.

Maugham's villa on Cap Ferrat was the most exciting house I'd ever seen. I'd been in bigger and more lavish joints on Long Island and in Palm Beach, but none of them had the beauty of appearing to be carved out of the landscape, like Maugham's did. It was built around a swimming pool, which was fed by fountains. The house was filled with the cool sound of rushing water, the mingled scents of tropical flowers, and color—the colors of the greatest of the French Impressionists and Moderns. Such paintings I'd never seen in a private collection before.

Our host, wearing only shorts and sandals, came bounding downstairs to greet us. Maugham was then fifty-four, but he looked no older than thirty-four. He was lean and brown and he sizzled with energy and good cheer. Aleck, I noticed, was relieved to see that the eminent author and I hit it off well from the start. I was on my best behavior, and so was Aleck.

Maugham wanted to show us the rest of his joint before giving us tea. He took us upstairs to the master bedroom, his pride and joy. It was situated so that he could dive out of his bedside window and straight into the pool when he woke up in the morning. This, I thought, was terrific.

247

While Maugham and Woollcott were turned away, discussing a painting on the far wall of the bedroom, I pulled off all my clothes and plunged into the water.

Looking up, I saw Woollcott looking hopefully at Maugham, to see if I had shocked him. Maugham's reaction was not what Aleck expected. He pulled off his shorts, kicked off his sandals, and dove into the pool to join me.

Maugham and I met several times afterward, at parties and in the surf, but after that summer I didn't see him again for eight years, and I was sure he would have forgotten me. At the opening of *Dead End*, in 1936, I spotted him during the intermission. He was sitting several rows behind me, with S. N. Behrman. I crawled back on all fours, monkey-fashion, across the tops of the seats. I was about to reintroduce myself when Maugham said, "Terribly sorry I haven't a banana for you, Harpo." He hadn't forgotten.

Aleck was pleased with my success at Cap Ferrat. Next, he allowed me to meet H. G. Wells. I got a bit confused about who this guy was, and in trying to make conversation I said, "I've heard a lot about your company, Mr. Wells. Especially out West, when I was on the Pantages-time. Every town we played in had a Wells-Fargo office."

I passed my Maugham, but I flunked my Wells.

In the middle of the summer I acquired a partner in crime. Ruth Gordon arrived at Antibes. Ruth was a special pet of Aleck's, and his special nickname for her was "Louisa." I remember he once took Ruth and me in his arms and said, "You two are the world, do you know that? Every man as pretentious as old Alexander should have at least one Louisa and one Harpo beside him always, to remind him of what really makes the world go round, and that everything else is pretending."

We did a pretty fair job of making Aleck's world go round for the rest of the season, Ruth and I. The first week she was there,

I borrowed Guy's car and took her for a spin through the country-side. I'd heard Aleck speak of a famous restaurant on a mountain-top at a place called St. Paul. I decided to take Ruth there.

I drove north. I got lost. It never occurred to me that Guy's jalopy could get lost in its own neighborhood. I assumed that it knew the roads so well that it could find its way *whonk-a-whonk-a-whonk* anywhere you wanted to go. Not so. We wound up driving from nowhere to nowhere.

Ruth's French was no better than mine. We kept stopping to ask people on the road, "St. Paul? St. Paul?" The natives gave us funny looks, shrugged, and went on smoking their pipes, milking their goats and tying up their haystacks as if they'd never seen us.

I took to asking, "Cincinnati? Cincinnati?"—and got a better response. People pointed, at least. But everybody pointed in a different direction.

Somehow, we finally made it up the mountain to St. Paul. We were famished. The restaurant was down a long flight of stone steps from the village square. The innkeeper was overjoyed at having two Americans for lunch. The gist of his welcoming speech was that we deserved to be served only the *spécialité de la maison, omelette au rhum.* Whatever the hell that was, we wanted it. Trusting souls that we were, we believed that anything with a French name was good to eat.

What we were served—after a soup with wine in it—was an omelet doused with rum. We lapped up the soup and the omelet. Ruth, it turned out, was just as vulnerable to alcohol as I was. When we finished the omelet, we were higher than two kites. The innkeeper insisted we have *crêpes suzettes.* When we finished the *crêpes suzettes,* which were prepared with brandy, we were skunk drunk. I remember staggering forth from the restaurant—Ruth and I helping each other up the flight of stone steps, which had lengthened considerably during lunch—and then walking around and around the village square so I could sober up enough to drive. I remember driving down the mountain and laughing like hell because the car had no brakes. I remember stopping to ask the natives the way to Galveston, Texas.

The next thing I was conscious of was being back at the villa and

249

Guy coaxing me to drink some thick black coffee that reeked of cloves. God and the patron saints of Harpo and Louisa had seen us home. They must have placed along the route somebody who knew where Galveston was. How else we could have made it I'll never know.

The postman cycled out to Galanon with a special-delivery letter one afternoon while we were playing badminton. Aleck must have been expecting it. When he saw the return address he made a joyful little gasp and threw his racket aside, conceding the game. He tore it open like it was money from home. As he read the note, he beamed and beamed and I thought he was going to dance one of his tippytoe jigs. Instead, he turned serious.

"Harpo," he said. "He's coming. He's coming to have lunch with us next Wednesday. Bernard Shaw!"

"Bernard Shaw?" I said. "Didn't his name used to be Bernie Schwartz? Ran the cigar stand in the Hotel Belvedere?" I was kidding, of course. I'd heard them speak of Shaw many times at the Round Table. He was an English politician or songwriter or something.

Aleck was in no mood for gags. He cut me off with a huffy stare, and trotted away to find the girls and tell them the great news.

The coming of Mr. and Mrs. George Bernard Shaw to Villa Galanon was Woollcott's supreme coup of the season. Everything had to be exactly right for the occasion. For Guy, preparing the Wednesday lunch was the longest and toughest battle he ever fought.

It took four days to decide on the menu. What made it so hard was the fact that Shaw was a vegetarian. How strict he was about his diet, Aleck didn't know. Ruth was sure that Shaw ate bacon. Beatrice didn't think so. Alice said there were all kinds of vegetarians, some liberal, some orthodox. The liberal ones ate fish and

250

fowl, only laid off red meat, and Shaw was certainly a liberal in every other respect, wasn't he? Woollcott did not agree.

On the fourth day they settled on omelet with truffles, broiled tomatoes and eggplants, asparagus, artichokes, green salad, hot breads, aspics, mousses, ices, cheeses and wild strawberries with thick cream.

Sounded pretty good to me. I made a rapid calculation. "You know something, Aleck?" I said. "A feed like this would have set Shaw back thirty-six cents at Max's Busy Bee."

That was my first and last contribution to the planning of the Great Lunch. I got the impression that Woollcott would be very happy if I would take my flytrap and leave, and not return until the honored guest had safely departed.

On the fifth day Aleck and Guy worked on the wines. On the sixth day Guy went to market. He shuttled from village to villa all day long, with load after load of precious bottles and groceries.

When Wednesday dawned, Aleck was as jittery as a girl getting ready for her first date. He went over the menu—which couldn't possibly be changed by this time—again and again. He couldn't decide what to wear.

The hour approached. All was in readiness. By now, Aleck looked elegant. He put on a wide Italian straw hat and a linen cape and got in the jalopy beside the gardener, who was substitute chauffeur for the day, and off they went to Antibes, to pick up the Shaws.

Alice, Beatrice and Ruth went upstairs to change. Guy was in the kitchen, screaming at the aspic to jell. I was alone—which, I guessed, was how everybody wanted me.

The hell with them. The hell with the whole affair. I went down the cliff to the little, sheltered cove we used for nude bathing, took off my clothes, and went for a swim. I came out of the water and stretched out on a towel to sun-bathe. I'd get dressed and go back up to the villa when I damn well felt like it. Maybe in time for lunch, maybe not.

I was startled out of my doze in the sun by a man's voice, blaring from the top of the cliff: *"Halloo! Halloo! Is there nobody home?"*

I wrapped the towel around myself and scrambled up the rocks to see who it was. It was a tall, skinny, red-faced old geezer with a beard, decked out in a sporty cap and a knicker suit. There was a lady with him.

"Where the devil's Woollcott?" the guy asked. Without waiting for an answer he said, "Who the devil are you?"

I told him I was Harpo Marx.

"Ah yes, of course," he said, with an impish grin. He held out his hand. "I'm Bernard Shaw," he said. He caught me flat-footed. Instead of shaking hands he made a sudden lunge for my towel, snatched it away, and exposed me naked to the world. "And this," he said, "is Mrs. Shaw."

From the moment I met him, I had nothing to hide from George Bernard Shaw.

Aleck came roaring back to the villa, wild-eyed and wringing wet with flop sweat. The Shaws had not arrived at the hotel, as expected. Aleck had waited for a while, then tried the railroad station, where he learned that a couple answering the Shaws' description had hired a driver to take them to Villa Galanon.

He fell all over himself apologizing to Shaw about the mix-up. "Nonsense, my boy," said Shaw, playing it straight for Woollcott but with a twinkle on the side for me. "We had a grand reception here. We were met by a naked jackanapes, your immodest Mr. Marx. A bit shocking, but quite grand!"

The luncheon too could only be described as grand. It was a one-man show. Shaw's performance at lunch was the most remarkable I'd ever seen, onstage or off. Ruth, Alice and Beatrice were entranced. Aleck was in heaven.

I'd never heard a voice as superb as Shaw's. He played it like an organ. This guy was no ham, but a real actor. He had expressive, graceful hands, magnetic eyes, and the plastic face of a comic.

The dining room became his stage. He flung himself in and out of doorways, making exits and entrances. He dashed around like Fairbanks, he danced and shuffled like Chaplin, he swooned like Duse, as he told story after story, acting out all the parts. He recreated scenes and plays, and he brought to life the famous characters he had known over the past fifty years—from Disraeli and Lenin to Darwin and Huxley, from Gilbert and Sullivan to Liszt and Debussy, from Oscar Wilde to Henrik Ibsen.

Only two people at the table dared to interrupt him—his wife and me.

Every time Shaw strayed onto the subject of Ellen Terry (which was fairly often), Mrs. Shaw would tap a finger on the table, slowly, steadily and ominously. If her husband didn't get the message she started thumping her spoon on the table, and she wouldn't stop until he changed the subject. I hadn't been aware of Shaw's famous "friendship" with Miss Terry, but the thumping of the Mrs.' spoon told me all I needed to know.

At one point Shaw admitted, a bit shamefacedly, that he hadn't written a play since *The Apple Cart*, and that he doubted if he would ever tackle another. This sounded to me like a terrible waste of talent. What this guy needed was a little encouragement. So I said, "How about it? Why don't you write another play, Shaw?"

There was a deathly silence. Shaw leaned across the table and fixed me with a piercing look from beneath the bristly hedges of his eyebrows.

In a stage whisper that would have filled Madison Square Garden he said: *"Got an idea?"*

Then he threw back his head and laughed so hard I thought he'd strangle. At that moment a great mystery was solved for me. Since I had first met the guy I had been trying to figure out whether or not he was wearing a tie under his beard. Now I knew. He wasn't even wearing a collar.

He asked why I was staring at him so oddly. "I just discovered," I said, "that you couldn't have sat downstairs at Loew's Delancey Street Theatre."

Shaw asked for an explanation. The downstairs seats were strictly high class at the Delancey Street, I told him. A man had to be wearing a tie to sit downstairs. Otherwise he had to sit in the balcony. The assistant manager of the theatre used to stand by the entrance, sorting out customers according to their neckwear. The older guys in the neighborhood all wore beards, and you used to hear the assistant manager, as he lifted the beards of the customers coming in, checking for neckties: "Upstairs . . . Downstairs . . . Upstairs . . . Downstairs. . . ."

Shaw said he would have been flattered to join the upstairs crowd at Loew's Delancey Street, with the sensible chaps who knew what a beard was for.

This time it was Woollcott who tapped a finger until the subject was changed. It was a hint for me to get the hell out of the act, so Shaw's one-man show could continue.

The lunch lasted three hours. When the guests departed, driven to Antibes by the gardener, the rest of us sat in silence. We were spellbound by the great man's presence long after he had gone. Aleck was first to speak. He sighed and said, "Well, what did you think of him?"

The only person prepared to answer was Guy, who was gathering up the wine bottles. As social arbiter of the Villa Galanon, Guy assumed the question was directed to him. He shrugged and said, "*Il est présentable,*" and went on about his business.

I was the Shaws' chauffeur for the rest of their stay in Antibes. We spent a lot of time together. I always drove the old bus the way it was used to being driven by Guy, and I'm afraid I gave the Shaws some pretty wild rides in the open jalopy. Bernard Shaw hung on grimly. He turned pale a few times, but he never complained. For a guy of seventy-four he was a wonderful sport.

Mrs. Shaw was just as good a sport. She usually sat by herself in the back seat, holding onto her hat with one hand and clutching a rolled-up umbrella with the other. She never commented about the way I drove—except to make sweeping signals with her umbrella whenever I stopped or turned. She waved and jabbed it around as briskly and efficiently as any Fifth Avenue traffic cop.

One day Shaw and I drove to Cannes, where a friend of his, Rex Ingraham, was directing a movie called *The Three Passions.* We only wanted to watch the shooting for a while, but Ingraham had other ideas. He shanghaied us and put us to work as extras. In our one and only joint appearance before the camera, George Bernard Shaw and I shot pocket billiards in a poolroom scene.

I'm sure the scene was cut from the picture. No audience could ever mistake us for extras, lost in the crowd. The way we shot pool we could only be taken for what we were—a couple of ringers, a couple of sharpies.

Aleck got sniffy and made like he was sore because I was spending more time with Shaw than he was. Actually, I knew that nothing tickled Aleck more than seeing me hit it off with one of his idols. He loved playing the game of Strange Bedfellows. "Harpo Marx and Bernard Shaw!" he used to say, with that smirking chuckle of his. "Corned beef and roses!"

When it came to parties, Aleck took his people-mixing seriously. Making up a guest list was an involved job. He wasn't happy until he came up with a balance of personalities that would make an evening perfect.

Unbeknownst to Aleck I took the liberty of adding to the guest list for his farewell dinner for the Shaws. I invited Sir Oswald Mosley and Peggy Hopkins Joyce.

Mosley, who later became the leader of the British Nazi Party, had some peculiar political ideas even then, and he wasn't too popular on the Riviera. Mrs. Joyce, on the other hand, was easily the most popular broad on the coast of France—although not at literary dinner parties.

Shaw was amused when my two extra guests showed up. The girls were amused. So was Woollcott, but he wouldn't admit it because he hadn't thought of the mixture first.

I lost a pal, with Shaw's return to England. But I gained a play-mate—Peggy Hopkins Joyce. Peggy was no spring chicken, but she was still quite a dish. She seemed to take a shine to me, after the evening at Galanon, but damned if I could make any time with her.

I managed finally to get her over to the villa for lunch one day when I was there alone. She was friendly and chatty and seemed to enjoy being with me as always, but that was the extent of it. I turned on the charm and took off my shirt and showed off my tan and my muscles, but it was no dice. No contest, no conquest.

Then, as she was about to leave, a lucky thing happened. She fell for my pet canary. She said she loved canaries, and mine was just the sweetest thing she'd ever seen.

"Peggy," I said, "he's yours. Please accept him as a gift." She was delighted. "However," I said, "it'd be better if you didn't take him home with you now. Being out in this hot sun would kill him. Tell you what I'll do. I'll bring him over to your place this evening. Say around seven o'clock?"

To my surprise she said yes. She went even further. "Why don't you stay for dinner?" she said. "It'll be informal, just the two of us, but I don't think you'll be bored."

I didn't think so either.

The bird and I arrived at her villa promptly at seven. She was wearing a slinky Oriental outfit, silk pants and jacket, with nothing underneath except Peggy Hopkins Joyce. It wasn't hard to see why she had come as far in the world as she had without a degree from Vassar.

There were just the two of us for dinner, but it was not exactly a tête-à-tête. The servants outnumbered us by about six to one. Then, when they cleared the table, Peggy said, "Shall we have our brandy in the sitting room, where nobody will bother us?"

My heart was pumping so fast I couldn't speak. I just nodded my head, trying to play it suave and casual.

Five minutes later I was reclining beside her on a harem-size divan, with a flunky waving a fan over us. She gave me the eye, snuggled deeper into her nest of silk cushions and whispered, "Peggy wants to have a little fun, Harpo. Will you help Peggy have a little fun?"

"You name it, honey," I said. On the brink of conquest I had found my voice again.

She dismissed the flunky and told him to douse the overhead lights on the way out. When he went out she sighed, slithered over closer to me, and ran a finger down the length of my arm, turning me into a cozy mass of shivers. *Well, old sport,* I said to myself, *you've got it made. The boys in Lindy's should see you now!*

Then she surprised me. She rang for the butler. She said to him, "You may bring the books now." The butler bowed and left the room.

Books? I didn't get it. Dirty books maybe?

The butler returned. He laid a stack of six books in my lap, bowed, and departed. The books were beautifully bound in hand-tooled leather. I looked at the titles. The titles were: "Mutt and Jeff," "Bringing Up Father," "Krazy Kat," "Tillie the Toiler," "Barney Google," and "The Katzenjammer Kids." They were collections of comic strips—not the dirty kind, but the kind that appeared in the funny papers.

Peggy gave a little giggle and curled up on the divan with her head on my shoulder. "Read to me, Harpo," she purred.

I read.

I read through the whole damn stack of comic books, beginning to end. Peggy Hopkins Joyce didn't know how to read, but she sure knew her literature. She knew it by heart. Whenever I made the slightest mistake, she corrected me.

The first mistake I made was to leave out the sound effects in a sequence where Jiggs came home late from playing poker and eating corned beef and cabbage and got waylaid by Maggie with her rolling pin.

"No, no!" Peggy howled, interrupting me. "You didn't read it all! You didn't read the 'Bam! Bang! Sock! Pow!' part!" I backtracked and read the bam-bang-sock-and-pow part and she was happy again.

I caught hell for leaving out a couple of glubs, half a dozen zowies, and a flock of zams, ulps and gulps, but otherwise I managed to struggle through the books without a hitch. And all the time Peggy kept tittering and squealing and fiddling with her toes and squirming all over the divan. No doubt about it. She was having her fun.

When I closed the covers on the sixth and final volume, I was exhausted. I stood and said that I'd enjoyed the dinner and thanks very much but it was getting late and I'd better be heading back to Galanon.

"Oh, no, Harpo!" said Peggy. She jumped up and ran to a massive carved chest and pulled out a drawer as big as a coffin. It was filled to the top with loose newspaper clippings.

"Look!" she said. "They're all about me! Here—" she scooped up half a bushel of clippings into her arms—"start reading these!"

My male pride had taken enough of a beating. I said, politely but forcefully, that I had to go home. I got away from Peggy Hopkins Joyce's love nest as fast as my legs and Guy's jalopy could take me.

Mrs. Joyce's record in the boudoir was more impressive than Benny Leonard's in the ring. But being more the literary type myself, I never made the list of her conquests.

August was the social month. It was a season within the season, a time of tea *dansants*, garden parties, cocktail parties, dinner parties, pajama parties, fancy-dress balls and formal receptions.

Aleck laid down the law. I had to do something about the way I dressed, at least be halfway presentable socially. He made an appointment for me with a tailor in Cannes to have a dinner jacket made.

I had a dinner jacket made. The material I picked for it was pool-table felt, and it had big brass buttons. Right away I became

known on the Riviera as "the American with the green tuxedo."
I was now a man of a certain distinction. I made every guest list
except one throughout the rest of the summer.

On the high-society circuit I met a new type of character. I met
a guy who owned the world's only Rolls-Royce with a built-in,
flushing john under the back seat. I met a dame whose villa had
two swimming pools, one for anybody and another one stocked
with live salmon for her pansy friends to swim in. My favorite
characters were King Alfonso of Spain and his Anthem Man.
King Alfonso was tone deaf. He couldn't tell Chopsticks from
the "William Tell Overture." So he traveled with a special aide
whose only duty was to give the high-sign whenever the Spanish
national anthem was played, so Alfonso would know when to
salute. Being a King's Anthem Man was the best occupation I'd
heard about since I myself had been Grandpa's Tin Can Swinger,
repairing umbrellas.

An American canning heiress steamed into Cannes on her yacht
and took over a hotel to throw a costume party. Aleck sent regrets.
He couldn't make it because he was entertaining Otis Skinner,
the distinguished elder statesman of the American stage, that
evening. Ruth and I decided to go anyhow, to uphold the honor of
Galanon.

Woollcott and Otis Skinner were having brandy when I came
downstairs in costume, on my way to the party. When Mr. Skinner saw me, he gagged on his cognac. I was "The Spirit of Toilet
Paper." I was bedecked from head to foot with rosettes of toilet-
tissue. The rosettes were spangled with official stamps of the
French government. (The saying was, you couldn't move your
bowels in France unless you got a government stamp first.) My
sash was a water-closet chain, with a placard saying TIREZ hung on
front, and I carried a roll of toilet paper like a muff.

Ruth came down to join me. She was going as a pregnant baby
doll. Before she could explain her costume, Aleck asked Mr. Skinner if he wouldn't like to finish his brandy out on the terrace, and
Mr. Skinner allowed as how he would like to very much.

It was a good party. With my eye-mask on, nobody recognized
me except Somerset Maugham and a guy I'd gambled with at

259

Monte Carlo, who got very drunk and kept following me around lighting matches and trying to set fire to my costume.

The next day our hostess steamed out of Cannes for New York. Hated to eat and run, she said, but there was a darling baby elephant on her yacht, and she had to get him home. She had bought the elephant in Africa for the purpose of pulling the lawn mower on her estate in Palm Beach. Let the Vanderbilts top *that*, she said. (Two weeks later, coming into the harbor, the poor baby elephant took one look at the skyline of New York and keeled over dead.)

When the canning heiress left, Daisy Fellowes, the sewing-machine heiress, steamed into port and took up the slack. Daisy had two yachts. She had a "decent-sized" one, with the displacement of a destroyer and a crew of sixteen, and a "dinky" one, which had a galley only big enough to serve a dozen voyagers. If Daisy liked you, she had you to lunch on the dinky yacht. If she *really* liked you, you were invited to dinner on the big yacht, after which you didn't get ashore for at least a week.

Daisy threw a series of parties in her "beach house"—a thirty-room villa in Antibes—at a hundred guests a throw. If a dame showed up with a gown remotely the same color or same design as hers, Daisy would disappear, then reappear in a dazzling new creation. One night she changed her outfit five times.

This Daisy was a charmer. She was like an Irene Castle with a French accent. Daisy would have been charming whether she'd been loaded with moola or not. It was just nice that she happened to be, like a chocolate éclair having frosting on it.

I remember once, as a party came to an end at dawn, she pursed her lips and rolled her eyes and said to those of us who were left, "You are all so talented. You write or dance or act or sing. But I do *nossing*." Whereupon Woollcott chuckled and replied, "My dear, I have heard different."

I was lucky enough to be invited to Daisy's big yacht. I stayed on board for ten days. The anchor never came off the bottom of the Mediterranean, but it was a very interesting voyage.

Elsa Maxwell barreled onto the Riviera to give a party under the auspices of the Monte Carlo casino. Elsa always had to do something different. Since there was no beach below the casino, only a shelf of pebbles sloping into the sea, she decided to give a beach party. She talked the casino into having a huge rubber mat made. She had the mat laid over the pebbles, and proclaimed it "Rubber Beach." The high point of Elsa's beach party was the entrance of Sidney Lejon and Gertie Sanford—not down the cliff but from the sea, on surfboards. Sidney was wearing white tie and tails and Gertie a shimmering taffeta evening gown, and as they swooshed onto the shore they were illuminated by searchlights while the casino band played "Over the Waves" from the top of the cliff.

The low point was reached not long afterwards, when Elsa's matting began to rip apart against the pebbles, and Rubber Beach became a sloshy mess, with everybody getting soaked up to the ankles and tripping over the shreds of rubber and bruising their knees and shins. It was a different kind of a party, all right.

The most exclusive soiree of the season was a dinner party at the Eden Roc Hotel. It was so exclusive that only Aleck, of our crowd, was invited. He gave the rest of us the needle for not being asked. We accused him, in turn, of turning into a social snob. Ruth Gordon and I decided we'd better go to the shindig too, so Aleck wouldn't lose the common touch. Naturally, we didn't tell him about our plans.

We crashed the gate of the Eden Roc by going in through the kitchen and apologizing to the chef for having goofed and taken the wrong entrance. Once inside, Ruth and I played it straight, and nobody questioned our being there. We were seated at a balcony table, with our backs to the railing. I could hear the sea washing the shore directly beneath me. Directly across from me sat Alexander Woollcott, who said nothing, only glared.

There was a waiter in scarlet livery for every couple at the dinner. When we finished the soup, our waiter came out with our second course, which was a whole poached salmon. The salmon was laid out on a bed of watercress on a gleaming silver tray, as lovely as an Irish corpse. Before serving it, the waiter lowered it between Ruth and me for us to inspect and admire.

I smelled the fish. I made a Gookie. I grabbed the tray from the waiter and heaved the salmon over my shoulder and into the Mediterranean Sea.

"Don't think I care for the fish," I said. "What's on the Blue Plate tonight?"

I got a laugh from everyone in the joint except the waiter and Woollcott. Aleck gave me a look of disgust, and I heard him say to the dame sitting beside him, "I don't know. I've never seen that vulgar person before in my life."

The society page of the next day's paper was given over entirely to the swanky shindig at the Eden Roc. Mlle. Ruth Gordon and Monsieur H. Marx were listed among the honored guests, but Monsieur A. Woollcott was not. We razzed the bejesus out of Aleck over this, after we read the paper to him. We must have gone too far. Aleck stomped out of the room. He returned with his poodle, Candida. He handed me the leash and said, "Kindly see to her comfort while I'm gone. She prefers her breakfast kidneys lightly broiled."

Saying no more, Aleck vanished from the Villa Galanon without a trace.

He had disappeared a couple of times before, that summer. It was after one of his disappearances, as a matter of fact, that he had brought the poodle home. We never bothered to look for Aleck when he went on the lam. He deserved to have a secret hideout, considering all we made him put up with at the villa. We were mighty curious, nevertheless, about where his secret hideout was.

I took good care of Candida during her master's absence. One day I took her along when I drove to Nice, and there a strange thing happened.

I was wandering through side streets, casing the shops, when I became aware that I was no longer leading the dog. The dog was leading me. She knew exactly where she was going. She led me to the door of a large, white house with shuttered windows.

A dame came out of the house. She and the poodle recognized each other. She talked to Candida in French and Candida wagged her tail—in French too, presumably. Then the dame spoke to me. I knew enough French by now to get the drift. Any friend of the poodle's was a friend of hers, she was saying, and wouldn't I please come in?

I went inside. The house was a high-class bordel, and Candida's lady friend was the madam. Candida had another friend there, too. In the whorehouse parlor was Alexander Woollcott, in silk robe and slippers, reclining on a black velvet couch and—I swear to God—being fed grapes by one of the girls of the establishment.

Whatever Aleck did, he did in style.

In the last two weeks of the season we got footloose and itchy and made excursions all over the map, following our whims. We would drive a hundred kilometers or more to hunt down a country inn we'd heard was famous for something like leek soup or *salmis* of gamebirds.

When Noel Coward wrote he was leaving London for the Riviera, we journeyed through the night to Paris to catch him between trains and give him a surprise welcome to France. I met his boat train disguised as a ragged, bearded street musician, playing a miniature harp. Aleck concealed himself in the shadows of the station to spy on the scene. What I had in mind was to latch onto Noel, playing as badly as I could, to see if I could annoy him to the point of calling a policeman.

Noel stepped off the train. I stopped playing and held out my hat for tips. Without seeming to pay me any special attention, Noel dropped a sixpence into the hat and said, "I've never seen you looking better, Harpo old boy. Now tell me where the devil Aleck is."

Our last excursion was to Naples, so Beatrice could pay one last visit to her favorite acquaintance in Italy—the *sensitivo* in the Naples aquarium. The *sensitivo* was a fantastic kind of shellfish. It drew into its shell whenever any strange object came near it, then poked out of its shell when the object was pulled away—all in a weird, synchronized movement. Beatrice could watch it and play with it for hours. The real reason she was so fascinated, she said, was that she knew a lot of people who were *sensitivos*. She refused to name any names, however.

Leaving Beatrice alone with her friend in the aquarium, Aleck and I drove on down the coast to Amalfi, to look for a cliff-top café we'd heard about. It was said to have the finest view of the Mediterranean sunset of any place in Italy. We found the joint and had a good time there. Aleck never forgot this little trip of ours. Five years later he wrote about it in *The New Yorker*. This is what he wrote:

> ". . . I fell to thinking of a sundown at Amalfi long ago, where you seek at the top of a cliff a restaurant once patronized by Enrico Wadsworth Longfellow. It is a sheer ascent of two hundred steps, and barefoot natives fight for the chance to carry you up in chairs. I was embarrassed by their obvious conviction that they would need relays to get me to the top. They were nervously managing the last twenty steps when I was aware that popular interest in their heroic attempt had shifted to the chair behind me, in which I knew Harpo Marx had been making the ascent. There were such shrieks of local pleasure that I had to turn and look. Grinning in the seat was one of the shabbiest of the bearers. Harpo was carrying *him* up. . . ."

Aleck neglected to finish the story, however. We reached the top just as the sun began to set. It was probably a gorgeous sunset, but I couldn't say. As soon as we got to the terrace we looked for the table the farthest away from the view, sat down, got out the peg-board and the cards, and started a game of cribbage.

Neither of us would admit it, but we were homesick. We'd had enough of the sea and the sun and the international life. The bam-bang-sock-and-pow part was over, until another summer. It was time to get back to the other side, the home side, of the million-dollar playground.

CHAPTER 16

Playground Condemned

THE VOYAGE HOME on the *Ile de France* shaped up to be a quiet, dull passage. It would have been just that, too, if I hadn't been undone by a good deed I did.

Everybody seemed to have blown his wad on the Continent that summer, and there wasn't much money on board. I happened to have a few bucks left, but the only action going on was a game of two-handed stud between an elderly Connecticut real-estate developer and a handsome young Brazilian. They made it plain they didn't want me in the game.

So I kibitzed. Right away I saw that the Brazilian was fattening up the American for the kill. He let him win a little at poker, then persuaded him they should change the game to craps. He let the old man make a few passes, then began to switch the dice on him and take him on a ride to the cleaners. It was very interesting to watch. The Brazilian was slick, but not too fast for me.

I got the old man aside at dinner and told him he was being swindled by the worst kind of shark, a dice-switcher. He thanked me and went to the Brazilian and accused him of cheating. The Brazilian challenged the real-estate man to a duel. He'd never been so insulted in his life. He put on such an act that the old guy wound up apologizing to him and turning on me. He said I ought to be reported to the captain for being a disturbing influence on board the ship.

The next day they were back at the crap table and the chips were moving faster than ever—in one direction, from North America to South. I was reminded of a fact I'd known for a long time: Nobody resents being called a sucker more than a sucker.

I turned my attention to pleasanter things, namely, the girls on board. I settled on a good-looking kid from Omaha who was a ball-bearing heiress. (And didn't Woollcott have fun with that one!) She was a lot of laughs and, since she didn't drink, a cheap date. I congratulated myself. It was going to be an inexpensive crossing. I would arrive in the States with almost all the dough I had when I left France.

Then, suddenly, my little affair became a triangle. Who should horn in but the old guy from Connecticut. It may have been the sea air, or he may have been sore at me still, but the old goat turned into a wolf. He puffed and panted after Miss Omaha and pestered her out of her mind. If he'd been twenty years younger I'd have clipped him one.

The Captain asked me to organize the entertainment for the last-night-out party, which was thrown to raise money for the Seamen's Home. Going over on the *Roma* back in May I had staged a hell of a show, with a big auction, and we'd collected a couple of thousand bucks. This time it was different. Everybody sat on their hands and their pocketbooks. Nobody volunteered to perform. Nobody offered anything to be auctioned off.

I got an idea. I would set up Miss Omaha in a booth and auction off kisses. Might make ten or fifteen bucks per kiss. Wouldn't raise anything like two G's, but at least there'd be something to turn over to the seamen.

The auction began. I should have known what would happen, but I wasn't prepared for it. The Connecticut Yankee sat down in the front row, leering and drooling. He made it plain he wasn't going to be outbid for a kiss. He got up to twenty-five bucks and nobody else wanted to go any higher. The girl said, under her breath, "My God, Harpo—raise the bid! I'd rather die than be kissed by that old wolf!"

So I made a bid of thirty myself. He barked back with fifty. I raised him five. He raised me twenty-five. I stuck with him, but at a hundred I got cold feet. Miss Omaha tugged at my sleeve. She begged me not to stop. Her pride was at stake, she said. So was her faith in me. I couldn't let her down. I didn't.

After two more rounds the guy up and quit on me. He hadn't counted on this kind of competition. So I won the kiss. What had been costing me nothing for three days suddenly cost me a hundred and fifty-five smackers. I turned the auction over to somebody else and went to my stateroom and straight to bed. I'd have to borrow cab fare from Aleck to get home from the pier. It was the most expensive crossing I ever made.

It was good to be home. The first thing I did was to get out my harp. I hadn't realized how much I'd missed the old monster until I touched the strings again. This had been our longest separation.

Frenchie cooked me a feast. Minnie and I swapped stories. She had to hear a full report on the Riviera, and she had to give me a full report on her poker club. It seemed a little sad that Minnie, who used to be fired up and full of fight over bookings and billings and special effects, had nothing left to talk about except her poker club. I asked her if she didn't miss the old life.

Miss it? Why, she'd never left it, she said. Right now she was working up a new act, a single, that she was going to push all the way to the Palace. "Who is it?" I asked. "Anybody I know?" Sure I knew him. It was the chauffeur. "Don't laugh," Minnie said quickly. "He's got a voice as good as Lou's ever was. Just needs a few dance lessons and a season or two on the road and he'll be ready for the Big Time."

Minnie didn't believe a bit of it and she knew I didn't either, but she loved the sound of the words. For a minute there she was back in fighting shape. Then her eyes lost their snap and, for the first time, my mother looked old to me.

My reunion with Chico, Groucho and Zeppo was on the stage of the 44th Street Theatre. Sam Harris had a new show for us, and I hardly had time to unpack my trunk before rehearsals began. The new show was *Animal Crackers*. It opened in October and became our third straight Broadway hit.

The only low note of the season was struck early in November by twenty-one million strangers, the people who voted for their Herbert Hoover instead of my Al Smith. Al Smith was to me one of the greatest living Americans. I simply couldn't believe the figures when the report came in that he had failed to carry even New York State. At what had been scheduled to be a victory rally at Yankee Stadium, but turned out to be a wake, I played "The Sidewalks of New York" on the harp. It was the only time my own playing ever brought tears to my eyes.

But these weren't times for sour grapes or bitter feelings, and the defeat was soon forgotten. Anyway, Franklin Roosevelt had won the governorship in Albany. This was one of the few Roosevelts around I hadn't met, but Aleck knew him and so did F.P.A. and they were pretty wild about him and said he was a guy to watch.

On Thursday night, November 22, the Woollcott mob was gathered at Alice Miller's. I joined them as soon as the show was over. I was ready for an old-fashioned, island-style evening of quizzes and games. But what it turned out to be was a surprise party for me. November 23 was my thirty-fifth birthday.

Aleck's present was the high point of the party. The present was a set of stationery he'd had printed up. The letterhead across the top said: HARPO DUER MARX. Beneath this were two photographs—"Mr. Marx at Home" and "Mr. Marx at Work"—from my Chicago days. Damned if I knew how Aleck had got hold of them. I hadn't seen the pictures myself for years. The final touch was a column that ran down the left side of the paper, entitled "A Few Tributes to Mr. Marx." The tributes were: "Why do we all love Harpo Marx?"—*Somerset Maugham*; "I was much embarrassed by Harpo Marx"—*G. Bernard Shaw*; and "Harpo Marx is one of the Four Marx Brothers"—*Percy Hammond*. Hammond, the theatre critic on the New York *Tribune*, was never exactly a fan of ours.

I had to thank Aleck in my own way for the stationery. He'd gone to a lot of trouble to have it made, so I should go to a little trouble to show my gratitude. A chance came a couple of weeks later, when Aleck dropped by my dressing room to walk me home after the show. I noticed that his black, broad-brimmed impresario hat was exactly the size of the comedy Spanish hat I wore in the second act of *Animal Crackers*—a ten-gallon, striped sombrero covered with gold and silver spangles and shaped like a volcano.

As we left the dressing room I switched hats on him. He didn't feel the difference.

I suggested we walk through Times Square. It was a warm night for December and a big crowd was out, milling around under the lights. This was a spectacle I'd seen a thousand times, but it never failed to give me a thrill. Tonight there was an extra added spectacle—Woollcott, the fat blinking owl in the opera cape, crowned with a hat as flashy and gaudy as the marquee of the Capitol Theatre.

Going up Broadway Aleck was delighted that so many people recognized him and smiled at him. It was the only time I ever saw him mellow enough to smile back at the public.

At the corner of 57th and Park we said good night. Aleck walked contentedly away, his stripes and spangles lighting up as he passed beneath a street lamp.

I thought maybe he'd never find out why he'd been such an attraction on Times Square, which would have been a terrible shame. But at three in the morning the phone rang. Woollcott snapped the familiar, libelous phrase I was hoping to hear, and hung up. He had just discovered I had switched hats on him. For all I know, he'd been walking the streets of Manhattan and smiling at the people who stopped to stare at him ever since we'd parted, at midnight.

I went happily back to sleep. Harpo Duer Marx had been avenged.

Nineteen twenty-nine was bound to be the greatest year in modern history. It began with a New Year's Eve party at the Swopes'. When the first day of January dawned, it was so beautiful out that we moved the whole party into Central Park and played croquet.

It seemed as if the New Year's Eve party never did break up. The inner circle of the Algonquin gang took to meeting every week night backstage at the 44th Street Theatre. From there we'd migrate to Woollcott's place or Swope's, to Ruth's or Alice's or Neysa's, and the fun and games would go on until morning.

There wasn't room for the gang in my place. I had moved into a new penthouse and it was already crowded—with mallets, balls, harps, paintings, plants, flowers, birds, fish, and piles of the rocks my poodle brought back from his daily walk. The effect was like jamming the Villa Galanon, gardens, animal life and all, into the old 93rd Street tenement. It was my kind of joint.

I could afford to live in this kind of style because the Marx Brothers had just been signed by Paramount Pictures for three movies—talkies, no less—for seventy-five thousand dollars per movie. Our first picture, *Cocoanuts*, was shot in New York that spring, between performances of *Animal Crackers*. "Shot" was just the word for it. All they did was point a camera at us while we ran through our old stage version of *Cocoanuts*.

Still, it wasn't as simple as it might sound for the producer, Walter Wanger, or the directors, Joseph Santley and Robert Florey. There were many long delays in the shooting, due mostly to the unexcused absences of Chico from the set. Since nobody had bought tickets to watch him, Chico figured there was nobody to squawk whenever he ducked out to consult with his bookie or play a few hands of pinochle. The trouble was, Chico would forget to come back if the action was good. Then Groucho, Zeppo and I would wander off looking for him. Sometimes Chico returned while we were gone, and he'd say the hell with it—if that's all we cared, he'd take the rest of the day off too.

270

When Santley and Florey hit the jackpot and had four Marx Brothers on the same set at the same time, and the camera got going, the shooting would be interrupted every time we started improvising. It wasn't that our ad libs weren't funny. The trouble was, Florey couldn't help breaking up. When he laughed, he laughed so hard he drowned out everything else on the sound track. Laughing left him very weak, so he would have to lie down to regain his strength before they could call a retake. This would give Chico a good chance to duck out to see how the action was going, which would soon send the rest of us out looking for Chico.

Wanger solved Florey's problem by having the directors use hand signals, from inside a soundproof glass booth. We still played to Florey, however. When he flew into a fit of silent convulsions we knew we had done something good. It was the weirdest audience we ever played to.

Then Wanger solved the Chico problem. He had the four cells used in the jail scene bolted to the studio floor. He had four signs made, one for each cell—CHICO, HARPO, GROUCHO and ZEPPO—and he had a telephone installed in the one labeled CHICO. Now Chico could call his bookie any time he felt like it, without bringing production to a standstill.

Between takes we were locked behind bars and the directors were let out of the booth. When shooting resumed, the directors were put back in their glass cage and the stars were let out of their jail cells. Too bad they didn't film the filming of *Cocoanuts*. It would have been a lot funnier than the movie was.

Summer came. *Animal Crackers* took a vacation. (This was long before theatres were air-conditioned.) The Woollcott mob's permanent, floating New Year's Eve party moved up to Vermont. Neshobe Island was even lovelier than I had remembered it, and even livelier than it had been two summers ago.

Fall came. The permanent party took the launch to the mainland, got on board the Delaware & Hudson, and played Hearts all the way back to the city. Another new season began in New York, another grueling nine months of all-night poker and all-day croquet, Round Table lunches and Long Island weekends. It was back to the grind of cooking up puns and practical jokes, needling Woollcott and embarrassing Kaufmann, and playing the newest party game—The Market.

There were grave responsibilities to face too. There were harps to be restrung, plants to be watered, poodles to be walked, and the decision on whether or not to take the Cubs over the Athletics at six-to-one in the Series.

The prospect of what lay ahead was somewhat changed, however. Sam Harris decided to take *Animal Crackers* on tour. We would rehearse a couple of weeks in New York, to get the show back in shape and break in the new people, then hit the road to Boston in mid-October.

During the last week of rehearsal the Marxes met for a rare family reunion in Zeppo's apartment. The seven of us hadn't been together for an evening for nearly four years—a lot of lost time to make up for. Frenchie spent the morning marketing and the afternoon cooking, out on Long Island. He arrived at Zep's place with pots and pots of our favorite food, still warm and steaming.

While we ate (and how we ate!) everybody caught up on everybody else. The state of Frenchie's wardrobe. (He could match the Prince of Wales, suit for suit.) The state of Gummo's business. (He was now a successful dress manufacturer.) What Groucho had had published lately. (His squibs and vignettes were appearing in all the big columns.) Chico's latest acts of generosity. (To his

272

favorite charity, the Impoverished Pinochle Players of America.) Zeppo's latest idea for an invention. (He was scheming and conniving to get out of show business.) My status as a bachelor. (The family never gave up trying to marry me off.)

The star of the evening was Minnie. Minnie was in her element. She had been having a little heart trouble, but you'd never know it. She wore a new blond wig, and the color and the sparkle of twenty years ago had returned to her face. She told stories we hadn't heard since 93rd Street. They had never sounded funnier. Then she got to remembering the one-night stands in Texas and the air-domes in Mississippi, and we worked off the dinner (we'd been eating steadily for two hours) by singing "Mandy Lane," then doing *School Days*, then winding up with seven choruses of "Peasie Weasie."

Minnie felt so great she was hungry again and damned if she didn't sit down to eat another dinner. Being loyal sons every one, we sat down and joined her.

To work this one off we started playing round-robin ping-pong—running around the table and taking turns with the paddles, trying to keep the ball in play. This was a wacky enough game anyway, but with Minnie shrieking every time she skidded around the corner of the table and her wig slid over her eyes, it knocked us out.

It was suddenly very late. Frenchie collected his empty pots. We all kissed Minnie as if she were our favorite girl after the nicest date we'd ever had, and the two of them left for Long Island.

Half an hour later, as I was about to leave Zep's apartment, they were back. Frenchie was carrying Minnie in his arms. She was in a coma. She'd had a stroke.

It happened while they were driving across the Queensboro Bridge. Minnie was complaining to Frenchie that she didn't feel so hot. She should have known better than to eat so much. Then she gave a sharp gasp and slumped over in the seat. Her mouth moved but she had lost her voice. Frenchie, for once, was in complete command. He didn't waver. He ordered the chauffeur to stop. He jumped out of the car and halted traffic in both lanes on the bridge. They turned the car around and headed back to Zeppo's.

The doctor arrived and examined Minnie. She was in critical condition, he said, but there was no advantage in taking her to a hospital before morning. Until then she had to be kept as quiet as possible. He wouldn't leave her side. The rest of us could see her one at a time, for a few minutes at a time, when he gave us the signal. Minnie couldn't talk, he said, and we shouldn't be shocked if she didn't appear to hear our voices, or even recognize us.

At two in the morning I was waiting for my turn to go into the bedroom. The doctor came out and said, "You'd better go in quickly. She doesn't need me any more."

Minnie's eyes were open when I came in. She was looking at me without seeing me. I called to her. She still didn't see me. I said, "I've come to pin the carnations on Mr. Green's cottage, Minnie." Then she saw me. She did the hardest thing she had ever done in sixty-five years of doing the impossible: she smiled. Her lips trembled. Her eyes were glazed with fear. But two tiny stars twinkled through the glaze, and she smiled.

The smile went quickly out. Her fingertips fluttered against the bedcover. She was trying to say something. I knew what she was trying to say. I reached over and straightened her wig, the new blond wig she had bought especially for tonight. The smile came back for a second. Then it faded, and all the life in Minnie faded with it.

I took her into my arms. I don't remember what I said, or thought. I only remember I was crying. Minnie was dead.

Woollcott came to Woodlawn Jewish Cemetery along with the rest of us, after the services in the city. He walked beside me, his hand over my arm, but he spoke only one word to me the whole day. During the procession to Minnie's grave, he stopped and pointed to a headstone that had the name KELLY chiseled on it.

"Spy," he said.

I probably laughed in spite of myself. But I was hurt, frankly, that this was all that Aleck had to say, that he had nothing else to offer me the one time I could have used some plain, common sympathy.

The next week I realized I'd underestimated my friend Woollcott once again. He hadn't been able to express what was in his heart during the funeral. That was no time, he must have felt, for a ham actor to speak his piece. He spoke his piece four days later—not as an actor, but as a writer and a friend. This is what he wrote:

> *A short history of the magician's daughter who was the managing mother of the Four Marx Brothers. . . . Last week the Marx Brothers buried their mother. On the preceding Friday night, more from gregariousness than from appetite, she had eaten two dinners instead of the conventional one, and, after finishing off with a brief, hilarious game of ping-pong, was homeward bound across the Queensboro Bridge when paralysis seized her. Within an hour she was dead in her Harpo's arms. Of the people I have met, I would name her as among the few of whom it could be said that they had greatness.
>
> She had done much more than bear her sons, bring them up, and turn them into play actors. She had *invented* them. They were just comics she imagined for her own amusement. They amused no one more, and their reward was her ravishing smile.
>
> She herself was doing sweatshop lace-work when she married a tailor named Sam Marx. But for fifty years her father was a roving magician in Hanover, and as a child she had known the excitement of their barnstorming cart rides from one German town to another.
>
> Her trouble was that her boys had got to Broadway. They had arrived. Thereafter, I think she took less interest in their professional lives. When someone paid them a king's ransom to make their first talkie, she only yawned. What she sighed for was the zest of beginnings. Why, I hear that last year she was caught hauling her embarrassed chauffeur off to a dancing school, with the idea of putting *him* on the stage. In her boredom she took to poker, her game being marked by so incurable a weakness for inside straights that, as often as not, her rings were missing and her bureau drawer littered with sheepish pawntickets. On the night *Animal Crackers* opened

she was so absorbed that she almost forgot to go at all. But at the last moment she sent her husband for her best wig, dispatched her chauffeur to fetch her new teeth, and, assembling herself on the way downtown, reached the theatre in time to greet the audience. Pretty as a picture she was, as she met us in the aisle. "We have a big success," she said.

Minnie Marx was a wise, tolerant, generous, gallant matriarch. In the passing of such a one, a woman full of years, with her work done, and children and grandchildren to hug her memory all their days, you have no more of a sense of death than you have when the Hudson—sunlit, steady, all-conquering—leaves you behind on the shore on its way to the fathomless sea.

She was in this world sixty-five years and *lived* all sixty-five of them. She died during rehearsals, in the one week of the year when all her boys would be around her—back from their summer roamings, that is, but not yet gone forth on tour. Had she foreseen this—I'm not sure she didn't—she would have chuckled, and, combining a sly wink with her beautiful smile, she would have said, "How's that for perfect timing?"

Aleck said nothing to me about writing a eulogy of Minnie. I didn't know about it until I looked through the copy of *The New Yorker* tucked inside the going-away present he'd had delivered to me on the train, the night the company left for Boston to start the road tour. The going-away present was an RFD mailbox, with HARPO DUER MARX stenciled on it. As always, he did it in style, a style that was Woollcott's and nobody else's in the world.

We didn't let our spirits sag. Minnie would have been furious if we had. Fortunately we had support from an outside source, the stock market. The market kept rising and we kept buying, on margin, to stay on top of the golden wave of prosperity.

I got my market tips from Groucho. Groucho got his from his friend Max Gordon, the New York theatrical producer, and passed them on to me. While we were in Boston with *Animal*

Crackers Groucho lost touch, temporarily, with Max Gordon. So he settled for tips from an elevator operator in the Copley Plaza Hotel, which he duly and loyally passed on to me. We spent more time on the long-distance phone with our brokers than Chico did on the local phone with bookies.

Our stocks were rising like the price of whisky in a gold rush. I was now worth a quarter of a million dollars, at the rate of $68.50 per average invested share.

After the week in Boston the show moved to Baltimore. The Baltimore papers began to report strange rumors about the market. My broker was cautious on the phone, all of a sudden. Instead of chirping, "Buy, buy, buy" he began to say, "It might be wise to commence covering margins."

A bunch of scare-talk. This wasn't a boom that was going to go bust. The market was a solid institution and I was being advised by the country's best authorities—Alexander Woollcott, Bernard Baruch, Max Gordon, Groucho Marx, and the elevator operator in the Copley Plaza Hotel. I kept on buying. My stocks kept on rising.

Our next date was Pittsburgh. We got into town on Sunday, the 27th of October. When the market opened on Monday, my thirty-five thousand shares were worth an average of $72 per share. But when the market closed their value had changed. The market didn't merely close that day. It got the hook. It flopped. It crashed.

Immediately a wire came from my broker in New York: FORCED TO SELL ALL HOLDINGS UNLESS RECEIVE CHECK FOR $15,000 TO COVER MARGINS. I hustled the fifteen G's together and got it to the broker. Now, I figured, I had survived the crisis.

I was wrong. The next morning another SOS came from New York. Same message. Same amount. Somehow I scraped it up and sent it off. On the third day of the week the third wire came: ADDITIONAL FIFTEEN THOUSAND DOLLARS TO COVER MARGINS. On Thursday morning Groucho gave up. He was completely wiped out. I didn't see him until lunchtime, when he greeted me with "Get your telegram today?" His laugh was hollow, and there was an empty look in his eyes.

I had gotten my telegram, all right. It wasn't just another SOS.

277

It was the yelp of a guy going down for the third time. The message was: SEND $10,000 IN 24 HOURS OR FACE FINANCIAL RUIN AND DAMAGING SUITS. MUST HAVE $10,000 REGARDLESS WHETHER I CAN SELL YOUR HOLDINGS.

In raising the dough for the three checks I had already sent, I had scraped the bottom of the barrel. I had liquidated every asset I owned except my harp and my croquet set. I had borrowed as far in advance as I could against my salary. My market holdings had shriveled to an average worth of one dollar a share. But this was based on quotations, not resale value. As assets they were probably worth a medium-sized bag of black jelly beans.

I was flatter broke than the day the Shubert unit died in Indianapolis. Then I at least had seven cents in my pocket, and I didn't owe anybody any of it. This was a lot worse. I had much more to lose. I had much farther to fall. How in God's name could I raise ten thousand bucks in Pittsburgh, Pennsylvania?

Zeppo had an idea. He told me to stop moping around the hotel. After the show, he said, he'd take me to the best source in town for raising the kind of dough I needed. "Leave all the arrangements to me," said Zep. "Only one thing you can do—bring along some burnt cork tonight." I was mystified, but Zep would tell me no more.

I had a hunch about the kind of place he'd take me to, and the hunch was right. Shortly before midnight we went on board a gambling boat in the Ohio River.

When I got inside I felt sick. The sight of gambling, after the way I'd been cleaned out that week, was too much for me. I told Zeppo I was grateful for his good intentions, but no, thanks. I didn't have the stomach for it. I couldn't even look a royal flush in the face.

But Zep said, "We're not here to gamble. We're here to meet a guy I know."

The guy was the operator of the riverboat, a pleasant fellow named Milt Jaffe. From the way Jaffe sized me up when we were introduced I could tell that Zep had briefed him about me and my problem.

We went into the lounge and talked for a while, about this and that. The subject of money never came up. Zep said to me, under his breath, "We've got to warm him up a little." Then he said to Jaffe, "I've got a great idea, Milt. Let's get up a game of Pinchie Winchie."

Jaffe was willing, but baffled. "Pinchie Winchie?" he said. "I haven't got anybody here who can deal that, I don't think."

"It's not that kind of action," said Zeppo. "But a lot of laughs, eh, Harpo?"

I agreed that it sure was. Pinchie Winchie! My God, I hadn't played that game since back in the old Chicago days! Now I began to see what Zeppo had set me up to.

Zep said it would be more fun if we got a fourth for the game, so Jaffe brought in one of his dealers, who happened to be on a relief break.

The rules were simple, we told them. I started by pinching the dealer, who sat next to me, like on the nose or the cheek or the ear, and saying "Pinchie Winchie!" The dealer then had to pinch Jaffe on the same spot, and Jaffe did the same thing to Zeppo. When it came my turn again I made a new Pinchie Winchie on the dealer, pinching or poking him someplace else, and the new Pinchie Winchie had to go around the circle, exactly as I had done it. We kept going around and around as fast as we could, until somebody made the wrong pinch and had to drop out. That's all there was to it. Silly, maybe, but it took a lot of quick thinking.

So off we went. We hadn't gone three times around before Jaffe was laughing so hard he damn near fell off his chair. The dealer chuckled politely. It was obvious he didn't think the game was *that* funny. In fact he gave the impression he thought his boss had gone nuts.

What the dealer didn't know was that I was palming a hunk of burnt cork. Every time I gave him a Pinchie Winchie he got a new black smear on his kisser.

By the time the dealer's face was smudged beyond recognition, Jaffe was too weak from laughing to stand up. Zep and I declared the game a draw, then took the dealer into the can so he could see himself in the mirror. The dealer washed up. Now that he was in on the gag he was dying to get another game going.

279

When we returned, Jaffe had not only recovered but had lined up a new victim, another dealer. The second game was better than the first. The two dealers hated to leave after it was over, but they said it was time for them to go back on duty. The hell with that, said Jaffe. He'd declare their tables closed. They stayed.

The Pinchie Winchie circle got bigger and bigger. Whenever a fresh customer came on the boat Jaffe would grab him off for a victim. Some of them were pretty tough-looking customers, gambling addicts desperate for action. But when Jaffe said, "You're going to play Pinchie Winchie," they played Pinchie Winchie. He was a guy they all loved and respected.

What a night he had! Jaffe was absolutely drunk with the game. Every round struck him funnier than the last one. Every time I made a smudge on some innocent guy's face, Jaffe would explode all over again, tears in his eyes, doubling over, stamping the floor and crossing his arms and slapping his back.

At two o'clock he ordered all gambling stopped and we moved our game into the main casino. By three o'clock the casino was a bedlam. There were twenty-some players in the circle. The latest victim, the guy I was smearing, was one of the richest guys around, the owner of a glass plant. The one before him had been a bootlegger, who was probably even richer. Around the circle, gamblers, dealers, shills, bouncers, deckhands, moonshiners and financiers were pinching, poking, jabbing and belting each other with wild glee, screaming "Pinchie Winchie!" and rolling on the floor and laughing like a pack of loons.

By four o'clock Jaffe simply didn't have the strength to play another game. His voice was down to a croak, his eyes were red from crying, and he was gasping for breath. With reluctance, he closed the boat for the night.

When all the customers had left, Jaffe beckoned me to come into his office. He closed the door, opened a wall safe, counted out one hundred C-notes, snapped a rubber band around the stack of bills, and handed the dough to me.

"Zeppo says you need ten G's," Jaffe croaked. "That right?"

I laid the dough on his desk. I had to be sure of what I might be getting myself into. I asked him what he wanted for security.

"No security," said Jaffe.

"What's the interest?"

"No interest."

"What do you want me to sign?"

"Nothing."

"So what's the catch?"

"No catch."

He stuffed the money back in my hands and said, "The one thing I'd like to ask in return is something I'm in no shape to handle."

"What's that?"

"Another game of Pinchie Winchie," said Jaffe.

Within a year I had paid Jaffe back the ten thousand, in installments. With the last installment I sent him a little gift. He wrote me a note of thanks, but he still didn't answer the big question. Why had he lent me, a guy he'd never met before, that much dough without security of any kind? It was thirty years before I saw Milt Jaffe again. Not until then did I learn the answer.

I left Pittsburgh broke but not ruined. I had a few debts to pay off but no threats of lawsuits, and I had good, steady work. I was one of the luckiest citizens in all of America. My Great Depression lasted exactly four days, the last four days of October 1929. When times got so rough that, as Groucho said, "the pigeons started feeding the people in Central Park," headliners in show business kept on working. I was lucky enough to be one of them.

So my depression came to an end. But so, alas, did the world I had lived in and loved for the five years, five months, and nineteen days since the morning a ham actor called me on the telephone and said, "The name is Woollcott." Martial law had been declared against us, against Croquemaniacs and Thanatopsians and

Sitters of the Round Table, and all the other over-aged children of our world. We were under house arrest. The sentence was the abolition of the 1920's.

Life would no longer be, ever again, all fun and games. The bam-bang-sock-and-pow part was over, and so was the permanent, floating New Year's Eve party. Our million-dollar playground had been condemned.

The hard truth of all this didn't sink in until we were playing Cleveland, Ohio, following Pittsburgh, and I got a call from Woollcott—collect. The fact that he called collect was the first jolt. It was his way of telling me he'd come out of the crash in worse shape than me.

His voice sounded strangely tired and sad. I thought: *Somebody in the mob has died.* But it was nothing like that. "I'm home alone with a terrible case of the cringes," Aleck said. "I'm calling you to make a confession."

I asked him what had happened. "Harpo!" he wailed. "Dear, dumb Harpo! Remember last spring when we took up a collection at the Thanatopsis to buy a present for the Hacketts' baby boy?" Sure, I remembered. "Remember, you all entrusted me to select the present and deliver it?" Yes, that too. "Do you know what I bought? Harpo, do you know what I gave the innocent little Hackett?" No, that I didn't know.

"I gave him a share of United States Steel," said Aleck. "I can never forgive myself."

That was when I knew it was all over.

CHAPTER 17

Hollywood Bachelor: Early Struggles

For three years we stuffed audiences with *Animal Crackers*, from Broadway to Chicago and points between, north and south. We had, to put it mildly, overexposed ourselves. So when Paramount offered us a new contract, which called for us to make pictures on the West Coast, we grabbed the deal and made our escape to California. The year was 1931.

On arriving in Los Angeles I checked into the Garden of Allah. The Garden of Allah, a collection of palm trees, bungalows and apartments grouped around a swimming pool built in the shape of the Black Sea, was at the time the most famous oasis in the stucco desert of the movie colony.

It was a hangout for Hollywood bachelors, actresses between marriages, and transients from the East like F. Scott Fitzgerald, Dorothy Parker and Robert Benchley. I considered myself one of the New York transients. After a picture or two I'd be back where I belonged, in friendly Algonquin territory.

However, along with a couple of thousand other transients, I somehow never got home. Without knowing what was happening to me I turned into a Californian—which I still am, after twenty-nine years.

Woollcott once described the Garden of Allah as "the kind of village you might look for down the rabbit-hole." It was a pretty mad place, all right. The night life in and around the miniature Black Sea kept the scandal writers supplied with more juicy items than they could use. But you couldn't prove it by me. I slept through everything. The shooting schedule called for me to be on the set at Paramount by eight o'clock in the morning, which meant I had to be up at six. It took quite a while for a city boy like me to get used to the farmers' hours they kept in Hollywood studios.

So my little bungalow in the Garden of Allah was a peaceful retreat. It was the best place to practice I ever had—until a piano player moved into a bungalow across from mine and shattered the peace.

I was looking forward to a solid weekend of practice, without interruptions, when my new neighbor started to bang away. I couldn't hear anything below a *forte* on the harp. There were no signs the piano banging was going to stop. It only got more overpowering. This character was warming up for a solid weekend of practice too.

I went to the office to register a complaint. One of us had to go, I said, and it wasn't going to be me because I was there first. But the management didn't see it my way. The new guest, whose playing was driving me nuts, was Sergei Rachmaninoff. They were not about to ask him to move.

I was flattered to have such a distinguished neighbor, but I still had to practice. So I got rid of him my own way.

I opened the door and all the windows in my place and began to play the first four bars of Rachmaninoff's Prelude in C-sharp Minor, over and over, *fortissimo*. Two hours later my fingers were getting numb. But I didn't let up, not until I heard a thunderous crash of notes from across the way, like the keyboard had been attacked with a pair of sledge hammers. Then there was silence.

This time it was Rachmaninoff who went to complain. He asked to be moved to another bungalow immediately, the farthest possible from that dreadful harpist. Peace returned to the Garden.

I didn't really know until much later how sharp my intuition had been. I found out that the great pianist and composer detested his Prelude in C-sharp Minor. He considered it a *very* Minor piece of work. He was haunted by it everywhere he went, by students who butchered it and by audiences who clamored for it, and he wished he'd never written it. After playing the damn thing nonstop for two hours I knew exactly how he felt.

The only other character who disturbed the peace that year was Harold Ross. One night I woke up thinking I heard a rattlesnake in the bungalow. It turned out to be Ross, who had just arrived from New York, shaking a cup of dice by my window. He was hot for a game of backgammon. We started to play. Every once in a while Ross would jump up and look outside and bellow, "Where are all those beautiful goddam Hollywood women I've heard so much about?"

I kept reassuring Ross that he wouldn't see any in this joint. The Garden of Allah was a home for quiet, clean-living bachelors like me. He snorted and called me a goddam liar and kept bellowing for the beautiful goddam broads.

I decided to shut him up. When he went to the can I telephoned one of the local madams and ordered her to send around three of her choicest call girls. The girls arrived half an hour later, and they were pretty choice, too. But Ross was not impressed. He was furious. He handed each of the girls a twenty-dollar bill and growled, "Go home, girls. Can't you see I've got a shut-out going?"

Shut-out notwithstanding, I took him for two hundred bucks. Ross could no more beat me at backgammon than he could beat Woollcott at cribbage. In the morning, when it was time for me to go to work, he picked up his dice and his board and stormed out of the bungalow, muttering that he should never have set foot in "this pesthole of pettifogging vaudeville actors and fallen women." The editor of the most sophisticated magazine in the country, *The New Yorker*, talked like the hero of an old-fashioned melodrama, and he meant every word he said.

285

We settled into Hollywood to stay awhile. Frenchie came west. He took a bungalow in the Garden of Allah and got busy putting together a California wardrobe and tracking down California pinochle players. Zeppo spent his time starting up an agency for movie talent, with the Marx Brothers as his first clients. This was such a good idea that he eventually persuaded Gummo to come West to be his partner, and Zeppo announced that he was through forever with acting as soon as our Paramount contract ran out.

Zeppo had his office on Sunset Boulevard. Not to be outdone, Chico, Groucho and I opened an office of our own in Beverly Hills and hired ourselves a secretary. Our office was over a real-estate brokerage, up a flight of creaky stairs. I was still a city boy who believed that stairs belonged only in tenements. Otherwise you took an elevator. So I preferred to do my business on the street.

When I whistled from down below, Rachel, the secretary, lowered my day's paper work out of the office window in a basket, on a rope. I then sat on the curb of Beverly Drive attending to bills and correspondence. When I'd finished reading my mail and writing checks and memos, I'd reload the basket and whistle twice and Rachel would pull up the rope. It was a very efficient office. I never saw it.

According to Ruth Gordon, who visited the coast during this period, Rachel had only three duties: (1) get book for Groucho, (2) get fourth for bridge for Chico, and (3) get girl for Harpo.

Our secretary's job was not that simple, but maybe Ruth had reason to think so—at least so far as (3) was concerned. Rachel kept a little black book for me. Whenever I had a date I'd phone in certain data afterward so it could be filed away for reference. My trouble was, as always, my memory for connecting names with faces. To me, Hollywood was still a town full of pretty broads all named Miss Benson.

I worked out a code, to save time and office work. Whenever I took a new girl out I reported her name, address, phone number and code category back to Rachel, who filed the information in the little black book. The code categories were "Coloratura Soprano," "Lyric Soprano," "Mezzo Soprano," and "Contralto."

Rachel never admitted it, but I think she cracked the code. It got to where I'd call for a check on a dame who'd been fishing around for a date, and Rachel would consult the file and report with pleasure, "Oh *yes*, Mr. Marx! She's a Coloratura Soprano!" Or another time she'd check and say, "I'm *terribly* sorry, Mr. Marx, but I have her down as a Contralto." My category of Contralto was for dames who turned out to like women better than men.

It was a great system, while it lasted. It broke down when I met a gal who was in a category all by herself. When I met her, the others could—and did—go to hell, and the little black book became about as valuable to me as a 1920 Staten Island telephone directory.

Little black book notwithstanding, I was working very hard during this period, both on the movie set and off. This was when I finally got up the courage to play the clarinet in public, and worked it into my act. Naturally, I didn't play it straight. What I did was rig some special tubing along my clarinet from mouthpiece to bell, leading into a hidden container of liquid soap. Halfway through a piece I would flick a valve, and bubbles would come out along with the music. This went over pretty well, even though it limited my clarinet repertoire to one number—"I'm Forever Blowing Bubbles."

Meanwhile other transients showed up from New York, and my old croquet partner from the Woollcott mob, Charlie Lederer, had resettled in California to work for the Hearst Syndicate.

There were croquemaniacs out on the coast, like Sam Goldwyn and Darryl Zanuck, but for old Eastern pros like Lederer and me the thrill of croquet was gone. It wasn't the same without the Katzenjammer Kids. The velvety greens of Hollywood were no challenge to us after the hills we'd shot over at Sands Point and the trees we'd banked around on Neshobe Island.

In Hollywood, Lederer stuck to Ping-pong, a game at which he was a whiz and at which he was quite a hustler. I turned to golf, at which I was not much of a whiz, which was too bad, because I was certainly a hustler at heart.

It was through Lederer that I joined a new kind of mob, the Hearst Crowd. William Randolph Hearst, Charlie's boss and the giant among American publishers, had gone Hollywood. His primary interest in the movies was the career of a charming young actress named Marion Davies. Miss Davies' beach house in Santa Monica became field headquarters for Hearst's Hollywood invasion, and it was there that I first met the Crowd.

Well, we didn't actually meet. My initiation was a costume ball to which I went, uninvited, as Kaiser Wilhelm. I won second prize. Nobody knew who I was except Charlie, who had smuggled me in.

It was fun for a while, playing Mystery Man to the hundred most famous people in Hollywood. But I had to cut out early, before I keeled over from suffocation and exhaustion. I must have been wearing fifty pounds of disguise: spiked steel helmet, bald wig, mustachios, nose and chin putty, uniform with medals and epaulets, knee-high boots, studded sword-belt and a three-foot ceremonial sword. When I got tired going around goosing everybody with the sword, I could only keep it from dragging on the floor by walking on tiptoe. Even more tiring was holding the monocle in my eye. My face hurt more than my feet did.

Charlie came to my rescue. He said he'd found a lift home for me with two of his "favorite people," who also had to leave early.

I rode off with them in a monstrous limousine. It was not very comfortable. I sat between husband and wife. They were plastered. I was sweltering, and I couldn't move. The spike of my helmet poked against the roof of the car. My sword was jammed against the bottom of the front seat. Now I knew what a pig felt like roasting on a spit.

288

Very soon I felt much more uncomfortable. The guy said to me, "We're sailing for Europe on Thursday, Harpo." His wife said, "Wednesday!" He didn't contradict her. He merely hauled off and socked her across the face. I caught it in the mush with his elbow. She hauled off and socked him back. I got a mouthful of her costume. I pulled down the visor of my helmet. But I still didn't feel safe. The guy and his wife were screaming such vile things that I got scared one of them might tear my sword loose and try to hack the other one to bits. This wouldn't be so healthy for me, since I was the battleground.

They fought all the way home. The chauffeur wasn't the least concerned. He told me not to worry. They fought like this every time they got tanked up, he said, which all Hollywood knew was at least four times a week.

I couldn't believe anybody could be as drunk as these two characters without passing out. When we pulled into the driveway of a mansion in a ritzy section of Beverly Hills and the chauffeur opened the limousine doors, I was sure they'd fall flat on their faces. But no. They ran into the house, her chasing him, slamming doors and still screaming. Now, I figured, the chauffeur would drive me on to the Garden of Allah.

But no. The chauffeur closed the car doors and disappeared into the night. I was stranded.

To make matters worse, the visor on my helmet was stuck and I couldn't raise it. When I tried to yell at the chauffeur to come back, my voice sounded like a belch in a bathtub.

There was only one way I could get home, which was three miles further east. I would have to hitchhike. There were no such things as cabs cruising Beverly Hills at night. I couldn't take a bus because I didn't have a cent on me. All the pockets in the costume were fake. There was no place to carry anything.

Walking was out of the question. I couldn't have staggered three blocks, let alone three miles, with the junk I had on me. Besides, I couldn't see so good through the slits in the helmet visor.

So I had to hitchhike. The sight of Kaiser Wilhelm in full military regalia thumbing for a ride at midnight on Sunset Boulevard stopped traffic, what traffic there was, but nobody stopped long enough to pick me up—until a police car came along. The police were very happy to pick me up.

For the next three hours, first in the car and then in the station house, the cops gave me a workout. One of the cops got a jimmy and pried up the helmet visor. He took a look at me, made a face, then slammed it down again. Everybody laughed. Very funny.

The cops thought they had me on every charge in the book. I had no money or identification on me: suspicion of vagrancy. I had caused delays in traffic: suspicion of being a public nuisance. When I explained why I was in costume and where I'd been, the cops said, okay, they'd telephone Miss Davies and see if I was on the guest list. I told them to forget it. I'd crashed the party. Aha! Suspicion of illegal entry.

I persuaded them to call Chico. They asked Chico if he had a brother who called himself "Harpo." Chico said he did. Did he know where Harpo was? He had no idea where he was. When had he last seen him? When he went to visit him in the Gloversville, New York, jail. What was the charge *that* time? Fraud, forgery and petty larceny, said Chico. What was Harpo's last known address? The cop repeated it as Chico gave it to him: "Happy Times Tavern, Merrick Road, Long Island, New York." Could he describe the brother? The cop wrote down the description: *Big mop red curly hair. Cross-eyed. Mute. Can't talk. Not too bright.* Only one item—the last one—checked out with me. Otherwise: Suspicion of being an impostor.

The cop thanked Chico, apologized for having disturbed him at such a late hour, and asked that he please cooperate in doing all he could to locate his real brother Harpo. Chico thought for a minute, then said, "Is there a reward?"

The cops, convinced they'd made the biggest haul since the capture of Geronimo, started to grill me. I promptly fell asleep, which proved that I was a pretty cool customer, all right.

They woke me up by whanging my sword on my helmet, and I thought, *I've had it—they've shut the door of the clink on me!* But I was still in the station house. Standing there staring at me was Charlie Lederer. He was shaking his head. He said, "Drunk again, poor bastard. All right, officer. I'll be responsible for him. I'll help him home and sober him up."

I should have known better. Charlie was too good a friend to be trusted.

I went with Lederer—an invited guest this time—for a weekend at the Hearst Ranch, up at San Simeon, California. This was a place you had to see to believe. When you saw it, you couldn't believe it. It was more like a mythical kingdom than a ranch. I wouldn't have been surprised if I had seen Ben Hur and Messala in their chariots racing around the formal gardens, Julius Caesar getting a rubdown by the Roman bath, Michelangelo touching up the paint on the chapel ceiling, Henry the Eighth sitting and burping at the head of the banquet table, or Robin Hood and his men swarming out of the hills to hold up the joint.

We got to San Simeon at night. We had to identify ourselves to the guards at the entrance before we could get through the gate. I found myself thinking I should have brought my passport. After driving forty minutes we arrived at the main castle. There a hostess met us and assigned us to rooms, like in a Catskill Mountain hotel. I slept in a bed that had belonged to the court of Louis XIV. What a shame it couldn't talk.

In the morning I couldn't find Charlie, so I followed the crowd to breakfast, and from breakfast to the tennis courts, where Mr. Hearst was playing. Lederer, the louse, was already there. I saw why he'd ducked out on me. He was having breakfast beside the court with a beautiful babe. I joined them. Lederer paid me no attention.

But when the phone on their breakfast cart rang, Charlie waved at me and said, "Answer it, Harpo, like a good boy." I answered it. Somebody wanted Marion Davies. I said, "Marion *Davies?* I don't know anybody here by that name."

That did it. The beautiful babe said, "Who the hell do you

think I am?" Charlie introduced us. She was, as I had suspected, Marion Davies. The only other time I'd seen her she'd been in costume, the night of the beach-house party.

Miss Davies and I got along fine together, and I was invited back to San Simeon many times.

One thing we had in common was a knack for gymnastics. One rainy weekend Marion and I practiced acrobatic stunts in the main library, after pushing a lot of junk out of the way. The junk included carvings of jade and ivory, silver chalices, and medieval parchments. We got a little wild sometimes and knocked a few books off the shelves, but we were careful not to break anything. Marion's diamond necklaces and bracelets kept falling off, and we kept picking them up, but as far as she knew she didn't think she lost any.

Charlie Lederer came by once while we were taking a break, getting our wind back. He picked up a book we had knocked to the floor.

"This is something even you might like, Harpo," he said. "You want it? Take it. What the hell—Mr. Hearst has more books here than he can ever get around to reading."

I was very happy to take it. Nice leather binding. Big print. Looked like a story I might get a kick out of. I stuck it in my pocket.

It was still in my pocket at cocktail time. When Mr. Hearst came in to preside over cocktails—the only time he talked to "minor" guests—the first thing he saw was the book sticking out of my pocket. "Where did you get this?" he said, taking the book away from me. I told him Charlie Lederer had given it to me. "Have you read it, Mr. Hearst?" I said. He nodded. I said, "Any good?"

Hearst didn't answer me. He put the book in his own pocket and walked away. I knew I had been chastised by the Master of San Simeon, but I didn't altogether know why.

After dinner I found out why. The book was a copy of *Gulliver's Travels*. It was a first edition, printed in 1726. Mr. Hearst had paid thirty-one thousand bucks for it at an auction in England. The next time I went in the library the books were all behind steel-mesh screens. The screens were locked with combination locks.

Charlie Lederer, who happened to be related to Marion Davies, was one of the privileged few who had the freedom of the Ranch. He got away with murder.

Once Mr. Hearst's guest of honor was the Governor of California. The first course at dinner was a fruit salad served in individual scooped-out pineapples. In the Governor's pineapple, on top of the fruit salad, there was a note. The note said: *If you know what's good for you, don't eat this!"*

Charlie's gag was not very subtle. The Governor of California was, at the time, getting threatening letters from all over the country for having given a pardon to Tom Mooney, the famous alleged bomber.

The dining hall in the San Simeon castle was grand enough to have suited King Arthur and all his knights and all their ladies. When you came into dinner, ten-foot logs were blazing in the fireplace and hundreds of candles were burning in giant silver candelabras. Candlelight flickered against the historic battle flags that flew from the beams, against the gleaming top of the seventy-foot-long banquet table, and on the little islands of glassware that dotted the length of the table. Each of these little islands was composed of a bottle of ketchup, a bottle of horseradish, a diner-type sugar dispenser, a water glass full of paper napkins, and pepper shakers in the shapes of Mickey and Minnie Mouse.

The first few times I ate in the dining hall I couldn't tell if the food was cold or not because I was so hot. I was a newcomer to the Ranch, and not an Important Person, so I was made to sit with my back to the fireplace. The fireplace was sixty feet high. It was big enough to park a Fifth Avenue bus in, and one dinner's fire consumed two whole trees. Every meal there was a race for me, to see if I could eat fast enough to make up for the weight I was sweating off.

I begged Charlie to use his pull to get me assigned to a new seat. Charlie kept trying. Finally the Boss relented, and I found my place card down at the cool end of the table. That meant I'd been accepted. I had passed the test of courage under fire and now I belonged to the Hearst Crowd. Now I could tell about the food. It was just as magnificent as the setting.

One weekend I was delighted to find that the guest of honor at San Simeon was George Bernard Shaw. The two of us had a great time reliving our days together at Antibes during the crazy, pre-Depression summer of '28. That was only five years earlier, but so much had changed since then it was like we were talking about events of the distant past.

Shaw cut quite a figure at the Hearst Ranch. Nothing about the joint fazed him. He seemed to be equally amused and offended by it. As dyed-in-the-wool a Socialist as he was, I don't think Shaw regarded San Simeon as proof that the Capitalist System was evil. He looked upon it as a monstrous freak: the biggest playpen ever built, stuffed with the most outrageous toys a child ever had to play with.

By the same token, some of the other guests at the Ranch weren't fazed by Shaw, either. One afternoon he and I were strolling around the edge of the indoor Roman pool. A blond dame, the bride of a well-known movie actor, was in the pool alone, riding on a blown-up rubber sea horse. When she spotted Shaw she splashed water toward him and yelled, "Hey, Whiskers! Come on in for a dip!"

The night after Shaw left there was a sudden snowstorm at San Simeon. Charlie and I watched the stuff pelting down onto the illuminated statuary outside the library window. We got the same idea at the same time. We scouted through the castle and "borrowed" ten fur coats from ten lady guests. We went out into the courtyard, through the falling snow, draped the naked sculptured broads with fur coats, and went to bed content that we had done a very gallant deed.

The effect in the morning was quite spectacular—the snow on top of the fur coats on top of the statues. There was another effect too. It was the first time I ever saw Mr. Hearst get sore at Charlie Lederer. In front of everybody, at cocktail time, he demoted Charlie to a seat at dinner by the fireplace.

March 1933 was a month of upheaval and melancholy. First, the unseasonable storm at San Simeon. Then the closing of the banks by President Roosevelt. A week after that Frenchie had a bad heart attack and was taken to the hospital, and the first day I was allowed to visit him was the day of the calamitous Long Beach earthquake.

While I was in Frenchie's hospital room one of the bigger shocks of the earthquake hit Los Angeles. His bed, which was on wheels, began to spin around the room. For some stupid reason I tried to push it back where it belonged, and wound up pinned to the wall. Frenchie was more worried about me than about himself. I told him not to worry. I never had it so easy, I said. Every time the earth shook my harp was home playing by itself. I was being saved a whole day's practice.

Two weeks later Frenchie was dead. It was a time of great sadness for all of his sons. We had realized far too late how much of what we had made of ourselves we owed to Frenchie. Over the years we had pawned his shears, gobbled up his delectable food without any thanks, scorned him for peddling lappas and for his lousy tailoring, and razzed him over his cockeyed card playing. But Frenchie never stopped smiling, and his smile was like a secret radiation. All of us who were exposed to it were affected for life. We had burned into us the meaning of loyalty and forgiveness, and of the futility of anger. I loved this man.

It was wonderful to find out that Frenchie's last day on earth was one of his happiest days. He had taught his nurses how to play pinochle, and in the last game he ever played he bid four hundred and made the bid.

In the middle of July I was up at San Simeon with Charlie Lederer. It was scorching hot. Charlie and I were lounging beside one of the outdoor pools. Nobody else was in sight. We were bored. We didn't know what the hell to do with ourselves.

Charlie got an idea. "What do you say we go drop in on Aleck at Bomoseen and scare the pants off the old fraud?" he said, and I said, "Let's go." I hadn't seen Woollcott for nearly two years.

Charlie finagled a Hearst limousine and we drove to the San Francisco airport. We flew to New York. It was a fast flight for those days—only three stops coast to coast. In New York we chartered a seaplane. We flew north to Lake Champlain. We hired a driver to take us to Bomoseen. At Bomoseen we rented a skiff and rowed to Neshobe Island. On the island we sneaked up through the bushes. We heard the *tonk-clunk, tonk-clunk,* mutterings and curses of a croquet game. We recognized the voices of Alice, Neysa, Beatrice and Aleck. Charlie and I took off our clothes. We burst out of the bushes onto the court, whooping like a couple of naked savages.

Aleck was reclining against his croquet mallet, using it like a shooting-stick. He glanced over at us, without so much as a flicker of recognition. He turned back to the game.

"Alice," he said, with a steely trace of annoyance in his voice, "it's your shot, my dear."

Charlie and I went back into the bushes and put our clothes back on. We rowed back to the mainland dock. We were driven back to Lake Champlain, where the seaplane was waiting for us. We flew back to New York, where we caught the next plane west. With stops at Chicago, Kansas City and Denver, we flew back to San Francisco, where the limousine was waiting for us. We drove back to San Simeon, where we stretched out beside the pool.

"Thought Aleck looked fine, didn't you?" said Charlie.

"Never looked better," I said.

"Never," said Charlie.

That subject being closed, we wondered what the hell we could do with ourselves now.

One reason I was welcome at the Ranch, I'm sure, was because I was an ardent New Dealer and so—in 1933—was William Randolph Hearst. But neither of us was half the Franklin Roosevelt fan that Aleck Woollcott was. Aleck took over the New Deal as if the whole thing was his idea from the beginning. He was a particularly good friend of Mrs. Roosevelt, and he flounced in and out of the White House like he owned a piece of the joint.

Early that fall he called me from New York. He'd just learned, he said, that President Roosevelt was about to carry out his campaign promise of recognizing the Soviet Union. That was nice, I said, and what else was new? Nothing, said Aleck, except that I was going to Russia. I told him he was crazy. I didn't even want to go to Winnepeg, Manitoba, let alone Russia. I liked California. I liked the sunshine. I liked the people. I liked the language. I intended to stay in California.

Aleck wasn't listening. "I've decided," he said, "that Harpo Marx should be the first American artist to perform in Moscow after the U.S. and the U.S.S.R. become friendly nations. Think of it!"

I was thinking of it. I was shivering.

"They'll adore you," Aleck went on. "With a name like yours, how can you miss? Can't you see the three-sheets? 'Presenting Marx—In person'!"

"Why the hell don't you go?" I said. "They love ballet over there. You could do your 'Itto Wabbit in de Sunshine' dance. They'll adore you."

"Listen, you faun's behind," said Woollcott. "I've already started pulling strings for you to get a visa. I suggest you be in New York not later than ten days from today." I made a nasty sound. "Besides," Aleck went on, "I haven't seen you for two desolate years." He avoided any mention of the unscheduled, hit-and-run visit Charlie and I had made to Neshobe Island that summer. He would have lost face if he had.

"Let me see," I said. "Where will I be ten days from now? Might be at the beach house in Malibu. Might go down the coast for a little fishing. Or I might just sit right here and watch the broads go by in their bathing suits. Anyhow, I'll send you a postcard."

Ten days later, of course, I was in New York City. Forty days later I was in Moscow. Woollcott had spoken.

CHAPTER 18

Exapno Mapcase,
Secret Agent

GETTING INTO RUSSIA in the fall of 1933 was not easy, unless you knew somebody who knew somebody in the Soviet government. In my case, Woollcott had reporter friends in Moscow who were on good terms with Maxim Litvinov, the Foreign Minister of the Soviet Union. Knowing somebody who knew somebody in the White House didn't hurt either, and my visa came through two weeks after I arrived in New York.

I had been busy in the meantime getting together a complete set of costumes and props—not knowing which of my acts they'd go for in Russia—and trying to work out an itinerary with the New York office of Intourist. After a couple of days of haggling, the Russians decided that everything should be worked out after I got to Russia. They gave me a letter to the director of the Moscow Art Theatre and wished me luck.

It was like heading for Texas to play one-night stands—no itinerary, no bookings, no dates, no guarantees. But also, this time, no Minnie either.

Aleck came to see me off, and gave me another letter of introduction, to the Moscow correspondent of the New York *Times*,
Walter Duranty. I couldn't be in more capable hands in Russia,
he assured me. Aleck also had a piece of "miraculous news." I knew
he was bursting to tell me something, but he saved it until the
very last, as a sort of going-away present.

"Harpo," he said, "I've come to the end of the search. I've
found her at last. I've found Miss Flatto, your female warden
from P.S. 69 or whichever school it was whose second grade you
escaped from."

"Yah?" I said. "No kidding? Does she remember me?"

"Can your ego suffer a blow?" he said. "Miss Flatto, alas, does
not remember Adolph Marx. But she will. We have a date for
tea, the three of us, the day you get back from Muscovy."

And so, with that to come home to, I headed for the Soviet
Circuit, aboard the S.S. *Albert Balin*.

It was a rough crossing, stormy all the way to Hamburg. Of
the eleven passengers on board, only three, including me, turned
up regularly at mealtime. It was hard to tell whether the others
were sicker from the rough seas or from having watched the captain
eat. The captain of the *Albert Balin* was a big Prussian with a
droopy mustache. His favorite food was sauerkraut cooked in
champagne, which he slurped up by the ton for breakfast, lunch
and dinner. When he got going good you couldn't distinguish the
sauerkraut from the mustache, and he was noisier than a leaky
bilge pump. It was enough to keep a sensitive passenger below
on the smoothest voyage.

I passed the ten days noodling on the ship's piano, playing solitaire, and wondering what the hell I was doing headed for Russia
alone, with a harp, a trunk full of props, and letters to two people
I had never met. Naturally, I was mighty curious about the place.
As it was to most Americans, the U.S.S.R. was as much of a
mystery to me as the other side of the moon. It was there. It had
to be there. But what it was like, I had no idea.

Old Russia had produced Tchaikovsky, Rachmaninoff, Irving
Berlin, and Chico's mother-in-law. You got the impression it was
a country where everybody sat around between sleigh rides, drink-

ing tea with raspberry jam, playing guitars and having friendly, loud arguments about which steppe or which swamp was the Garden Spot of the Earth. But New Russia? The impression was vague, from the little you could read in the papers—Bolsheviks looting palaces, driving tractors, and being shot by firing squads for making dirty looks at the Commissar.

Well, I consoled myself, Shaw had been there and so had Woollcott, and they'd come back in good shape.

I had planned to take my time getting to Moscow after we reached Hamburg, sort of mosey through Germany and see the sights. I did not mosey, however. In Hamburg I saw the most frightening, most depressing sight I had ever seen—a row of stores with Stars of David and the word *"Jude"* painted on them, and inside, behind half-empty counters, people in a daze, cringing like they didn't know what hit them and didn't know where the next blow would come from. Hitler had been in power only six months, and his boycott was already in full effect. I hadn't been so wholly conscious of being a Jew since my *bar mitzvah*. It was the first time since I'd had the measles that I was too sick to eat.

I got across Germany as fast as I could go.

On the train out of Warsaw I found another American, a guy who could speak Russian. He'd been back and forth from New York to Moscow several times, trying to drum up an export business in radios and spark plugs, and he knew the ropes. He asked me how light I was traveling. When I told him, he tipped me off that I'd have to pay for excess baggage at the Russian border.

Then he did me a favor. He lent me a hundred rubles, which I could repay when we got to Moscow. The Russians were itching to get their hands on American money, he said. He had a hunch I could save a lot of dough if I insisted on paying in rubles instead of dollars.

Some favor. Some hunch.

It was night when we got to the Polish-Russian town of Negoreloye, where we had to change to a Russian train. Everybody was ordered off and lined up by the border inspection station. It was freezing cold outside. It must have been thirty below and wasn't much warmer inside the station, a wooden shed with newspapers tacked over the cracks in the walls. When it came my turn at the Inspector's desk, everything seemed to be in order: passport okay, visa likewise. Good. I was dying to get on the train. Then the inspector handed me a form. It had my name on it, a lot of figures, and at the bottom, "Twenty-five dollars."

"Bog-gosh," said the inspector, which I interpreted to mean "baggage."

"How many rubles is twenty-five bucks?" I said, hauling out my roll of Russian bills. The inspector jumped to his feet and grabbed the money out of my hand. He yelled orders and pushed buttons. Bells rang. Buzzers sounded. Boots clomped all over the place as guards came running.

They hauled me off to another shed. The officer-in-charge, a goon with so low a brow that his nose seemed to grow out of his hairline, questioned me through an interpreter. Where did I get the rubles? A guy on the train lent them to me. What was his name? I didn't know his name. I was lousy at remembering names. I was lying, the Russian colonel said. Tell the truth now: where did I get the rubles? I gave him the same answer.

A squad of guards lugged my trunk and harp into the shed. "Open the trunk, please," said the officer. I unlocked it and the Russians began unloading it. When at first they only found a raincoat and an assortment of pants, shirts and ties, they were obviously disappointed.

Then they hit the jackpot. From the trunk they removed four hundred knives, two revolvers, three stilettos, half a dozen bottles marked POISON, and a collection of red wigs and false beards, mustaches and hands. More bells rang. More buzzers sounded. Whistles blew. More officials and more guards came clomping into the shed.

They started grilling me again. Would I please explain why I was transporting weapons and disguises? I told them they were all

302

props for my act. Act? What act? I said I had come to Russia to put on a show. Americans do not entertain in Russia, they said. I had better tell the truth. And I had better tell the truth about where I bought my rubles too. The law was that dollars and rubles could only be exchanged in Moscow. Illegal exchange was a serious offense. It undermined the economy of the Soviet Union.

Then they asked me what was in the harp case. When I told them, they ordered me to open the case and play something, to prove I was a harpist. This would have been my salvation any other time, any other place, but not in an open shed when it was thirty below zero. I was so stiff from the cold that I couldn't get my gloves off. All I could do was run my gloved hands up the strings a couple of times and pray that somebody there would recognize the professional touch.

There wasn't much to recognize. One of the guards ran *his* hands up the strings and got exactly the same music out of the harp that I had. The officials shook their heads and smirked. Then they got into a hot argument. I didn't need an interpreter to get the drift of it. They were debating whether to have me shot now or wait for morning, when the firing squad would have clearer aim and would waste fewer bullets.

I didn't know what the hell to do. This was one spot that no crazy stunt could get me out of. Besides, I didn't have any burnt cork on me to start a game of Pinchie Winchie with. So I began to yell. I knew my rights! Take me to the American consul! Was this a free country or wasn't it? I knew of course that I had no rights here and that there were no American consuls anywhere in Russia, which was not a free country, but I kept on yelling, because I didn't know what else to do and because it made me feel a little warmer.

Then things got a lot warmer. The officials settled their argument. They turned on me, scowling, and Colonel Low Brow said, "Take all your personal belongings and come with us, please." I shrugged, trying to appear nonchalant, but my knees began to wobble. The only personal belonging I cared about right then was my skin.

"Where are we going?" I said.

I never got the answer. My friend from the train, who'd been looking for me, walked into the shed. He quickly explained, in Russian, about the rubles. Yes, he had lent the money to me. No, I had not given him any American money for it. It was simply a loan to be repaid in Moscow. And where did he get his rubles? In Moscow, through legal exchange, during his last trip to Russia.

The officials accepted his explanation. Only at one point did they look suspicious, like they might throw the guy's story out the window. That was when he told the Russians I was a great popular artist in the United States. They had heard me play the harp. This was a great artist?

I paid the twenty-five bucks, American money, and got on the Moscow express. The train was unbelievably crowded, ten and twelve people to each six-passenger compartment, and it stank of disinfectant, but I thanked God I was lucky enough to be on it.

I woke up as we were coming through the outskirts of Moscow the next morning, and had my first real look at Russia. It was all gray—the city, with its acres and acres of unpainted wooden shacks, the wisps of smoke rising from each shack, the sky, and the snow that covered everything. It did look like the other side of the moon should look—gray, flat, and spooky. The spooky part of it, I realized, was not seeing tall buildings or telephone poles anywhere, only the occasional skeleton of a tree between the train and the horizon.

We began to pass factories, and electric lines appeared as we came closer in. It looked more like a city, yet it didn't look like a city at all. I couldn't figure out what was still missing, which made it seem spookier than ever.

Two minutes after the train came to a stop in the station, a Russian dame showed up in my compartment looking for me. "Mr. Marx, please?" she said. I identified myself and she shook my hand. "I am Comrade Malekinov," she said. "I am your guide and interpreter for the duration of your visit to the Union of Soviet Socialist Republics. Welcome. This way, please, for inspection of passport and visa." Her English was pretty good.

I had to look at her twice to be convinced she *was* a dame. She wore a man's double-breasted overcoat, which hung below the tops of her galoshes, a gray fur hat, steel-rimmed glasses, and not a smidgin of make-up. The only color on her face was the blue of the rings under her eyes. Her eyebrows were unplucked and so was a patch of whiskers growing around a mole on her chin. I had to study her for quite a while before I decided she was very young, probably not more than twenty-five.

While I was getting my things off the rack she said, "Any questions, please?"

"Yah," I said. "Do you mind if I call you Miss Benson?" She thought for a minute, then closed her eyes and nodded and said, "That is a joke."

"No joke, honey," I said. "I'm going to have trouble with a name like yours."

"My name is Com-rade Mal-e-*kee*-noff," she said, one syllable at a time, like a teacher talking to an idiot pupil.

We compromised. For the next six weeks I called her "Melachrino," which I could remember because it was the brand of cigarettes I was smoking at the time. On one thing she never compromised. In my presence she never once laughed or cracked a smile. Later, when I had Russians rolling in the aisles with my pantomime bits, I used to sneak a look at Melachrino, watching from the wings. She would be nodding her head with her eyes shut. I couldn't hear her but I knew she was saying to herself, "That is a joke." The nicest thing I can say about the Russians is that Melachrino wasn't a typical one.

We rode to the hotel in a government limousine that must have been a reject from the Stanley Steamer assembly line. Melachrino acted like it was her first ride in a car. She kept rubbing the cracked upholstery and saying, "Beautiful! Beautiful, beautiful machine!" I was more interested in Moscow itself, but the springs of the seat were shot and I was sunk way below window-level. The windows were frosted over solid anyway. So all the way to the hotel

I admired the back of Comrade Driver's head, which was shaved to the bone, and the cone-shaped vases of artificial flowers on the door posts—something I hadn't seen in a car since Frenchie's old Chevy.

I had been in a lot of crummy little hotels in my time, but the Moscow Nationale was the first crummy big hotel I ever checked into. The guy behind the desk saw that I was not too impressed by the looks of the joint. He apologized, explaining that a new hotel for international guests was being built, but wasn't ready yet. Ah, but it was going to be magnificent!

Nothing worked in the Nationale except the people. The heat was always going off, along with the hot water. The elevator was always "temporarily out of commission," and the telephone system kept breaking down. The only thing you could be sure of getting was ice water, usually out of both taps. But the service was overwhelming. While a Comrade Mechanic scratched his head and banged at the elevator mechanism with a monkey wrench, six women, all built like brick backhouses, carried my things up five flights of stairs, trunk, harp and all.

Naturally, I felt they deserved a fat tip when we got to the room. Melachrino was incensed. "The degrading practice of tipping is unknown in the Soviet Union," she said, and made me put the money back in my pocket. The dames who had carried my things gave her dirty looks and trudged back downstairs.

I started unpacking. Melachrino made no move to leave. I excused myself and went into the can. When I came out she was still there. What was the score? Was she going to be my roommate? I got the picture of her at night, curled up on the floor like a dog at the foot of my bed.

Somehow the idea penetrated that I wouldn't mind being alone for a while. She left, saying that I only had to telephone the desk when I needed her and she would be in my room instantly. With almost any other broad in the world this would have been a very cozy arrangement. But with Melachrino, Comrade House Dick had nothing to worry about.

I couldn't locate Walter Duranty by telephone, even with the help of the Nationale operator. So I decided to go out for a walk—alone—and take a look at Moscow. I didn't make it alone. Before I got out the front door of the hotel, Melachrino was beside me. She gave me a stern look but said nothing.

Walking down this main drag, toward the Kremlin, I realized now what was so eerie about Moscow. There was no roar of traffic. The streets were jammed with people, but nearly empty of cars. Whenever a government limousine or truck drove by, its sound was muffled by the snow which was packed onto the road and piled high along the curbs. It was like seeing a silent movie come to life, with no titles or background music.

Another thing I couldn't get used to was the sight of women doing all the heavy labor—women shoveling snow, chopping ice, hauling trash, driving trucks, working on construction with hods and wheelbarrows. They all looked alike, squat and round, their heads tied in scarves, their bodies bundled in layers of men's clothes, their feet swaddled in burlap tied with strips of rags.

Everywhere, in front of small shops and big stores, there were lines of customers waiting to get in. Unlike New Yorkers, Muscovites on line didn't jostle or gripe. They just shuffled quietly and patiently in the snow. Everybody in Moscow seemed to be concentrating on what he was doing, even when he was doing nothing.

Many people stared at us, but never with any change of expression. At first I thought it was me, so obviously a foreigner, that they were curious about. Then I realized that it was not me, but Melachrino. More specifically, they were staring at her karakul hat, unpatched overcoat and fur-lined galoshes, which marked her as a high-up comrade.

I wanted to explore some of the side streets, but my guide kept me walking a straight and narrow path down the main drag, which was, I believe, Tverskya Street. Once in a while I got a glimpse, through an alley, of what she didn't want me to see. Behind the stone buildings on Tverskya Street, on both sides, were awful jumbles of slums—rickety tenements, unglassed windows covered with lumber scraps, wrapping paper and tattered blankets, and in front of the tenements, heaps of refuse burning in the snow.

"You must realize," said Melachrino, "that this is only the first year of the new Five Year Plan. There is much to be done. It will be done."

From what I had seen of the Russians during my first ten hours in the country, I had no doubt that it would be done.

I got too hungry and cold to walk any further, and decided to do the Kremlin some other day. On the way back to the hotel, we stopped at a government clothing store, so I could buy something warmer to wear. There was the customary long line in front of the store. Automatically, I got on the end of the line. Melachrino grabbed me and took me straight into the store. "Party members and honored guests of the Soviet Union have priority," she said. The people waiting out in the cold didn't seem resentful when we bypassed them. Melachrino didn't bother to apologize or explain, and nobody made the least complaint. The only person unhappy about it was me. I thought it was dirty pool.

I bought me a fur hat, fur coat, and fur-lined galoshes, all for forty dollars. Back on the street, wearing my new outfit, it came to me why the bear was the symbol of Russia. The only way a Russian could survive the winter was to dress like a bear.

We had dinner at the Nationale, and it was pretty good—all the caviar I could eat, hot cabbage soup, boiled potatoes and boiled fish, black bread, tea, and jam. The jam, of course, was for the tea, not the bread. All during my stay in Russia, in all the restaurants I ate in, the food was pretty good—which means I didn't get tired of caviar, cabbage soup, boiled potatoes and boiled fish, black bread, tea and jam. The breakfast menu, which didn't vary much either, consisted of stewed prunes, hard rolls and coffee. Russian coffee was the only thing I couldn't take. It tasted like it was brewed out of burnt potato skins.

Again I had no luck getting in touch with Duranty. I asked Melachrino to come on up to my room and we'd kill the evening and have a few laughs. This was a new bit of English to her, and while she wiped her glasses she scowled and practiced it: "We shall kill the evening and have a few laughs. Yes, certainly."

Upstairs in the room she put on her overcoat and hat and sat on a straight chair—her way of warning me there would be no monkey business. I got out the harp and did a few warm-up arpeggios and glissandos. I stopped to stretch my fingers. Melachrino said, "Whose music have you played?" I told her it was Beethoven. "Yes," she said. "Certainly. Beethoven." I did some more warm-ups. "Whose is that music?" she said, and I told her that it was Tchaikovsky. Melachrino shut her eyes and nodded her head and said, "Beautiful! Beautiful!"

After a while I kicked her out, telling her I wanted to go to bed early. I was curious about something. Half an hour after she'd gone I went down to the lobby. There she sat, in a corner facing the stairs, overcoat and hat still on, reading a book. She looked up at me sharply, I smiled and waved at her. She nodded her head and, having seen that I was not dressed to go out, went back to her reading.

No doubt about it, she was a government spy. But that was okay with me. I had nothing to hide, nothing that the Soviet Union would want to find out. Still it was a creepy feeling, knowing that every move you made was watched and that every word you spoke probably went into a report to the secret police.

In the morning I talked on the phone to an English correspondent from Reuters, who told me that Walter Duranty was in Leningrad, and wouldn't be back in Moscow for another week. Before I hung up I said, "Okay, Melachrino, honey, come on up." The Englishman was puzzled. Nobody else on the wire was. Melachrino was in my room in two minutes.

"Take me to the director of the Moscow Art Theatre," I said. I handed her my letter of introduction from the Intourist people in New York. She read the letter and said, "Yes, certainly. Comrade Director will be expecting you."

I had decided not to wait for my American contacts. I'd get

the show on the road by myself. That's what Minnie would have done—gone straight to the local manager.

The office of the director of the Moscow Art Theatre was behind one of the proscenium boxes. It was the classiest room I'd yet seen in Russia: thick carpet on the floor, polished furniture, pictures on the wall. But it was freezing cold. Russian rooms were either overheated or underheated. This one was underheated.

The director read my letter. He didn't speak English. Through Melachrino he said he had been expecting me. But what did I do?

What did I do?

"Yes," he said, "what type of actor are you?"

"I guess you'd call me a comedy actor," I said. I began to wonder what kind of an introduction I'd been given from the characters in New York.

"Pantomime?" he asked me, and I said yes, I did pantomime.

The director said all right, then, how about me giving him a little demonstration. I would love to, I said, but I'd have to get some props from my hotel before I could do any kind of an audition.

"Very well," said the director. "Get your accessories and return tomorrow morning at eleven o'clock. We shall be happy to judge your performance."

So I came back the next morning with costume, wig and a hundred or so knives. The director had the rest of the staff with him, six or seven stony-faced characters who were a tough audience if I ever saw one. I got into costume, planted the knives up my sleeves and said I was ready for the stage.

"No," said the director. "Not on the stage. You will perform here."

I asked if somebody would volunteer to be my straight man for the bit. "No," said the director. "We must see you perform alone. To perform alone is the only true test of the pantomime artist."

So I had to play both parts, straight man and comic. I made some faces, winding up with a Gookie, then shooks hands with myself to start the knives dropping. The silverware fell to the carpet of the office, not with raucous clatter but with polite, soft thuds. Nobody cracked a smile. The room was deathly silent. Cold as it was there, I was drenched with flop sweat. It was the most miserable performance I'd ever given.

The director asked if I was finished. I nodded my head. He looked at the Stone Faces. Almost in unison, they shrugged. "You will please return tomorrow morning at eleven o'clock," said the director. He got up and left the office and his assistants got up and followed him.

Melachrino helped me pick up the knives. She made no comment.

The next morning I was there at eleven. The director said my juggling of the cutlery was not exceptionally clever. I said I could do any of a dozen different bits, but they wouldn't mean anything without an audience.

"I shall be the judge of what your acting will mean to an audience," he said. "You will please return tomorrow morning at eleven o'clock."

I decided that of all the routines I did, the clarinet bit would be the funniest without an audience. On my fourth visit to the Moscow Art Theatre, the Stone Faces were already waiting for me in the director's office. I had Melachrino explain that I was accompanying a girl singing, "I'm Always Blowing Bubbles," and they would have to imagine the voice part. I started playing the tune straight, then flipped the special valve on the clarinet and let the bubbles come out.

The director and all the assistant directors studied the bubbles as they floated through the room. When the last bubble burst on the floor, they looked up at me, grim as a jury in a murder case. Melachrino said something to them in Russian. They shrugged it off, whatever she said.

They had a brief conference. They sat staring at me for a while, then the director said: "We will let you know. Please be here tomorrow morning at eleven o'clock."

What I felt like saying wasn't translatable, so I said, "This time I'll let *you* know, Chief. Maybe I'll come back and maybe I won't."

The director got up and left the office and his assistants got up and followed him. Melachrino watched them go. She shook her head. "I told them it was a joke," she said. "Please believe me. I told them."

"Yah, thanks," I said. "You were one hell of a claque, honey."

The jig was up. I didn't give a damn who was going to be the first American to play the Soviet circuit. I only knew it wasn't going to be Harpo Marx. I told Melachrino to use all the pull she had to get me reservations out of Russia on the next train to Poland. I went to my room to pack.

I called the man from Reuters and a couple other correspondents I'd become friendly with, to tell them good-bye. All three of them begged me to stick it out. Not a chance, I said. The Russians didn't understand me and I didn't understand them. I'd never been so humiliated, not by the crudest, crookedest manager in the smallest-time vaudeville house in the sticks.

I was packed and ready to take off, waiting for confirmation of my train ticket, when I got a telephone call from a lady with a British accent. I missed her name when she introduced herself, and figured she must be the wife of one of the correspondents.

She told me she'd just heard I was in town to play, and she thought it was wonderful. I told her it had sounded wonderful to me once, but now it was all over, before it began. I was on my way out of Russia.

"But you mustn't leave!" she said. "You don't know how we're looking forward to seeing you. Whatever has made you change your mind?"

I told her briefly and as politely as I could about my four-day run-around with the Moscow Art Theatre.

She wasn't surprised. "That's not the theatre for you," she said. "You were sent to the wrong people."

Well, then, I asked her, where should I have gone? "I couldn't say for certain," she said. "But we'll put you straight. My husband will be back from Washington in the morning, and I'll see to it that you're his first order of business."

"He's got connections here?" I said.

There was a pause. Then the dame with the English accent said, "Perhaps you didn't catch my name, Mr. Marx. I am Ivy Litvinov. My husband, Maxim, is the Foreign Minister. I know he'll be terribly sorry he wasn't in Moscow to greet you. The conference with Mr. Roosevelt has lasted far longer than he thought it would."

I don't know what I said after that. I only know I agreed to put off leaving for twenty-four hours. Right after I hung up, Melachrino ran into my room. She was so pleased that she almost smiled. I couldn't tell, however, whether it was the postponement of my departure that pleased her, or the fact that she'd had the honor of snooping on a conversation with the wife of the Foreign Minister. At that time the prestige and power of Comrade Maxim Litvinov was second only to that of Comrade Joseph Stalin.

I stuck to my room in the morning, practicing the harp and waiting for the call that might keep me in Russia. No call came. After lunch I asked Melachrino up and I played "Waltz Me Around Again, Willie" for her. I told her it was Rimski-Korsakov and she said it was "Beautiful, beautiful, beautiful."

Still no call. I put the harp back in the case and told Melachrino to go check on my reservation like a good little spy. She shook her head and sighed, but off she went.

There was a knock on the door. "Come on in, honey," I said, "I'm decent." It wasn't Melachrino who came in. It was a delegation of eleven Russians, *smiling* Russians.

One of them, a tall young guy who looked a little like George Kaufman said, in English. "Mr. Marx? We are at your service." He bowed and all the rest of the delegation bowed. They looked eagerly at the trunk and the harp case, and my first thought was that they'd come to carry my baggage downstairs to the limousine.

Then the tall guy said, "Let me introduce your staff. My colleagues ask to be forgiven for not speaking English, but they too hope we shall have a long and happy association together." The names of the guys all sounded like "Bensonoff" to me. After I shook hands with them, the spokesman made the rounds again, introduced them by titles: "Producer. Director. Assistant Producer. Musical Director. Writer. Arranger. Stage Manager. Company Manager. Scenic designer. Assistant Director. I myself am a writer."

Litvinov had said the magic word. The next day I went to work—on the stage, not in anybody's office.

And on the next day, at 7:50 A.M., to be exact, while I was having my prunes, rolls and tea in the hotel dining room, Russia became—officially—a friendly country. That was the prearranged time for the pact worked out between Litvinov and Roosevelt to go into effect. The United States now recognized the Soviet Union, and the U.S.S.R. now recognized the U.S.A.

Suddenly, the whole complexion of Russia seemed to change. It didn't look so gray any more. It didn't seem nearly so cold out.

During the rehearsal period, Walter Duranty returned to Moscow, along with another American writer, Eugene Lyons. They were wonderful to me. Woollcott was right. I couldn't have been in more capable hands. No road show ever had two better advance men than mine, Duranty and Lyons. Duranty took me to meet William Bullitt, who'd been appointed as our first ambassador to the Soviet Union. The Bullitts had me to dinner. The Lyonses had me to dinner. Ivy Litvinov promised to have me to dinner as soon as her husband had a free evening. Seems he was sort of tied up with the Boss. Trying to explain some of the items on his Washington expense account, I figured. But obviously he had, as his wife had promised, made me his first order of business on coming home.

I felt like a heel for having announced, the week before, that I was going to take it on the lam out of Russia.

My show was staged in a small but well equipped—and well heated, by God—State theatre. We put on a preview performance for the international press, the big shots of the People's Culture Commissariat and the American "official family" in Moscow. Ambassador Bullitt was the guest of honor. We made such a hit that we had to put on a second preview.

Then we had our opening for the Russian public ("public" in this case meaning Party members in good standing who could con the Commissariat out of tickets). We were a great success. It went over twice as big as either preview. On the morning after, Melachrino read me the review in *Izvestia*. It was the most flattering thing written about me since Woollcott's piece in the New York *Sun*, back in 1924.

I knew I'd done pretty well. My type of comedy had been surefire with audiences from London to Broadway to L.A., and I had found that people laughed the same way all over the world at pantomime. I was confident and I was well prepared.

One thing I wasn't prepared for, however. I never knew any people who laughed as easily as the Russians. Maybe laughter was more of a luxury to them than to anybody else. Maybe they were starved for it. I stopped trying to figure them out. Walking the streets, working, or waiting in line, these were the most self-concontrolled people I had ever seen. In the theatre, the same people couldn't hold themselves in. Every move I made threw the joint into a new riot. The director of the Moscow Art Theatre, the guy who'd almost auditioned me out of town, still had tears in his eyes from laughing when he came back to congratulate me.

It sure as hell hadn't been easy to put my act together in Moscow. I had never in my life worked harder for an opening. The Russian sense of humor was a wonderful thing once you got it going for you. But how to get it going? That was the catch.

They had assigned me four spots in the show, which was to be sort of a revue. I decided I'd do a harp solo first, to introduce myself, and next do the clarinet-bubbles bit. In act two I'd do a comedy pantomime bit, and for my last spot I'd go back to the harp and keep playing as long as the crowd wanted more.

The part I'd have the least trouble with, I thought, would be the pantomime. Not so. It was the only part that gave me trouble.

The scene I worked out was the opening of *Cocoanuts*, with a few variations thrown in out of *I'll Say She Is*. I come to check in at a hotel. I tear up the telegrams and the mail. I decide I'm thirsty. I take a swig from the inkwell on the desk. The ink—after I've swallowed it—tastes like poison. I make a Gookie. I need an antidote. I take out a rubber glove, inflate it, and milk it. The milk does the trick. I feel great now. I jump on the straight man's shoulders and throw pens like darts until I hit a plaque on the wall and a bell rings and I win a cigar. Blackout. The second part of the scene was the old knife-dropping routine. For a local-gag finish, I dropped, not a silver coffeepot, but a miniature samovar.

The first time I ran through my bits, at the first rehearsal, the staff applauded the harp solo. They howled and clapped when the bubbles came out of the clarinet. But throughout the comedy scene, which I had worked on all night with my Russian straight man, they sat on their hands. When it was over they smiled politely, nothing more. *Oh, no*, I thought. *Here we go again!*

The English-speaking writer who looked like Kaufman lumbered onto the stage. "Your movements are extraordinary," he said. "But please forgive us. We don't know the story. If I may say so, the point eludes us."

"Point?" I said. "There isn't any point. It's nothing but slapstick. You know—pure hokum."

"Yes, yes, of course," he said, like he understood, which he didn't at all. "But may I ask why you were compelled to destroy the letters? Why did you drink the ink, knowing it was ink? What was your motive for stealing the knives that belonged to the hotel?"

I was flabbergasted. I'd done these pieces of business hundreds of times, and this was the first time anybody had ever asked me *why* I did them. "All I know," I said, "is that if something gets a laugh you do it again. That's all the reason you need. Right?"

316

Now the Russian was puzzled. He said, "No."

I said, "No?"

He said, "Forgive me. Perhaps it is different in your American theatre. Here you must tell a story that answers the audience's questions, or your performance will fail."

Well, what the hell. It was them that had to cover the nut, not me. It was their crowd I had to play to. "Okay," I said. "If you think I need a script, cook one up. I'll go along with it. But remember—on the stage I don't talk."

He gave me a big smile. "My colleague and I will write the scene," he said. "Don't be afraid. We won't change your part. We will simply give it a purpose. You understand, don't you?"

I said, "Yah, I understand," which I certainly did not.

So the Russian writers—I called them George S. Kaufmanski and Morrie Ryskindov—cooked up a script. They didn't fool around with any of my stuff, as Kaufmanski had promised. What they did was add three extra parts, a doctor, a dame and the dame's jealous husband. They made with the drama between my bits of business. What I had planned as two one-minute black-outs became a ten-minute, two-act play. My net working time was still two minutes. The rest of the time, while the actors declaimed, I froze—waiting for the director to throw me a cue to go into my next routine.

I had no idea what the doctor, the dame or the dame's husband were saying in Russian. I never did find out. When I asked Melachrino she said, "It is not important to you." When I asked George S. Kaufmanski he shrugged, smiled, and changed the subject. It was weird, to say the least, to be the star in a play you didn't know the plot of, or what a single line meant.

The writers called the rest of the staff in for a run-through of their Moscow Art version of *Fun with Harpo*. Here goes nothing, I said to myself. You just couldn't tinker with my kind of hokum without taking all the comedy out of it.

But I'll be a son of a bitch if it didn't knock them out of their seats.

It was the same way with the full house, the night we opened for the "public." While the supporting actors declaimed, between comedy bits, nobody in the audience stirred. Nobody rattled a program or coughed. When the dramatic part was over I could see the heads nodding out front and the eyes turning toward me. At this point I only had to wiggle an eyebrow to bring the house down, that's how ready they were to laugh. I didn't give a damn what the plot was about. It was a comedian's dream.

At the end of the show the audience stood and clapped and I lost count of how many curtain calls I took. The critic in *Izvestia* wrote that I received "an unprecedented standing ovation, lasting ten minutes." I wasn't timing them, but it seemed to me that the crowd never would quiet down and go home. Maybe they dreaded leaving the theatre, to face the icy streets and their drafty apartments, and figured as long as they kept applauding and I kept coming out for a bow they could stay warm.

No other success ever gave me quite the same satisfaction. Besides, it happened on my fortieth birthday.

What had been two weeks before a city on the other side of the moon was now my new home town. I got a hell of a kick seeing the posters all over the main streets advertising the show, and recognizing my name in Russian print. It looked like this: *XAPIIO MAPKC.* The nearest I could come to pronouncing it, from the way it looked, was "Exapno Mapcase."

So I was Exapno Mapcase, the Toast of Moscow.

The show played for six weeks in Russia. We did two weeks in Moscow, a week in Leningrad, a week of one-night stands in smaller cities, and a final two weeks in Moscow. The variety acts that filled out the bill were changed each week, along with the actors in my "play," but two regulars stayed with me, the girl singer and the straight man. The straight man was no Groucho, but he spoke High German as well as I spoke Plattdeutsch, and we could communicate, after a fashion.

No matter where we played, the Russian audiences never let me down. The only times I let them down were when I refused to do a third or fourth encore of "Rose Marie." During the winter of 1933-'34, everybody in Russia was singing "Rose Marie, I love you." The song had swept the country. Every act on every bill gave it a rendition. It was sung by baritones (for whom it was written), by male sopranos, and by female tenors—all of whom seemed to have mustaches and legs that would support a pool table.

I got the chance to see a few other productions, on nights off and afternoons when I had no matinee. Soviet vaudeville was heavy on acrobats, wire walkers, kazatski dancers, jugglers and trained animals. Actually, the People's Vaudeville was a watered-down stage version of the People's Circus. The circus was by far the most popular kind of entertainment.

I managed to see two legitimate plays. One was a Chekhov production at the Moscow Art Theatre, which I had a hard time following even with Melachrino's subtitles. The other was an antireligious play called "The Seventh Regiment Goes to Heaven," which was staged like a Shubert extravaganza. I had no trouble following this one. The obscene characters they made out of saints and apostles turned my stomach—and kept the rest of the audience in stitches from beginning to end. I have never been strictly religious, but the memory of this performance still makes me sick.

After I became a hit, Melachrino was suddenly a lot more relaxed, and I could now go off by myself almost any time I wanted to. One day when there was no matinee I ducked out and went looking for some kind of action. In front of a good-sized theatre, one I hadn't been in yet, there was an unusually long line of people. The line wasn't moving. No tickets were being sold. It had to be something sensational with this many people waiting for a chance to get in.

Since the day I bought my outfit at the government store I had become used to the idea that foreigners didn't stand in line. I went up to the box office and waved a dollar bill in the window. The cashier grabbed the buck and gave me a ticket. *Valootye*—foreign currency—worked like magic in Moscow.

The house was packed, and noisy. Most of the audience were

standing or walking around, chatting, drinking and eating. Others were sleeping or reading. I had apparently come in during the intermission. Yet the curtain was raised and the stage was lit. Oddest of all was the setting on the stage. There was a small table and a chair. On the table were two telephones, and a bunch of knickknacks. Behind the table was a large, tilted mirror.

It was the longest intermission I ever sat through. Fifteen minutes passed. Twenty minutes. Twenty-five. Nobody seemed to mind waiting that long for the next act.

Then a buzzer sounded. People damn near trampled each other to get back to their seats. In thirty seconds the theatre was silent as a tomb. Everybody was watching the empty stage.

A boy, maybe ten or eleven years old, walks out from the wings. He sits at the table. He picks up the receiver of one of the telephones. He listens for a while, then hangs up without saying anything. He moves one of the little props on the table. The joint is so quiet I can hear my wrist watch ticking. The boy moves another knickknack. A guy comes out, walks to the footlights, announces something to the audience, and the joint goes wild.

People jump to their feet. They yell and throw their hats in the air and embrace each other. The guy who made the announcement shakes hands with the boy and the cheers are deafening. This is absolutely the craziest show I ever saw.

Finally it dawned on me what I had been watching. A chess match.

The kid on the stage, I found out, had been playing the Polish chess champion and the Ukrainian champion, by long-distance telephone. It was nice to know the home team won, but it would have been nicer if I could have gotten my dollar back.

On the eve of his departure for Washington, the new Soviet Ambassador to the United States, Alexander Troyanovsky, gave a dinner party for the American colony in Moscow. The date was

November 30, and damned if he didn't feed us an old-fashioned Thanksgiving dinner. I must say a stuffed turkey with all the trimmings was a welcome relief from the endless caviar.

Troyanovsky went to a lot of trouble to make certain the dinner would be the McCoy, down to the last detail. The detail that gave him the most trouble was celery. His research staff told him there had to be celery chopped into the stuffing and celery stalks as a relish, along with olives and sweet pickles. The staff had dredged up sweet potatoes, cranberries and pumpkins. But they struck out on celery. As far as they could find out, with the help of the Ministry of Agriculture, not a stalk of the stuff existed in the Soviet Union this late in the year.

A diplomatic courier was dispatched on a special mission. His orders were to head west and keep on going west until he found a supply of fresh celery. He didn't find any until he got to Warsaw. He telephoned the Kremlin that he had the goods. At the border he was met by an armed guard, who hustled him onto a Red Army plane. At the Moscow airport another guard hustled him off the plane and into a limousine. The celery arrived in the Ambassador's kitchen in time to go into the stuffing.

It was a fine dinner and a grand gesture. We had recognized the Russians for only two weeks and already they were buddying it up with us like we were old allies.

All this made the foreign newspaper guys hopeful that they could start digging for their own news in Russia, instead of sitting around waiting for handouts. They had no reason to doubt—yet—that the Reds would live up to the terms of their pact with the U.S. In the pact they promised to encourage the exchange of ideas and information. They also pledged "to refrain from propaganda against the policies or social order of the United States."

The foreign correspondents rented an apartment in Moscow as a sort of cooperative clubhouse. That's where they spent most of their time, huddling by a feeble wall stove and playing poker, while they waited for the green light from the Kremlin that would permit them to get into Siberia. Siberia was the biggest mystery in all the mysterious Soviet. The Reds hinted it was a place of miracles, where factories, even whole cities, were carved out of ice

321

and rock. The Westerners suspected otherwise—that Siberia was a continental prison camp, where a million political exiles were used as slaves.

Ambassador Bullitt kept working at getting travel clearances for the reporters. The Kremlin kept promising they were coming through. But as far as I knew, no correspondent ever got to Siberia.

I got into a poker game with them one night. My luck was good, but I came away a loser. We played for rubles, not dollars, and Russian paper currency was so thin it would disintegrate after being handled a few times. It was the first time I lost at poker due to the money wearing out.

You could buy a lot of rubles for an American dollar, and if you spent them before they wore out you could get some good bargains. Cablegrams were a good bargain. I sent cables back home to everybody I knew, by the bushel, at approximately two cents per wire.

Some got through uncensored, some didn't. One which didn't get through at all was a cable to Woollcott: "HAVE GONE THROUGH TOUGHEST WICKET. NO LONGER DEAD ON RED. EVERYTHING BUCKETY-BUCKETY. EXAPNO MAPCASE." This must have kept the lights burning all through the night at the counterspy department of the GPU.

I finally got to see the inside of the Kremlin, thanks to Duranty's pull. (This was twenty years before the Kremlin was to compete with Disneyland for tourist dollars.) The exhibits there of Czarist treasures were fantastic. By comparison the Hearst Ranch at San Simeon was a collection of souvenirs from Atlantic City. In my wildest dreams I couldn't have imagined such a display of riches—crowns, jewelry, robes, coaches, all so dazzling they knocked your eye out. There was more wealth here, by American

322

с **18** по **24** ДЕКАБРЯ 1933
Только 7 ДНЕ

АРПО МАРКС

М. Д. КСЕНДЗОВСКИЙ

СЕРГЕЕВА и ТАСКИН

НАРОВСКАЯ

НАЦУИТИ

ИСАЯМИ

3 ОСВАЛЬД 3

3 НАСТЕЛИО 3

2 РУФ 2

Alias "Exapno Mapcase," I'm a headliner on the Caviar Circuit. Poster for a one-night stand out of Moscow, December, 1933. Below: A tender moment with Thelma Todd, in the movie *Horse Feathers*.

A most revealing scene in *Animal Crackers*. Below: Little did we know when we filmed *Duck Soup* (left) and *Horse Feathers* that we'd wind up featured on the Late, Late, Late, Late Show.

Penquin Photo

Innocent bystander watches Edgar Kennedy and small friend exchange slow burns, in *Monkey Business*. Below, *Go West*. Groucho: "Don't you love your brother?" Chico: "Nah, I'm just used to him."

Penquin Photo

"Chorus" (left) and "Property Man" in *Yellow Jacket*. My first venture into the legitimate theatre, which came close to breaking up a beautiful friendship.

Harpist and piano player compare notes at an Air Force base during the Korean War.

I sit for Salvador Dali. Below:
the result, one of the prizes in
my art collection.

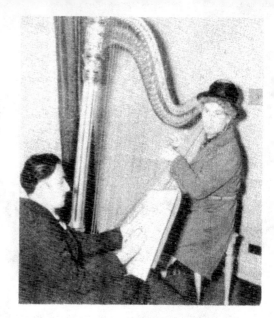

John Munn

Two canvases from my do-it-yourself collection. The clown is one of my latest. I painted the accordion player during my Early Chicago Period (circa 1926).

The honeymooners. Susan and I in 1936, not long after our masquerade upstairs in the firehouse.

S36 8=MA NEWYORK NY 26 101P

HARPO AND SUSAN MARX=

 701 NORTH CANON DRIVE BEVERLYHILLS CALIF=

1950 MAY 26 AM 11 07

DEAR HARPO AND SUSAN GIVE HIM MY LOVE=

 ALEXANDER WOOLLCOTT.

by WESTERN UNION

SQ193 12 SC=BZ NEWYORK NY

MR AND MRS HARPO MARX=

 701 NORTH CANNON DR BV=

CONGRATULATIONS ON YOUR SON. DOES HE NEED A BROTHER? WIRE

TERMS LOVE=

 OSCAR LEVANT.

The arrival of Billy makes us a family. Below, he visits his old man on the set of *The Big Store.*

Opposite page, from north to south: Jimmy. Alex, Minnie. Above, left to right between takes on *A Night in Casablanca:* Uncle Chico, Alex, Uncle Groucho, Jimmy, Billy, and the proudest father in Hollywood (holding Minnie).

Christmas, 1947. It was so much fun we couldn't bear to take the lights down and kept on celebrating Christmas all through 1948.

Family group, Beverly Hills. Jimmy is the Little Leaguer, Alex the Cub Scout, Minnie the Brownie, Billy the sophisticated teen-ager. Mom's cool smirk is due to the fact that she knows damn well this is the first time I've ever seen the inside of an encyclopedia, and who am I trying to kid?

Christmas, 1953. Mom says there *is* a Santa Claus.

John Munn

Where seldom is heard a discouraging word—El Rancho Harpo, 1960. The Marxes (from Jimmy, left, to Alex, right) and their livestock: three head of horses, two head of dogs, and one head of Siamese cat.

"... and the world is mine."

standards, than in the vaults of the Chase National Bank. By Soviet standards it was worthless, except as a bunch of trophies.

One of the Czarina's robes, which swept to the floor in a train, was lined with ermine and covered solid with pearls, thousands upon thousands of perfect pearls. One of the Czar's coaches had solid gold wheels. It was lined, inside, with gold leaf and studded with pearls and emeralds.

The walls of the Czarina's bedroom in the Summer Palace were covered, every square inch of them, with icons. Another room was constructed of pure amber—floor, walls and ceiling. Visitors had to put on slippers to enter it. According to the guide, the amber had been a present to the Czar from the Kaiser. In return, the Czar had sent the Kaiser three matched soldiers, magnificent specimens six-feet-five inches tall, for his personal use. How the Kaiser used them the guide didn't make clear.

In still another room I was surprised to see, in the midst of all the magnificence, snow blowing in through broken windows. The guide explained that street fighters had thrown rocks through these windows during the Revolution. He then pointed out what were to him the only precious pieces in the entire exhibit. On the carpet, on the far side of the room, lay the rocks the Bolsheviks had heaved. The rocks had not been touched since the day they had come crashing through the windows, sixteen years ago.

So many contradictions, so many contrasts! The Russians were at the same time the warmest and the coldest people I'd ever met, the most serious and yet the easiest to amuse.

During the show one Friday night I was surprised to see one of the stagehands wearing a *yarmilke*. Remembering the anti-religious play I'd seen, I asked Melachrino to ask the stagehand if it was true there were no *shuls* (synagogues) in Moscow. The guy looked at his feet, which were bound with strips of rags, and gave an embarrassed shrug. "These keep me warm enough," he said.

I realized Melachrino had misunderstood me. She thought I'd said "shoes." I corrected her and she rephrased the question. This time it was easier for the guy to answer. "It is true there are no *shuls*," he said. "But there are no pogroms, either." He wished me a good Sabbath and I wished him the same.

323

The day before the company took off for Leningrad a stranger came to my hotel room. He'd seen the show and he wanted to thank me personally for the pleasure I'd given him. The guy was unmistakably Russian. His clothes, just as unmistakably, were not. They had style, and they fit him. The suit he was wearing, a dark worsted job with a narrow red stripe, seemed strangely familiar to me. I looked at the label over the inside pocket. Sure enough—the suit had been made by Benham, a theatrical tailor in New York City.

Something about that suit rang another bell. What it was I couldn't dope out. I asked the guy, through Melachrino, how he came to be wearing clothes like this. A distant relative had sent them from America, he said. I asked him what the relative's name was. He told me. It was Chico's mother-in-law.

The suit with the red stripe had been mine. I remembered it now very clearly. I'd had it made by Benham during the run of *Cocoanuts*, and it had vanished, one night, from my dressing room. I hadn't reported the theft because I felt that whoever swiped it, whichever night watchman or janitor, needed it a lot more than I did.

I had to come seven thousand miles from home, to the heart of Soviet Russia, to find out that Chico was still the same old share-and-share-alike Chico of 93rd Street, who could smell money through wallpaper!

We took the day train from Moscow to Leningrad, and this trip was like a dream to me. The landscape we passed through was a continuous, miraculous unfolding of scenes from Christmas cards. Against an unearthly white backdrop, miniature tableaux flashed past the proscenium of my window. A horse pulling a *droshke*, the driver bundled in furs. A clump of pine trees hung with masses of icicles. A half-buried village, with the red onion bulb of what used to be a church poking up out of the snowdrifts. Children, little fur-balls of children, skating on a frozen pond, the smoke from their open fire rising straight into the windless, pale gray sky.

Thick snow began to fall, as if a curtain had been pulled to end the dream. I came back to reality.

There was a giant samovar at the end of the car. Passengers were serving themselves glasses of steamy, hot tea. I had a glass of tea, waiting hopefully for the snowstorm to stop. A guy came along renting radios. I took one. I put on the earphones. All I heard was the clacking of the train wheels. It continued to snow. I went to sleep with the clacking earphones on. I woke up when the attendant came by to pick up the radio. It was dark. Melachrino said we were coming into Leningrad.

Compared to Moscow, Leningrad was a picture-book city. It was a city of bridges, palaces, cathedrals and monuments, criss-crossed with frozen rivers and canals—exactly the kind of place you expected to arrive at after a trip through a Christmas landscape. I didn't see any slums in Leningrad, but then, I didn't have much time for sight-seeing. My advance men, Duranty and Lyons, had spread the word that I was one of Litvinov's personal projects, and I was wined and dined—well, tea'd and caviar'd—all over the place.

I did get to spend an afternoon in the Winter Palace, which was the scene of the beginning of the Revolution back on November 7, 1917. One wing of the palace had been turned into an art museum. I wasn't prepared for the paintings I saw in this museum. I saw Raphaels, Titians, da Vincis, Botticellis, Rembrandts, and an amazing collection of French Impressionists.

I couldn't help comparing the exhibit here with what I had seen in the Kremlin. All the time the rest of Europe was producing immortal works of art, the Czars of Russia had apparently been too busy hustling themselves solid-gold coaches to patronize any artists except the icon makers. Most of the icons I saw were pretty gruesome. So, in a different way, were most of the modern Soviet paintings. Maybe there wasn't a moral here at all, just the sad truth that the Russians were lousy painters.

We barnstormed out of Leningrad, playing towns like Novgorod, Malaya Vishera, Vyshni Volochek and Kalinin. This was the rough equivalent of making the midwinter swing from Fargo to Spokane on the Pantages-time. I say "rough" because it was even colder than Montana ever was, and I never saw a single poolroom.

The audiences couldn't have been warmer, however. I got a tremendous satisfaction out of going into the hinterlands of the Soviet Union, where no Marx Brothers picture had ever played—where, in fact, nobody had ever heard of any non-Russian Marx except Karl—and scoring a hit.

It was also satisfying to discover that in small towns I could cash United Cigar Store coupons, which I had a supply of in my prop trunk, for rubles—at the dollar rate of exchange.

Still, it was good to get back to Moscow.

It was a triumphant return. The house was sold out for every performance of my second stand in Moscow. I could do no wrong. I got so cocky I refused to play "Rose Marie."

After the curtain came down on the last scheduled performance, the audience wouldn't let me go until I played six encores. It was late when I got to the hotel that night. There was a message for me: "Please telephone Mr. Litvinov. Urgent."

Mr. Litvinov, when I called, said he owed me an apology. He was delighted to have seen me so many times socially, but he was deeply disappointed that he hadn't once been able to see me perform. The pressures of his office had been simply overwhelming. This I knew. Every time I'd been with the Litvinovs, at tea or lunch or some reception, he'd gotten a call from the Kremlin and had to duck out. Stalin kept the craziest hours of any boss a guy ever worked for.

Litvinov said he'd like to ask a tremendous favor of me. Would I—could I—put on an extra performance tomorrow night? Nothing

326

could stop him from seeing it. "Please don't misunderstand me," he said. "This is not a command performance. It is a humble personal request."

I told him I'd be honored to, as long as it was okay with the rest of the company. He laughed. "For the rest of the company," he said, "it will be, I'm afraid, a command performance."

At curtain time, the next night, there was one empty seat in the house—the guest of honor's. We waited. Then Ivy Lee Litvinov sent a note backstage from her box telling us to go ahead. Her husband had been called to the Premier's office, she explained, but he would be in the theatre in a few minutes.

We did the first half of the show. At intermission time Mr. Litvinov still hadn't shown up. We waited. The audience, as Russians were apt to do whenever there was a delay in a theatre, turned the intermission into a party. They walked around in small groups, gossiping and arguing, drinking tea and vodka and eating snacks.

After an hour passed, Litvinov appeared in his box, smiling and making apologetic gestures. The audience cheered him and went quickly to their seats.

It was the best house I had yet played to in Russia. I think I gave them their money's worth. I couldn't tell from the stage, however, whether the Foreign Minister was enjoying the performance or not. When I came out for my first encore my heart sank. The guest of honor's box was empty. Litvinov was gone and so was his wife. I attacked the harp without much enthusiasm.

When I finished the piece, I noticed there was something peculiar about the audience. They were applauding but they weren't looking at me. They were looking at Comrade Maxim Litvinov. He was standing onstage, just behind me. He came over to me, put an arm on my shoulder and made a brief speech, in Russian. Then he turned to me and said, "You have given us precious moments of pleasure, Harpo. We shall be forever indebted to you. On behalf of the U.S.S.R. I thank you."

He held forth his hand. I shook it. A cascade of steel knives tumbled out of his sleeve and clanked to the stage.

The audience exploded with one great shriek. It was the biggest laugh this bit ever got. The only time I ever played the straight man, I got my biggest laugh. And my comic was the Foreign Minister of the Soviet Union.

On the morning of my last day in Moscow Walter Duranty telephoned to ask if I would please meet him at the Embassy. The Ambassador would like to say good-bye to me.

In Mr. Bullitt's private office the three of us drank coffee—good, American coffee—and talked about this and that. At one point Bullitt said, casually, "Harpo, could you do me a favor? I'd like these delivered back to the States, in person." He held up a thin packet of letters tied with string.

I said I'd be glad to. I reached for the letters. Bullitt didn't let me have them.

"It's not as simple as you might think," he said. "This packet must get to New York undetected. No one—no one—must know you have it. It will be strapped to your leg, under your sock. You still want to do it?"

Sure I still did. Why not? Nobody would ever suspect me of being a diplomatic courier. Exactly why he was asking me to do this little service, Bullitt said. "So who do you want it delivered to?" I asked, and he said I didn't have to worry about that. I would be contacted as soon as I got home.

"Okay," I said. "Strap me up."

We bound the packet to the inside of my right leg and secured the straps with adhesive tape. "Just forget you're carrying it," said the Ambassador. "Except," he added, "when you go in the shower."

He thanked me, wished me bon voyage, and we said good-bye. Duranty dropped me off at the hotel. Melachrino was waiting in the corridor outside my room. Boy, oh boy! I thought. Wouldn't she pop her cork off if she knew that I was now a secret agent too!

"Honey," I said. "I forgot to tell you something. I'm also a spy. I'm smuggling the designs for the Ford tractor out of Russia."

She closed her eyes and nodded her head. "That is a joke," she said, and I agreed. It wasn't very good, but it was a joke.

Melachrino took off her overcoat, her galoshes, her karakul hat, and her glasses, and sat to watch me finish packing. It was the coziest she had ever been with me. I gave her a big, dirty wink. She quickly put her glasses on, and that was the end of our intimate affair.

She watched intently while I packed the presents I'd bought to take home. It was quite a haul: several pairs of black leather gloves, replicas of the Czarina's crest, silver tea-glass holders, teaspoons and cigarette cases, icons, chess sets, peasant embroideries, carving sets with ivory handles, fur hats and fur-lined boots.

I felt guilty. I hadn't bought a thing for Melachrino. "Hey, Spy!" I said. "I want you to have something for a souvenir. What would you like? Anything in the trunk—you name it."

She shook her head. "I have everything I shall ever want," she said. "I cannot accept gifts, thank you." She got up and ran her fingers caressingly down the wall of the hotel room. "You see?" she said. "This is as much mine as anybody else's. This is my gift."

She said it with defiance. Yet she sounded wistful too, and gave herself away. Tomorrow, when I was gone, she'd be back in her chilly flat and back in the routine of whatever dreary office she worked out of. No more luxuries of the Hotel Nationale, limousines, diplomatic receptions, trips to Leningrad, or backstage chats with big shots from the Kremlin.

I closed the trunk. Melachrino put on her hat, overcoat and galoshes and shook hands with me. She had, apparently, completed her mental inventory of everything I was taking back, the details for her final report. Beyond this she had nothing further to do.

329

"Good-bye, Mr. Marx," she said.

"Dahsvedahnya, honey," I said, and she said, "It has been a great number of laughs." I closed my eyes and nodded and she marched out of the room to her next assignment.

That afternoon Eugene Lyons and his wife came to say good-bye. They insisted on driving me over to Pushkin Square and having me do the knife-dropping bit by the statue of Pushkin. Then, for the Soviet cameramen, I stuffed knives up the sleeves of the statue and they photographed Pushkin doing my act.

Later, Duranty and a guy from the Embassy came to take me to the train. The harp and the trunk had gone on ahead, lugged out of the hotel room by the usual platoon of squatty women wearing *babushkas* and surplus uniforms from the army of Genghis Khan.

In the station Duranty said it might amuse me to know that the *Izvestia* critic who reviewed my Moscow opening had just been executed for a crime against the State. But he hadn't been shot for raving about my decadent, bourgeois comedy. He'd been shot for making an illegal exchange of rubles and *valootye*.

Until Duranty told me that, I had actually forgotten about the packet of letters strapped to my right leg. Now it felt like a manacle. When the Poland express pulled out of the station I was thinking of nothing else. So I really had had a close shave at the border, that night I entered Russia. I was clutched by a sudden chill. What if Low Brow and his crew were on duty when I crossed over on the way out, and they recognized me? Suppose they gave me a working over, just for old time's sake? What would happen when they found what was hidden on me? God Almighty! What had Woollcott gotten me into?

I could hear myself saying to Melachrino, eight hours earlier, "Yah, it's a joke, honey." Some joke. I was scared. I was so scared I fell asleep and slept through the dinner hour.

The next thing I heard was a gruff voice saying, "Marx! Marx! *Tovarich* Marx!" I opened my eyes. It was daylight. The train was stopped. The voice belonged to a Red soldier of the border guard. I recognized him from two months ago, and he recognized me. He jerked his head to signify I should come with him. I put on my coat and hat, took down my suitcase, and followed him off the train.

By this time most of the other passengers were lined up by the inspection station, waiting to have their papers checked. I asked the guard, in pantomime, if I hadn't better get on line. He told me, in the same language, "No." He led me into the station. There, waiting for me, was my old friend Colonel Low Brow.

"Your passport, please," he said through his interpreter. I handed over my passport. Low Brow gave it to a soldier, who disappeared with it.

The colonel said, "Please come with me to headquarters."

I couldn't think straight. I may have walked straight, but I felt like a seasick unicyclist condemned to ride the deck of a ship in a storm. We came to headquarters. Low Brow opened the door and motioned me to go in. I went in. Waiting for me, standing in the middle of the office, was a Red officer who must have been at least a field marshal, a beefy guy decorated with an equal number of scars and stars. He was squinting hard at me and grinding his teeth.

I said, "Any of you fellows know any verses to 'Peasie Weasie'?" The general looked at the colonel. The colonel looked at the interpreter. The interpreter said, "Please?" I didn't answer him. I couldn't.

The general broke into a diabolical grin, which with all the scars on his face looked like a map of the Rock Island Railroad. He grunted and waved toward a table on the other side of the office. On the table, around a hot samovar, were bottles of wine and vodka, stacks of bread, pots of sour cream, and platters of caviar, herring, sausages, pickles and *piroshki*.

The general issued an order. "Eat," he said. "It's your last chance. In Poland they eat like pigs."

With no further ado the general obeyed his own order. That's

331

why he'd been grinding his teeth. He couldn't wait. In fifteen minutes he had consumed half the goodies on the table, washed down with half a bottle of vodka. I didn't do too badly either, having missed dinner on the train.

Colonel Low Brow reassured me, while I was eating, that my papers and baggage were being processed by his men. An honored guest of the Soviet Union, he said, must not be permitted to wait in line. When three other officers came into headquarters they were surprised to see me there. The colonel set them straight on who I was. I could recognize the words "*Tovarich Marx*" and "*Tovarich Litvinov.*" Name dropper.

A soldier brought in my papers, and the interpreter said, "It's train time, please." The general licked sour cream off his fingers and waved me good-bye. The other officers crunched my hand, one by one, and I was escorted over to the Warsaw express. I was stuffed and groggy when I plopped onto my seat. I had nothing to be scared of now, I told myself, but a delayed reaction set in and I began to shake. Knowing no other cure for my condition, I shook myself to sleep.

If the trip from Moscow to Leningrad had been a dream, the trip from Moscow to New York was a nightmare, every kilometer of the way. I had originally planned to stop over in Paris for a week or so, then hop over to London to meet Chico, who was due there in the middle of January to do a series of appearances.

My secret mission changed my plans considerably. I stopped only when I absolutely had to, and for no longer than it took to change trains. I was so conscious of what I was carrying under my sock that I favored my right leg, without thinking, and I caught myself walking with a limp. I'd always been an inconspicuous type guy offstage, but now people seemed to stare at me as if I had forgotten to put my pants on.

It was amazing how many counterespionage agents I could

identify, by their dark looks and shifty movements, on trains and in stations. I must have spotted altogether six hundred agents, give or take half a dozen. The most dangerous ones, I knew, were not the dark and shifty characters. They were too obvious. The ones to watch were the characters like the guy who rushed up to me between trains, slapped me on the back and said, "*Hey*, boy! Am I glad to see another Yankee Doodle Dandy! Are you comin' or goin'?" I was goin'. I got away from him fast. Pretty clever, trying to throw me off my guard like that. But not old Mapcase. I was onto his game.

The ocean crossing took seven days, according to the records of the French Line. According to me it took seven months.

I laid down a strict rule when the boat left Le Havre. I must leave the stateroom only to eat, and for no other reason. But after the second day out I overruled myself. It was a choice of getting caught or going stir-crazy. For two days I did nothing except play solitaire and make bets with myself on how long it would be before the ship hit another big wave. When I found myself checking the papers on my leg every time I turned up a face card, I knew I was going nuts.

I got to brooding about those eight weeks in Russia. Even after I had become a local celebrity in Moscow I couldn't shake off the awful feeling (it hits you in the pit of the stomach) that I was being watched wherever I went, by eyes I couldn't see. I never, not for a minute, felt I was really alone. I was a stranger who had stumbled into a deadly conspiracy, who had to be kept from finding out what the plot was all about. The worst part of it was knowing that, if I wasn't within hollering distance of the American Embassy, I had nobody to turn to for help. I couldn't call a cop or a lawyer, or complain to the government, or appeal to the guys I was working with. They were all part of the plot, every last one of them. The actors as much as everybody in the audience. The charming Litvinovs as much as the unsmiling Melachrino and the scar-faced general at the border. The devout Jewish stagehand as much as Comrade Stalin.

What tipped me off to the Russians were the things I admired them for at first, their ability to concentrate, their frank curiosity, their enthusiasm in the theatre, their capacity for hard work, their respect for regulations. Wonderful qualities, but deadly—deadly because I did not come across, among the thousands of Russians I saw, one screwball, one crackpot, one wise guy, one loafer, or one sorehead. I never saw anybody do anything just for the hell of it. I never saw anybody pull a spontaneous gag.

Like George S. Kaufmanski had said, a bit wasn't funny merely because it got a laugh. It had to have a reason to be truly funny. Well, the Soviets were too wound up with reasons to suit me. It was a shame they couldn't have gotten the job of the Revolution done and still had a few kicks along the way. What Moscow needed was one big hotfoot—just for no reason at all.

It was only during my last few days there that I began to make any sense out of the impression Russia had made on me. The more I thought about it the worse the feeling in the pit of my stomach got. I knew it wouldn't go away until I got to the Polish border and breathed the fresh, free air of the Western world again.

Then came the meeting in Ambassador Bullitt's office. And here I was, four days out of New York City, an American citizen on a friendly French boat, locked in my stateroom and acting like a fugitive lunatic. This was ridiculous.

I was making myself all the more conspicuous by hiding out. It was a smooth crossing for winter. There was a congenial crowd on board. So what was the famous, fun-loving harp player locking himself in his stateroom for?

I let myself out. I decided to play it nonchalant. I should mix it up. Circulate. Roam the ship and case the broads, like I was any old spy named Joe. I played a few rubbers of bridge, talked to elderly couples who looked trustworthy—and cased the broads.

There wasn't so much to this cloak-and-dagger business, I told myself, once you got the hang of it. The main thing was to act like you didn't have a worry in the world. Still, I slept with my socks on, and took showers with my right foot sticking out of the bath compartment, standing like a ballet dancer with the gout.

The voyage dragged on, and on. The waves got farther apart and the ship's clocks slowed down. I couldn't sit still long enough to play a hand of bridge. I circulated. I roamed. I fidgeted. The stewards and the waiters and the bartenders were growing darker and shiftier by the minute. I began to wonder about the elderly couples in the library. They were the ones to watch. Trying to throw me off my guard.

Twenty-four hours to go. Twelve hours. Time to change to city clothes and pack my suitcase. Time to make a final check of the straps around the packet. Might get jostled getting off the boat, or in customs.

There was a knock on the stateroom door. I tried to pull my pants leg down the same time I jumped to my feet, and I fell flat on my face. I missed busting my nose on the edge of a chair by an inch.

It was only the steward. "One hour from docking," he said.

"God bless you," said I.

A lot of corny lines had been written about the Grand Old Lady of New York Harbor, and what the sight of her meant to a traveler returning home. Now I knew how true they were. When I saw the Statue of Liberty, out of the porthole, I couldn't think of anything corny enough to say to her. She may have been nothing to seagulls and pigeons but a big, green latrine, and nothing but a menace to ferryboat captains—but to me she was the most beautiful broad in the world.

In thirty-five minutes we'd be tied up at Pier 88.

Somebody knocked at my door. It wasn't the steward's polite rapping. This was a solid belt that said, *Open up or else!* I didn't have to open up. The door was flung open. Two hulking, stony-faced bruisers came in the stateroom, slammed the door behind them, and turned the lock. I hadn't seen either of these guys at any time during the voyage. They were dressed for going ashore, and carried their hats and overcoats. One of them carried a black brief case. They both wore suits with padded shoulders, plenty bulky enough to conceal holsters and pistols.

335

They stood there for a minute or so without speaking, towering over me, glaring at me, waiting until they were sure nobody had followed them.

The one with the brief case said, in perfect English, "Marx, you have something we want. You probably have it strapped to yourself somewhere under your clothing. You will be good enough to remove it and hand it over."

Well, Exapno Mapcase, I said to myself, *you gave it a try but you didn't make it. The jig is up.*

Then the guys took out their wallets, flipped them open, and showed me their identification. They were agents of the Secret Service. The United States Secret Service.

I pulled up my pants, ripped off the tape, unwound the straps, handed over the dispatches from Ambassador Bullitt, and gave my leg its first scratch in ten days. It was a beautiful scratch, sheer ecstasy. It was all the reward I wanted for what I had done.

When the ship tied up at the pier it was announced over the loud speakers that there would be a short delay before passengers could debark. I was the only passenger who knew the reason for the delay. It was to allow me to be the first to go ashore. The ship's officers saluted me as I stepped off the boat. I walked down the gangplank, followed by the two agents. I turned and waved back at the passengers crowded against the rail. Without knowing why, they applauded me. What a finish!

The agents led me straight through customs, stopping only to flash their wallets and to explain that Mr. Marx's baggage was tagged for diplomatic priority. Now I was even more ecstatic—on account of my trunk was full of illegal rubles and hot icons.

On the pier, on the free side of the customs barrier, were Gummo and his wife and Aleck Woollcott. When the Secret Service boys saw I had friends waiting, they shook hands with me and said, "Sure appreciate this," and "Glad it didn't put you out any," and then ran down the pier toward the street.

Aleck was so glad to see me and so stunned by the way I had been escorted off the boat that he couldn't speak. He waggled his head and grinned and held up his hands and puffed with pride. Gummo and Helen hugged me and kissed me. It was a wonderful homecoming.

Now I could say it and mean it: it had also been a wonderful trip.

One thing, only one thing, was missing to make the triumph complete. I was a Secret Agent who didn't know what his Secret was. I had no idea whatsoever what might have been in the envelopes I had carried, strapped to my leg, all the way from the other side of the moon.

I still don't know. I never will, of course.

CHAPTER 19

The Oboe under the Blanket

MISS FLATTO, REST her soul, had died while I was in Russia. Aleck was heartbroken, but I felt it was merciful that we never had a chance to meet again and relive those exasperating days of P.S. 86. As it was, Miss Flatto was able to pass peacefully on, blessed with happier memories.

The day I got back I took a suite in a hotel on Central Park West, dumped my loot there, and went with Woollcott to have dinner with as many of the mob as he could round up. Waiting for us in the restaurant were Adams, Broun, Benchley and Dorothy Parker. A little later George Kaufman came in. He was carrying a newspaper clipping and he had a mean and sour look about him.

When I started to greet him, Kaufman put a finger to his lips and shushed me. He sat down, laid the clipping on the table, swatted it with the flat of his hand, and took out his watch. I could only see the headline on the story:

HARPO MARX SCORES BIG HIT IN MOSCOW
First American Popular Artist to Entertain Soviets
Receives Ten-Minute Standing Ovation

Every time I tried to speak, Kaufman shook his head and held up a hand to stop me. Otherwise he sat perfectly still, glowering at his watch. The others were as puzzled as I, and the table went quiet. The waiter brought drinks. Woollcott told him we weren't ready to order yet. Time passed. The waiter came back. Woollcott said we still weren't ready. Kaufman hadn't moved. I said, "George—" He silenced me with his hand. Around us, other diners finished eating and left, and new customers took their places. Kaufman was still in a trance, as if he was hypnotized by his watch.

After what seemed like an hour he put the watch in his pocket, turned to me and said, "That was ten minutes, Marx. The Russians applauded you for ten minutes, eh?" He snorted, took the clipping, got up from the table, and left the restaurant.

It was gratifying to see that my friends were so proud of my newest success.

Benchley also gave me the business that night, in a sneakier way. We were sitting around having coffee when Benchley cringed at the sight of a luscious blonde who was heading his way. The girl was on the make for him and made no bones about it. He tried to shake her off, but she stuck to him like flypaper, to the vast amusement of Woollcott.

Then Benchley said, "I'd like you to meet my idol, dear, the famous Harpo Marx," and the next thing I knew, Benchley had beat it and the blonde was stuck to *me* like flypaper.

Well, frankly, I saw nothing to cringe about. After eight weeks of looking at dames with mustaches and pool-table legs, my resistance was pretty low. I asked the girl if she'd like to come up to my place for a nightcap. She said she'd love to. Aleck beamed with approval. Normally he would have been furious at my breaking up a party to run off with a nitwit broad. Something was cooking. There was a smirk behind Woollcott's smile. But that didn't slow me up. I'd been away too long. I left with the blonde.

When we got to my hotel suite the blonde acted like she'd also been away too long.

"Mind if I make myself comfortable?" she said. I said, "Go right ahead." She did. In five seconds flat she slid off her coat, unzipped her dress, and pulled off her slip. She wore nothing under her slip.

I undertook to get equally comfortable. I didn't get very far. The blond dame was looking at me strangely. I then saw she was gripping something in her hand. It was a small penknife. The blade was open and it was pointing toward me. I grabbed her wrist, broke her grip, and took the knife away from her.

She started to cry. "Please!" she said. "Can't I just *scratch* you a little?"

I'd heard of dames like this, but I'd never been exposed to one before. I made a quick tour of the suite and picked up every weapon in sight—a bottle opener, a letter opener, a nail file, a pair of nail scissors, even the hotel key. When the blonde saw what I was doing she made a lunge for me, her fingers hooked like the talons of a hawk, and ripped open the front of my shirt.

I ran into the bedroom and locked the door. I had an idea. I undressed. I slathered myself from head to foot with hair oil, so the blonde couldn't possibly—I thought—get a grip on me. I came out of the bedroom, a greased pig with a bathrobe on.

I had thought wrong. The blonde gouged me good, right through the hair oil. I retreated back to the bedroom. She started pounding on the door for me to come out and give her some fun, just a *little* fun. She wouldn't give up. I wouldn't give up either. I got another idea. I opened my trunk and got out the outfit I'd bought in Moscow and put it on.

When I opened the bedroom door the blonde gawked at me, groaned, and stopped crying. I then gawked at myself in the mirror on the door, and all desire flew out the window. Hair oil was oozing from under my karakul hat, running down my face and onto the collar of my fur coat. The fur coat hung down to the ankles of my fur galoshes. It was a very funny sight.

Wallowing like a bear on snowshoes, I went over and sat beside the naked blonde on the sofa. She didn't say a word. She just stared at the impenetrable fur that covered me and wistfully flexed her fingers.

"Listen, honey," I said, "why don't you get dressed and go home?"

340

She stared at the fur a while longer, then shrugged and said, "All right." In five seconds flat she pulled on her slip, zipped up her dress, put on her coat, and walked out of the suite.

What the hell, I said to myself. If nothing else it was nice to know that my old act worked just as well backwards as forwards—picking up cutlery instead of dropping it.

The old mob was still full of hanky-panky, after all these years, but their gags were fewer and farther between. They weren't the same crazy Katzenjammers of the 1920's. They had changed along with the times. Seven or eight years ago we would have wound up an all-night party in Aleck's apartment arguing about croquet or the stock market, or making up wild puns and nasty menus. Now we wound up talking (they did, I mean—I still listened) about the NRA, the CCC, FDR's last Fireside Chat, and Fiorello La Guardia, the new mayor of New York. Sooner or later Adolf Hitler entered every conversation, which killed it, and everybody went home wrapped up in his own depressing thoughts.

The first night this happened it got me thinking of what I had seen in Hamburg. I saw again those poor, frightened bastards staring out of windows with the Star of David painted on them, and I went home and threw up.

Woollcott, of course, had appropriated all rights to the story of my trip to Russia. He kept calling me up and ordering me to join him, at lunch, at cocktails, or at some party. If I didn't feel like going out, he'd say, "But you *must* come! I'm with people who still haven't heard 'The Adventures of Harpo in Sovietland!'" As soon as I got to wherever he was, he'd launch into the story. I never got a chance to get a word in. I would have gotten tired of hearing it, but the story got better every time around.

It was after one of these sessions that I weighed myself in a penny arcade and my fortune card read: YOU TALK TOO MUCH. REMEMBER—SILENCE IS GOLDEN.

341

I was in no hurry to get back to the coast. With F.P.A. I went to Philadelphia to catch the out-of-town opening of *Dodsworth*, which Sidney Howard had adapted from the Sinclair Lewis novel. Max Gordon—Groucho's old investment counselor—was the producer, and I watched the opening performance from the back of the house with Max. As producers have always done and always will do during an out-of-town tryout, Max paced back and forth during the whole show, sweating out each line and each piece of business, and trying to read the audience's mind.

Every few minutes he'd stop, look sharply toward the stage, then write something on a slip of paper. Memos like this, I knew, were on-the-spot decisions that could make a success out of a tottering wreck of a play. By the third act his pockets were bulging with them.

When the final curtain came down, Max ran for the stage door. One of the little slips fell out of his pocket. I picked it up to take back to Max, and I couldn't resist reading it. Who knew? This might be the single stroke of theatrical genius that would give Broadway its newest hit.

The memo said: "Send shirts to laundry."

When I returned to New York there was a cablegram waiting for me. It was from Chico, who was still in England. His message was desperate: DYING FOR SPORTS NEWS. CAN'T GET RESULTS HERE. PLEASE SEND PAPERS. I devoted the rest of the day to fulfilling Chico's desperate request. I scoured the city and bought copies of the London *Times*, London *Observer*, Manchester *Guardian* and the *Scotsman*. In each paper I underlined scores of association football, rugby and cricket matches, and shipped the whole batch off to Chico. I cabled him that the papers were on their way with the latest results, and wished him the best of luck.

Suddenly I was in a hurry to get back to the coast. Our next picture commitment at Paramount was several months off, and I had no professional reason for being in Hollywood, but I was itchy and restless. New York was no longer a great place in which to do nothing. People were hopeful, but the Depression still hung over the city, and it was a raw, runny-nose winter. When I heard myself griping about the weather I became acutely aware of being a transient in New York, a displaced Californian. Everybody was busy except me. I went home.

The Garden of Allah, after the snows of Moscow, the sleet of the North Atlantic and the slush of New York City, seemed more like the Garden of Eden. The sun was an old friend I hadn't seen for five months. The miniature Black Sea was crawling with gorgeous broads. Even the palm trees were beautiful.

Daytimes, I spent hours without interruption at the harp, getting back in shape. Nighttimes I spent hours on the town—a hot Hollywood sport in cream-colored suit and rakish skimmer, swinging a cane—getting a few other techniques back in shape.

I joined the Hillcrest Country Club and shot at least forty-five holes of golf per week. I rented a beach house, laid out a wooden floor for a badminton court and enclosed it with a wall to keep the wind out. Charlie Lederer was a regular weekender at the beach house, along with Sam Goldwyn, Walter Wanger and John Gilbert. When it got too dark for badminton we moved inside for bridge or backgammon.

But damn it, I was still itchy and restless. Something was wrong with this picture. It came to me what was wrong. I had been cooped up too many years in hotel rooms, staterooms, apartments and bungalows. The happiest days I could remember were when I lived in the rambling clubhouse on Neshobe Island, and in the Villa Galanon on the Riviera.

I might be a bachelor, but bachelor quarters were not for me. I was a house man. A big-house man.

I rented a furnished mansion that belonged to a retired queen of the silent screen, in Beverly Hills. It was a tremendous place. All my worldly possessions, harp and case included, fit into the hall closet with plenty of space to spare. There must have been twenty rooms in the house. I never knew how many for sure. Every time I set off to count them I either got lost (my sense of direction never was very good), or I got tired and decided to finish counting some other time—then forgot to mark my place.

It was after his first visit to my new joint that George Burns warned the boys at Hillcrest: "Don't go to Harpo Marx's without an Indian guide." Somebody played the straight man and asked why not. "I'm at Harpo's the other night," says George. "I ask him where the can is. He says, 'Follow me—I know a short cut.' Not knowing any better, I follow him. By the time he gets me there I need a change of clothes already."

But George had to admit that, once there, it was worth the trip. In the master bathroom the john sat on a raised marble base, like a Roman throne. Hanging next to it, on a silver chain, was a silver-plated police whistle. The queen who had built the house had a morbid fear of prowlers, and she was always hearing prowlers when she was least prepared to cope with them. Burns had other ideas about what the whistle was for, but they cannot be printed.

The grounds were spacious and beautiful, and there was a huge swimming pool, arched over by a graceful Japanese bridge.

I went on a spree redoing the joint to my taste. I stocked it with cats, dogs, birds, tropical plants and a pool table. I hired a gardener, a cook, two maids and a butler. I was now prepared to undertake a brand-new role: Host.

It wasn't hard enticing guests to come to my dinners and parties. After operating for ten years as a mooching bachelor, I was in a position at last to pay at least some interest on all the hospitality I had enjoyed. People I had known took immediate advantage of this, and so did a lot of people I had never met before. It was Open Season on Harpo.

There was never an empty guest room. There was never a

moment of silence. Something was going on at any given time, around the clock—harp, piano, badminton, swimming, arguing, eating, bridge, backgammon, poker, pool, or any of several more intimate types of action.

For wayfarers from the East like Sam Behrman, Sam Harris, Moss Hart, Max Gordon, Alice Miller, Ruth Gordon, Dorothy Parker and the George Kaufmans, my house was the Beverly Hills Algonquin—always good for a night's lodging, a hot meal, a spot of talk and a game of chance. For immigrants like Charlie Lederer, Charlie Brackett, Ben Hecht and the Gershwin brothers, it was a clearinghouse for news from the old country, New York City. For Burns, Benny, Jolson, Holtz, Cantor, Jessel and the Ritz Brothers, it was a combination Retreat for Retired Vaudevillians and Hillcrest Annex. To me it was a nifty hangout. It was the first hangout I ever had that I didn't have to take a cab home from.

Before I knew what was happening, my joint changed from a nifty hangout to a snooty resort. I became a fad, a social lion, which was the last thing I had in mind. I detested snobs as much as I detested publicity hounds. Well, I wanted a house. I had asked for it.

Actually, the guest who would have been most welcome of all never showed up. Aleck was now the "Town Crier" on radio—sponsored by Cream of Wheat—and between broadcasts he rode the lecture circuit. When I wrote him to get his pratt out to Los Angeles, he replied with a carbon copy of his schedule for the first half of the following month. After listing two broadcasts and eight lectures in ten days, the schedule wound up with:

14th: Lecture, Toledo.
15th: Lecture, Detroit.
17th: Broadcast from Chicago.
18th: Death of Mr. Woollcott, as thousands cheer.
19th: Dancing in the streets; half-holidays in all the schools, bank moratorium.
20th: Burial at sea.

Acting in *Duck Soup,* our last picture for Paramount, was the hardest job I ever did. It was the only time I can remember that I worried about turning in a bad performance. The trouble was not with the working hours, the script, the director, or the falls I had to take (I never used a stunt man or a double). The trouble was Adolf Hitler. His speeches were being rebroadcast in America. Somebody had a radio on the set, and twice we suspended shooting to listen to him scream. Hindenburg had died. Hitler was now absolute dictator of Germany. He threatened to scrap the Versailles Treaty and create a German navy and air force. He threatened to grab off Austria and part of Czechoslovakia. He threatened to go beyond the boycott and revoke the citizenship of all Jews.

I never knew until then what the emotion of pure anger was like, how it felt to be sore enough to want to hit somebody in cold blood. A lot of people I knew were shocked that I was so shocked. Nothing would really come of the dictator's threats, they said. He was all bluff and hot air. His act was nothing more than a bad imitation of that other comic, Mussolini.

I knew better. I had seen faces, those faces in Germany, that most other people had not seen. And now I remembered: I had been tipped off even earlier than that. It was Sam Harris, sweet, gentle Sam, who had opened my eyes to this evil thing festering in Germany, before I sailed for Hamburg in the fall of '33. Sam had been reading the news from there, every word of it in every paper he could get hold of, and he had come to a conclusion.

"Harpo," he said, "that Hitler is not a very nice fellow." It was the most vicious thing I had ever heard Sam say about another living person.

Things got quieter in my house of the silver whistle. I got firm and stopped inviting everybody who invited me to invite them. Open house was okay for holidays, but not seven days a week, twenty-four hours a day.

346

The peace was wonderful. It was wonderful to have some privacy again. But I didn't expect it to last, and it didn't. The peace was broken by the strangest young man to enter my life since the day Seymour Mintz came skittering on a bias down 93rd Street, looking for a new partner.

One evening during a small dinner party for seven or eight people, the butler told me I was wanted on the phone. He didn't catch the gentleman's name, he said, but it was apparently a matter of great urgency.

I picked up the phone and said, as I always do, "Yah?"

A voice I had never heard before, a raspy, nasal, mumbly voice that sounded like somebody playing an oboe under a blanket, said, "Harpo? I'm coming over."

"Who the hell is this?"

"This is Oscar Levant, is who the hell this is. I'm coming over. Now."

"Oscar who?"

"*Levant*, you musical illiterate."

"Oh, yah, I've heard George and Ira speak of you. Well, good luck on your next concert."

"I don't play concerts. So how do I get to your place from here?"

"Look, Benson, whatever your name is. I'm sorry, but I have guests. We're in the middle of dinner."

"That's all right. Don't wait for me. I've eaten already."

"Look—why don't you call up the Gershwins?"

"That's where I'm calling from. George and Ira are out on a heavy date playing Ping-pong and I'm here alone. So I'll see you in five minutes."

"Look—maybe tomorrow, huh? How about it? You free tomorrow? All three of you come over. Lunch, dinner, you name it. I told you—I have guests tonight, a party."

There was a pause, then an anguished wail unwound out of the phone receiver: "*Look, you son of a bitch! You can't leave me here alone!*"

I knew I wasn't going to stop him. "All right, all right," I said. "Come have a cup of coffee with us."

Oscar was there in five minutes. He had a cup of coffee, and then decided to stay a while longer. He stayed for one year and one month.

I was too slow on the trigger and too soft in the heart. I knew more about Oscar than he knew I did. I'd been briefed about him by the Gershwins, and by the Kaufmans too. Oscar idolized George Gershwin. For years he had been tagging after him like a kid brother. He carried his music for him and turned the pages for him when he practiced, and for years Gershwin was the only composer Oscar himself would play. Back in New York, Ira and George had lived in a double penthouse on Riverside Drive. Oscar, without being invited, decided he should board with them. For ten months he didn't miss a meal. Then one night that fall he jumped up from the table in the middle of dinner and said, "Hate to eat and run, but you'll have to excuse me." With that he bolted out of the penthouse and the Gershwins didn't see him or hear from him until sometime in the middle of winter.

Not long afterward, the George Kaufmans acquired him. Oscar turned up at their Bucks County place—uninvited, of course—for a weekend. Late on Saturday night, he suddenly turned on Kaufman and sneered that he'd been insulted enough. He was leaving. He headed for the door. Then he made an about-face and came back into the room, taking off his coat. "I'm not going after all," he said. George asked him why not. Oscar said, "I just remembered. I have no place to go." He stayed for the rest of the week.

What can I say about Oscar Levant that hasn't already been said, mainly by Oscar himself? For one year and one month he declared my house his house. For one year and one month he ate my food, played my piano, ran up my phone bill, burned cigarette holes in my landlady's furniture, monopolized my record player and my coffeepot, gave his guests the run of the joint, insulted my guests, and never stopped complaining. He was an insomniac. He was an egomaniac. He was a leech and a lunatic—in short, a *litchi* nut.

But I loved the guy.

He honestly believed he was taking what was coming to him, and nothing more. This was not to be confused with generosity, which Oscar didn't know how to accept. If anybody offered to help him out, his favorite reply was, "Do me a favor—don't do me a favor." But if it was he who asked the favor it was all right. Oscar was utterly unable to enjoy an equal relationship with anybody. It had to be one-sided, on his side, with the single exception of George Gershwin. Once I understood this and accepted it, I found Oscar to be one of the most rewarding men I had ever known. I lost a house, but I gained a friend.

My higher education, after a lapse of five years, was resumed. I took up learning things from Levant where I'd left off with Woollcott. The amount of knowledge Oscar carried in his head was fantastic. I never came up with a question he couldn't answer. I never saw him stymied by any subject anybody ever brought up in his presence. And if anybody had the nerve to say he knew more than Oscar about music, psychiatry or baseball—well, he was in for a scorching blast of sarcasm, followed by an all-night solo discourse which would leave the challenger hanging on the ropes and feeling like a punch-drunk moron.

I had never been exposed to such a mind as Oscar's, not even at the Algonquin Round Table. He had wit and talent to burn. Sometimes I think he literally did. When he fell into his periodic silences, brooding over his coffee and chain-smoking cigarettes, he might have been burning off excess talent, along with all the witticisms he'd never have time to make.

When Oscar wasn't brooding he was doing everything at once. Like the time I came downstairs and saw him reading from a book on the piano rack while he was playing Bach and listening to a new recording of a Beethoven concerto. He would sing along with the Beethoven, then sing a couple of bars of Bach, then read a passage out loud from the book. He'd chuckle over what he had read, wince when he hit a clinker on the keyboard, and close his eyes in ecstasy over a lovely phrase on the record—all damn near simultaneously.

You'd think that here was a man lost to the rest of the world. But in the middle of this triple performance he'd say, without looking away from the book, "Harpo, why don't you loathe me like everybody else? Don't you like me?"

Other times I'd bust in when he was practicing and say, "Hey, Oscar! Here's a buck. Play me some Chopin."

Oscar would cut short the Bach or Rachmaninoff or Gershwin or whatever he was working on, and play one of my favorite Etudes or Nocturnes—all the way through, and beautifully. He never failed to do it for me. He never failed to take the dollar, either.

At sight-reading music he was a wizard, absolutely inhuman. One evening I had the Kapinsky Trio, a famous concert ensemble, in to play for my guests after dinner. Oscar had never done chamber music, but he couldn't resist giving it a fling. After the first piece he took over at the piano. I thought: *For once you're going to make an ass of yourself, kiddo.* Not Oscar. He sight-read through volumes of Mozart, Schubert and Brahms—music he had never read before, much of it music he had never heard before. His playing was concert perfect. Piano blended with violin and cello as if the three had performed together for years. Those of us in the room who knew Oscar were proud of him, and not alto-gether surprised. The members of the Kapinsky Trio were knocked for a loop. They'd never seen such a phenomenon.

The rarest gift Oscar had to offer was not his virtuosity, but something very few people were fortunate enough to receive—his smile. He didn't give it often, but when he did, it was sunshine in Moscow. His mouth untwisted into a grin, his eyes squinched and twinkled, he ducked his head as sheepishly as a kid caught in some mischief, and in this startling flash of warmth you realized that Oscar, for all his sarcasm and sullen cracks, didn't really mean to hurt anybody except himself.

There was little I could offer Oscar in a nonmaterial way, except to listen to him. But that may have been the most precious gift I could have given. It certainly wasn't cheap.

Well, I did get to show him a little of Southern California. One of Oscar's phobias was the outdoors. He regarded Nature as a gigantic plot to persecute Oscar Levant, and avoided the outdoors along with evil hoodoos like physical exercise, hats, the number thirteen, the words "lucky" and "death," and any mention of his childhood.

Oscar had been in California for three months when I found out he had never seen the Pacific Ocean. He was in a strangely cheerful mood that day. When I suggested we go out to the shore and case the ocean he said okay. He supposed it was part of his education—like looking at the sky, which he also meant to do someday.

We drove to the Palisades and parked at the edge of the cliff, where the panorama of mountains, beach and sea was unspoiled by any signs of civilization. The water was a sparkling blue and calm. Catalina Island, forty miles away, stood out like a sharp, brown rock. The western horizon was distinct as a line drawn with a ruler. No boardinghouses, bathhouses, refreshment stands or boardwalks anywhere in sight. It was magnificent.

Oscar gave it a long look. He gave a whistle of disbelief. He said, "What do you know—a Gentile ocean!"

My favorite indoor sport was getting Oscar into a battle of wits with guys who could give him a run for his money. When I became resigned to the fact that Oscar was going to be there anyway, I built dinner parties around him, playing Woollcott's old game of People-Mixing. One of the parties I remember best was the night of the Maxes. The guests were Max Gordon, Max Reinhardt and Maxie Rosenbloom.

When dinner was over we took our coffee to the library. I said to Max Gordon: "Max, Oscar says you're the lousiest producer on Broadway," and then sat back to watch the fireworks.

Those were the last words I spoke until five o'clock in the morning, when I said good night. One of the Maxes—Reinhardt— had left. The second Max, Rosenbloom, was fast asleep on the pool table. The third Max was still at it with Oscar. Levant was just warming up, but Gordon was fading fast. It was the damnedest cockfight you ever saw. They had fought over The American Drama, The American Novel, Schopenhauer, Dutch Schultz, Harry Hopkins, The War in China, Homosexuality Among Prize Fighters (they tried to wake up Maxie for a statement but couldn't rouse him), Dizzy Dean's fast ball, and—finally—The Anxieties, Compulsions and Hostilities of Oscar Levant. Max began to wobble in the middle of Compulsions, and from there on it was no contest.

One reason Oscar talked through so many nights was that he wouldn't have gone to bed anyway, not before four-thirty or five in the morning. He had acute insomnia. It took at least three pills to put him to sleep. When he got up, early in the afternoon, he'd be so woozy from the sodium amytal that he'd start chain-drinking coffee immediately, which kept the vicious cycle going. After fifty cups of coffee, his average for a day, he'd be so hopped to the gills with caffein that he'd have to take the pills to knock himself out.

Technically Oscar didn't live with me, since he never slept at my house. At this I firmly drew the line when he first decided to move in. All the facilities I had were his except the bedrooms. So he took an apartment in another part of Beverly Hills, where he slept, etc., and he bought a secondhand Ford to commute with.

On nights when I had no guests, and Oscar had nothing to go home to except his sleeping pills, he would hang around long after I had gone to bed, reading, brooding, and—when the loneliness got unbearable—making phone calls, regardless of the hour. In the morning when I got up he'd be gone. I could tell how late he'd stayed by how many cigarette butts were crammed into the ash trays and how warm the coffeepot was. But no matter how late it had been, he'd always show up at two-thirty the following afternoon, bright and surly.

Once, while I was puttering around before retiring, Oscar called up his ex-wife Barbara at her home on Long Island. Barbara had been remarried for some time. Her husband was Arthur Loew, of the famous movie-theatre family. When she recognized Oscar's voice, she was furious. She asked him why he'd woken her up in the middle of the night. It was 4 A.M. in New York.

"Just wanted to ask you something," said Oscar. "Well?" said Barbara. "What's playing at Loew's 86th Street tomorrow?" said Oscar.

Naturally, she hung up on him. Oscar turned to me and said, "I have a feeling she still loathes me, Harpo. Nothing definite, but a very strong feeling."

An exceptional guest, always a lodger as well as a boarder at my house, was S. N. Behrman, who put in several stretches on the coast writing screenplays. I never knew two guys more unalike than Sam Behrman and Oscar Levant. Sam was precise, punctilious and thoughtful. He was a scholar and a connoisseur, a true cosmopolitan-type intellectual.

Sam never understood why two adults like Oscar and me could get so worked up over boys' games like baseball and boxing. He gave up trying to reform us, but never gave up hoping that we'd outgrow such things. Sam always looked on the hopeful side of life. He was as up-trodden as Oscar was down.

Sam and Oscar had one thing in common, however. They were terrible drivers. One night the three of us went to a party at the home of the late Sonya Levien. I went with Oscar, in his beat-up Ford. Sam, who had to leave early, followed in his rented Cadillac. When the party broke up, long after Sam had left, Oscar went for his car. He came yip-yipping back to the house. His car had been stolen! I helped him look for it. He was right. The Ford was gone.

While we waited for the cops to come, the car thief telephoned, asked for Oscar, and made a full confession. The thief was Sam Behrman.

Driving home, Behrman had suddenly become aware that a car was following him. It didn't appear to be a police car, so Sam tried to shake it. He made several quick turns, then tried to outrace whoever it was. Fast as he went, the other car stayed on his tail. He decided to zoom for home.

The car followed him all the way into the driveway and stopped right behind him. Sam was in a sweat, and very apprehensive. He dreaded any kind of violence. But he was also by this time very sore. Instead of bolting for the house and calling the police, he went to have it out with his pursuer. But the car behind him was empty. It was Oscar Levant's Ford, locked bumper-to-bumper to the Cadillac.

Sam remembered then: in parking, back at Sonya Levien's, he had whanged back into another car. But bashing other cars was a common occurrence with Sam, and he'd said nothing about it to anybody.

The only damage done was to Behrman's good nature. He was given a blistering three-hour verbal beating by Oscar. The subject was "Infantilism, or the Use of the Automobile (Mother Symbol) as an Instrument of Hostility."

When Behrman returned to New York after that stint in Hollywood he left a big emptiness in the house. Oscar and I both sensed this, and talked ourselves into an awful case of homesickness. We decided to take the cure: a trip to New York. We packed our bags and got on the eastbound Chief.

I had the lower berth and Oscar the upper in the Pullman. It was midsummer, and hot as blazes the first night out. It was going to be rough for normal people to sleep, let alone insomniacs. In this respect I wasn't normal, of course. I had no trouble. The last thing I remember before drifting off was Oscar thrashing, groaning and rattling his bottle of sleeping tablets in the berth above me.

An hour later I woke up. Oscar was hanging over my berth, his head poked upside-down through the curtains, screaming at me. I asked him what was the matter.

"You son of a bitch," he said, "I don't mind your sleeping, but do you have to *smile* in your sleep?"

What the hell, I said. If that bothered him, why didn't he stop looking at me?

354

"Doesn't make a damn bit of difference," said Oscar. "Even if I don't look at you I lie up here *knowing* you're down there smiling. I've taken five pills and I can't take any more and you're driving me out of my mind."

I knew it was no gag. This kind of torture was as real and as painful to Oscar as if he'd been put on the rack. "Look," I said, "I'll sleep on my stomach with my face to the pillow. Would that help?"

"Try it," he snapped. I turned over. Oscar retreated back into his berth and all was quiet. After a few minutes, he called down, "Much better!" A few minutes after that we were both asleep.

Aleck was on his island for the summer and he was expecting us. He was eager to meet my "young musician friend," of whom he had heard so much. Oscar had reservations about Woollcott, but after the build-up I gave him all the way across the continent, he was eager to meet my old "father-transference figure."

We stayed in New York only long enough to catch a train for Bomoseen. The nearer we got to Vermont, the worse Oscar's anxiety got. He sat in the dining car drinking coffee and sulking. He refused to look out the window. When we got off at Bomoseen he was too shaken to speak. On board the launch crossing to the island, he gripped the seat and stared in frozen panic at the bottom of the boat.

When he got on Neshobe Island he was a wreck. Aleck came down to the dock to meet us. Oscar offered him a limp, sweaty hand and muttered something unintelligible. Then the shock of where he was hit him with a jolt. Never in his life had Oscar been so out-of-doors.

"Birds!" he wailed. "There are birds here! The sickest creatures on God's earth! Trees! Even the trees are psychotic! Bugs! Don't tell me there aren't any insects here because I know there are!" He grabbed my arm. "Harpo," he said, "what have you done to me? Take me away from here. *Take me away from here!*"

He wouldn't stay on Neshobe even long enough for a cup of coffee. We took the launch to Bomoseen and the next train to New York City. Oscar was sunk in a black pit of depression. He spoke not a word to me, not until he'd called his East Coast analyst from Grand Central Station and made an emergency appointment for a two-hour session.

When he came out of the phone booth he was already at peace with himself. He gave me one of his rare, warm grins and said, "Isn't it great to be back?" He never made any mention of the grim trip to Woollcott's island, ever again.

We hung around New York for a couple of weeks. I had no facilities that Oscar could mooch, so he used me in other ways. Mostly, I was useful to him as a decoy to pick up dames. Going down Broadway, Oscar would walk three steps behind me. When a good-looking dame passed by he'd yell, "Hey, Harpo! Harpo Marx!" I would stop. The dame would stop. Oscar would rush up and ask her if she'd like to meet his friend, the famous Harpo Marx. Before the dame got to meet the famous Harpo Marx she'd be off and running with Oscar Levant.

One girl he picked up was a chorus girl in a night club. Oscar spent every night in the club where she worked, and their dates would begin at three in the morning, after her last show. This fit just fine into Oscar's cockeyed schedule of living and sleeping. The only trouble was, the girl lived way the hell out in Brooklyn, which denied him the pleasure of seeing her home. Oscar was not exactly a big spender, mainly because he didn't have what to spend. So at the end of a date he'd give her a kiss and a nickel for the subway.

One night I went to the club with Oscar. After he picked up his broad, the three of us went to Lindy's, where we sat around having cheesecake and coffee. When she said it was time for her to go home we discovered it was raining hard outside, coming down in sheets.

Oscar, in a flash of gallantry, announced he would send her home in a cab. It was the least he could do on a night like this. He had the waiter summon a taxi driver from the street. When the cabbie came dripping over to our table, Oscar asked him what the fare would be to the address in Brooklyn. The driver said that since he couldn't count on a return fare from any place that far out the trip would cost seven-fifty.

Oscar let out a howl. *"Seven-fifty?"* he said. "Ridiculous! This girl's a *virgin!"*

He gave her a nickel and sat out the rest of the night in Lindy's.

During scenes like this I was apt to forget about the other sides of Oscar. Then something would happen to remind me that no matter what else he did or how many people he humiliated, he was still a genius like none other I had ever known.

Toward the end of our stay in New York I went with Oscar to Harms, the music publishers. While we were there a stranger came in. Oscar recognized the guy and greeted him with the sweetest, sincerest smile I'd ever seen him give to anybody. The man was Russian, from his accent. They talked awhile, then Oscar asked the guy if he wouldn't please play the first movement of his Second Piano Concerto. Oscar said he'd heard it a few times, and liked it, but he'd never tackled it himself. The Russian was happy to oblige.

Halfway through a passage, he stopped playing. He'd forgotten his own concerto. Oscar was so impatient that he pushed the guy off the stool, took over at the piano, and finished the movement—without once faltering or faking. "Bravo!" said the guy who'd written it. "Extraordinary!"

Finally, Oscar introduced me to him. He was Sergei Prokofiev, probably the greatest Russian composer since Tchaikovsky.

When I got back to California, the lease on my Beverly Hills joint ran out, and I was informed that it would not be renewed.

When I told Oscar I had to move, he said, "Harpo, I am profoundly disappointed in you. This is the dirtiest trick anybody has ever played on me." He walked out of the house, got in his

Ford, and drove away. He arrived at the Gershwins' place just in time for dinner.

For one year and one month I had spent scarcely one waking hour out of earshot of the mumbly, nasal rasp of Oscar's voice, the oboe under the blanket. Three years later it became familiar to all America, when Oscar appeared on the radio program "Information Please." Subsequently he became a fairly regular panelist, and his success on the show brushed away enough of his phobias to give him a brand-new charge of confidence.

It was not until 1942 that the guy who'd been one of the best musicians in America for nearly twenty years became, at last, a concert artist. My loss was the public's gain. Lucky—if you'll pardon that horrifying word, Oscar—public.

CHAPTER 20

Cherchez la Fleming

Susan.

I didn't catch her last name. She was seated next to me at a dinner party at the Sam Goldwyns'. Frankly, I was surprised at the Goldwyns, people of their position being coy with me and playing matchmaker. It seemed like every place I was invited to, some unescorted starlet just "happened" to be seated next to me. And every time it happened, an item would appear in Louella Parsons', Hedda Hopper's or Winchell's column a day or two later.

"What's this about Harpo Marx and Bibi Bensonne?" they used to write. "Insiders say they aren't kidding." Or, "Flash! Look for an altar-cation to brew between Paramount's twinklingest new starlet and Hollywood's most eligible bachelor—initials, B.B. and H.M.!"

I was a bachelor because that was the way I chose to live. The only thing I was eligible for was to vote. I didn't mind giving a hopeful kid a boost. I didn't mind when a press agent quoted me as saying I had worked in a picture with the "lovely and glamorous Miss So-and-so, who has all it takes to become a star." Any girl with good looks, healthy organs and not too many inhibitions had

359

all it took to become a star in the 1930's. But when people insisted on marrying me off to those nitwits, it made me sick.

I earned as much money as I needed. I had more offers of jobs and parts than I could possibly accept. I had friends, hundreds of good friends. I had a full social life. I had a satisfying private life, and I intended to keep it private. I never would speak or appear out of costume before the public. I got no satisfaction whatever from seeing my name in print, unless it had to do with a Marx Brothers picture. The very last thing I wanted in this world was personal publicity.

But the matchmakers and gossips wouldn't leave me alone. What the hell did everybody who was married have against a guy who wasn't? Why did they feel it was their God-given duty to see that every bachelor got hitched? I didn't sneak around trying to trick my married friends into getting divorced.

Anyway, this night at Sam Goldwyns', the starlet-bait was named Susan. The lovely and glamorous Miss Susan-So-and-so.

I wasn't sore at her, but I was sore at the Goldwyns. Thanks to them I was a sitting duck for the columnists again. There'd be an item in somebody's column the next day. Suppose I happened to like this kid? I couldn't make a date with her if I wanted to. If we were seen together a second time we'd be in front-page headlines. What could I do? What I usually did on nights like this—ignore the girl without being unfriendly and, when I had to, talk to her without getting personal.

One thing I had to give the Goldwyns credit for. They had the good taste to pick me out a beaut. It was impossible, I soon found, to ignore this Susan. She was a stunning brunette with a soft, fair complexion and a gorgeous figure, and she had something besides good looks. She gave signs of actually being bright. She had an easy, honest laugh. And she still hadn't caught the Hollywood affliction of "table-hopping eyes." When she talked to you she didn't gaze around the room to see if anybody important was watching her. She looked at you directly, and challenged you to look straight at her. There was something taunting and impudent about the way her eyes sparkled. This I liked.

360

In nearly every respect the girl was un-Hollywood-like, and re-freshing. She didn't want to talk about agents, contracts, who was having an affair with who, or even about herself. Mainly, she wanted to talk about me.

"You're so New York," she said. "You're not one of those Beverly Hills wolves. I can't stand them!"

I hated to disappoint her, but I had to confess that I too lived in Beverly Hills, along with the rest of the bums. "I know," she said. "Near the corner of Elevado and Bedford. Oscar Levant stays with you. He drives a Ford with only one headlight working. You have a big white dog with black spots. I think the dog was with you in *Horse Feathers*."

"Yah," I said. "His name is Kayo. How'd you know?"

"I've seen all of your pictures three times," she said. "The Marx Brothers are my favorite act and you're my favorite Marx Brother."

"I mean about where I live, and Oscar and his car," I said, and she said, in a stage whisper, "*I'm a prowler*."

I told her she'd better be careful. I had a morbid fear of prowlers and kept silver police whistles hanging on chains all over the house. "Why silver?" she wanted to know, and I told her that in Beverly Hills the cops wouldn't come unless you blew on a silver whistle.

This was a dame I could go for. I said, "Do you play croquet?" She said, "You mean what the old folks do with the long sticks down in St. Petersburg, Florida?" Well, so she wasn't perfect. I could still go for her.

For a while she stared at me without saying anything. "You've done something to your hair," she said, finally. "You wore it a lot longer five years ago."

"Yah?" I said. "How do you know? I never played straight. You never saw me without a wig, honey."

She raised her eyebrows and puckered her lips. Her eyes were teasing me. "You don't remember, do you?" she said.

"Remember what?"

"Five years ago—the first time you saw me."

I didn't remember.

"I went to see *Animal Crackers*, in New York. You picked me

361

out of everybody in the audience and gawked at me—like this."
She popped her eyes and let her mouth hang open. "You didn't
take your eyes off me for one whole scene, and everybody was
looking at me instead of the stage. I was so embarrassed I wanted
to die, and at the end of the scene I got up and left the theatre.
Then afterwards I found out it was part of the act and I was
lucky to be the one you picked out for a stooge in the audience
because you always looked for the prettiest face you could find.
That was when I made up my mind I was going to meet you and
apologize in person for walking out on you. We met on Sixth
Avenue in front of the Ziegfeld Theatre, during an intermission
of some benefit. Remember now?"

I didn't. I shook my head.

"It's just as well. When I was introduced to you, I was so
shocked I could hardly speak. You looked like a wild man. Your
hair stuck out in bushes from under your hat. You gawked at me
like you were starving and I was a lamb chop. Before you even
got my name straight you asked me for a date. I was a kid of
twenty and a starry-eyed fan, and I was scared enough of you in
the first place. But to find out that the great Harpo Marx, who
was so sweet and appealing on the stage, was in real life a wicked
old fiend! I think the only words I spoke to you were 'How do
you do, sir?' and 'Oh, no, sir!' "

"Are you still scared of me?"

"Try me."

I gave her my evilest leer. She shook her head solemnly. I tried
a depraved Gookie. She laughed. "Guess I've lost it," I said. "No
longer wicked."

"I'm no longer twenty," she said.

But she didn't look much over twenty, and now, as I looked at
her, something stirred in my memory. The scene of five years ago
began to take shape—the lights of the marquee, the theatre crowd
milling around during the intermission, and emerging out of the
crowd the glowing figure of this little enchantress.

"Excuse me," I said, trying to put the whole picture together.
"When Mrs. Goldwyn introduced us tonight I didn't get your last
name. All I caught was 'Susan.' I'm awful on names."

"I know," she said. "You call everybody Benson, don't you?" This girl certainly had the book on me. She must have had more scouts than Notre Dame.

Then she said, "Fleming. My name is Susan Fleming."

Fleming!

I made a face, this time unconsciously, and she said, "What's so funny about a name like that? What have you got against Fleming?"

"Nothing," I said. "I recommend it highly. Everybody should flem at least once a year."

It was true I had nothing against her name. It was also true that "Fleming" had a very special meaning to me. I had hardly known Susan long enough to tell her what it was. So I vamped and faked until the subject was changed, hoping she'd forget about my strange reaction.

I had known many women in my life, in varying degrees of intimacy, but there had been only one I'd ever felt serious enough about to want to marry. She was named Fleming.

When I first came to Hollywood, I had met an extraordinary girl named June Fleming. We went steady for nearly four months. June was an active, independent gal. She was a crackerjack tennis player, and she flew her own airplane—a real competitor and a hell of a lot of fun to be with. I decided I wanted to be with her for the rest of my life.

We had a date for a Saturday night, which was my deadline for proposing to her. On Friday, June crashed into a mountain flying back from Palm Springs and was killed.

Susan Fleming.

So what about this one? She was the first girl I'd met in a long time that I wanted to keep on seeing for a long time. But I wondered if the name might be a bad omen.

It was tough to beat down the temptation to ask Susan for a date. After dinner I found out she was no mere starlet. In her newest picture, *Million Dollar Legs*, she was doing the lead—and boy, was she equipped for the title role! I also found out that her sitting next to me was not the Goldwyns' idea, but her own.

Still, I resisted. Whether I was a jinx to Flemings or they were to me didn't matter. I couldn't take a second chance. I had to be sensible. We said good night, and that was that.

That, however, was not that, not at all. Two mornings later Susan Fleming called me up. She was very angry. Her voice sizzled and crackled, and I was afraid sparks might shoot out of the telephone and burn my ear. "*Mister* Marx," she said. "I take back everything I said to you at the Goldwyns'. You *are* one of them. You're nothing but a publicity-crazy, ambitious, big-headed Beverly Hills wolf."

She sizzled and crackled on, with more unladylike variations of the same theme. She sputtered out and I got a chance to get in my first word, which was: "Yah?"

That was all I got in. She was off again. Who was I kidding? What a dope she'd been to fall for my line! A man who didn't put on airs? A lover of the simple life? "Phooey!" she said. "A fraud! I know all about you and your friend Winchell. I know the whole story of how you had to dress him up in a costume to sneak him into *Cocoanuts* when the Shuberts had him on their black-list."

"Yah?" I said, and she said, "Yah! Don't try to play innocent. Don't tell me you didn't read his column this morning. You probably have it pasted in your scrapbook already. Well, I want to serve you notice here and now, *Mister* Marx, that I will not stand for being used as an excuse to get your stupid name in the paper."

I laid the phone receiver down gently, and went to get the papers from the breakfast table. When I came back she was still squawk-squawking. I found the item in Walter Winchell's column: "West Coast spies report Harpo Marx, Hollywood's most reluctant bridegroom, huddling and cuddling with actress Susan Fleming, the cutie with the Million Dollar Legs. Weakening mebbe, Harpo? . . ."

I felt like jumping up and down and yelling *whoopee!* Instead, I kept yelling "Miss Fleming!" until she stopped yapping. Then I said, "Miss Fleming, I must ask you to get off the wire. I have to call my lawyer right away, or you might be in trouble."

"Trouble? Me?"

"Trouble. You. I have advised my attorney to bring suit against you and your press agent for invasion of privacy."

"My *what?*" she said. "I'd starve before I stooped to hiring a press agent!"

That did it. All resistance, good sense and superstition flew out the window. I didn't give a damn what any columnist wrote. I didn't care if we hit the front pages. I was going to see my second Fleming again.

"Tell you what's the best idea," I said. "Let's settle out of court. How about if I pick you up at seven tonight and we find some quiet place to eat?"

She thought for a moment, then said, "How formal shall I be? What kind of a 'quiet place' do you have in mind?"

"I have in mind a nice little spot out in Malibu."

"Your beach house?"

"Well, it happens to be a short walk from there, now that I think of it."

"I was right the first time. You're not a bum. You're still a fiend."

"Seven o'clock?"

"Seven o'clock. You don't mind if Mother comes along?"

"No—that's swell. I'll bring Jimmy Fidler and that'll make four for bridge."

"You still haven't told me how formal."

"I'll be wearing a black tie."

"Oh, goody me. I get to dress up twice in one week. Seven o'clock?"

"Seven o'clock."

When I arrived at Susan's apartment I was wearing a black tie. I was also wearing a bushy black wig, a derby, striped trousers, cutaway coat, a sweatshirt, ballet slippers (which I always wore when I performed, so I could feel the harp pedals), and one black sock. The other sock was my tie.

Susan met me at the door. She was dressed fit to kill, in a turquoise evening gown. I threw her a Gookie. She smiled pleasantly and said, "You can tell a New Yorker anywhere by the cut of his clothes. Isn't it disgusting the things men wear in public out here? Come on in—Mother's dying to meet you."

Mrs. Fleming said she was thrilled to meet somebody she'd admired so much for so many years. She didn't bat an eye over my costume either. She gave me a warm smile and then excused herself. She said that Susan and I had a big night ahead of us and she didn't want to deprive us of one minute of our fun.

The two of us had dinner at a place out on the coast highway where they knew me well enough not to be surprised when I showed up in disguise. After we'd eaten I said we might as well drop in at my beach house, it being so near by. Susan said, "Oh, goody me! I've always wanted to see a Malibu love-nest. I've read so *much* about them in the papers."

We took off our shoes and walked down the beach. Susan clutched the hem of her evening gown to keep it from dragging in the sand. She held her dress higher than she really needed to and walked with a swing and a lilt, singing to herself, and oh, my God, it was the loveliest sight I had ever seen! And oh, my God, didn't she know it, too.

I unlocked the beach house, let her in, and switched on the light. She stopped singing. "Well," she said. "Bachelor hall."

"Yah," I said. "Sorry the tiger-skin rug is out at the cleaner's."

She cased the joint inch by inch. She inspected the card tables, which were littered with dirty beer glasses, coffee mugs, ash trays jammed with cigar butts, score sheets and pencil stubs. She appraised the bamboo furniture, piece by piece. She went into the kitchen. She examined the mess in the sink. She took inventory of the cupboard: half a can of coffee with no lid, two cracked coffee mugs, a set of fake buck-teeth, a pile of sugar cubes from various restaurants, a box of dog biscuits, a pair of tennis shoes, a jelly glass full of pennies, a toothbrush and a bagel hung on a hook, and three racks of poker chips. She took inventory of the refrigerator: eight bottles of Vichy water, two bottles of beer, some tubes of oil paints, an empty, unwashed milk bottle, a bottle of hair oil, a jar of peanut butter and a jar of cold cream, half a dozen badminton birds, one egg, one green orange, one black avocado, and in the compartment labeled EXTRA COLD, one homesick Russian karakul hat.

She said nothing, just kept inspecting. When she went to case the bedroom I grabbed a broom and did a fast job on the living-room floor. It was covered with sand, with enough bare footprints on it to make a dandy set for *Robinson Crusoe*. After I'd swept the pile of sand into the fireplace, Susan laughed. She'd been watching me from the bedroom door. She was in her stocking feet, still holding up the hem of her evening gown.

"I suppose," she said, "you think I'm going to say, 'What this place needs is a woman's touch.' Uh-uh. I love it the way it is. I'm also supposed to push up my sleeves and tie on an old shirt of yours for an apron and pitch in and do the dishes and dust and tidy up. Right? Uh-uh. I'm going to sit right here and watch you while you put on a pot of coffee and build a fire."

She sat at one of the card tables, shoved the junk to one side, put her shoes on the table, plunked down her elbows, rested her chin on her hands, and gave me that I-dare-you, teasing look of hers. When she did that she could have melted me through an asbestos wall.

I put on a pot of coffee. I got a load of driftwood from under the deck, threw it in the fireplace, and lit it. While I waited in the kitchen for the coffee to get done I called to Susan, "Mind if I take off a few things and get comfy?"

"Mind?" she called back. "I've got my shoes handy and I know which way the highway is. Why should I mind?"

So I took off a few things—the derby, the wig, and the cutaway coat. I untied my tie and put it back on my foot, where it belonged. I brought out two mugs of coffee, set them on the card table, took her shoes off the table and set them on the floor.

I sat down, facing her. "Okay, honey," I said, "what'll we play first? Gin?"

"Never mind what first," she said. "Exactly what do you have in mind to play second?" I gave her a Groucho eyebrow-waggle, implying I had all kinds of naughty games in mind. Susan said, "You, Mr. Marx, are what my mother calls 'a speedy fellow.' Do you always work this fast the first time you take a young lady out?"

I had to laugh.

"Me—*speedy?*" I said. "You've got me confused with my brother Chico. He's the speedy one in the family. I'm the slow worker. Not slow and steady, just slow. When we were kids, I never had a girl unless Chico got one for me and we double-dated. Then, all I could think of to talk about to my date was my meerschaum pipe, and how it took me four months at least to turn it from white to brown. While I was talking about my pipe, Chico would make some pretty good time with his girl. Then, while I kept on talking about that damn pipe, Chico would make some pretty good time with my girl too. By the time I was ready it would be about three hours too late and I'd put on my derby hat, rub up my sty, and go home.

"I'm so speedy," I said, "that I have to set an alarm clock to catch a Leap Year."

Susan didn't laugh. She said, "Were you lonely when you were young?"

"Well, I was a lone wolf, never had a lot of friends. But I liked it being alone."

"What about now? Do you still like being alone?"

"Tell you the truth, I've forgotten what it's like. You ought to hang around my joint a while. I couldn't be alone if I wanted to be."

She looked me square in the eye. "No," she said. "You know what I mean. I mean not being married, not having a family. Is that the way you like it?"

I shrugged off her question. The conversation was getting uncomfortable. But she wasn't to be shrugged off. She asked me again. I said, "Yes, that's the way I like it."

"Haven't you ever met anybody you wanted to marry?" she said. When she said that it was like the fire went out and the room was as cold as the ocean. I got up to take the cups back to the kitchen and get my coat. I said, "Do you always talk about getting married the first time you go out with a guy, for Christ's sake?"

"Okay, okay!" she said. "Forget I said it. I've got my answer anyway. Shall we go now?"

"Yah," I said. "Let's get the hell out of here."

When I took her home she invited me in for a real cup of coffee, but I turned her down, and we said good night by the door. We were both a little depressed. We'd started out the evening like two balls of fire, then wound up a couple of clinkers. "Guess I wouldn't have made Chico's list," said Susan, and I said, "Guess not." She squeezed my hand and I brushed her cheek with a kiss, and I ran down the steps to the car thinking, *Well, that's the end of the second Fleming.*

The end? I wasn't kidding myself a bit. By the time I got home I was already wondering what her name would sound like if I changed it slightly, and I decided it wouldn't sound bad at all.

Susan Fleming Marx?

I didn't see Susan for quite a while after our first date. She was busy on a new picture, and I didn't want to bother her until she'd finished shooting. The real reason, of course, was that I was ashamed of the way I'd behaved that night in the beach house. There I was alone with the most appealing gal I'd ever met, loving every minute of it—and when she happened to utter the word "marry" I'd got cold feet.

Me, Harpo Marx, age forty-one, the guy who'd held his own with the world's sharpest playwrights, playgirls, authors, editors, artists, foreign ministers, ambassadors and gamblers, me, Harpo, acting like a scared teen-age kid! When was I going to grow up?

I was finding it increasingly hard to kid myself about anything. It was shortly after I met Susan that Sam Behrman came west and stayed at my house. I was never happier to see Sam. (Real reason: any kind of diversion helped. I couldn't get Susan out of my mind.) Then, when Sam left and the joint got too quiet, I came down with a bad case of homesickness and took off with Oscar for New York. (Real reason: I wasn't ready yet to face Susan, and New York was a dandy place to escape to.) After two weeks in New York I was dying to get back to California, because I didn't trust anybody else to look after my plants and pets that long. (Real reason: I was ready to talk to Susan.)

I called her the minute I got home. She said she'd be delighted to see me again. She'd been hoping to hear from me ever since that nice evening we'd spent together at the Goldwyns'. No mention of the evening at Malibu. I took her out dining and dancing the next night, and the next, and the night after that. I took her to the ritziest spots in town, and we went formal. Never before had I dressed up in proper dinner clothes three nights in a row. For twenty years I had been a social freak, a scarecrow in sports shirt, slippers and green pool-table jacket. I now discovered it was very satisfying to be Proper. (Real reason: Susan liked the way New York men wore their clothes.)

She was gay and gracious. I was gay and gallant. Each time we said good night we told each other what a wonderful time we'd had. She'd give my hand a quick squeeze and I'd give her a quick kiss on the cheek. Neither one of us had the nerve to bust through the silly impasse we were in. Still a couple of clinkers.

Then I was told the lease on my house was not being renewed. I decided to take an apartment, temporarily. This was a wise move for two reasons. There wouldn't be room for guests, which would give me more time to practice on the harp. In an apartment I could live from month to month, not too expensively, while I took my time finding exactly the house I wanted. (All right, so there was a third reason: I could bring Susan Fleming home without worrying who'd be hanging around, or who might bust in unexpectedly.)

I boarded all my animals except Kayo and took a terrace apartment in Sunset Towers, which was a kind of vertical Garden of Allah. As soon as I moved, a drastic change occurred in the rela-

370

tions between Susan and me—drastic, but so subtle that for a while I didn't know what hit me.

One day she called up and asked if I could do her a big favor. She was up for the lead in a new picture, the toughest part she'd ever tackled. She'd just got the script and given it a quick look and it scared her. If she came over would I help her with it? Help her learn the lines and coach her in the role? Of course, I said. She came right over.

We worked together every afternoon for a week. I sat in a director's chair with the script and fed cues to Susan while she paced around the terrace, emoting, with Kayo plodding at her heels every step of the way like a devoted fan, which he was. Each day somehow we put in less and less time on Susan's part, and talked more and more about ourselves. I told her about my family's mad life on 93rd Street, about the parade of jobs I was fired from when I was the boy least likely to succeed, my awful debut at Coney Island, the Chicago days, the vaudeville days, my crashing the gates of the world of Alexander Woollcott, my career as an artist and my career as a professional listener.

I couldn't tell her enough about Minnie. Susan insisted on hearing, again and again, all the stories I could remember about my mother—Minnie the mastermind, putting Groucho and Gummo on the stage and Chico on a piano stool, and kidnaping me and shoving me into the act. Minnie on the road. Minnie's battles with managers and booking agents. Minnie's inspirations for special effects. Minnie at our Broadway opening. Minnie as a wife. Minnie as a poker player. The story of Minnie's last hours on earth.

Once Susan said, "Do you think you'll ever find another woman quite so wonderful as your mother?"

"I'm looking," I said. I didn't finish the sentence. What I wanted to say was, *I'm looking at her now*, but I lost my nerve.

I finally got Susan to open up about herself. Her life had been a long, frustrating search for a real home. Her father was a mining engineer, and the Flemings were always on the move. Every time Susan, who was an only child, managed to make friends in a new place, the family would have to pull up stakes and move to another part of the country. Her father was a fine draftsman and amateur artist. Susan had inherited his talent, and the most fun she had as a kid came from drawing, and watching her father work with pen and brush. Those were lonely years for a girl as full of pizazz as Susan. When she got older, art didn't seem satisfying enough and she turned to acting.

"Now," she said one afternoon, "I'm not sure an acting career, or *any* career, is the answer. It's only something to escape to. I'm tired of moving and running. What I want to do is settle down. You know what I mean? Don't you feel the same way?"

"I better go feed Kayo," I said. This was dangerous talk.

After the week of rehearsing on the terrace, I went out and played golf with George Burns. George took me seven holes to two, which ranked as the upset of the year. He could only conclude that I was sick. When I paid him off he said, "What the hell's the matter with you, Harpo? You're walking around in a coma like you're two days dead and nobody's had the heart to tell you. You'd better go to the coroner for a checkup."

I told George I felt great, never felt better. He shook his head. "Don't even know what hit you, huh?" he said, and left the locker room.

That was when it dawned on me. Now I knew what had hit me. I was so much in love with Susan that I couldn't think straight. And because I couldn't think straight I hadn't seen what she was up to. Susan was out to hook me. She was using every trick in the book. Flattery. Sweet talk. Sneaky talk about loneliness and marriage and settling down. Softening me up for the kill. I was being courted and I was weakening.

Now I saw how insane this last week had been—*me* coaching *her* in a dramatic part. Me, who hadn't spoken a line onstage since *School Days!* I knew as much about the interpretation of an acting role as my dog did. I couldn't even read the lines straight. But Susan hadn't objected—oh, no. It was all a scheme to get me where she could work on me. And I fell for it bing-boom-bang.

She wasn't after my dough or my name. She was after me. She loved me as much as I loved her, that I was sure of. But damn it, I wasn't ready. I was a slow worker, a slow thinker, a slow decider.

I had a lot more thinking to do before I decided it was time to change my way of living.

So this was the new pattern of our relationship: Susan attacked. I encouraged her to keep after me, because I couldn't bear to be away from her. But every time I found myself on the point of giving in I got cold feet and escaped. When I escaped, she pursued, and began to attack again. She was not about to give up, and neither was I.

Susan Fleming Period.

I liked her the way she was and I liked her name the way it was.

My first escape was from Sunset Towers, where I was too easy to corner, to the home of the producer Joe Schenck. Joe, at the time, was rattling around in the most lavish bachelor quarters in Hollywood. His house was an Oriental-style palace, built to his special needs. It was a combination gym, sanitarium, harem, and gambling casino. He even had a suite of rooms "just for bowel movements," complete with masseur's table, steam bath, and enough hygienic gadgets to equip a small clinic.

Joe had been after me for a long time to move in with him and become a full-time partner in fun. That was a job I didn't measure up to, however. It would have taken three guys to keep up with Schenck, the way he gambled and the stakes he played for, and the way he played the field with the broads.

When I flunked out as a playmate, Schenck made it plain that he still wanted me to share his palace. I guess he wanted to keep me around for laughs. Now and then I sat in on his poker sessions, until I got dizzy from the size of the pots. But mostly I kept to myself—and Susan.

It was like having a private house. Joe turned over a complete wing of his joint to me. I got my menagerie out of the vet's and turned them loose, hauled in a couple of truckloads of potted plants, and before long I was living in a marvelous, upside-down mess. Siamese cats flew all over the place and roosted on the

373

mantelpiece. While the cats flew, the myna birds walked and pecked at spots in the design of the Persian carpet (which Joe had paid eighty-five thousand bucks for), the two monkeys slept in my wardrobe trunk, the turtle ran around in circles, and the poodles tried to climb trees. Kayo, disgusted with all of them, sat glowering under the easel—which he associated with Susan, the light of his life.

The first time Susan saw my palatial slum at Schenck's she said, "It's exactly the way it should be! Please—never let a woman's touch wreck it!" I never heard a more loving or more insincere statement in my life.

It was here that Susan met Oscar Levant. Oscar never forgave me for pulling the rug out from under him in Beverly Hills, but we still saw each other fairly often. About Susan he said, after first meeting her, "Harpo, she's a lovely, lovely person. She deserves a good husband. You'd better marry her before she finds one."

Oscar didn't move in on me at my new location because he had nothing in common with my host, and Oscar was a man of principle. He never sponged off anybody he didn't admire. When I gave Oscar a tour of the palace, wing by wing, suite by suite, he wasn't impressed. But he thought he ought to make some kind of nice comment since I chose to live there. "Well," he said, reflecting on all the wonders and facilities he had seen, "I'll say one thing about Schenck. He certainly knows how to shit."

Susan's pretext for coming around was so we could paint and draw together. She could do cartoons of me and I could do oils of her and that way we could save on models' fees. Before long, Susan's talk began to turn toward the same subject—marriage.

This time I was lucky. I didn't have to move to escape. I went to work at Metro-Goldwyn-Mayer.

The Marx Brothers had been in a rut. Our last three pictures, *Monkey Business, Horse Feathers* and *Duck Soup*, were all the same kind of patchwork of gags and blackouts. We were making a pleasant amount of loot but we were standing still. One more picture of this type and the law of diminishing returns would set in and we'd be on our way out. What we needed was a good, strong producer who'd give us a change of pace.

The family agents, Zeppo and Gummo, were beating the bushes for the right man, but it was Chico who flushed him—out of a bridge game. He was a skinny, intense, bright-eyed young guy named Irving Thalberg. Chico said that anybody who was that good a bridge player was good enough to produce our pictures. The fact that Thalberg was the head of production at Metro-Goldwyn-Mayer was incidental to Chico.

In 1935, Thalberg had plans to produce personally three new movies: *Romeo and Juliet, Mutiny on the Bounty,* and *The Good Earth.* Now he added a fourth to his slate: *A Night at the Opera,* with the Marx Brothers.

Our trouble, Irving said, was that we were a big-time act using small-time material. We belonged in "A" pictures, not in hodge-podge, patchwork jobs. Our movies should have believable plots, love stories, big casts, production numbers. We were afraid this would take us out of our element, but Thalberg said: "Don't worry about a thing. You get me the laughs and I'll get you the story."

This Thalberg was no "boy genius," as some people called him. He was a tough, smart cookie, a hard-working, mature man, and he was a perfectionist. When the first draft of our script was turned in, we thought it was terrific. Thalberg thought it was good, but not half good enough. The only way to get it in proper shape, he said, was for us to take it on the road and test it with live audiences.

So we hit the road with *A Night at the Opera.* Thalberg was so right. Some of the writers' favorite bits didn't get a snicker. They were cut. On the other hand, stuff that we ad libbed on stage, as in the "stateroom scene," went into the shooting script. As written—a bunch of guys jamming into a stateroom for no very good reason—this bit failed to get a laugh on stage. The writers got very depressed over it and decided to cut it. We decided, however, to give it one more chance.

So this night we did it our way. Groucho, ordering a meal from a steward while being jostled into the corner of the jammed-up stateroom, said, "And a hard-boiled egg . . ." I honked my horn. "Make it two hard-boiled eggs," said Groucho.

The audience broke up, and as simply as that, a dud became a

375

classic. The stateroom scene is still the best remembered of any bit the Marx Brothers ever performed.

We opened in Salt Lake City. Between shows I came across something new, tropical fish for sale in a ten-cent store. I spent a buck on a glass bowl and a pair of little pink fish, thinking this might add a bit of life to my dressing room. When a gang of reporters came backstage for interviews, one of them asked me about the fish. Was that a hobby of mine? he asked.

"Oh," I said, "more than a hobby. These two baby fish are my dearest friends, and I wouldn't think of leaving home without them. Why, I couldn't open if I didn't know they were waiting for me in my dressing room."

So a wire-service story goes out coast to coast about Harpo Marx, the tropical fish expert. Starting the day the story appeared, I was swamped with catalogues from hatcheries, pitches for testimonials, and letters from all over the country asking my advice on feeding and breeding tropical fish, and offering to swap guppies for mollies. This went on for weeks. The first thing I did when I got back to Hollywood was to install an aquarium in my joint. Another case of an actor coming to believe his press clippings.

To tell the truth, the Salt Lake City goldfish were good company on the road. They were the brightest spots in the long hours between calls to Susan.

We came back to L.A. with the show in tiptop shape—all shook down, tried out, tested and proven. But this was only the beginning. Working under Thalberg was twenty times harder than anything we'd ever done before.

Things were different at Metro. Sam Wood, who directed A Night at the Opera, was a perfectionist, as everybody under Thalberg had to be. He'd shoot a scene twenty times, from twenty different angles, before he'd go on to the next one. And every time he was ready to shoot, whether it was Take One or Take Nineteen, he'd give us the same instructions: "Okay, boys—go in there and sell 'em a load of clams!"

It was rougher on me than anybody else because of the stunt work my part called for. I had to swing on ropes sixty feet above the camera, teeter along the edge of a drop thirty feet high, and run straight up a twenty-foot curtain trusting in the strength of two almost invisible strands of wire. I acquired an aversion to clams.

This was the age of specialization at M-G-M. One day while we were recording a production number, the music director for some other picture came in and asked if he could borrow a B-flat chord. With him was a young guy whom I recognized as a tenor who once sang in our chorus. The orchestra obligingly played the requested chord, and the tenor sang a B-flat, two measures long. The visiting music director said, "Thanks a lot," then took the tenor and left.

Much later I found out that the tenor was the High Note Singer for Nelson Eddy (or "Eddie Nelson," as Louis B. Mayer always called him), who was then making *Naughty Marietta*. One of Eddy's songs ended above the register of his voice, which stopped at A, so the B-flat had to be dubbed into the sound track. Too bad it wasn't steadier work. Otherwise I would have added Eddie Nelson's High Note Singer to my private roster of wonderful jobs, along with Alfonso's Anthem Man and Grandpa's Tin Can Swinger.

It was during the shooting of *A Night at the Opera* that Arnold Schönberg came to town. Schönberg was a famous modernist composer who'd been hounded out of Germany by Hitler. He was desperately broke. Arturo Toscanini had appealed to Sam Behrman to see if he couldn't help the composer find work in Hollywood. Behrman paid Schönberg's way to the coast, and he wrote me to do everything I could to get him a job at M-G-M.

I gave Thalberg the pitch on the famous composer who'd just arrived on the coast. Thalberg was then producing *The Good Earth*. He still hadn't assigned anybody to compose the score, and he said he'd be happy to have Schönberg in for lunch at noon the next day. I warned Irving that this guy was one of the world's great musicians, and quite an eccentric, and he shouldn't be kept waiting one minute. Irving was notoriously late for appointments. But he gave me his word he would be punctual for Schönberg.

At a quarter to twelve the next day I went to Thalberg's office.

Irving was there. At twelve o'clock he buzzed his secretary and said he was about to have a very important conference and there must be no interruptions. We waited. Twelve-fifteen, twelve-thirty, and no Schönberg. Irving ordered lunch brought in. We ate. Finally, at one o'clock, the composer showed up. He was wearing a hat and an overcoat (it was warm and summery out) and carrying a violin case.

Schönberg explained why he was late. His English wasn't too good, and the guards at the gate had trouble with his accent. Instead of escorting him to Thalberg's office they sent him to the waiting room for studio tours. After half an hour of following a guide around the lot with a pack of tourists, Schönberg began to suspect he'd been misdirected. He broke away and found Thalberg's office by himself.

When we'd all finished lunch Irving got right down to business. What he was most concerned about was special background music for one of the scenes in *The Good Earth*. He described the scene, and gave it the full treatment. A woman working in a rice field begins to scream. She's giving birth to a baby. And just as the baby comes into the world, there's an ominous roar. It gets louder and louder. The locusts are swarming! Billions and billions of them, blackening the sky and casting the shadow of famine over the land!

Irving finished with the scene. Schönberg, still reeling from the labor pains in the rice paddy and the billions of locusts, blinked and said, "My dear Thalberg, if all these things are happening, you do not need music." He got up, put on his hat and overcoat, picked up his fiddle case, and walked out of the office.

Every time I saw the composer—on the lot, in the lobby of his hotel, on the streets of Beverly Hills—he was wearing overcoat and hat, and carrying his violin case. I couldn't figure out why he had his violin with him everywhere he went. He never volunteered to play it. He had no concerts scheduled. The only reason I could think of was that it must have been a Stradivarius, too valuable even to leave in a vault.

One night he showed up at the Gershwins', and I decided to solve the mystery of his fiddle once and for all. I asked him about it, point blank. Schönberg smiled and opened the case. It contained four Ping-pong paddles and a collection of Ping-pong balls. "One must be prepared," he said. "One can never tell where one might find a table."

The Gershwins' basement was my regular nighttime hideout when I was pulling the escape act on Susan. There was a Ping-pong table there, two pianos, and a built-in kibitzer—Oscar Levant. It was the best clubhouse in town.

The day we finished shooting A Night at the Opera, Susan came a-courting. The battle was on again, and hotter than ever before. This time her tactic was touting me onto buying a house. It was nice of Joe Schenck to let me stay this long, she said, but hadn't it been too long? Didn't I feel a little guilty about it? Didn't I owe it to my dogs, cats, monkeys, birds and turtles to provide them with adequate space? Didn't I want a place where I could entertain my friends properly? Didn't I want a place I could call my own, and be proud of? Didn't I want a place with room for a pool table?

The answer to all these questions was, of course: Yes.

It was the most logical thing in the world that I buy myself a house. But, I said, there was a slight financial problem. I couldn't lay out dough for a house as if there wasn't a future to worry about. We'd made our first picture at M-G-M. Our first high-budget picture. Thalberg was taking a big gamble on us. But suppose it didn't pan out? Suppose we were a flop? Paramount certainly wouldn't take us back. Nobody would want us.

"Do you have any doubt it'll be a hit?" she said, and I had to tell her that I did have doubts. It hadn't even been previewed yet. Nobody—not Irving Thalberg or L. B. Mayer—could guarantee that a picture would be sure-fire, nobody except the audience.

"Suppose the audience eats it up at the preview?" she said. "That would clinch it, right?"

"Yah," I said. "I suppose it would."

The sneak preview of A Night at the Opera was given at a theatre in Long Beach. All the Marxes were there, along with all the top brass of M-G-M. When the titles flashed on the screen the audience laughed. It was the last time they laughed. For their money the movie was a dud, a turkey, a flop. When it was over we all stood on the sidewalk in front of the theatre, clustering around Thalberg, in a daze. This was something that hadn't happened to us since the night we laid an egg on the stage of the Royal Theatre, sixteen years ago. We couldn't figure it out.

I saw Thalberg whisper something to a couple of his assistants. The assistants run into the theatre. They come out with the film, in six cans. Thalberg announces to all the mourners on the sidewalk that the picture is being shown again, in the theatre across the street. He refuses to accept the verdict of one audience. He has too much at stake in this deal. We all walk across the street, dragging our feet.

So we ran the movie a second time. The difference was like night and day. This time the audience laughed when the titles came on and they never stopped laughing until the end, when they whistled and applauded. It was emphatically a hit picture. The executives of Metro-Goldwyn-Mayer hugged and kissed each other. Chico tore off to call his bookie. Groucho said, "At last! Now I can complete my set of *The Book of Knowledge!*"

My date said to me, "Now you can buy our house, Harpo," and I said I sure could. Delayed reaction. Three hours later, lying in bed, I realized that Susan had said *"our house."*

I didn't fight it. I went house-hunting, on my own. Soon after the movie was released I found a place I liked in Beverly Hills, and bought it. Not until the papers were signed and I held the deed did I tell Susan about it. I took her over to show off the joint. It looked very big and very empty and I didn't have the vaguest idea what I wanted to do with it, but Susan said, "Perfect! The kind of a house I knew you'd pick out. I can see exactly how you're going to furnish it and decorate it. You don't need to tell me your plans. I know."

She kept a stiff upper lip while I showed her the layout, until we came to a room that had obviously been used as a nursery. There she broke down. She stood looking out the window with her back to me, and she said, "Harpo, when are you going to ask me to marry you?"

"Any day now, honey," I said. "Any day."

"What day?"

My feet got cold. There were many reasons, I said, why we shouldn't rush into such a serious venture. We had to have time to plan, time to outfox the press. If we didn't play it close to the chest the publicity could murder us. We wouldn't have a minute of private life.

"All right," she said, "so let's start planning."

"I am, honey, I am. I'm thinking hard about it right now."

She sat on the ledge of the window in the bare nursery. "Go ahead and think," she said, giving me her I-dare-you look and swinging a foot. "I don't mind waiting. I have nothing else to do for the rest of the day—or the rest of the year—or the rest of my life."

"Let's get out of here," I said. "I have to go home and feed the turtle."

The next day Gummo called me up, apologetically. Metro, he said, had the wild idea that I should go to Europe and do a series of personal appearances to plug A Night at the Opera before it was released over there. He'd told them I never wasted my time with that kind of exploitation, but they insisted Gummo should at least ask me and so he was now asking me, and what else was new.

I said, "How soon can I leave?"

Gummo told me I was kidding. I told him I wasn't. He asked me what the hell I wanted to go to Europe for. I said I had to take it on the lam, and he shouldn't ask any questions. So he asked questions. Who was after me? The income-tax people? Worse than that, I said. What was the rap? Was it serious? It was serious. What was the worst I could get? I could get life, I said.

"Oh," said Gummo. "Susan." My silence told him he'd guessed it. "I'm on her side, you know," he said, "and I think you're running away from the nicest thing that ever happened to you.

But you're my client and I work for you and I'll get you on the Friday plane to New York, and then I'll do my best to find a nice fellow for Susan while you're gone."

"You do that," I said.

I got a lot accomplished before I left. I huddled with the architect, the decorator and the landscaper and gave them final approval of all their plans. When I came back my new place would be remodeled, redecorated, furnished and landscaped, ready to move into.

I took Susan to dinner to tell her good-bye. She took my leaving very bravely, I must say. She said she knew how it was with anybody in my position. My life could never be entirely my own. When the studio said jump, I had no choice but to jump. It was terribly unfair, but she understood. The only thing she felt sad about was my poor house, the thought of it sitting there so empty and forlorn all the time I was gone.

"You'll be surprised what'll happen to the house while I'm gone," I said, and this cheered her up immensely.

It was not altogether a cheerful evening, however. On the eve of our being so far apart we had never felt so close together.

Rome was my first stop on the Continent. Dull time. Next stop was Milan, where M-G-M had rigged a night of publicity stunts for me at La Scala Opera House. Milan was memorable only because I drank too much peppermint liqueur at dinner. The liqueur had a delayed, disastrous effect on me in the middle of the opera, at which I was the guest of honor. I stuck it out only because I was able to make a deal with the men's room attendant for his trousers. I'm still not sure what was performed that night. The only name that comes to mind is *Il Purgativo*.

Even Paris had few attractions for me this trip. All I can remember of my stop there was staying at the George Cinq Hotel, and my French being so lousy I couldn't get the name of the joint across to cab drivers—until I got the idea of saying "Hotel Joe Schenck, please," which worked like a charm.

I was glad to get to London, the last date on the tour. I had many good friends in England, Marx Brothers' fans dating from the night we opened at the Alhambra shortly after the First World War. One fan I wouldn't see this time, however, was the Prince of Wales.

The last time Wales had been in the audience Chico and I had done our "flash" bit. In this we're onstage looking for something we've dropped. Chico asks me for a flashlight. I act dumb. "The flash!" he says. "Where's-a flash?" I am very eager and anxious to please, but I keep pulling the wrong thing out of my coat—a flask, a flag, a fish, a flush (poker hand), a flute, everything but a flash. Finally Chico says, "You're-a impossible. Come on, help me look for it." Whereupon I haul out a flashlight, turn it on, and help him look for it.

On the following day a present arrived backstage from the Prince of Wales. It was a velvet-lined hamper containing a flask, a flag, a fish, a flush, a flute, the whole inventory of the sketch, including a flashlight.

Now, in the middle of 1936, he was no longer the Prince of Wales, but the uncrowned King of England, Edward VIII. He was being kept under wraps for the period of mourning between his father's death and his own coronation.

I was amazed when the stage manager told me, during the intermission of my first show, that His Majesty was in the theatre in a private box, screened off from the public. After the show a messenger brought back a note, signed "Ed. Rex," thanking me for an enjoyable evening and inviting me to a reception at the royal residence.

There were only six or eight people at the reception, which was informal. I got on line to pay my respects. When it came my turn I decided I shouldn't bow, not being an English subject. I gave the King my hand. The King, with a straight face, gave me his leg. It was an old switch I'd pulled many times in my act, but it was never more perfectly executed. This broke up His Majesty's dignity, and mine too. He loved our routines, and knew every one of them, and we had a great time just horsing around.

He certainly didn't act like a guy in mourning, or like he was awed by his new responsibilities. I'd never seen him so outgoing, so bouncy and full of the devil. Well, he had plenty to celebrate. It wasn't every day that an unemployed polo player became the King of England.

Except for that brief visit with Edward, I was miserable in London. It had been the longest, loneliest summer I had ever spent. Life had a big empty hole in it, and it wouldn't be filled until I saw Susan and heard her voice.

It was a long time coming, even for a slow decider. I made the decision. I was going home as fast as I could. I was going to marry Susan as fast as I could, and we would never be apart again. I knew now I wouldn't be able to survive another separation.

I stuck a change of socks and a toothbrush in my raincoat pocket, left my trunk behind to follow by slow freight, and hopped aboard a transatlantic plane.

I tried calling Susan from Floyd Bennett Field, New York, and again from Chicago, but got no answer at her apartment either time. I was sure she'd be waiting for me at the L.A. airport, since I'd wired Gummo when I was due in. She wasn't there. I tried her number. No answer.

When the cab pulled up at Schenck's place, I had a second thought and told the driver to continue on to Beverly Hills. So my homecoming wouldn't be a total letdown, I'd go have a look at my new house before I did anything else. I didn't recognize it when I got there. The plantings out front were lovely, but nothing like what I'd visualized from the landscaper's plans. The columns on the house were painted white. I distinctly remembered I had ordered them to be green.

384

Then I noticed a station wagon in the driveway, full of equipment. My God, I thought, are they still working on the joint? The job was supposed to have been finished three weeks ago.

I went inside. A guy was hanging drapes and some dame wearing a smock, tennis shoes and a baseball cap was supervising him. The dame turned around. It was Susan.

When we came out of the clinch and back down to earth I took my first good look around. The place had been remodeled, decorated and furnished, all right, but not according to any plans I'd ever known about. The woman's touch—*a* woman's touch— was everywhere. The total effect was gorgeous, but it was also totally unlike any place I could imagine calling mine.

"I made a couple of changes, here and there," Susan said. For once she avoided looking at me directly, choosing to look at her tennis shoes instead.

"So I see," I said. I was still in a state of shock.

"I knew you wouldn't mind," she said, and laughed nervously. "I've been here since six this morning. I was determined to have everything ready before you arrived. Well, I almost made it. Everything's done except getting these drapes up. You can move in tonight."

Then she took a deep breath and said, "Harpo, when can I move in?"

"Monday," I said, for no good reason. I had lost all track of time somewhere between London and Los Angeles. When we unclinched the second time I said, "What's today, honey?" and she told me it was Thursday, the 24th of September. I had given myself three days of grace.

When Sunday came I was still in a state of shock. I tried to calm myself by practicing, but I couldn't even manage to finish a chorus of "Annie Laurie." I took a crack at "Love Me and the World Is Mine" and drew a blank after the first two bars. Forgot completely how it went.

I hadn't moved into the new place. If I'd moved without throwing a party, people would have suspected that something was up, and I was in no condition to throw a party. So I stayed on at Joe

Schenck's making like it was business as usual, old Harpo at the old stand, in there selling 'em a load of clams.

Sunday afternoon Susan and I had a secret strategy conference in a diner on Santa Monica Boulevard. I said I would pick her up at her apartment at nine o'clock in the morning. If her mother was around, Susan would tell her we were going to make the rounds of the tropical fish dealers. I had to restock my aquarium after being away so long.

"Where *will* we go?" said Susan. "City Hall?"

"No, absolutely not," I said. "Every clerk there is a spy for some columnist. Before the ink got dry on our license, Louella and Hedda would be typing out the story. What we do is get in the car and keep driving until we get to a place where nobody wants to know anything about us except that we're over twenty-one and have two bucks on us."

The game was becoming kind of fun. Took me back to my days as a Secret Agent. While I paid the guy in the diner I said, "Sure was nice seeing you again, kid," and Susan—showing a lot of talent for this kind of work herself—said, "Sure was nice, Fred. Don't forget to remember me to the gang back in Azusa, all except Louella."

"Yah," I said. "Never could stand Louella, could you?"

When I got home I was proud of myself. I was proudest of the fact that I wasn't getting cold feet.

Joe buzzed me on the house phone and asked if I wouldn't like to join him for dinner and maybe a little poker afterwards. "Love to," I said. So what did you know? I was going to have a bachelor party!

I didn't eat much dinner, but I had two brandies afterwards, and sailed into the card game feeling lucky enough to take on Swope, Harry Sinclair and Nick the Greek, dealer's choice, stakes unlimited. When the brandy wore off I found I wasn't doing so well. I made a mental note to pull out of the game at midnight no matter how I stood. At midnight I was nearly even again. I pushed the deadline ahead to one o'clock. It was not a very lively game. Out of courtesy to me, nobody bet any big money. This wasn't right. I was cramping their style. I should have been in bed long ago. But I couldn't make the effort to get up and leave the table. At two o'clock I was still in the game. Three o'clock. Four. Paralysis was setting in, with all the symptoms of what I thought I'd licked. Cold feet.

The game broke up at six o'clock. When the others left Joe said, "How about a steam? A nice steam'll untie the knots and you'll sleep like a baby all day."

"Sounds great," I said.

Sitting in the steam cabinet I concocted some brilliant, logical excuses for not going through with the day's plans. I had nothing to wear. All my good clothes were either at the cleaner's or in the trunk which hadn't arrived from England. I wouldn't feel right about getting married without Zep, Gummo, Groucho or Chico being the best man. It wasn't fair to Susan to get married without somebody from her family being there. We should play it smart—announce our engagement, let the publicity die down, then get married in style. We had been engaged a total of three days. Who could really be sure how long a marriage based on a three-day engagement would last? We owed it to ourselves to wait.

It was nearly seven, and daylight, when I got to bed.

Three hours later I was awakened by somebody banging on the window. I staggered up to see who it was. It was Susan. She was wearing a wide-brimmed picture hat, pulled down over her eyes, dark glasses, a 1930-style beige suit and "sensible" flat brown shoes, and she had blanked out her features with face powder.

"Do you think anybody will recognize me?" she said. I said that I, for one, sure as hell didn't. I was ordered to hurry and get dressed. She said she'd wait in the car.

I did as she ordered. I grabbed the first things I could find, in my spare wardrobe trunk, and put them on. I looked at myself in the mirror. I was wearing a squashed fedora, bright red tie, striped shirt dickey, swallow-tail coat, khaki pants, and dark glasses. "The jig," I said to whoever that poor clown was in the mirror, "is up."

Susan was behind the wheel, with the motor idling. "South," I said. "Drive south." She headed south and I fell asleep.

Mrs. Adolph Arthur Harpo Marx!

When I woke up the car was stopped. "Where are we?" I said. "Santa Ana," said Susan. "It looks like a nice, safe place. Thirty-one and six-tenths miles from L.A."

We got our license from the city clerk—no waiting, no impertinent questions asked. I put myself down as "Adolph Marx," as an added precaution. Then off we went, cruising through town, going down the list of justices of the peace the clerk had given us. The first one we approached took one look at us and our weird getups and said he didn't know what the joke was—probably an initiation stunt from some college—but he wanted no part of it. The next one we located said to come back when we sobered up, and slammed the door in our faces.

The third guy was wearing a Landon button, and we walked out of his place before any words were exchanged.

We worked our way to the outskirts of town and to the bottom of the list before we found a justice who at least had the decency to ask to see our marriage license. He looked it over carefully and looked us over carefully. "Well," he said, "there's no law says how you have to dress up to get married. Okay, I'll oblige you."

He asked if we'd brought our own witnesses for the ceremony. When we told him we hadn't, he said, "Come on next door to the firehouse. We'll dig up a couple for you."

We went next door to the firehouse.

A fireman was snoozing on a cot beside the hose car. The J.P. shook him awake and told him to call up his wife and tell her to come on over to be the matron of honor. "Tell her not to expect anything extra, if you know what I mean," he said. "But at least she can have a good cry for herself."

The fireman put on a tie. The fireman's wife arrived, wearing a hat and carrying a bunch of chrysanthemums. When she saw us her mouth dropped open and she nearly dropped the flowers. *"Them?"* she said, and the J.P. said, "Them." It was all extremely uncomfortable.

But when they found out I'd forgotten to bring a ring, the awkward situation turned into a friendly little party. A bridegroom who forgot the ring could only be a harmless, overgrown kid, head over heels in love. The matron of honor lent us her ring.

Due to there being no fires on the outskirts of Santa Ana around noon on the 28th of September, 1936, the ceremony went off without an interruption. Adolph Marx and Susan Fleming were pronounced man and wife, upstairs in the firehouse. The fireman's wife cried. The J.P. kissed the bride. The fireman kissed the bride. I kissed the bride.

My punishment for squandering forty-two years as a loony lone wolf had caught up with me. As I had told Gummo, it was a serious rap. I got the maximum. Life. Sweet, sweet sentence!

We were about to drive away when the J.P. came running over to the car. "Say, Mr. Marx," he said. "Mind if I ask you a personal question? I've been thinking about your name, and it kind of rings a bell with me."

I tried to make a getaway, but I had the car in the wrong gear and it stalled. This didn't discourage the Justice. He caught up with us and said, "Marx, Marx, Marx—aren't you related to the folks that run the dry-goods store over in Orange?"

"Yah," I said. "Distantly." Susan blew him a kiss and we headed for home.

We kept our secret for over a month, from everybody except Susan's mother. I was still living at Joe Schenck's address, officially, and Susan at her apartment. Unofficially we lived in our house in Beverly Hills. Daytimes Susan spent helping me put the joint in shape, which was very generous of her. Nighttimes we locked ourselves in and kept the lights turned out, which was not altogether a hardship.

After a while the cloak-and-dagger game began to bore us. We were too good at it. Nobody suspected. Mainly, we were dying to tell our news to the world. The question was when? I got an idea. We'd pick a time when there'd be a big enough news event to crowd us into the back of the paper—like the national election, November 3.

To make the picture perfect, Alice Duer Miller arrived on the coast. The Irving Berlins had turned their place over to her and she decided to give a small dinner party on Election Night. When she called to invite me she said, "I do hope your charming young friend Miss Fleming will be free to come too," and I said I thought there was a pretty good chance she'd be free.

I hadn't looked forward to the first Tuesday after the first Monday in November so eagerly since the last time I collected wood for the Tammany bonfire on 93rd Street. I also had a financial interest at stake. Thanks to the *Literary Digest* poll, which had Alf Landon sweeping the country, it was possible to get a bet down on Roosevelt. I scraped together all my loose cash and bet the bundle on F.D.R., as a wedding present for Susan.

Returns were already coming in on the radio when we got to Alice's. I didn't want to upstage the next President of the United States, so I took Charlie Lederer aside and told him about us right away. Telling Charlie, I knew, was like telling the Associated Press. But as soon as I told him, he slunk away as if I'd touted him onto Dr. Townsend for President.

Soon after we finished dinner it was announced that the Democrats were in by a landslide. Alice rang the hostess' bell and out came the champagne. We filled our glasses. Charlie Lederer rose to propose a toast. We all prepared to drink to Franklin Delano Roosevelt.

But Charlie said, "I give you the bride and bridegroom, Mr. and Mrs. Harpo Marx." Nobody believed it. I had come prepared. I took out the marriage certificate and handed it around the table. Out came more champagne. Instantaneously, the party turned into a good old-fashioned Manhattan bash. The way they carried on you'd have thought it was me, not Roosevelt, who'd just carried every state except Maine and Vermont.

I slipped away to see what had happened to Lederer, who had disappeared. I found him on the telephone, reading from some notes. He was phoning the story to one of the Los Angeles morning papers.

The L.A. paper double-crossed me. They sat on our story until their Election Final was out. Then they slapped us across the front page in a banner headline (pictures on Page Three), and put out an extra edition to carry the story.

When the papers hit the streets I was amazed at myself. I wasn't the least bit upset. For a moment I even toyed with the idea of hiring a skywriter, and finishing the job in style.

CHAPTER 21

Most Normal Man in Hollywood

T HE YEAR WAS 1940. The scene: dinner at the David O. Selznicks'. The guests: Rose and Ben Hecht, Dr. Sam Hirshfeld, Susan and myself. The conversation had turned to psychiatry. Psychoanalysis was the current fad among the movie colonists, and no party was complete without a discussion of Freud, Oedipus, hostility, penis envy, and comparative rates of Beverly Hills analysts.

Rose Hecht asked for silence. She had a pronouncement to make. She pointed across the table at me and said, "There sits the only normal man in Hollywood."

The pronouncement was for the special benefit of Sam Hirsh-feld. Obviously, Rose expected the doctor to say something like *Hear! Hear!* or, *The only true words spoken tonight!* This was not his reaction, however. Sam said, "That's a pretty big statement, Rose. What evidence do you have to back it up?"

"Harpo," she said, "is one of the few men I know who hasn't spent an hour on the couch. He's the only man I know who hasn't even talked about being analyzed. He's happily married. His son has reached the age of two without once being taken to a child psychologist. Harpo has no enemies. He's never gone on a diet or taken a sleeping pill. He's not money-mad or driven by ambition. He's mature. He's *adjusted*. He's a breath of fresh air in a town full of neurotic exhibitionists and show-offs."

The doctor thought for a while. Then he began to laugh. "I'm not going to confirm or deny any of your evidence," he said. "But I'd like to tell a story about this 'adjusted' friend of ours, Rose. An incident that occurred last summer at Hillcrest . . ."

I knew the incident Sam had in mind, one I'd hoped he had forgotten. It was not one of my glorious moments. It happened one day when four of us were shooting a match-play round of golf—Joe Louis, the heavyweight champion; Lou Clayton, Jimmy Durante's old partner; Sam, and myself. On a par-three hole my drive landed in a sand trap. In blasting out I overshot the green by a mile. I conceded the hole, picked up, and waited for the others by the next tee.

Joe, Lou and Sam were good, consistent players. The only consistent thing about my playing was its eccentricity. When I was on my game, I was very good. When I was off I was lousy. This day I was off. I looked to lose a few hundred bucks, so I figured I might as well play it for laughs.

Near the tee there was a short length of watering hose, connected to a spigot embedded in the ground, and a pile of fresh clippings of leaves and grass. Not much to work with, but enough to improvise a little gag. I ran the hose up my pants leg, then stuffed my pants with handfuls of the clippings. When I heard the other three guys approaching I turned the faucet on with my foot. They came upon me in the act of relieving myself—with a phenomenal, powerful stream laden with green hunks of vegetation.

"Hey, Doc!" I said. "Maybe I better have a urinalysis. Do you think there's anything wrong with me?"

"Nothing a good psychiatrist couldn't cure," said Hirshfeld, who then broke up, along with Joe and Lou.

But if they thought the gag was funny then, they found it twice as funny the next day when they learned why I didn't show up at the club for another round. The "leaves and grass" I had stuffed in my pants were fresh clippings of poison ivy.

393

"Only normal man in Hollywood?" asked the good doctor, as he finished the story at the dinner table.

Rose Hecht stuck to her theory about me. "Well at least the *most* normal man," she said. "What happened on the golf course comes under the heading of 'boys will be boys.' What I was thinking of was a man in his important relationships—with the people he works with, with his wife, how he relates to strangers."

At this point I looked at Susan and she looked at me and we laughed. Now it was our turn to tell a story, on ourselves.

The summer after we were married we went down to the B-Bar-H Ranch in Palm Springs for a second honeymoon. It was very hot in the Springs. Sensible people stayed away, and the town was just about deserted. I finally found a golf course open, and shot a few holes alone. Back in the clubhouse I met a guy, a retired Admiral, who was as much of a golf nut as me and who was also looking for a partner. We made a standing date to play together.

That night Susan and I sat around wondering where to look for some fun. We had come to the wrong place for a gay time. "I know what I'm going to do," Susan said. "I'm going to dye your hair, Harp."

"Well, okay," I said. "but wait until I finish tomorrow's round of golf."

So I shot a round with the Admiral, with my hair still its natural brown. That night Susan went to work on it. It came out a flaming pink. The next day I was wearing a hat when I showed up on the golf course. Halfway through the round, while the Admiral was lining up a putt, I took off the hat. The old guy looked at me, made no comment, and sank his putt.

That night I had Susan go to work on me with a razor. The following day I took off my hat along about the eleventh hole. The left side of my head was still a luxuriant, flaming pink. The right side was shaved clean to the scalp. The Admiral made no comment.

On the fourth day the rest of my skull was shaved, except for a square pink patch over my left ear. On the fifth day the patch over my ear was dyed a shiny, jet black. The Admiral's game was steady as ever, and golf was the only topic of our conversation.

On the sixth day I turned up with my hat pulled down over my ears. Under the hat my head was shaved completely, smooth as an uncracked egg. But my golf date never showed up. I called the joint where he was staying. The desk clerk said the Admiral had checked out that morning, a week ahead of time, refusing to leave a forwarding address.

I went home looking like a dehydrated Erich von Stroheim, and that was how the Most Normal Man spent his second honeymoon. I'm afraid we gave Rose Hecht a pretty hard time with her theory.

The truth was, marriage hadn't changed me much at all. If anything it had brought out more and more of the Patsy Brannigan in me. Now I had a permanent claque to egg me on—a claque of one, Susan.

Dr. Sam Hirshfeld had become our family physician, and one of our best friends. I never knew a man who had more time and affection to give to other people, or more energy to give to his work—with enough left over to take on anybody, any time he could, at any game you wanted to name. This guy was half demon and half saint.

Years later, after Sam had passed away, Ben Hecht wrote: "His work as physician and surgeon was a small part of his activities. Through with his hospital rounds and his professional calls, Sam would dash off to some laboratory where he pursued the secrets of longevity and cancer cures. At midnight Sam would enter his home, stretch himself in his bed and read until dawn. His mind poked into all the corners of science and psychology, and mysteriously found time for poetry and novels.

"But Sam's chief activity was his side line of good Samaritanism. His patients were always his friends. He got them jobs, nursed them out of drunks, picked out babies for childless couples to adopt, induced roués to marry girls they had made pregnant, restored the egos of defeated writers and suicidal wives.

"As I write of him, I see again his wide grin, his tense eyes full of eagerness and wisdom, his trim and tireless body. He was one of my few friends who could beat me at badminton and beach racing. If not for his eyes, he could have passed for a prize fighter. . . ."

A gang of us used to go to the fights, baseball games or hockey matches—whichever was in season—once a week, and Sam was our ringleader. Hockey was his special passion among sports. He never missed a match unless he had to be in surgery or with a patient who was confined to bed. Patients who were ambulatory he often brought along with him to the hockey game. One such was our mutual friend Gene Fowler, the writer.

Fowler was a big, congenial, convivial guy who didn't believe in moderation in those days, particularly moderation in drinking. When he hit the bottle he stayed on a bat for weeks at a time. But Gene was also a wise man, wise enough to know that only the living got any enjoyment out of life. So when he felt a drunk coming on he placed himself in Sam's custody, and stuck as close as he could to Sam until the urge passed. If he slipped, Sam would be handy to give him a hypo to ease him back on the wagon.

One night Hirshfeld, Fowler and I went to a hockey game. Fowler swore he had taken his last drink. He even bought four bags of popcorn before the game—to absorb his craving for alcohol, he said. Everybody except Sam was impressed by this. The doctor was hopeful, but noncommittal. "We shall see," was his attitude.

By the end of the first period Gene, munching away at the popcorn, appeared to have lost the symptoms of his craving. He'd been close-mouthed and fidgety when he first got to the arena. Now he was cheerful and full of chatter. Sam was finally impressed. For the first time, he felt his patient was making some kind of progress.

In the middle of the final period, it became plain what kind of progress the patient was making. He was getting progressively drunker. Fowler was mysteriously but unmistakably plastered. Sam was baffled. Gene hadn't once left his seat, and Sam had kept an eye on him the whole time.

The doctor bore in to investigate. Now that Gene had won the battle of the booze, he didn't have to lie any more, and he happily made a full confession. Before the game started, he confessed, he had slipped into the men's room and doused a quart of bourbon over his popcorn.

Going through the parking lot after the game was over, Gene was feeling ultragenial. He was very pleased with himself and with the world. We passed a guy who was having car trouble. Gene stopped, stuck his head under the guy's hood, poked around, and yanked something loose. "Here," he said. "Here's your trouble, pal." He handed the guy the carburetor and walked on, overflowing with the spirit of human kindness.

Gene Fowler once tried to teach me the art of drinking. I didn't enjoy drinking, he said, simply because I didn't know how to do it right. It was best to start with brandy. Brandy, taken properly, could keep you glowing without actually making you drunk. The secret was in drinking it slowly enough. You took a sip, then squeezed an ice cube in your hand. When the ice cube melted, it was time for another sip.

I gave it a conscientious try. I got the first gulp down all right, but before the ice cube had melted I got to thinking about the second gulp and dreading it so much that I had to go throw up.

There was something wrong with my chemistry. Alcohol and Harpo didn't mix. This even applied to me as a bartender, when I entertained. Charlie Lederer once said that I could take a sealed fifth of rare old Scotch, uncork it, and pour it straight from the bottle—and by the time the liquor got in the glass the drink would be ruined.

For this reason I was never asked to join Fowler's mob, whose members included John Decker, John Barrymore and W. C. Fields, and whose common bond was the kind that bourbon was bottled in.

John Decker was an artist who was unbelievably facile with brushes and oils. He used to paint in the styles of the old masters as a way of picking up eating money, like other artists knocked out magazine covers or portraits of society broads. Decker's canvases weren't cheap copies of old masters. He had a genius for reproducing the feeling, the lights and shadows and depths, of the originals.

I got to know Decker well when he painted a series of me and my brothers after the manner of Gainsborough, Franz Hals and Rembrandt. While I was posing for him as "Blue Boy" he told me he hadn't seen his pal Jack Barrymore for a long time. Barrymore was in a serious decline. He was disintegrating physically and mentally, and he knew it. He was ashamed even to see his good friends and kept himself a voluntary captive of doctors and attendants.

I said, "You know, it might give the guy a shot in the arm if we got a gang together and took him out. We could have dinner at my house, then maybe go to the fights." Decker thought it was a wonderful idea. The only thing was, if Jack came, his girl would have to come along too. "Fine," said I. "We'll make it Saturday night." Decker checked with Barrymore's girl friend. She said Saturday was fine with her—as long as her husband came along too. Why not? said I.

The next day Decker told me it was all set with Barrymore himself. "You don't mind if Jack's masseur comes along too, do you?" he said. Of course I didn't mind. I knew that the rub man's main job was to control Barrymore's ration of drinks. The boss was allowed a small glass of watered vermouth every two hours.

One thing Decker warned me about. We should all drink freely in front of Barrymore. If we held back, or hid the bottles, he'd suspect we were treating him like a child, and—like a child—he'd get belligerent. I hired a bartender for Saturday. I told Susan that, all things considered, it might be a swell time for her to take her mother out to dinner and a show.

Everybody arrived on time: Barrymore, his girl friend, the girl friend's husband, his rub man, the rub man's wife, Decker, Fowler, and three or four guys I didn't know, the type which there was only one word for—"cronies." The Great Man strode into the house at the head of his entourage. He looked marvelous, lean and graceful as a college athlete. He strode through the joint delivering an eloquent and expert tribute to each of the paintings on the walls.

No matter where Barrymore stood, you had the illusion that he was under a spotlight. He was every inch, ounce and fiber a masterful actor. He was also a masterful magician. By the time we sat down to eat he was fried. He had stolen two drinks from me alone, before I'd had a sip of either one. I was under his spell and didn't know what had happened until it was too late.

During dinner I noticed that he was drenched with sweat. His shirt and jacket were soaked through, and sweat was streaming down his face. I told him to go ahead and take his coat off, if he was too warm. When he found my eyes he gave me the piercing, pained look of a wounded eagle. "My dear Marx," he said. "To perspire is a gift of Providence. It saves me the trouble of pissing."

After the fights we wound up having coffee and nightcaps in a crummy jukebox joint off Hollywood Boulevard, a place that had sawdust on the floor for atmosphere and therefore charged double for everything. Decker and Fowler said good night and left the party. The girl friend and her husband followed them. As host I felt it was my duty to stick it out to the end, along with the rub man and the cronies. It was two in the morning. Barrymore was trying to make time with the waitress, a blondine dame of about fifty with eyes too close together and teeth too far apart.

Finally I had enough, host or no host. When Barrymore pulled out his handkerchief, the piece of napkin the waitress had written her telephone number on fell out of his pocket. The last time I saw John Barrymore alive he was down on his hands and knees, groveling on the floor, weeping and snuffling, looking through the sawdust for a juke-joint waitress's phone number.

399

The passing of an ordinary man is sad. The passing of a great man is tragic, and doubly tragic when the greatness passes before the man does.

The mob that hung out in the Hillcrest Club was more my speed. A bunch of us had lunch there so regularly that we organized ourselves into a Round Table.

Members of the Hillcrest Round Table included Al Jolson, Eddie Cantor, George Jessel, Jack Benny, George Burns, Lou Holtz, Milton Berle, Danny Thomas, Danny Kaye, and four or five Marx Brothers. The doubtful Marx Brother was Chico. Chico turned up only once in a while, and never for very long, depending on how his business was going. Chico's business at the time was the daily pinochle game at the Friars Club. As of this writing, some twenty years later, it still is.

I've often been asked to compare the two Round Tables, the Algonquin and the Hillcrest, since I'm the only guy lucky enough to have belonged to both. Actually, there's no fair comparison to be made. They were different in every respect.

At the Algonquin anybody, male or female, who dropped by and was accepted into the conversation "belonged" to the Round Table. Contrary to legend, the talk at the Algonquin was not one continuous olio of sparkling wit. There were long stretches of serious talk and literary shop talk, and when the Algonquinites told jokes or made up limericks they weren't competing for laughs. It was their way of relaxing.

At the Hillcrest we had a fixed membership. It was strictly stag. The table was in the Men's Grill of the club, where no female dared set foot. If any dame had tried to invade our sacred territory she would never have returned. The language at the Hillcrest Round Table was seldom fit for mixed company.

There was little conversation, as such. It was a wide-open competition to see who could get the most laughs, a running game of "Can You Top This?" It was never dull. We had among us three of the funniest men of our time, George Burns, George Jessel and Groucho Marx. And it was among us, where no holds were barred, that they were their funniest.

For my dough George Burns was—and is—one of the truly great wits of America. Whenever George started rummaging in his trunk of vaudeville souvenirs, the competition all sat back to listen. Offstage, he didn't talk in gags. George was always original. He could tell the same story a dozen times without seeming to repeat himself. He had a prodigious memory for people, and he revived names and faces that everybody else has long forgotten.

Above all, he had the gift of instant satire. Yet George was a guy who didn't know the meaning of the word "malice." He's never been an "insulting" comic. When he tells a story on you, you love it. I ought to know. I've been one of his favorite subjects for twenty-five years.

The virtuoso showman of the Hillcrest Round Table was George Jessel. Jessel was "on" from the minute he stepped into the Grill, yelping something like, "What do you think I just heard on the radio! Somebody shot the President! Why would anybody want to shoot a nice man like McKinley?" He wasn't "off" until he'd strung together a three-hour monologue of jokes, take-offs, folk tales, reminiscences, blackouts and dialect bits, all equally hilarious.

With his humor, anything goes. But socially Jessel is a stickler for what is correct and proper. He has refused, all through the years, to call the Marx Brothers by our stage nicknames. To him Chico is still "Leonard," Groucho is "Julius," Gummo is "Milton," Zeppo is "Herbert," and I am either "Adolph" or "Arthur."

When Jessel launched into one of his monologues, even his friend Julius kept quiet. Otherwise Groucho was the Round Table's heckler-at-large. He "left-jabbed" us to death in his sneaky, soft voice, with his cracks and asides. No punch line was safe from Groucho's counterpunch. No man, at the Round Table or elsewhere, ever dared to slug it out with Groucho.

It's a pity that some of the classic meetings of the Hillcrest Round Table couldn't have been recorded for posterity. One day we hid a microphone in the matzohs before Jessel made his entrance. Unfortunately, George discovered it before he got wound up, and he clammed up. Yet, I suppose if any of our sessions had been recorded they'd still be lost. They would have suffered too much in the translation into printable English.

Late one Friday afternoon five of us were sitting at the Round Table, Burns, Jessel, Lou Holtz, Zeppo and myself. We weren't trying to top each other for laughs. We were trying to see if anyone could make Lou Holtz laugh at all. Lou's wife was divorcing him. He had just been notified of the settlement she insisted on. The way her lawyer talked, he was being stripped of every worldly possession.

As a result, his ulcer was kicking up something fierce. Every time he thought of the settlement he got another pang, and had to take a swig of some thick white medicine he kept in a bottle in his pocket. We hoked it up like a pack of clowns, but Lou didn't crack a smile. He kept thinking about that settlement and groaning and swilling down the white stuff.

Zep had an idea. "You know what you need, Lou?" he said. "A weekend in Palm Springs, where it's warm and dry. Lie around in the sun. Swim. Play a few holes of golf. Greatest tonic in the world."

Lou said he was ready to try anything short of the gas pipe. Zeppo made it sound so good that we decided we should all take off for the desert, then and there. I called Susan and told her I'd be home a little late—like two days—since I had to go on a mission of mercy with a sick friend.

We had an early dinner at the Round Table. When we were through I said, "There's room for all of us in my car. I'll drive. I know a short cut."

Burns looked apprehensive, but he piled gamely into the car with the others. I announced we'd be at the Springs well before midnight, what with the short cut, and off we went, just as darkness came on. Driving conditions weren't exactly perfect. The car was full of loud talk and cigar smoke. The windows steamed over so badly that I had to drive with one hand, hunched over the wheel, while I kept wiping a peephole on the windshield.

Still, time seemed to go pretty fast. I didn't realize how fast until Lou Holtz wailed from the back seat, "Harpo! Aren't we *there* yet? It's one o'clock in the morning and I'm running out of medicine and I'm freezing!" Like the rest of us, he was wearing golf slacks and a short-sleeved sports shirt.

I reminded Lou that nights got chilly in the desert, but it was a *dry* cold, good for you. I explained that I hadn't expected the roads to be in such bad shape. Must have been tearing them up for repairs. But cheer up—we'd be in Palm Springs any minute now.

Half an hour later I wasn't so sure myself. I stopped the car. "Boys," I said, "I think we're lost." "What makes you think we're lost?" said George Burns, and I said, "Because it's snowing."

I drove on, creeping through the snowstorm. At last we hit the lights of a town. It wasn't Palm Springs. It was Victorville. Victorville was about seventy miles from Palm Springs as the crow flies— if a crow could fly over the ten-thousand-foot mountain range that separated the two towns.

It was almost three in the morning when we piled into the lobby of a small hotel near the railroad tracks in Victorville. Nobody had anything to say, least of all to me. Lou Holtz took out his medicine bottle, looked at it sadly, shuddered, and gulped the last remaining swig of his precious white stuff. He was sick as a dog and turning blue from the cold. I felt guilty, and uncomfortable, so I hauled a harmonica out of my pocket and started to play "Waltz Me Around Again, Willie."

Lou put a hand on my arm, ever so gently. "Harpo, not now," he said in a soft, sad voice. "Anything else, but not the mouth organ. This is the low ebb of my life."

We put in a call for ten o'clock and staggered up to our rooms. I was exhausted from the strain of driving and went out like a light. But when I heard the ring of the morning call I woke up

403

fresh as a daisy. I jumped out of bed and went whooping from room to room rousing the other guys. I got 'em all awake before I noticed it was still dark outside. I looked at my watch. It was four-thirty. We'd slept a total of an hour and a half.

What I had taken for the ten o'clock call was the bell of a freight engine. We went back to bed, but not back to sleep. The freight engine kept clanging and banging all the rest of the night, beneath our windows.

Well, we did get to Palm Springs. Normally, it was a trip that shouldn't have taken over two and a half hours. By my short cut it took twenty-one hours and twenty-five minutes. But the weekend wasn't a bust. Lou Holtz did feel better. And George Burns acquired a new story for his Harpo file.

Burns and I were constant golfing companions in those days. I could always beat George. He made me feel like a pro. George found it impossible to take golf seriously, and he could always get a laugh out of me on the course. I made him feel like a great comedian. We were an ideal twosome.

The Hillcrest didn't regard us as ideal members, however. We had too little respect for Club regulations. One summer when the weather got unbearably hot, George and I took our shirts off on the course, which was against the rules. The Board of Governors wrote us a letter requesting that we desist from this flagrant violation. The day after we got the letter it was still hot, and we went back on the course and took off our shirts again.

We were called on the carpet and warned that if we did it again we'd be suspended. We did it again. We were suspended from the Club for two weeks.

The day the suspension was up, we gave our word we'd never break the rule about shirts again. This time we kept our word and kept our shirts on. But on reaching the third tee, we took off our pants. We had checked and found there was no rule against this. So we played eighteen holes in shirts and undershorts and nobody stopped us. Fortunately for all concerned the weather turned cool before the next meeting of the Board of Governors.

Only once did I have a serious fight with the club. That was when I led a campaign to revoke the by-law that only persons of the Jewish faith could be members. I am proud to say I won the fight, and Hillcrest ceased being a restricted club.

At Hillcrest I got to know a guy named Lee Langdon, who was one of the top-ranked bridge players in the country. Langdon had the idea of starting a bridge club, and asked my help in financing it and lending my name as a front. I liked the idea, and was happy to help.

The Beverly Hills Bridge Club was an immediate success. We rented high-class rooms on Wilshire Boulevard, and we had a charter membership to match the rooms. Most of the guys from the Round Table joined, along with the cream of the movie colony, everybody from Norma Talmadge to George Raft. We charged members by the hour to play. There was seldom an empty table. Before the club was six months old I got my investment back. I became a silent partner and devoted my spare time to golf again. Because of this I missed out on the most dramatic moment in the history of the bridge club.

I was paged this day in the Hillcrest locker room. It was Lee Langdon on the phone. He was almost too shaken to speak. He said, "For heaven's sake, Harpo, get over here as fast as you can. Don't even stop for a red light."

When I got to the joint one of the members, a heavy-set lady of forty or so, the wife of some movie producer, was sobbing hysterically. Two other dames were trying to comfort her, without much effect, and Lee Langdon was pacing the floor, wringing his hands. Lee whisked me into the office. "This is an awful crisis," he said. "We've got to think fast to save the club." Then he told me what had happened.

The fat dame was playing four-handed gin rummy with Harry Ritz and two others. When they finished a game and switched partners, Harry Ritz pushed back his chair to let this dame pass in front of him. When she did, Harry was overcome by a sudden, diabolical impulse. He bit her on the behind.

She let out a shriek and flew around the joint screaming that "this dreadful man" must be expelled from the club.

Lee said he couldn't expel Mr. Ritz from the club. Ridiculous. Harry was a charter member in good standing.

If he wasn't expelled, she said, she would walk out and form her own club and take half the membership with her, everybody who believed in paying for a safe and decent place to play in. Then she went into hysterics, and that's when Lee rushed to call me over.

We came out of the office to face the crisis. The dame fell on my neck. After I heard her side of the story all over again, I said, "I'm sorry, but Mr. Langdon and I have gone over the by-laws very carefully, and there's nothing there that says a member can't bite another member on the behind."

She was on the verge of going off again when I held up my hand and smiled and said, "*However!* However, we'll be glad to make it a rule from now on that anybody who does what Harry Ritz did will be suspended for six months."

"No," she said, dabbing at her eyes with a handkerchief. "It should be a *year's* suspension."

I said I thought a whole year was too stiff a penalty. Lee agreed. The dame said, "Well, I'll settle for ten months."

I said, "Eight months?" She folded her arms and shook her head.

The three of us thought it over for a while. Then I said, "How about if we compromise on nine months?"

"All right," said the dame. "I'll agree to that, but not a day less." She got up and marched triumphantly back to the card table.

So a new by-law was put on the books: "*Effective immediately, any member of the Beverly Hills Bridge Club caught biting an-*

other member on the behind will be automatically suspended for a period of nine (9) months."

To my great disappointment we never had an occasion to invoke the rule before the War came and the club was disbanded.

Unlike the wives of a lot of my friends, Susan was not a "country club widow." Something had happened to us to bring us closer together than we'd ever been.

The first thing we had agreed on, driving back from the Santa Ana firehouse the day we got married, was having a big family. Me, because I'd grown up in one and loved it. Susan, because she'd been an only child and dreamed through so many hours about belonging to a big family.

Three months later, we started making arrangements to adopt the first member of our family.

It wasn't easy. Susan and I shared a deep love—for each other, for life, for all living things. We shared a faith in the same Divine Power, even if we had no handy stage name to call Him by. Yet on the records we were incompatible. I was Jewish and she was Christian. Adoption agencies were sympathetic, but they warned us that because of our religious difference, the adoption procedures might be unusually long and involved.

We had nobody to turn to except our friends. They went to bat for us. Dr. Sam Hirshfeld led the fight. Marion Davies helped move mountains of red tape for us. Aleck Woollcott and Alice Miller wrote letters on our behalf. Swope was not content to write a letter. He thundered across the continent at the agency people, by telephone.

Still, we had to sweat through six heartbreaking months before we could bring our baby home. We had found him right away. He was pale and tiny, small for his eight months. The nurses were a little discouraged over him. He seemed listless. He never smiled. He refused to take solid food. But the moment Susan and I looked into his huge, somber dark eyes, we fell in love with him.

Susan leaned over his crib. The baby studied her face for a moment, then broke into a smile. To the nurse this was a minor miracle. She asked Susan if she wouldn't try feeding him. Susan offered him a spoonful of cereal. He gobbled it. We knew he was ours and he knew it too.

On a lovely morning in March 1938, we brought our son home. William Woollcott Marx entered our lives and changed our world.

Billy was the forty-seventh string on my harp. The first sounds he could distinguish were the sounds of music—of Susan's laughter, of my playing. Music has been his personal language ever since. When he was two his favorite bedtime story was "Annie Laurie," on the harp. By the time he was five he could sing all the melodies in my repertoire by heart. Call it a miracle or just plain luck, but Billy had chosen us just as surely as we had chosen him.

We had asked Woollcott to be Billy's godfather, and we had hoped that he could be with us when we brought our baby home. But Aleck's schedule of lectures and broadcasts was brutal as ever, so he performed his godfatherly duty by long-distance phone. While I held the phone to Billy's ear, he introduced himself as "Uncle Acky Wookie," sang "I'm Des a Itto Wabbit in de Sunshine," and concluded with, "May God bless you, Master William Woollcott Marx, and may your father fry in hell."

Before Aleck finished, Billy fell fast asleep. He was my boy. There was no mistake about it.

On Billy's second birthday I was overcome with nostalgia for the East. You'd have thought that parenthood would make me feel more deeply rooted to the West. But the effect was just the opposite. I guess it was the natural urge of a new father to show his family off to his oldest friends.

The only communiqué I'd had from New York in a long time was a letter from Sam Behrman. I came across the letter, unopened, between the pages of an old magazine in the reading rack in the can. It had been mailed five years ago. I must have received it about the time I was moving out of the Garden of Allah. What difference did five years make? It was still news from home, and it was nice to read that Sam was well and was planning a trip to Hollywood, and was anxious to hear all about my trip to Russia.

I answered Sam right away. My reply began, as I remember, "Yours of the past decade received . . ."

Not long after I found Behrman's letter, a telegram from another old friend arrived and stirred up memories of a more distant past:

GOING FROM NEW YORK TO ANTIBES THE LONG WAY AROUND VIA CALIFORNIA. YOU ARE ONE OF TWO PEOPLE I CANNOT LEAVE WITHOUT SEEING AGAIN. COCKTAILS FIVE P.M. BEVERLY HILLS HOTEL. BAISERS MON PETIT VESTON VERT.

DAISY FELLOWES

After I got somebody to translate *veston vert* for me I hunted until I found the green jacket with the brass buttons, and had it patched and cleaned to wear to Daisy's party.

Seeing Daisy Fellowes again was like reliving that whole summer of '28. She hadn't changed a bit. She was rich enough not to have to change, but more than that, she simply didn't want to. Her cocktail party in Beverly Hills was small and informal, but gay as any elegant bash Daisy had thrown on the Riviera.

The only guest I didn't know was a plain-looking, skinny dame in blue jeans who was sitting on the floor. She wore no make-up and her hair hung straight and needed combing. She was vaguely familiar to me, but I couldn't think where I might have met her. Antibes? Neshobe Island? San Simeon? Sands Point? Broadway? London? I couldn't make any connection.

Before I could get tipped off on who this broad was, I found myself sitting on the floor talking to her. From the questions she asked, she knew me all right and she knew most of my friends. I played along with her, and we talked circles around each other for half the party. The only clue I had was her slight accent. But

I couldn't place the accent. It might have been French. Or maybe Russian. For that matter, it could have been plain old 86th Street Yorkville.

When the party broke up we exchanged fond farewells. As soon as I got Susan outside I said, "For God's sake, do you have any idea who the dame is I was talking to on the floor?"

Susan gave me a very odd look, then burst out laughing. "That," she said, "was Greta Garbo."

Out of the blue, I got a summons from Woollcott. He telephoned to say he was taking the summer off to go on the stage, and that I was going to tour with him. "Nuts to that," said I, to which Aleck said, "We open in Marblehead, Massachusetts, on the twenty-third."

So I got to go east to show my family off.

The play was called *Yellow Jacket*. It was a "Chinese ritual drama," whatever that meant. To me the play made no sense whatsoever. All it lost in the translation was everything. Everybody wore embroidered mandarin jackets, pillbox hats, baggy pants, and silk slippers. When they weren't bowing and shaking hands with themselves they were galloping around on imaginary horses or singing songs that had so little melody you couldn't tell if they were off-key or not. There was a four-piece pit band, made up of two Chinese guitars, tom-tom and drum.

The leads were played by Fay Wray and Alfred Drake. Woollcott was "The Chorus"—a sort of master of ceremonies. My part was "The Property Man." What I really played was the part of the curtain. The only way the audience could tell a scene was over was when I came on stage and changed the props and scenery. I also (shades of Minnie and the Shubert Revue!) did the special effects. Like at the end of the third act, when after a lot of grunting and thrashing around, the hero and heroine climb up to heaven, leaving the heavy slumped on the floor, and I come out tossing confetti in the air to signify it's snowing. Between scene changes I lounged around onstage smoking a cigarette in a long jade holder, to add atmosphere. That was the toughest part for me. I had quit smoking. So I usually managed to park myself near the wings, where I went through the motions while Susan, out of sight behind me, blew the smoke for me.

I wore a Chinese costume, but insisted on wearing my red wig instead of a pigtail. Even so, nobody recognized me through the Oriental make-up.

The only thing I knew for sure about *Yellow Jacket* was that Aleck took it very seriously. This project was a crusade as holy to him as selling America on *Goodbye, Mr. Chips, Dumbo,* or Seeing Eye dogs. He brushed me off whenever I asked him what *Yellow Jacket* was all about. In so many words I was told that its depths of meaning were beyond my feeble comprehension, and I was a lucky clown to be on the same stage with such artists, and so be grateful and shut up.

After we opened I was more bored than sore. I tried hard to do my part and play it straight. *Yellow Jacket,* hell. It was more like *Strait Jacket.*

Then, during the second week, Alfred Lunt and Lynn Fontanne came to see the show. With those two friendly faces out front I couldn't resist doing a little something special. During Aleck's big solo scene in the third act, I had to sit downstage—the one time I had to do my own smoking. So this night when Aleck got going I fixed the Lunts with a popeyed stare, dragged on the cigarette and started blowing smoke bubbles. From the back, Aleck couldn't tell what I was doing. But when the laughs got bigger and bigger and the audience stopped watching him he knew I was up to something.

Aleck was so mad after the show that he couldn't speak to me without spitting. "I'm shocked," he said. "Shocked and ashamed. Your behavior is reprehensible and thoroughly unprofessional. It befits a cheap burlesque comedian." To make it worse, the Lunts came backstage and embraced me and said, in front of Aleck, that I was the most refreshing thing in the play.

I promised to be a good boy. I was genuinely sorry, but Aleck wouldn't forgive me.

411

Woollcott was staying in an apartment next to ours, on the second floor of a boardinghouse. Susan and I used to help him up the stairs to his apartment, pushing him from behind. I continued to help him up, but he stopped speaking to me socially after the incident of the bubble blowing. He spent all his spare time with Susan, whom he adored, and with Billy. Billy rendered him as soft and gooey as a gob of melted cheese.

But for me he didn't have the time of day. What the hell. He had nothing to worry about. I wasn't going to louse up his lousy ritual drama. The performances dragged on. It was worse than boring. It got to be humiliating. I was doing my damnedest to stick to the part, and people were giving me laughs in the wrong places. After each show I got a lecture from Aleck about my unprofessional attitude. But I was determined not to blow my stack.

It had to happen. It happened on closing night. The audience was packed with friends from New York, many of whom had come to see me, not *Yellow Jacket*. During the first act I could read their faces. They were puzzled and impatient, waiting for me to do something. Let 'em wait. I swore I wouldn't step out of character. Still I was prepared, if worst should come to worst.

It was something Aleck said between the acts that did it. I've forgotten what it was—probably a very trivial remark—but I felt it was one condescending crack too many. For the one time in all the years I had known him I got sore at Woollcott, good and sore.

In Act Three I did everything except drop the knives and chase blondes across the stage. Blowing smoke bubbles was only warming up. I was all over the place. I ogled the leading lady. I gave the leading man the leg-hitch. I did outrageous takes. I changed the props so often the actors never knew which scene they were doing. I came out with a fly swatter and swatted flies. This wasn't effective enough so I got a flit gun to finish them off.

When the warriors rode on, on their imaginary steeds, I galloped after them, honking my horn. When they rode off I followed them, sweeping behind the horses with a janitor's push-broom.

Then came the final scene. The hero and heroine started their ascent to heaven, stepping over the body of the heavy. My cue to start the snow falling. I filled the air with confetti. I shook confetti out of my sleeves, from under my hat, and from out of my pockets. I took off my socks and shook confetti out of my socks. That wasn't nearly enough, so I began dumping confetti by the bushel-basketful. Snow was piled so deep on the heavy that the poor guy could hardly breathe. When the curtain came down I was hopping around and slapping my sides to keep warm in the blizzard.

We took curtain call after curtain call. The audience wouldn't let us go. Aleck stuck it out like a trouper, but I could see the danger signals. His eyes were flashing and his jaws were grinding.

He waited until Susan came backstage and then he let me have it, in front of Susan. He didn't get very far. I turned on him. I told him what he could do with his phony Chinese horse opera, and all his snotty talk about unprofessional behavior.

Aleck's mouth hung open. His chin wobbled. He couldn't speak. This was a Harpo he had never known before. Neither had Susan. To tell the truth, neither had I.

I left him with a parting crack. "I'm beginning to see," I said, "what Harold Ross sees in you." I walked out of the joint still in costume and make-up. Susan exchanged looks of astonishment with Aleck, then followed me out.

Two hours later Aleck came puffing and grunting up the stairs, under his own steam. He knocked on the door of our apartment and tootled, "Uncle Acky's here! Bearing gifts for Master William and Mistress Susan and apologies for Little Harpo!"

He was there almost an hour and he still hadn't made any apologies. Damned if I'd make the first move. This time it was all up to him. I got out the cribbage board and a deck of cards. We started to play. Our minds were not on the game. Finally Aleck laid down his hand. "All right," he said. "I'm sorry. It was a great misunderstanding on your part, and none of your accusations were true, but still I'm sorry. May I explain?"

413

I nodded he should explain.

He began to run down the whole *Yellow Jacket* affair, from the beginning. What I said. What he said then. What I had the gall to say after that. By the time he got to the final performance he was no longer explaining. He was getting mad all over again. He got madder and madder. He started banging on the table. The cards and the board flew off onto the floor.

"Goddamn it!" he yelled. "If *you* don't like me, Harpo, there's no reason why anyone on earth should like me!"

I didn't say a word. I picked up the cards and arranged the deck. Aleck made a noise like a collapsing balloon. He picked up the cribbage board. "I believe," he said, "the last hand may be safely called a misdeal."

We started to laugh at the same time.

The upshot of it all was that the Marxes spent the rest of the summer on Neshobe Island.

CHAPTER 22

Exit Alexander

THE UNITED STATES went to war. I'd been ready to go to war for eight years, ever since the sickening trip I'd taken through Germany on my way to Russia. I was fired with patriotism and full of fight. I offered myself to the armed forces.

The armed forces wanted no part of me. I was reminded, tactfully, that I was overaged, undersized, and devoid of any military skill. I had no business in olive drab or Navy blue. The only uniform I was qualified to wear consisted of a plug hat, red wig, raincoat and baggy pants. The only weapons I could be trusted with were a rubber-bulb horn, a harp, a clarinet, and two sleeves' worth of knives.

I took the hint, and so that was how I fought the war. For four years I toured the GI Circuit. I traveled two hundred thousand miles and played for half a million troops and defense workers. I performed at camps, airfields, naval stations, hospitals, ports of embarkation, service centers, and war plants. I crossed the Continent so many times I lost what little sense of direction I had left.

What confused my itinerary even more than the long jumps was the audience. I say "the" audience because it was like playing to only one huge crowd. It had been broken up and scattered around the country, but it was still the same crowd. In the old days the act that followed you into a town always asked, "How were they?" You said they were wonderful, or so-so, or a bunch of bums who sat on their hands. If you said "Typical Boston audience" or, "They haven't changed in Pittsburgh," the other act knew exactly what you meant.

On the GI Circuit nobody had to ask. They were the same in Boston and Pittsburgh as they were in San Diego, Wichita Falls and Newport News. They were terrific. They were always ready to explode. All you had to do to light the fuse was walk on stage. From that moment on, they were yours. You could do anything— play "Nola" on your teeth, imitate Dorothy Lamour, tell a joke about the WACs, or juggle a stack of tin plates—and the house went off like an arsenal full of TNT.

When I first appeared at an army camp, I had the weirdest feeling that I'd been there before. Then I realized why. It was like playing for the Russians all over again, only more so. These kids were starved for laughs, like the audiences in Moscow and Leningrad. The difference was that the GIs didn't need plots or stories or reasons. They'd laugh at anything.

Of course nobody was half as good as the GI audiences made him look. For this reason a lot of young comics, dancers and vocalists I knew became war casualties. They made it big doing camp shows. They made it too big. When the war was over they didn't know, or had forgotten, how much hard work it took to win over a club full of drunks or to impress producers and casting directors.

While it lasted it was unbelievable. It was an entertainer's market. But for us on stage, it was also a time of deep heartbreak. I used to look out at the seas of young faces, with laughter rippling across them like sunshine, and marvel that any of them could even crack a smile, knowing what they were going through and what they were headed for. In my mind I saw them as thousands of Billies—not as the men they were but as the kids they had been just ten or fifteen years ago, hoping that Daddy would keep on playing and making funny faces and bedtime would never come. I couldn't help thinking that when bedtime finally came for some of these kids it would be a nightmare followed by an eternity's sleep. No explosions of applause were powerful enough to erase this awful reality.

I was reminded many times of what Captain Thornton Wilder, the playwright, had written Woollcott from his army post: "Nothing so lifts a soldier's morale as getting a letter from home, and nothing so depresses him as reading it."

My favorite Thornton Wilder story was the one about the time a little girl asked him what a war was. Wilder replied, "A million men with guns go out and meet another million men with guns, and they all shoot and try to kill each other." She thought that over, then said, "But suppose nobody shows up?" and for this Wilder had no answer.

When war was declared in 1939, and it became apparent that both sides were going to show up, the New York *Herald Tribune* held an emergency staff meeting. The managing editor said the first order of business was to pick a special correspondent to send to Europe. Somebody said, "How about sending Aleck Woollcott?" The others thought this was a good suggestion—everybody except Percy Hammond, the drama critic. "Be taking a chance," said Hammond. "Woollcott might not like the war."

As it turned out, Woollcott didn't get to review the hostilities for another couple of years. He was itching to go over, but Percy Hammond's warning prevailed. It had been too long since Aleck had worked as a newspaper man. He was paid for spouting opinions, not reporting facts.

Meanwhile, during the summer of '39, when Moss Hart was visiting Neshobe Island, Aleck said that the next Kaufman-Hart play ought to have a part for him. Hart was delighted with the idea. So was George Kaufman, and they went to work immediately. What they came up with was *The Man Who Came to Dinner*. The leading role, "Sheridan Whiteside," was not only written for Woollcott, it was written about Woollcott.

Aleck was ecstatic when he read the script. Then he reconsidered. He decided that it would be in bad taste for him to appear in a play in which he himself was the hero. The part was given to Monty Woolley. And a juicy part it was—a self-centered prima donna with the manners of a grizzly bear, who basked in the adulation of celebrities and eccentrics but chewed decent, ordinary people into mincemeat. It was Woollcott with bells on.

One of the eccentric characters was a half-illiterate practical joker called "Banjo." It wasn't hard to figure out who *he* was supposed to be.

After the show became a smashing success in New York, the temptation was too much for Aleck, and he signed to play the lead in the West Coast company of *The Man Who Came to Dinner*. The L.A. opening was a personal triumph for Woollcott in more ways than one. He proved himself a fine comic actor in a long, tough role. And by playing the Whiteside version of himself with such relish, he proved he was a human being who was aware that he had many faults and who wasn't afraid to laugh at himself in public.

This confirmed the theory I'd always had about Aleck. He was a great, big, wonderful ham, and people who took him seriously were people who took themselves too seriously.

Most actors slept till noon during the run of a play. Not Aleck. He was at work by eight o'clock every morning. He dictated letters and articles through lunchtime, then romped off to spend the afternoon with his friends. If he didn't come to my place, or Walt Disney's, or Charlie Chaplin's, he held court at the Garden of Allah, where he was staying. Kaufman, Hart, Charles Laughton, Robert Benchley, Dorothy Parker and Alice Miller were also staying there, so it wasn't hard for Aleck to get up a quorum. When he finished his night's chore onstage it was party time—eating, talking and gaming until the small hours of the morning. Then, no matter when he might have turned in, it was up and back to work at eight o'clock.

In March of 1940 the company departed for San Francisco, where they had a spectacular opening and settled down for a long run. Early in April, Aleck wrote Beatrice Kaufman: "I have enjoyed the past twelve months rather more than any year I can remember. I have, however, no idea to what to ascribe the fact that, ever since I started on this trek at the end of October, I have felt in better health than I have known in a dozen years. I feel elegant. It will startle you to learn that, after more than twenty years of fidelity to one cigarette, I now smoke another brand and that, for some unknown reason, I no longer belch. You would hardly know me." He signed the letter "Porky."

The week after he wrote those lines, all the dozens of years of excessive living caught up with Porky. He had a severe heart attack. It was Aleck's first illness since he was a kid fresh out of college, the time he'd nearly died from the mumps.

I was allowed to visit him briefly in the hospital in San Francisco. Aleck was a changed man. I had never seen him so subdued. He was more annoyed than frightened, but he was meek and docile with the doctors, and obeyed their orders to the letter. His annoyance was not so much over the illness itself as over the closing of his show.

"You won't believe it after the lousy job I did in Los Angeles," he said, "but I was beginning to be quite good. Another month and I would have been absolutely superb." He smiled. "I've even licked the hoodoo of that line in the second act—you know, the one which kept coming out, 'At Christmas I always feel the needy.'" We agreed that Aleck's fluff would have made a dandy subject for a Peter Arno cartoon—Arno's rich old club man, in fur coat and Homburg, moving up and down a breadline feeling the needy.

That was about the extent of our conversation. He was too tired to laugh.

Woollcott wasn't docile very long. That fall he came out of his retreat on Lake Bomoseen to electioneer for Roosevelt in the campaign against Wendell Willkie. Activity seemed to do more for him than rest, and not long after the election he was back on the road again in *The Man Who Came to Dinner*.

In the fall of '41, against all medical advice, he went to England. The old warhorse couldn't stay out of the fight any longer. He did a series of broadcasts over the BBC which the English, still reeling from the Blitz, found very heartening. When he returned to the States he went straight to the Midwest, where he shook up the isolationists and America-Firsters with fiery speeches proclaiming that the war in Europe was our war, like it or not.

This brought on a relapse, which was followed by an operation. The surgery was successful. He went back to convalesce at Bomoseen and began to mend very quickly. Soon came the Woollcott summons: Fly at once to the island, where Decembers were so wild and beautiful.

But before I could get there, the Japs attacked Pearl Harbor, we were at war, and I was on the road with my camp show.

Somewhere on the West Coast

A marine general, who looked old enough to have fought on the shores of Tripoli, entertained our troupe at his bungalow after the show. He hadn't seen the show, but he'd gotten a look at one of the broads in the troupe, fallen for her, and decided to throw us a party. At dinner I sat on one side of the general and the broad sat on the other side. The general was plastered. After he had his soup he gave me a blank look and said, "Who are you?"

I primped my wig—I was still in costume from the show—and said, "I travel around the country with these gorgeous dames, General, and I've come here to make a deal."

"What kinda deal?" said the general.

"I've got fifteen girls in my troupe and you've got forty thousand men in your camp," I said. "We could go partners in a whorehouse and make ourselves a bloody fortune."

The general grunted and turned to talk to the broad. A little while later he gave me a blank look and said, "Who are you?"

I gave him my story again. He grunted and turned back to the broad. An hour later, he gave me a blank look and said, "Who are you?" For the third time, I outlined my deal about the fifteen dames and forty thousand men.

"Funny damn thing," said the general. "Girl over here just said the same thing to me."

Somewhere in Arkansas

Early in the game I learned that nobody had more power on a military base than a civilian, and that no civilian had more power than a comic traveling with an all-girl band, like me. For this reason I never had any trouble getting a high-ranking officer to act as stooge in the knife-dropping act, wherever I played.

After the first show at this base, I said to the guy who'd been my straight man, "You did great out there tonight, Colonel. I've had John Barrymore play that sketch with me, and he was no better than you." Since the straight man did nothing more than walk on and shake hands with me, to start the cutlery falling, this was strictly a tongue-in-cheek compliment. But I should have known better. The colonel was stage-struck. When I arrived at the theatre to get ready for the second night's show, he was already in my dressing room, putting on make-up.

As a matter of fact I was pleased to see this. I had a favor to ask of the colonel. That afternoon while I was walking through the base I was surprised to hear somebody call my name. The voice came from the basement of a barracks. I looked down in the basement. It was a friend of mine from Beverly Hills, a young lawyer. He was in fatigues, swabbing out a latrine.

He told me he'd spent all the night before out on maneuvers, and he'd been socked with latrine duty as soon as he got back to camp. The guy was dead on his feet, and depressed. He saw no hope of ever rising above the rank of buck private. I told him not to worry. I'd try to help him.

421

So that night I asked the stage-struck colonel if I could bring a friend to the party he was throwing for the cast after the show. "Why, of course," said the colonel. "Any friend of yours is a friend of mine, Harpo."

When my friend turned out to be a draftee, the colonel was a bit taken aback. I had rousted the poor guy out of bed to come to the party (he hadn't slept for forty-eight hours), but groggy as he was, my friend was able to give the colonel an hour's free consultation. He showed the C.O. where he'd overpaid his last year's income tax by forty-five bucks and this was the kind of military know-how that impressed the colonel.

A couple of weeks later the guy was recommended for Officer's Training, out of the blue. He wound up assigned to Moss Hart's company of *Winged Victory*, where he met many influential people. Soon after he was mustered out—with the rank of captain—he was appointed a judge in Los Angeles.

Somewhere in New Jersey

An actor I had known slightly in Hollywood was a corporal in a Jersey camp. We hadn't been in camp two hours before he made a date to take out one of the gals—a former stripper—after the show. But that afternoon, because of impending troop movements, all passes were revoked and all personnel were ordered confined to the post until further notice.

The corporal was desperate. He really had it for this broad, and she was in a mood to reciprocate. So I went straight to the office of the base commander to plead the corporal's case. The colonel was a real Babbitt in uniform. Framed mottoes hung all over his walls, along with citations and awards going back to when he was an Eagle Scout. I could see I wouldn't get far with any buddy-buddy talk, so I tried the shock treatment.

"Colonel," I said, "I want to ask you a big favor."

"I am here to serve, Mr. Marx," he said. "What can I do for you?"

"One of your boys wants to lay one of my girls," I said, "and he can't get a pass tonight."

The colonel bristled, turned red, huffed and puffed and damn near strangled. But he was too good a soldier to duck the issue. He said, "How long do you estimate this—ah—maneuver will take?"

I shrugged and said, "You know as well as I do, Colonel. With some guys it might take only—"

He didn't let me finish. "All right, Marx," he snapped. "I'll see what I can do."

That night the corporal was watching the show from backstage when he was notified he was being put on special orders. The colonel had made him his personal driver for the rest of the night. After the show, the colonel offered me and the corporal's girl a lift in his car. The colonel indicated the broad should sit up front, then ordered the corporal to take us to the officers' club.

At the club the C.O. and I got out. The colonel told the corporal to find a nice, dark place to park, and to take his time about picking us up.

"You understand, I'm not authorizing you to go on an all-night maneuver," said the colonel, "but, shall we say, three hours?"

Three hours was fine with the corporal, just fine. Rank had its privileges but it also, at times, had a heart as well.

Somewhere in Indiana

I played my first GI hospital here, and it was not a complete success. I had been scheduled to entertain first in the psycho ward. The doctors warned me not to appear in costume. This was to be strictly a concert, a musical-therapy treatment. I walked through the ward beforehand, chatting and joking with the patients and passing out cigarettes, to gain their confidence. Except for the extreme cases, they were all eager for me to play. I called for the harp to be brought in.

Instead of taking the instrument out of the case and wheeling it into the ward, three GIs lugged it in, case and all, on their shoulders. They looked like pallbearers carrying a sealed black coffin. The poor bastards in the ward started to yell. Attendants ran in to quiet them. I ran out, behind the pallbearers. The musical therapy for the day was canceled.

Somewhere in California

Actually, the biggest laugh I got any time during the war was at this hospital. It was a new, six-story joint built around a courtyard. They decided I should play a concert down in the courtyard, where the patients could watch from the windows and balconies above.

In the center of the courtyard was a replica of the famous fountain of Brussels, with the statue of the little boy taking a leak. Whoever designed the hospital had had a stroke of genius to put this conversation piece where all the patients could see it. It exactly fit the mood of convalescing soldiers.

Before I came out to perform, I had a conference with the maintenance staff of the hospital. When I came out I didn't look at the statue. All through my comedy routine I failed to notice it. Then came the serious part of the program. The harp was brought out. I began to play "Annie Laurie," very softly. The audience, most of whom were hanging over me on the six balconies, was so quiet I could hear the splashing of the fountain.

The splashing annoyed me. I had to have utter silence. I stopped playing. I turned and saw for the first time the statue of the little *pisseur*. I gave him a reproving look. I put a finger to my lips, pointed to my fly, and waggled the finger at him. The spout from the statue fell away to a trickle, then stopped. The maintenance man at the water valve had timed it perfectly.

Nobody heard the rest of "Annie Laurie," not even me. The GI audience up above laughed themselves hoarse and the staff members sitting down in the courtyard had to duck flying crutches and nurses' caps. After this opening I wasn't able to get away without playing a full hour concert. I hope it helped their morale. It sure helped mine.

In the summer of '42 I worked on a USO committee in Hollywood while I waited to go back on the road.

In the middle of August, Susan and I went east quite suddenly, when I got a telegram from Woollcott. It was a three-word message: ALICE IS DYING.

I found Alice at home in New York, in bed, racked with cancer. Alice had known she was a terminal case for nearly three months, but she'd told nobody except Aleck. Aleck had decided on his own that I should know, to give me a chance to see her once again.

I spent two days at her bedside, for as many minutes at a time as her doctor would allow. The first day I saw her she had only enough strength to squeeze with her right hand, feebly, and to whisper. But the spirit of the old Butch still flashed within her. It hadn't weakened by one volt.

She was still gracious and gallant, and too good a sport to concede a single point, let alone the game, to the disease. She burned more from curiosity than fever. Alice wanted no truck with the past. This was no time for looking backward. Nations were at war, great events were taking place, and her friends were scattered all over the world. She had to know where everybody was and what they were doing. She squeezed from me everything I could tell her—from the state of Carl Hubbell's fastball to the Marines' progress on Guadalcanal.

On the second day, my visiting periods were cut shorter. Alice's whisper had faded. The only physical power left to her was the movement of her right hand. But through her fingers and through her eyes the current of her spirit still flowed. Although I did all the talking it was a warm, two-way conversation.

That evening, when I returned to her house, they told me she was dead.

Aleck was up at Neshobe Island. I'd been in touch with him throughout the vigil, but the end came on a wartime Saturday night, a time when I couldn't get a line through to Vermont. I sent him a wire.

A letter that Aleck wrote to Charles Brackett from Lake Bomoseen, tells more eloquently than I ever could about his reaction to Alice's passing.

"You must feel," he wrote, "that your world is being depopulated. I warn you that it is one of the penalties of lingering on this scene after fifty.

"Late at night on the next to the last Saturday in August, my dear Lilly Bonner and I were out on the terrace here relishing a fabulous moon. Through the windows, from inside, there came the muttering and card slappings of a gin rummy game with Dorothy Gish and Louis Calhern involved.

"The quiet of the lake was disturbed by the sound of Howard Bull's motor launch chugging towards the island. At such an hour this could mean only one thing—a telegram and an important one, too, or he would have let it go until morning. The Bulls sit in judgment on our telegrams and decide among themselves if there is any rush about our seeing them. So while Howard moored his launch at the dock, I told Lilly that Alice Miller was dead.

"It was on just such another August Saturday night fifteen years ago that the same messenger brought the same news about Gregory Kelly (then married to Ruth Gordon). I remember now how he found all the lights out and, calling through the window of the ground-floor bedroom in front, awakened Neysa. She came in and got me up and we put on bathrobes and put a log on the fire and sat until all hours talking about Gregory.

"I think you may guess with what courtesy and grace of spirit Alice made her exit. She had written me confidentially early in June telling me that the jig was up and thereafter our exchanges were on that basis. It was precisely as though she regretted having to leave early but whispered it behind her fan so as not to disturb the party.

"Finally I decided that Lederer and Harpo ought to be told. I am glad I did for Harpo came east ahead of schedule and was in time by forty-eight hours to be welcomed by her. The second day she could not speak but held his hand while he talked to her, squeezing it when she was most interested. I am proud to report that out of the topics in his repertory, she squeezed hardest for Charlie Lederer, myself, and the Giants.

"I've found it an enriching experience to read over the letters I've had from her in the more than twenty-two years of our association. The file began with a hand-painted Christmas card. As the accompanying verse addresses me as a Cribbage Pimp I assume that a check came with it but apparently I was not sentimental enough to file that, too.

"It is a bleak fact that there is now no such person in our world as Alice Duer Miller. . . ."

The one bright note in that trip east was Aleck. He looked terrific. He had all the zest and bounce of ten years before. His blood was again up to its full, rich count of white corpuscles (whipped cream) and red corpuscles (acid). The medics had given him the green light to come out of confinement and go back to work. When we left him he was apartment hunting in New York for a winter headquarters—his "Valley Forge," as he said.

My camp-show troupe had taken off without me, so I sent Susan home and joined an all-star company doing one-night stands for the War Bond Drive. At Soldiers Field in Chicago we played to a hundred and ten thousand people. While I was waiting to do my second bit on the show, one of the stadium hot-dog vendors came backstage to shake hands with me. "For my dough," he said, "you're the best one on the program." I felt complimented, since the others on the program were Mickey Rooney, Judy Garland, Fred Astaire, Lucille Ball, Betty Hutton, Kay Kyser and his band, and José Iturbi.

"Yes, sir, Mr. Marx," he said. "When you played on your harp I sold four times as many hot dogs as when anybody else was on the stage."

A modest man is made, not born.

On the 12th of September I was home again, and just in time for an unexpected reunion. Ivy Lee Litvinov was in town and had been trying to get in touch with me. I hadn't seen her since the night in the Moscow theatre, nine years ago, when her husband had popped on stage as a comic and turned me into a straight man. Maxim Litvinov was now the Soviet Ambassador to the United States.

We took Ivy Lee out to dinner at Mike Lyman's Restaurant. I put on quite a performance, mainly for Susan's benefit, re-creating my six weeks in Russia—from the trouble I had carrying rubles across the border going in and my fiasco with the Moscow Art Theatre to my final "command" performance. Because of Mrs. Litvinov, I omitted telling about what I carried across the border on the way out.

Mike Lyman had been hanging around the table. Finally he said, "Excuse me for interrupting, but I heard some news on the radio in the kitchen that you folks might be interested in. The Russian Army stopped the Germans at Stalingrad."

Ivy Lee Litvinov certainly was interested in the news. For the rest of the night, the champagne at Mike's was on the Soviet Union.

I hooked onto a troupe heading east. We pulled into Watertown, New York, on a cold, gray afternoon in January 1943. It had just begun to snow. After the show it was still coming down. The next morning I woke up early. From my hotel window I watched the sun rise. The city was covered under a deep white blanket of snow. Nothing moved. It was a beautiful sight.

A great idea occurred to me. I called Woollcott in New York City, at his apartment in the Hotel Gotham. When he stopped cursing me for waking him up in the middle of the night, I told him my idea. I was sure he'd call it an absolute inspiration.

"Aleck," I said, "I'm back in your neck of the woods, outside of New York here in Watertown. The snow's eight feet deep and it's gorgeous out—too nice to make the jump with the rest of the company on the bus. Know what I'm going to do? Hire a horse and sleigh for the trip!"

Aleck said, "Exactly where is your next jump to?"

"Boston," I said. "How about it? Hop over and we'll take the sleigh ride together. Jingle bells, the whole works."

He did not leap at the idea or call it an absolute inspiration. Instead, he took a deep breath, let it out with a sigh, and said, "Harpo, you didn't dawdle long enough in P. S. 86 to become exposed to the subject of Geography, did you?"

"No," I said. "Why?"

"My dear boy," he said, "this may come as a bit of a shock to you, but Boston, Massachusetts, is not on the outskirts of Watertown, New York."

I refused to let go of my notion. I asked him how about if I took a short cut through the city and picked him up there? He said, "Oh a *splendiferous* thought! I shall be waiting for you in front of the Gotham to come jingling up in your troika. You'll know me by my white beard and the white fur trimming on my red suit. I'm fat and jolly and tend to go around saying 'Ho! Ho! Ho!' to little children. Meanwhile, if you don't mind, I'm going back to beddy-bye. God bless you and keep you safe from anything as dangerous as knowledge."

He hung up.

Later that morning, on the road, I asked our bus driver how many miles he figured it was from Watertown to Boston.

"Oh, it'll be around three hundred miles," he said.

I asked him what it would be if we took the short cut through New York City.

The driver played it straight. "The short cut wouldn't add more than two hundred miles to the trip, Mr. Marx," he said.

When I got to New York after playing Boston, I was delighted to find Charlie Lederer in town. Charlie said Woollcott was being very stuffy. He was having Eleanor Roosevelt up for tea in his apartment, after which he was doing a broadcast, some sort of forum program. After the broadcast, Aleck had told Charlie, he was going straight home and to bed and he could not be seen until noon the next day, and then by appointment only.

So what were we to do? We went to Abercrombie & Fitch, bought two croquet mallets and four balls. We arrived at the Hotel Gotham at teatime and went up to Woollcott's floor. I rang the bell of his apartment. Charlie and I then started hitting the balls up and down the corridor in the best old Neshobe Island manner, whackety-whack.

Aleck opened the door of his apartment. He looked through me. He looked through Charlie Lederer. He paid no notice to the croquet balls bounding and ricocheting up and down the corridor. From inside I heard Mrs. Roosevelt's voice saying, "I'm sure I heard the bell, too. Is there nobody there?"

"Nobody," said Aleck. "Strange—nobody at all." He slammed the door shut.

Charlie and I picked up the red ball, the blue ball, the yellow ball, and the black, stuck the mallets under our overcoats, and departed.

Lederer was invited to go to a dinner party that night with the Alfred Vanderbilts. When he said that Oscar Levant was going to be there I invited myself to go too.

After dinner the host asked if we'd like him to turn on the radio so we could hear the broadcast Woollcott was on. Charlie said not to bother. We would have liked to listen, he said, but we hadn't been asked. Woollcott would be furious if he found out we'd tuned him in without an appointment.

Later in the evening, before the party broke up, somebody telephoned to ask if we had heard the news. The news was that Alexander Woollcott had been stricken with a heart attack while he was on a broadcast.

I rushed to the phone. The lines were jammed at CBS. Everybody in New York was calling there for the same reason. I kept trying until I got through, and finally got the name of the hospital where Aleck had been taken.

When I called the hospital I was told that Mr. Woollcott was dead.

Whack.

The program had been a panel discussion called "The People's Forum." The guest panelists were Alexander Woollcott, Marcia Davenport and Rex Stout. They were discussing the civilian's role in the war effort. Aleck revved up and went zooming off like a mad hornet, to attack his old "enemies within the gates"—the isolationists and anti-Rooseveltians of the Midwest.

In the middle of a sentence Aleck stopped talking. He turned very pale. He wrote on a piece of notepaper, "I am sick." He pushed the note along the table to Miss Davenport, who read it and signaled at once toward the director's booth.

Ten minutes of air time remained. While the discussion continued, Woollcott was helped out of his chair and out of the studio. He was laid on a stretcher and carried to a waiting ambulance. When he was brought to the nearest hospital there was nothing that could be done for him. He died just before midnight, January 23, 1943.

One crazy detail stuck in my mind. It still does. A guy at CBS told me that while Aleck was being carried to the street on the stretcher, he fumbled around until he felt the rim of his hat, his big, black impresario's hat, which had been placed on the dome of his stomach. When he passed out the door and into the night, he lifted the hat and put it over his face.

What was crazy about this was that it reminded me of what Jack Johnson had done the time Jess Willard had knocked him to the canvas in the arena at Havana, Cuba, back in 1915. While the referee counted him out, Johnson, who was supposedly unconscious, laid an arm over his eyes to shield them from the glare of the sun. Everybody who had bet on Jack Johnson screamed that the fight was fixed, that the champion had faked being knocked out and had done a lousy job at that. People with dough on Willard said that Johnson's covering his face had only been a reflex. He was seeing stars, not the sun, and didn't know what he was doing.

With Aleck, I've never been able to decide—whether he had deliberately shielded himself against the night, or whether it had been a reflex. He was too good an actor to tip his hand. After playing the role of himself to the hilt, in spades, why should he goof on his exit and give the critics a chance to pan him?

The funeral was short and uncluttered. Ruth Gordon and George Backer each spoke a eulogy, and Paul Robeson sang the Twenty-third Psalm.

When it was over nobody had to suggest where we should go. Without a word being said, we all went straight to the Algonquin. It was the last gathering of the Woollcott crowd, and it was our strangest gathering. Neither Neysa nor Dottie nor Ruth nor Beatrice nor George nor Frank nor Charlie nor the lone surviving Katzenjammer Kid knew quite what to say, and for me, for once, there was no use listening.

I was on my own. The fat, spoiled, moody, cantankerous, mischievous, gay, generous, loyal and loving smarty-pants son-of-a-bitch who had dragged me into a world I had no business being in had ditched me. Like approximately one million other people, I felt sorry for myself when Aleck Woollcott died. But I guess that's the way it is. When you lose something irreplaceable, you don't mourn for the thing you lost. You mourn for yourself.

CHAPTER 23

Life on a Harp Ranch

I CAME TO REALIZE fully, with Aleck's passing, what his friendship had done for me more than anything else. It had kept me young. When he died my first reaction had been that he had ditched me and I was left all alone. But I wasn't, of course. The slack had already been taken up, by Susan and by Billy.

Now, six years later, there were three more Marxes in the house to keep me from growing up. In the fall of 1943 we had brought home our second son. We named him Alexander. In 1944, James Arthur and Minnie Susan had joined the family.

It was a crowd Aleck would have fit right into. We didn't run a very proper or conventional household, but the joint was never dull either.

At the end of the war we enlarged our house. We threw out the butler, disconnected the buzzer on the dining-room floor and got rid of all the rest of the Beverly Hills nonsense and converted the dining room into a poolroom.

The next thing we threw out after the butler was Dr. Spock.

I was the same kind of father as I was a harpist—I played by ear. But I've been lucky on both scores. The harp has given me a decent living and my children have given me more pleasure than I ever thought a man could possibly have.

What rules we had, as a family, stemmed from the fact that all of us had been adopted by each other. We've always had equal amounts of gratitude and respect mixed in with our love for each other. Susan, an only child who never had any roots, and I, a lone wolf who got married twenty years too late, were adopted by the kids as much as they were by us.

Somehow, without lecturing or threatening or studying any books, we all followed the same rules, from the time the kids were very young:

> Life has been created for you to enjoy, but you won't enjoy it unless you pay for it with some good, hard work. This is one price that will never be marked down.
>
> You can work at whatever you want to as long as you do it as well as you can and clean up afterwards and you're at the table at mealtime and in bed at bedtime.
>
> Respect what the others do. Respect Dad's harp, Mom's paints, Billy's piano, Alex's set of tools, Jimmy's designs, and Minnie's menagerie.
>
> If anything makes you sore, come out with it. Maybe the rest of us are itching for a fight too.
>
> If anything strikes you funny, out with that too. Let's all the rest of us have a laugh.
>
> If you have an impulse to do something you're not sure is right, go ahead and do it. Take a chance. Chances are, if you don't you'll regret it—unless you break the rules about mealtime or bedtime, in which case you'll sure as hell regret it.
>
> If it's a question of whether to do what's fun or what is supposed to be good for you, and nobody is hurt by whichever you do, always do what's fun.
>
> If things get too much for you and you feel the whole world's against you, go stand on your head. If you can think of anything crazier to do, do it.
>
> Don't worry about what other people think. The only person in the world important enough to conform to is yourself.
>
> Anybody who mistreats a pet or breaks a pool cue is docked a month's pay.

I think Woollcott would have liked the way we ran our joint. It was pretty much the way he ran his island. I know for sure that my father and mother would have approved. Our house, like the old tenement back on 93rd Street, was seldom without the sound of music or laughter, or questions being asked, or stories being told.

Billy, Alex, Jimmy and Minnie have turned out to be healthy, inquisitive individuals with minds of their own. I'm proud of them. I'm the most fortunate one-foot skater, undersized rent-kicker, self-taught harpist and nonspeaking actor who ever lived.

I felt a little pang when I turned fifty-six: Aleck had just turned fifty-six when he died. Susan and the kids didn't let me mope very long over my age. They turned on the Christmas lights in honor of my birthday, and the pang went away. It was nowhere near Christmas, and the lights were hung in a jacaranda tree in the patio, but this was our joint and this was the way we ran it. The jacaranda was the pride and joy of our patio. It was big enough to provide shade for the Ping-pong table all day long, and every spring it burst with clusters of delicate lavender blossoms. A useful, graceful tree it was. On the Christmas when Minnie and Jimmy were three, we strung the jacaranda with colored lights. The kids were so enchanted by the lights that we didn't have the heart to take them down. So we left them connected in the tree, and turned them on whenever we felt like declaring a holiday.

The lights were turned on for all of our birthdays, for Sam Goldwyn's birthday, St. Patrick's Day, April Fool's Day, Bastille Day, California Admission Day, Harry Truman Winning the Election Day, Alex's Learning to Swim Day, and Uncle Chico Wins at Pinochle Day. For two years we averaged about fifteen Christmases a year.

Finally the wiring began to fall apart, and we had to have the lights taken down. Billy, who was twelve, watched the handyman remove the lights with great fascination. Billy led a rich, full life, and he had little opportunity to enjoy such spectacles as a handyman up in a jacaranda tree, climbing from limb to limb. I'm afraid we made heavy demands on Billy, as parents are apt to do when their first child shows unusual talent. At the time he was taking piano lessons, riding lessons, lifesaving lessons, golf lessons,

435

dancing lessons, dramatic lessons, arts-and-crafts lessons, and special instruction in musical theory and composition.

Now he realized his life wasn't full enough. Something wonderful was missing. So when the handyman dropped down out of the jacaranda, with the strings of lights coiled over his shoulder, Billy, who hadn't missed a step of the operation, said, "Sir, who did you take your climbing lessons from?"

We got the point. It could be just as bad to give a boy too much as to deny him everything. We relaxed considerably after the jacaranda episode.

As the kids grew up, they turned our place into a zoo. We had poodles, dachshunds, collies and mutts—finally settling on mutts as our favorite breed. To maintain the balance of nature we kept the cat population up to equal strength, and threw in a monkey for good measure. Minnie raised hamsters. The boys and I built an aviary in the back yard. At one point, we had over a hundred birds there, behind a cat-proof screen. For a while we kept parakeets in our master bedroom, but they were oversexed to the point of distraction, and had to be exiled to the aviary.

The only troublemaker we ever had among our pets was Siegel the Sea Gull.

One day I was driving to work along Motor Avenue, the street that separated the El Rancho and the Hillcrest golf courses. I stopped when I saw a large white bird flopping around beside the road. It was a sea gull with a busted wing. Apparently he'd been knocked out of the air by a slicing golf ball.

(I was reminded of the time Sam Goldwyn was having a bad day at Hillcrest. Sam was working hard at correcting his slice, but no matter what he did, the ball kept fading on him. Before teeing off on a short hole over near Motor Avenue he asked his caddie's advice—should he use a wood or an iron? "That depends, Mr.

Goldwyn," said the caddie, "on which course you're playing—Hillcrest or Rancho.")

Anyway, I got the wounded gull in the car, covered him with a blanket to restrain him, and rushed him to the infirmary at M-G-M. The doctors there were undecided whether they should put the bird's wing in splints or amputate it. The vet wasn't much help. He was great with Rin-Tin-Tin III's mange, bog spavins on cowboy horses, or loss of appetite in lions that were supposed to devour Christians, but he was helpless with sea gulls.

While the medics argued, word of the crisis got around the studio, and all production ground to a halt. I called in the one guy I was sure would know what to do—Sam Hirshfeld. Sam came right over. He said that if they didn't amputate immediately there was danger of a fatal infection setting in. As the patient's guardian, I gave Sam permission to operate. In a room packed with Metro-Goldwyn-Mayer's highest paid stars and executives, Dr. Hirshfeld performed the wingectomy. When he finished, they applauded. Paul Muni never played a more stirring scene before the French Academy at Warner Brothers.

When I brought him home we named him Siegel, in honor of our producer friend Max Siegel. Dr. Hirshfeld had done a fine job on Siegel. Of course the bird could never fly again, but in all other respects he was a hale and hearty sea gull. Too much so, it turned out. He became a tyrant. He strutted around the joint like he'd come to collect the rent. He had the dogs and cats buffaloed. They backed away from his sharp tongue and his sharp beak, and he stole their food right and left. The monkey wouldn't come down out of the jacaranda tree when Siegel was on the march.

At the same time Siegel got less popular with the management. He took over the swimming pool as his private john. He kept it so messed up that the guy from the pool company advised us the rates would have to be raised for the monthly cleaning. It got worse. The rates went up again. The pool people really cleaned up on Siegel.

We'd become very attached to the fat old one-armed bandit, but he had to go. So we made a present of him to Zeppo, who was

437

then living on a ranch. There Siegel lived out the rest of his life. He died, apparently, of old age—but not until he'd spent a contented year keeping three dogs scared out of their wits and causing Zeppo's pool-cleaning rates to be raised.

It's always been George Burns' theory that Siegel was a stooge for the Paddock Pool Company.

To see our children develop, day by day, into four distinctly different characters, was like watching a continuous show, full of suspense, surprises and comic relief. I watched the characters with mixed wonder and envy.

Bill was the most predictable one. There had been no doubt about his being a musician since he was two years old. By the time he was thirteen there was no doubt he was going to be a damn good one. He already knew more about the harp than I did, or ever would. Under his influence I began to change my style. I realized I'd been faking for all these years, covering up my lack of musical knowledge with gooey arpeggios and flashy glissandos. Bill showed me the straight harmonies I should have been playing instead, and brought me up to date—out of the ricky-ticky 1920's— on my jazz beat. He was making an honest harpist out of me. He was making me work.

While Bill was turning into the musician I might have been, Alex was turning into the mechanic I could never have been. Alex was a tinkerer, a kid who could talk to machines in their own language. I never knew what the word "industrious" meant until Alex came along. He wasn't happy unless he had a hip pocket full of tools and something that needed fixing. School didn't come easily to Alex. But, being a challenge, it intrigued him. He tore into math and history as happily as he tackled a leaky faucet or a bent sprocket on his bicycle. For a busy beaver, Alex was remarkably unstuffy. He was, in fact, the nonconformist of the family, and whenever he had to conform he played it for laughs to save his pride.

Jimmy preferred thinking to tinkering. He was strictly a theory man. Where Alex was an engineer, Jimmy was a pure scientist. He had more fun designing something on paper or building a scale model than working on the real thing. Like Susan, he had a fine talent for draftsmanship. And Jimmy, although he was the nearest to an introvert among all of us characters, was probably the best natural athlete in the family. As a kid he developed a powerful golf swing and was a formidable switch hitter in Little League baseball.

Minnie was the one most like me. Nothing ruffled Minnie. Life for her was a dreamy, easy-come easy-go, day-to-day business. Unfortunately, this attitude prevailed in her school work, just as it had half a century ago with me. Unlike me, however, Minnie was smart enough to bring home a good report card anyway. Minnie's great love was the animal kingdom. She talked to animals like Alex talked to machines. With people she preferred to listen.

Come right down to it, our continuous show in Beverly Hills was not so different from the show the other generation of Marxes put on back on East 93rd Street. With each new day we all took off on our own, because we all had different notions of how a day ought to be spent. But no matter how far apart we strayed, we were sooner or later brought together by the sound of music or laughter, or by the urge to get some kind of a game going. Just as in the tenement flat, there never seemed to be time for jealousies or anger. Living conditions were a few thousand times improved over the East Side. The only meaning "hustle" had any more was "to hurry up." But we were no more orthodox than the old East Side characters were. We were the same breed of Happy Hooligan.

In one department we were certainly no different—Fatherly Discipline. Only once did I bring myself to the point of spanking one of the kids. It was Jimmy. He'd left an awful mess in the garage after putting together a model airplane and he'd been warned he couldn't do anything else until he'd cleaned up. He tried to sneak off on his bike for baseball practice. I intercepted him and sent him back to clean up.

439

The next thing I knew, smoke was coming out of the garage. Jimmy had swept the scraps into a pile and set fire to them. He thought he'd save time by burning the stuff on the spot, instead of hauling it to the incinerator.

We beat the fire out, then I sat him down for a serious talk. I explained what a dangerous, thoughtless thing he had done. Jimmy agreed that he'd committed a major offense, all right. I told him he had to be punished for it, and he said he thought so too. I asked him what kind of punishment he would recommend if he were the father and I were the son.

"Well, spanking, I guess, Harpo," he said. To the other kids I was "Dad," but Jimmy never called me by any other name except Harpo.

"How many spanks?" I said.

He thought it over and said, "Six."

"All right," I said. "Let's go up to your room and get it over with."

Jimmy was very cooperative. He assumed the position. I raised my hand for the first blow. I almost got cold feet. In my mind the scene suddenly changed to a dingy tenement hallway. Frenchie was shaking his whisk broom under my chin and saying, "*I'm going to give you, boy. I'm going to break every bone in your body!*" I reminded myself again of what Jimmy had done and that wiped away the fantasy. Our property could have been destroyed. Somebody might have gotten badly burned.

I brought my hand down with a mighty whack.

Jimmy howled—not in pain, but in protest. "Hey! That's not *fair!* You didn't tell me you were going to spank *that* hard. You should have given me a *sample* before you asked me how many spanks. Six is too *many.*"

"How many would you have said if I gave you a sample?"

"Three," he said. I gave him two more whacks. Jimmy said, "They weren't as hard as the first one, Harpo. Better give me one more." I gave him one more. He then got up and told me how sorry he was about the fire and all. He'd done it, he guessed, to "show" me. But now, he guessed, I'd showed him.

At dinner that night it was Jimmy, not me, who told Minnie

and Alex what he had done, and what I had done. They were impressed. I never had another occasion to take a hand to any of them.

Susan was much firmer than me. She was not averse to delivering a swat on the rear, now and then, to show the kids she meant business.

Like me, however, she was opposed to all-out spankings. And like me, she only had to do it once, when it was a serious matter of safety. This time the culprit was Alex. She caught Alex riding his Flexi-Racer in the middle of the street after dinner one evening in winter, when it was getting dark. She hauled him in the house and gave it to him good. Much as it hurt Susan, it hurt Alex a hell of a lot more. He had a fair complexion and extremely sensitive skin.

Five minutes after the deed was done, Susan heard a blood-curdling noise outside. She ran to investigate. There was Alex sitting on his haunches in the middle of the driveway, rocking back and forth to fan his fiery little bottom, and screaming into the night, "Help! Murder! Police! I been *kilt!*"

In one respect I was luckier than a lot of fathers. Having battled every kind of audience for forty-odd years, I knew that if you got 'em laughing you had 'em. It was the same with kids. Keep 'em laughing and they'll do anything for you.

Susan and I decided we would tell our children they were adopted as soon as they could understand any speech at all. It had to be the very first thing they learned about life. We'd seen some pretty sad cases, where parents were afraid of the children they had adopted—afraid, as they put it, that the kids "might turn on

441

them"—and kept putting off telling them the truth. When they were told too late, the kids really did turn, full of resentment and a feeling of being unwanted. The results were tragic—unhappy early marriages, delinquency, even alcoholism.

Billy was fourteen months old when he joined the family, and he already knew, by the time he learned to talk, that he had come from someplace else. Before he was able to ask questions about that "someplace else," we told him all about it. He accepted it for what it was, a fact of life. It was like learning that the sun went down at night, and night was the time for sleep, and that Mommy loved Daddy and they both loved Billy just as much—nothing more, nothing less.

Alex, Jimmy and Minnie each came home to us as babes in arms. We started telling them where they had come from when Alex was two, and Jimmy and Minnie were scarcely a year old. We told it in the form of a true-adventure bedtime story. By the time they were four and three, they couldn't go to bed without hearing "The Story," as we all came to call it.

They used to sit around Susan and me on the bedroom floor, curled up in their bunny-type pajamas, while we told The Story. We played it for suspense, like an old-fashioned cliff-hanger, and how they loved it!

Alex's eyes would be glittering, because he knew he came first. "Poor, poor Billy," Susan would begin. "Growing up sad and lonely, not having a little brother to play with. We had to find a little brother for Billy—not any little brother, but the *right* one, whose name would be Alex and who would have yellow hair and pink cheeks. Well, we looked and we looked. We looked at this baby boy and that one, but no—not one of them was Alex. Then one day Dr. Hirshfeld called on the telephone and said, 'I think I know where you can find him!' So Daddy and I packed our suitcase and got on a train and rode all day and all night, and then we got off the train and rushed to the place that Dr. Hirshfeld told us about. There they showed us a little boy. We looked at him—"

Susan would pause for effect. Alex would be hunched over and shivering from the terrible suspense.

442

"—and what do you know! It was Alex! We bundled him up and took him on the train with us and all three of us traveled all night and all day and then we came home and Billy had his little brother and wasn't sad and lonely any more."

Alex would let out his breath and smile with relief. He'd been found! Now it was Jimmy's turn to squirm and hold his breath.

"But Billy was six years older than Baby Alex, and he would run out to play with the older boys, and now Alex was going to be sad and lonely if *he* didn't have a little brother to play with. So we began looking and looking for a little brother for Alex—not any little brother, but the *right* one, whose name would be Jimmy and who would have bright, shiny brown eyes. Well, we hunted all over. People showed us babies, and they said, 'Is this the one you're looking for? Is *this* the one?' But none of them was the right one. We began to think we would never find Jimmy. Then one day Dr. Hirshfeld called on the telephone and said, 'I've heard about a baby boy, and I think he's the one you're looking for.' So Daddy and I got on the train, and this time we rode three days and three nights, and we said, 'Wouldn't it be awful if we got there and the baby they showed us wouldn't be Jimmy?' Well, we got off the train and rushed over and they showed us this baby, and oh, my goodness—"

Susan would shake her head. Jimmy would be biting his lip and clenching and unclenching his hands.

"—it wasn't our Jimmy. We started to leave, and then they said, 'Maybe we showed you the wrong one. Maybe *this* is the one you're looking for.' And what do you know—it was! It was Jimmy!"

Jimmy would smile and clap to hear he had been found at last, but Minnie would be beside herself waiting to hear the end of the story. The excitement would be so unbearable for her it was absolutely delicious.

This is where I usually took over. "Alex had his kid brother now, and somebody to play with," I would begin, "but what Alex and Jimmy wanted now more than anything else in the world was—"

"A *baby sister!*" Minnie would whisper, breathlessly.

443

"—a baby sister. Not just any old baby sister, but a little doll named Minnie, who was happy and gay and who wanted three brothers, the same as they wanted her. Well, it's not easy, you know, to find a baby girl like that. We hunted and hunted, all over town, and looked at all the baby girls, but we couldn't find Minnie. Then one day Dr. Hirshfeld called on the telephone and said, 'Hurry over, fast! I think I've found the one you're hunting for!' So Mom and I hurried over fast, and Dr. Hirshfeld showed us this little girl. And what do you know! It wasn't Minnie at all."

Minnie would stuff her hand in her mouth so she wouldn't blurt out the ending, and spoil the mystery.

"So we came home, feeling sad, and told Alex and Jimmy we hadn't found their sister, and maybe we never could. Dr. Hirshfeld called up again, and again, but every time we went to look it was the wrong baby girl. Then one day Aunt Gracie Burns called us up all the way from New York City, and she said, 'I think I've found the girl you're looking for!' and we said, 'What's she like?' and Aunt Gracie said, 'She's a little doll, happy and gay,' and we said, 'Yes! That sounds like our Minnie.'

"Well, we were in such a hurry to see her that we couldn't wait. So we didn't go to New York on the train. We told them to bring Minnie to us on an airplane. And the very next day a nurse got off the airplane and brought the little girl to us. But the minute we looked at her, she began to cry and yell, and her face got red and she wasn't happy or gay at all. 'You'll have to take her back on the airplane,' we said. 'This isn't Minnie. You brought us the wrong baby.' But then do you know what happened?"

Minnie's eyes would be shut tight. She'd be nodding her head and wiggling all over the joint trying to contain herself.

"What happened was, the little girl fell fast asleep—she was so tired from the long airplane ride. And I looked at her, and in her sleep she was smiling a happy and gay smile, and she was the most beautiful little girl you ever saw. I yelled, 'Hey, Mom! Come here quick! It *is* her, after all! It's Minnie!' "

When we had finally recognized her and decided to keep her, Minnie would be exhausted from the ordeal, exhausted but walking on air. Now that all three of them had been found, they had something wonderful to take to bed with them and dream about, and there was seldom any squawk when the lights went out.

Alex, Jimmy and Minnie never tired of hearing The Story. Long after they outgrew bedtime stories they would ask us to tell them The Story at least once a week. When they reached their teens they still wanted to hear it a couple of times a year. By then, of course, Susan and I had worked it into quite a show. What with all the touches and gimmicks we'd added over the years, we could have followed Alfred Hitchcock and kept an audience holding onto their seats.

Alex was about twelve when one day he came to me while I was playing the harp. He looked troubled. I stopped playing and asked him what was eating him.

"Oh, nothing, Dad," he said. He stared at the harp pedals like he'd never seen them before. He didn't know what to do with his hands.

I reminded him of our rule. No holding back. If he had something to say, out with it.

"Well, Dad," he said, "we've been talking about The Story, Jimmy and Minnie and me. And, well, there's something none of us ever said to you that we ought to have. And, well, me being the oldest we voted I should come and say it to you."

My heart was in my throat. Maybe the truth was coming out, after all these years. Maybe we'd made a big mistake. Maybe we had told the kids too much, too soon.

I said, "What is it you want to say, Alex?"

He finally got up the courage to look straight at me. He took a deep breath and said, "Thanks. Thanks for adopting us."

My heart went back where it belonged, and it's stayed there ever since.

When Billy was thirteen he happened to be with me once when I went through our safe-deposit box in the bank vault. I happened to come across his birth certificate. I showed it to him. Billy read it, then broke out laughing, and handed it back to me. I asked him why he was laughing. Oh, nothing, he said. It was only that the family name he'd been born with struck him as sounding very funny.

That was the beginning and the end of Billy's curiosity about his origins.

One night when Minnie was doing her geography homework she said to Susan, "Hey, Mom—where was I born? Maybe I've been studying the place where I was born and didn't know it."

Susan told her. It was a small city near New York. Minnie located it in the atlas. "Must be a real dump," she said. "It's only got a little dot by it, not even a circle or a star."

For a while it was a running gag with Minnie. Whenever I had to go east on a date, her last words to me would be, "Don't forget, Dad—give my love to my old home town when you fly over it!" Then the gag wore out, and that was the end of Minnie's inquisitiveness.

A year or so later Minnie came home from school one day very amused. A girl friend had asked her what it felt like to be adopted. "Of all the silly questions!" said Minnie. At first she'd told her friend that there was no "feeling" about it. Then Minnie corrected herself. Yes, there was. You felt you were the luckiest person in the world, if you were adopted. You hadn't just happened to your family, like most kids. You had been picked, out of hundreds of candidates. You were somebody very special. "Gee," Minnie said to us, "I hope I didn't make her feel bad. I certainly didn't mean to."

When Alex and Jimmy asked to see their birth certificates, they reacted quite differently. Jimmy read his with no comment, and shrugged it off like it was a piece of last year's homework. Alex's reaction was delayed. A couple of months later he came to me and said, "Dad, if my father was killed in the war, doesn't that mean I would have been in his will? Hadn't we better hire a lawyer and find the money that should come to me?"

I tried to explain to Alex that some lawyer would have found him a long time before this, if he had any inheritance coming to him. But Alex kept the notion alive that he was a missing heir for over a year before he threw in the towel, and admitted that I was right.

Of the four children, Alex has always been the most money-conscious—probably because he's needed the most dough, to keep himself in machines and tools and parts. They cost a lot more than Billy's piano scores, or Minnie's feed for her animals. As for Jimmy, he had the cheapest tastes of all. His rockets he got for Christmas or his birthday. When he wasn't rocketing, he was perfectly content to curl up with a book from the library, or play himself a game of chess, or help Susan work on her rose-bed.

The only time Jimmy ever splurged was once when he bought ten new trees for our lot and planted them himself, because he thought our landscaping looked a little skimpy.

We never gave any of the kids any money outright. There was no such thing as an "allowance" in our family. If anybody needed money he damn well earned it, doing odd jobs at home or on the outside. He could spend a third of what he earned—if we approved of the expenditure—and the other two thirds went into a savings account. We laid down the law that nobody could make a withdrawal from his savings until he was sixteen, and then only subject to our approval.

Alex may have had moola on the brain, but he wasn't a mercenary kid. One of his jobs was to maintain the sprinkler system—no minor job in a dry place like Southern California—and to turn the water on every morning before he left for school. One night at dinner he announced that he could no longer accept any

447

money for turning the water on in the morning. We asked him why not. He said because the water got turned off while he was in school, by the gardener. It was wrong that he should get paid for a job that he only started, and never finished.

His sense of right and wrong was an amazing thing. At the age of thirteen, Alex had as many principles as any guy who ever ran for President—the difference being, he stuck by every one of his.

The old man, meanwhile, was being housebroken. Susan and the kids were doing a neat, subtle job on me. I stopped going to the fights. I didn't go to the ball park unless I took the family along. I had already stopped smoking. And now I even laid off gambling.

Around the time I first met Susan, I maintained a second telephone, strictly for talking with the bookies in Kansas City. I used to bet on baseball, basketball, football, hockey, Davis Cup matches, bridge tournaments, flag-pole sitters, anything anybody gave odds on. But no more.

I won't say my family completely reformed me. I continued to bet on the Democrats in any election and the New York Giants in any pennant race or Series. But this was a matter of conviction, not looking for a quick buck, and this was the extent of it. I woke up one morning and discovered I was no longer a gambling man. I was a one-hundred-percent family man.

For one thing, I had not married a gambling woman. Susan was, she was frank to confess, an utter coward in any kind of a game where money changed hands or where winning was a religion. The one time she tried to play poker she shook so that she kept dropping her cards. The one time she played croquet with me, at the Goldwyns', we gave her such a hard time over a shot she missed that she spent the rest of the night in tears. Whenever she played bridge with me she never stopped humming. When I asked her why, she said she hummed to cover up how scared she was that she'd make a stupid play and I'd be sore at her. It was like whistling past a graveyard.

Well, so Susan kept humming and the next thing I knew I had stopped playing for big stakes. The real reason I stopped, I know, had nothing to do with her being chickenhearted or my feeling sorry for her. I stopped because I was having too much fun at home, and had no desire to go out looking for action.

I was living, through my kids, the kind of childhood I never had myself, and always wished I could have had. There was a time when I believed that entering the world of Aleck Woollcott had made this up for me. But that wasn't the same. Aleck had probably been right when he called me an arrested adolescent. There was no place for adolescents in the world of Billy, Alex, Minnie and Jimmy, however. Here I could be a bona fide kid.

Here I wasn't arrested, either. I was making progress. It was as if, after sweating out fifty-five years in Miss Flatto's room, I had finally been promoted to the third grade.

Our ranks decreased by one. Bill—no longer "Billy"—went east to the Juilliard School of Music. He had graduated from Beverly Hills High and he'd advanced as far as he could go in the music department of the University of California at Los Angeles. His professor of composition at U.C.L.A. recommended him to Juilliard, probably the toughest conservatory in the country, and Bill was accepted.

I don't know who Juilliard was tougher on—Bill or his old man. What chords he brought home when he came back on vacation! He had me pulling sounds out of the harp I never thought were possible. When I had the modern harmonies licked, he sprang his original pieces and arrangements on me and really had me sweating. Bill ran through them on the piano, patiently, over and over, while I translated them to the harp, by ear. He worked out a system of writing down music for me by letters, the names of the strings, and left me plenty to work on when he went back to school.

What he had done was a revelation to me. He had given voices to the full range of the instrument. He had produced tonal colors, shimmering, jangling, glowing, booming, that gave me goose bumps. My son, at the age of nineteen, was one of the few composers living—for that matter, one of the few who ever lived—who knew how to write for the harp.

It was a hell of a shame that Minnie never knew what a fantastic return there would be one day on the forty-five-buck investment she had made back in 1915, the time she decided that a harp might add some class to "The Six Mascots in *School Days*." When I unlocked the mysterious black crate in the freight depot at Aurora, Illinois, I certainly had no inkling of the kind of future I was opening up.

Even with Bill gone we were bursting the fences in our Beverly Hills joint, what with rocket labs, workshops, studios, kennels, rose gardens and practice putting greens. The kids would soon be entering high school. It was the time to move. Which way to go? Only one way—out. Out of the city. Los Angeles wasn't big enough to hold us.

Which way out? Palm Springs, by unanimous vote. We'd been spending a lot of weekends down there, and had fallen in love with the desert. Besides, I had a couple of things going for me in that part of the country: grapefruit and a golf club.

The grapefruit was Zeppo's latest deal. The remarkable Zep had done it again. In the years since he quit being a professional Marx Brother, Zep had come into his own many times over. Actually, his first achievement was becoming a professional Marx Brother. When he jumped into the act (to replace Gummo during the First World War), the rest of us had nearly fifteen years' stage experience behind us. Zep had none. Besides, he hated every aspect of show business, including actors. But he stuck it out to the end of our Paramount contract—through four years in vaudeville, three Broadway shows, and five movies.

His first venture on his own was a talent agency on the West Coast, which Gummo later helped him run. Their roster of stars and directors was surpassed only by the giant agencies in Hollywood. After a few years Zep sold out to the Music Corporation of America, the biggest of the giants, for a profit in seven figures. He took a hunk of this dough and went into the breeding of Thoroughbred horses, an enterprise he knew a total of nothing about. He bought a huge farm, complete with training track, and stocked it with stallions and brood mares of his own selection. The Thoroughbred business did so well he soon got some very tempting offers for it. He sold out for a fat profit.

Meanwhile he'd built himself a workshop, so he could fool around with some invention ideas he had. He came up with a new-type gasket for a certain hose connection in airplanes. It didn't sound like much to me, but it did to the U.S. Air Force. After the horse farm was sold, Zep expanded his workshop into a manufacturing plant with a force of two hundred and fifty employees. The gasket works he sold to one of the big aircraft companies—for a nice profit, needless to say.

Now he decided to take it easy. He built himself a lovely home in Palm Springs, where he could retire in comfort. Not long after moving down, he headed for the Salton Sea, one day, to go fishing. He never got there. On the way he saw a sign saying "260 Acres for Sale." He stopped to inquire. It was two hundred sixty acres of dust and tumbleweed. Zep bought it. He had the idea of covering it with grapefruit trees.

He knew less about raising grapefruit than he did about breeding horses, but in three years' time he was one of the most successful citrus ranchers in the Coachella Valley. Zeppo offered the rest of us shares in the business. I was happy to have a piece of any of Zeppo's action. So now I was in grapefruit.

That's when we started going to the desert so often. Had to oversee my acreage and protect my interest. At the same time, I had become the ringleader of a bunch of guys from Hillcrest who had the idea of starting a new golf club somewhere near Palm Springs. The fancier clubs down there were restricted. We wanted to put up a course that would be the equal of any, but where everybody would have an equal right to play, regardless of his faith or the color of his skin.

We bought property for the course in Cathedral City, six miles southwest of the Springs, and that was the beginning of the Tamarisk Country Club. I personally bought ten acres of sand and scrub at one corner of the layout, and that was the beginning of El Rancho Harpo.

Our new home, a timber-and-stucco house at the end of a long lane of oleanders, was finished in the spring of 1957, and we moved in. The happy hooligans became desert rats.

It was a dream home in every respect. There was a wing for the kids and a wing for Susan and me. Between the wings was a huge, vaulted living room, with facing walls of glass. To the west we looked across the swimming pool and the open desert to the backdrop of the San Jacinto Mountains. To the east we looked through a screen of eucalyptus trees to the fourteenth hole of Tamarisk.

Minnie, at last, could have horses. Jimmy had enough space for a whole rocket range. Alex had an irrigation system and a house full of automatic gadgets to tinker with. Susan had room to paint. And I had an eighteen-hole golf course.

The setting for our lives had changed drastically, but we hadn't changed our ways. The Marxes carried on at the harp ranch just as we'd always carried on, and always would.

I felt I should do something very special to dedicate our new joint. So one August afternoon, when the temperature was over 110° and the golf course was deserted, I piled into the golf cart with my clubs and a supply of fifty balls and drove off to the

452

fourteenth tee. Before teeing up I took off my shorts and shoes. I was determined to be a Famous First—the first naked man in history to fire a hole-in-one.

I didn't make it, but I came damn close. I came within six inches, to be exact, of immortality.

We had Gracie and George Burns down for Thanksgiving that year, to make up for Thanksgiving the year before. The year before, our new place hadn't been finished and we were living in an apartment court in Palm Springs. Susan bought a tremendous turkey, then found it was too big to fit in the refrigerator. I had a solution. We could lock it up overnight in the harp case, outside. There it would keep cool, and the dogs and cats couldn't get at it.

Well, the Burnses arrived the next morning. It came time to put the turkey in the oven. I went to get it. The harp case was gone. Then I remembered why. The harp case was on the list of things we'd asked the porter to put in storage so the place wouldn't be cluttered up for the holidays. I couldn't find the porter. The storage room was locked. I had to go back to the apartment and announce a change of plans. We were taking the Burnses out to dinner, on account of the turkey being missing.

"Missing?" said Gracie. "Where were you keeping it?"

"In the harp case," I said.

"Where else?" said George.

But a year later we gave them a real, home-cooked feast. While we were having coffee, I said, "I almost forgot. We found some marvelous grapes yesterday. These you have to taste. You never had such grapes." But neither Susan nor I could find them. Then it came to me where I had stashed them. When I brought the grapes to the table, Susan asked me where they'd been.

"In the jewel case," I said.

"Where else?" said George.

It also amused George, for some reason, to find my harp standing in the bathroom. This was a very practical setup, however, and no gag. The first two things I did every morning were to practice the harp and go to the john. This way I could do both at the same time and save a lot of steps. Who said I didn't know any good short cuts?

At Cathedral City I learned I was a better disciplinarian in effigy than I was in person. We had a lot of trouble getting grass to grow around the house, mainly because of the birds. Every time we reseeded they flocked around and had themselves a free lunch. Somebody suggested we put up a scarecrow. We did. Alex constructed a frame, and I dressed it with red wig, plug hat, red tie, floppy raincoat and baggy pants, and stuck a horn in its belt.

The next morning the biggest flock of birds we'd seen yet were out on the lawn. But, by God, they weren't pecking for seeds. They were just sitting there looking up at the scarecrow. Obviously, said Susan, they were waiting for him to play the harp.

When he didn't play, they gave up and flew away and never came back. We finally got a decent crop of grass.

The kids' favorite holidays were Christmas and Susan's birthday. Thinking up presents for Mom became quite a family hobby. On the first birthday she celebrated in Cathedral City, she got a record haul. Alex gave her a case of Jello (Alex never got enough Jello; he was crazy for the stuff). I gave her an adding machine (Susan did all our bookkeeping). Jimmy gave her a stamp machine (she handled all the correspondence too), and Minnie gave her a set of hair clippers (no special reason except they were on sale). By way of thanking us for a wonderful birthday, Susan gave us all haircuts. She's been the family barber ever since. Not one of us has ever gone to a barber shop again.

When I asked her what she wanted for Christmas that year she said that, just for once, she'd like money. She'd like a thousand dollars to spend any crazy way she felt like—on paints, brushes, sewing-machine attachments, curtain fabrics, rose bushes, whatever. To Susan, who was very practical with dough, this sounded like a mad splurge.

It would have been dull to put a single envelope under the Christmas tree for her. That was no kind of present, and lousy showmanship. So I went to work long before Christmas, up in town at the Hillcrest.

Early in December, mysterious Christmas cards addressed to Susan and marked *Personal* began to trickle in. Ten of them came, altogether. Inside each card was a check made out to Susan in some odd, meaningless amount—like $82.97, $73.33 or $26.58. Each was signed by some absolute stranger, a name that meant nothing to her. She decided not to worry me about the checks until after the holidays, so she hid them. She herself was plenty worried. She was sure it was some kind of new extortion racket.

On Christmas morning she found seven more cards with checks inside, beneath the Christmas tree. These checks were also made out to her for odd amounts, but they weren't signed by strangers. They were signed by George Burns, George Jessel, Danny Kaye, Harry Ritz, Eddie Cantor, Jack Benny and Milton Berle. Susan puzzled over them for a minute. Then she gave me a sly smile. She ran to get the mysterious checks hidden in her dresser drawer, and her adding machine.

The seventeen checks added up to one thousand bucks on the nose. She said it was her nicest Christmas ever.

That year we promised the kids they could stay up until midnight on New Year's Eve for the first time. But then I got to thinking about it. I didn't mind their staying up this late, for one night, but I was afraid Susan and I wouldn't be able to make it. We loved holidays, but we were a couple of reformed night owls. I had become such an early bird that I could seldom stay awake long enough to see Groucho's television show, which came on at the ungodly hour of ten.

On the morning of December 31 I was the first to get up, as usual. Before retiring to the john to practice, I went through the house and set all the clocks ahead three hours. When the rest of the family woke up, they kidded themselves about oversleeping and nobody knew the difference.

At nine o'clock on New Year's Eve, our clocks struck twelve. I poured everybody a sip of champagne. We sang "Auld Lang Syne," toasted 1958, kissed each other, and the kids ran off to bed. While I was turning out the lights I heard Minnie say, "Hey, Jimmy! I think I'm drunk!" Jimmy said, "Nah, you didn't drink enough to get a charge. It's just the wee small hours that makes you feel dizzy."

It's a classic corny joke that a guy who's married more than ten years always forgets his wedding anniversary. He comes home from work that day and finds his wife dressed to go out, and she gets mad as a hornet when he doesn't know why she's all dolled up.

Not so in our family. For some reason Susan and I invariably pull a switch. It's me who remembers. When I come to the breakfast table on the morning of September 28, after harp practice, I am wearing a squashed fedora, a bright red tie over a striped shirt-dickey, and dark glasses. When Susan sees me she gives a start, gasps, clamps a hand over her mouth, and hurries off to change. When she comes back to the table she has on her floppy big picture hat, 1930 vintage beige suit, cotton stockings and sensible brown shoes, and her face is whitened out with powder.

We keep our wedding outfits on all day long. The part of the day that gives the kids the biggest kick is when we come home after I have taken Susan out to dinner. They have to hear all about it—where we went, what trouble we got into, whether anybody recognized us, how many laughs we got—and then they have to hear all over again the story of how we got married, upstairs in the Santa Ana firehouse.

The most gratifying part of it to me is the way the kids accept our cockeyed kind of celebration and fall right in with the spirit of it. I've heard other children, who have a hell of a lot less hokum to put up with, say, "Boy, have we got a couple of screwy creeps for parents!" or, "*Criminy!* Why can't they act their age?" Not ours. If their father ever acted his age they'd disown him.

I hadn't moved to the desert to retire, not by a long shot. I no longer did movies (our last picture, A *Night in Casablanca*, had been made some years ago), but I kept up a fairly busy schedule of concerts, benefits and guest appearances, and once or twice a year Chico and I would go off on a club date together.

The most expensive benefit I did was for the pension fund of the Palm Springs Police Department. After the show I found thirty-two of my knives missing. The cops had stolen them, for souvenirs.

The highest-priced club date Chico and I ever played (or so we thought, at the time) was for the Texas oilman Glenn McCarthy, in his snazzy Shamrock Hotel in Houston. McCarthy offered us a choice of thirty-five thousand dollars—seventeen thousand five hundred a week for two weeks—or an interest in his newest natural-gas field. Chico didn't bother to figure the odds. The only important figure here was the twenty-seven-and-a-half percent deduction for depletion rights. We told McCarthy to keep his cash. We'd take this other deal.

Sure enough, royalty checks started coming in from the Texas Gas Corporation later that year. They still come in, at the end of every quarter.

I happened to be in the Hillcrest the day after I'd gotten a royalty payment, and I had the check in my pocket. I spotted a table of bankers, a couple of whom I knew pretty well, having lunch. I went over to their table. "I'd like to tell you guys something that might surprise you," I said. "You probably think all actors are shnooks when it comes to handling money. We throw it away as fast as we get it because we don't have any business sense. Well, I want you to know this isn't true, at least not about me or Chico."

Then I told them about the choice the oilman had given us down in Texas—thirty-five G's cash or two interests in a gas field. "You think we grabbed the loot?" I said. "Not us. We settled for the long-range investment, and we've been getting quarterly payments ever since. Maybe you still don't believe an actor could be this smart. Well, gentlemen, I have documentary proof on me. Here's my latest royalty check—and it happens to be a hundred percent higher than what I received for the previous quarter."

I showed my check to the bankers. It was for thirteen cents. The previous check had been for six cents.

The next one I got that year was made out *"to the amount of exactly $0 and 01 cents."*

I'm afraid nobody ever took me seriously as a man of finance. Like the time I told the local telephone operator to please get me the Beverly Hills office of Merrill Lynch, Pierce, Fenner and Smith, and she said, "Do you know his first name, Mr. Marx?"

I even had trouble convincing Jimmy that I was a good risk. While we still lived in the city, I was once driving home from the desert. I was late, so I stopped by a roadside phone booth to tell the family when to expect me. The only change I had on me was a dime. I told the operator to reverse the charges.

It happened that Jimmy was alone in the house when the phone rang. The operator said, "I have a collect call from Mr. Marx. Will you accept the charges, please?"

Jimmy said, "What's a 'collect call'?" and the operator said that meant the party answering the call would pay for it, not the party making the call.

"You mean *me?*" said Jimmy. "*I'm* supposed to pay for it?"

The operator said that was the general idea. Would he then accept the charges?

"Heck, no," said Jimmy. "I can't pay for it."

I told the operator to please explain to him that it was his father calling. The operator relayed this to Jimmy.

"My *father?* Well, let *him* pay for it!" he said, and hung up.

It was a sparkling clear morning in May. After the kids went off to school I felt like practicing an extra hour or so before shooting a round of golf, so I moved the harp out by the big west window. While I played, I watched our three mutts take their daily swim. It was a funny thing. Every morning, as soon as the kids left to catch the school bus, the dogs came yipping and galloping around the house and dove straight into the pool. Their habits were no more conventional than their masters'.

Susan was in her room, sewing, working on a dress for Minnie's first dance. The dogs climbed out of the pool, shook themselves, and ran off to look for the horses, to see if they could get up a friendly game of tag. The only sound was the sound of the harp. There was no wind outside. The nearest thing to any movement was the changing of the shadows on the mountains, as the sun rose in the sky. I was surrounded by peace.

I got to thinking as I played about how lucky I was to be who I was, where I was—an old faun's ass of sixty-five, the father of four children aged from fifteen to twenty-two, sitting in an air-conditioned house, admiring the spectacle of the California desert while I made music, with nothing more to worry about than whether I should keep on making music and enjoying the view and then play nine holes of golf, or quit now and play eighteen holes. I decided to keep practicing.

It was a decision Woollcott would have approved of. Golf was one game he had no regard for. Of course he never had much regard for the harp either—particularly as played by me—but it was better than golf. Aleck had been very much in my mind recently. The past Tuesday had been the anniversary of what I used to call my Gentile *Bar Mitzvah*. It was thirty-five years ago Tuesday that Woollcott had invited himself to my dressing room, introduced himself, and taken me over to the Hotel Algonquin to "meet a few friends."

I jumped back to the present when I heard myself ripping off a showy glissando—the kind I thought was sensational thirty-five years ago, but the kind that Bill would give me hell for today.

Now I was thinking how proud Aleck would be if he could see William Woollcott Marx today. Bill had done a hitch in the Coast Guard, after studying two years at Juilliard, and now he had his own apartment in Hollywood. He was a man of independence. He insisted on paying his own way, all the way. There wasn't much dough in writing serious music, so to support himself while he kept composing, he played jazz piano in all kinds of offbeat joints around L.A. and hustled arranging jobs. In his spare time he worked out new numbers for me, with the idea of our putting an album together. Bill had found his place in the world, and it was a good place.

The other three were going to find their places too. I had no doubts about any of them. Minnie, at fifteen, had announced to us what her future was going to be, in no uncertain terms. She was going to marry a guy who raised horses. Period. She was already making sure she'd have the proper qualifications. After school and on weekends she worked for the local vet.

Jimmy was looking forward to college. We'd been kidding him about his top-secret, hush-hush rocket-fuel project—until he won first prize in a big regional science fair. He knew what he was doing, and there was nothing funny about it.

Alex was more vague about college. He was as obsessed with cars as Minnie was with horses. He had one specific ambition. College or no college, he was going to own and operate his own garage some day. It was going to be called "Lou's Garage." When we asked him why "Lou's," he said he didn't know—it just sounded like a good name for a garage. That was the kind of reasoning that the Alexander he was named for, who died the year Alex was born, would have adored.

The dogs jogged back in sight, their tongues hanging out, looking for a shady place to plop down for their siesta. The sunbathing mountains were losing their early-morning wrinkles. That meant it was getting on toward golf time.

I was playing very badly anyway. I was lousy, in fact. I plucked an awful clinker of a chord. Another one. My God! I thought—I'd better start putting in this extra hour every day.

460

I couldn't have been sloppier if I'd been playing with mittens on. Then all of a sudden I couldn't play at all. I felt a pain in my middle. The strength went out of my fingers. I felt sick, very sick.

I called to Susan. She came as far as the doorway, looked at me, then ran back to her room and telephoned for the doctor.

The doctor thumped me and tapped me and checked all my vibrations. I told him I felt like a kettledrum being tuned up for a concert. He looked under my eyelids and examined other secret places. I said I couldn't decide now whether he was a kettle-drummer or a customs inspector. He ran the sharp end of a finger-nail file up the bottoms of my feet, hard. I said, "You still haven't found where it itches. Could you tickle me on the left foot again, and this time wobble it a bit?"

The doctor didn't laugh. He didn't even give me a bedside smile. He said, "Mr. Marx, I'm a great admirer of yours and I'd love to sit here and crack jokes with you. But I must tell you the blunt truth. You have had a heart attack."

I said, "Bad?"

He said, "I don't know. I don't think so."

But when I said, "Quote me any odds?" he shook his head and gave me a sickly bedside smile.

It wasn't bad. It was what is known as a "mild" attack. I was re-examined, cardiographed, checked for cholesterol, prescribed for, put on a diet, and sent to an L.A. hospital for six weeks of "precautionary bed rest."

The specialist who'd taken me over gave me a pep talk the day I checked into the hospital. He said the one thing that would help me most was something I could only prescribe for myself. I should retire.

I asked him what he meant by retire. He spelled it out. No more work. No more engagements of any kind. No more golf. No more harp. Nothing but pure, full-time leisure.

I said I thought this was a pretty stiff rap, considering the offense—one lousy bellyache. He said, "Think about it some more." I did. I thought about the last days of Frenchie, and of Aleck. I thought about all the days to come for Susan, and for Bill and Alex and Minnie and Jimmy.

"Okay," I said. "I guess you're right. The first thing I'll do when I get up out of this bed and put on my clothes and go home is retire. Then what do I do?"

"What's the most relaxing thing you've ever done in your life?" he asked me.

"Taking off my shoes and lying on the grass and flying a kite so the string tickles the bottom of my feet," I said, without any hesitation.

The doctor said, "Harpo, the best piece of medical advice I can give you is this—go fly a kite."

It didn't sink in until the doctor left, and I began to reflect on the meaning of the decision I had made. Retirement. This meant good-bye. Good-bye to the closest companion I ever had, a companion who'd given me thousands of hours of exasperation, botheration and pure joy—my harp.

And what about my name? Shouldn't I maybe have it changed now? How about *Adolph Ex-Harpo Marx?* No. Not a very good gag. I couldn't come up with anything better, so I went to sleep.

CHAPTER 24

The Return of Pinchie Winchie, or, You're Only Young Forever

I WAS ON A plane headed for Las Vegas. I wasn't going to Vegas to perform, or play golf, or gamble. All these were pursuits I had given up for life. I was traveling as a tourist, a tourist with nothing special to do and nobody special to do it with. I had some idea of kibitzing the action in the casinos, taking in a few of the shows, lying around in the sun for a while—but beyond that, nothing.

I had been retired for nine months now. My costume was in mothballs. My harp was in storage. My golf clubs I had given away. I didn't miss any of these things. The only things I had lost by retiring were my tan and a little weight. I might have looked pastier, and saggier, and older, but I was back in good health, and that was the only important thing. That was why I told myself I had no regrets about the decision I had made on the first day of my first stay in the hospital.

463

The plane landed at the Vegas airport. The other passengers walked up each others' heels in their hurry to get off. Yet they were hardly a gay crowd. All of them had a hollow-eyed and hungry look, and they talked under their breaths. They were indistinguishable from suckers going to the slaughter of the gaming tables anywhere—Monte Carlo, Covington, Juan-les-Pins, or the old Saratoga Springs. But they happened to be going to Las Vegas, and I happened to be the only tourist among them, and they bored me.

Briefly, I considered getting on the next plane out of there and going back home. I nixed the idea. Susan's insinuations had been pretty plain. It would be better for everybody if I didn't hang around the house for a while.

Actually, I had retired three times in the past nine months, after a total of three heart attacks. The first and second times I got sprung from the hospital I called it quits but I never quite believed it. Now, after the third time, I believed it. This was for good.

The summer after my first illness had been a period of discovery for me. First, I discovered I didn't miss playing the harp, not a bit. Second, I took up painting again, and found it very exciting. Third, I found that time passed just as fast doing nothing as it had when my days were full of activity.

When I was released from the hospital, we closed up the house in Cathedral City. Susan packed the kids into the station wagon and off they went on a camping trip through the Rockies. I took a quiet bachelor apartment in West Hollywood, where I could devote the summer to adjusting to my new life, under the eye of my doctor.

I made my own breakfasts, usually had lunch at Hillcrest, and for dinners I made the rounds of the family—from Bill's place to Groucho's to Gummo's to Chico's. Between meals I painted, I read, I watched TV, I napped, or I did absolutely nothing.

The nearest I came to playing anything was taking pills at night. I was on a complicated, round-the-clock schedule of drugs. The line-up beside my bed was formidable—pills and capsules of all sizes and shapes, to be taken at different intervals. I hated to turn on a light during the night, so I practiced with the bottles until I could tell them apart by the sound they made when I shook them. I got an alarm clock with an illuminated dial. Whenever the alarm went off for a pill-time I only had to reach behind me and shake the bottles until I heard the right one, take my capsule or tablet, reset the alarm, and go back to sleep.

I'm probably not the first guy who ever played the harp by ear and certainly not the first to play the piano that way, but I don't know of anybody else who can play pills by ear.

I was turning out four and five paintings a day. I worked in water colors, a new medium for me. I'd taken it up while I was in the hospital, where I first felt the urge to paint again, and where oils would have been too messy. Water colors were fun, but I was getting into a rut. Every summer landscape I did turned into Vermont as seen from Neshobe Island. Every winter landscape looked like Watertown, New York, as seen from a hotel window. Every figure I did turned into a guy in the rain under a black umbrella. The black umbrella had no significance except that it was the best way to cover up the guy's face when it didn't turn out right—and it never turned out right.

What I needed was a fresh approach. I should switch to another medium. I didn't want to mess up the apartment with oils, so I got a bunch of art books to see what else there was. I found the perfect medium. The inspiration for it came partly from the art books and partly from the new diet my doctor put me on. For breakfast I could eat the whites of two eggs. This presented the problem of what to do with the yolks. The answer: paint in casein, which could be prepared with the yolk of an egg.

It got me out of the rut. My painting loosened up to the point where I could do abstractions. To me this was a big step forward. But everybody who saw my collection asked if I wouldn't please paint them "one of those charming figures with the black umbrella." I could have sold them by the gross.

465

That was when I discovered how I was different from most people. Most people have a conscious mind and a subconscious. Not me. I've always operated on a subconscious and a sub-subconscious.

By August I was in another kind of a rut. I was homesick. With every postcard I got from the family, from Arizona, Colorado or Montana, I felt worse. I now spent more time at the Hillcrest than I did painting, but that didn't help much. The only guys who hung around there after lunch played cards or shot golf. The Round Table was often empty by two o'clock. George Burns was producing television programs and getting up a show of his own to do in Reno and Vegas. Jessel wasn't around long enough between hops to Seattle, Minneapolis, Tallahassee and Tel Aviv to ever get a monologue going. Benny was busy. Cantor was busy. Berle was in New York. Danny Kaye was overseas. Groucho, when he wasn't working on his new book, was doing his TV show. And Chico, of course, was unavoidably detained at the Friars Club. Everybody was busy but me.

When the end of summer came and I drove home to Cathedral City, it was like coming back from Russia. Susan and the kids arrived the next day. My exile was over.

Susan and I converted the utility room next to the garage into a two-man studio. Now, every morning after the kids left for school, the dogs jumped into the pool and Mom and Dad went to paint. We were ideal partners in a studio. She preferred oils and she was a hell of a draftsman. I preferred non-oil paints. I couldn't draw worth a damn, never could get anything in perspective, so I had to let my colors do all the talking. I admired her drawing. She admired the way I used color.

But I couldn't stick with it very long. The joy of homecoming was wearing off. I'd start out painting up a storm, sloshing wild strokes onto my board, then I'd peter out. I'd wander through the house. I'd go out and talk to Minnie's horses and scratch the dogs behind the ears. I'd take a tour of the acreage in the golf cart to inspect the trees we'd planted. I'd come back to the house and look for something to read. I couldn't find anything that would hold my attention. I'd turn on television. Nothing but old movies and soap operas. I'd go back to the studio. Susan would be halfway through a new painting. I'd look at what I'd started two hours ago and I'd throw it in the trash.

I knew why I was restless. I was itching to get my fingers on the harp strings. I was itching to grip a golf club again. I'd been kidding myself. Why the hell should I sit around and read and paint? I was, as they say, living on velvet anyway.

One day I gave the strings a swipe when I passed the harp. The next day I paused to play a couple of chords. The day after that I sat down and played a chorus of "I've Got Rhythm." On the fourth day I practiced for half an hour, then went out and putted a golf ball around the swimming pool.

That afternoon, I found out later, Susan made a frantic call to Gummo. She told him I was showing symptoms of sneaking out of retirement. She made him promise that he'd turn down all offers for me to perform, no matter where or for whom or for how much loot, before word of them got to me. Gummo promised.

Susan's call was not really necessary. On the fifth day I had another heart attack, much like the first one, and I was carted off to L.A. for another six weeks flat on my ass in a hospital bed.

When I came home it was the same story all over again. I swore I was retired for good. I went back to painting, and for a while I painted like a fiend. Then I got restless. I got the itchy fingers. I started to practice again. I felt so great I called Gummo and told him I was ready to take on any date, anywhere—TV, clubs, benefits, anything. Gummo said he'd let me know as soon as anything came in. He was lying, of course. Susan, alarmed over my symptoms, had already talked to him and made him renew his promise that no offer of work should reach my tender ears.

I spent quite a bit of time in the city, at the Hillcrest. I got talking to producers and agents there, and that's how I found out about the plot between Susan and Gummo. Several guys asked me how come I was turning down jobs. I told them I wasn't—on the contrary, I was looking. That wasn't the way they got it from Gummo, they said.

This burned me up. But before I could do anything about it, I had another attack. This one hit me while I was in downtown Palm Springs, shopping with Susan. I felt like I'd been flattened by a sandbag.

The doctor made no bones about it. This was no "mild attack." It was an acute coronary.

The day I came out of the hospital I called Gummo myself. I told him I was no longer a client of his, or of anybody else's. I had had it. I had finally had some sense scared into me. I was putting the harp in storage, along with my costume, and I was getting rid of my golf clubs.

"I hope to God you're serious," said Gummo. "Couple more rounds like this and you'll have retired more times than Sarah Bernhardt."

"I was never more serious in my life," I told Gummo.

I went back to painting, and put in an hour or two a day working on notes for my book. I went over to the county seat, Indio, and put in for unemployment insurance. I took my pills and stuck to my diet and my rest schedule like a good boy.

Before I knew it, I came away from a weekly examination with a clean bill of health. The doctor said I'd made a damn near unbelievable recovery. Susan said even she was amazed, having watched me improve in front of her eyes, from day to day.

"It's that old Nightingale blood," I told her. "It's pulled me through again."

Then the hours began to drag, especially while the kids were in school. I couldn't sit still. But every time I got up to do something I found there was nothing I really wanted to do. Thank goodness the harp wasn't there to tempt me. Smartest thing I ever did, having it put away.

If only the kids were here, I'd say to myself. *Then there'd be a little life around the joint.*

But when the kids came home it wasn't much different. At first they thought it was swell having their old man around the house all day. I thought it was great being there whenever they were, and for a while it was. I did card tricks, taught them back-gammon, and listened to all their gripes about school.

Then it got tiresome. For the first time, I realized that kids could be terrible *nudges.* Hanging around expecting you to enter-tain them. Hanging around asking questions. Mainly questions they had no business asking.

"Feeling better today, Dad?"

"Can I get a pillow for you, Dad, or bring your slippers?"

"If it costs so much to keep your harp in storage and they charge so much for insurance, why don't you sell it? Why did you want to play the harp in the first place, instead of like a trumpet? Anyway, aren't most of the harpists who play the harp ladies and not men?"

"Why was Mr. Woollcott so fat in all the pictures? Didn't his doctor make him go on a diet, like your doctor?"

"What did you do at night when you were a boy, if there was no TV then?"

"Well, if there wasn't any TV, how did you find out who won the election on Election Day?"

"Why do you say it's important that all of us finish high school when you didn't even finish grade school? Didn't it mean so much in those days?"

"Is it true that Uncle Groucho went on the stage before you did?"

"Were Minnie and Frenchie their real names or just their nicknames like yours and Uncle Chico's and Uncle Gummo's?"

"Who's the oldest man you ever met in history? President Franklin D. Roosevelt? If they hadn't shot Abraham Lincoln would you have met him?"

"If it was so cold in the winter when you were a boy, why didn't you move to California instead of to Chicago?"

"If you agree with Uncle Zeppo every time he says show business stinks, how come you went on the stage instead of having a career?"

"Sure you wouldn't like a pillow, Dad?"

"If you didn't finish grade school did that make you a juvenile delinquent? You weren't a juvenile delinquent, were you? Because if you'd had a prison record Mom wouldn't have married you and they would have blacklisted you from making movies, right?"

"Yes, but you would have had a lot more interesting stuff then to put in your book, right?"

"How are you feeling *now*, Dad? Any better?"

I stood it as long as I could. I was a good-natured guy and a tolerant father, but they were driving me off my nut. It got to where I had to shut them up and barricade myself in my room to get any privacy.

Then Susan began giving me the needle. I should get out of the house. Do this, do that. Ride the golf cart over to the course and watch them shoot golf. I told her the game didn't interest me any more, not in the least. Go into town more often and see more of the old gang at the Hillcrest. I told her the Hillcrest had changed. It was a dull place.

"Any worse than here?" she said. I shrugged. "Harp," she said, "are you bored?"

I said yes. Frankly, I was.

"Do you know what anybody who's bored really is?" she said.

"What?"

"He's a bore."

The short discussion that followed was very close to being a fight. This, I said to myself, wasn't my old Susan. Something was eating her. She was turning on me the same as the kids.

To keep peace in the family, I said I'd decided to go away for a couple of days. Susan asked me where. The first place that came to mind, for no good reason, was Las Vegas. She thought that was a splendid idea, much as they'd all miss me. She

470

couldn't conceal how pleased she was that I was going away. I wished I could feel the same.

So I flew to Vegas.

It wasn't half as bad as I had expected, that night. After dinner I wandered through the casino in my hotel. There was something sweet and restful about the clicking of dice and chips and roulette wheels, like hearing crickets at sundown. Looking at the patches of green felt on the blackjack and crap tables, I knew how a country boy must feel upon seeing his first green fields after being stuck too long in the city.

But I didn't weaken.

I went across the Strip to another joint. There, in the lounge next to the casino, quite a crowd stood around a TV set, watching the fights. I joined the crowd. One of the bosses (you can always spot them in Vegas) came over from the casino and stood in front of me to see how the fight was going. His silhouette had a very familiar shape.

I knew this guy. Even from the back I recognized him, and I hadn't seen the guy for thirty years. The last time—the only time—we'd met was on a gambling boat in the river off Pittsburgh, Pennsylvania. It was Milt Jaffe, the guy who'd saved my skin by lending me ten thousand bucks that night in 1929.

I nudged him in the ribs. "How's chances of letting me have ten G's?" I said, in a con man's voice. Jaffe didn't turn around. He gave me a vague, impatient gesture with the back of his hand. I nudged him again. This time his gesture was definite. It meant I should get lost. I nudged him a third time. "If you loaned me ten G's once why can't you do it again?" I said.

Without removing his gaze from the fight on the TV screen, he sidestepped away from me. You had to be a thick-skinned diplomat to handle drunks and crackpots in Las Vegas. They might turn out to be well-heeled customers. You couldn't take a chance by offending them.

471

When the bell rang for the end of the round and the crowd relaxed momentarily, I piped up, in a loud falsetto: "Pinchie Winchie!"

As he turned, even before he saw me, Jaffe yelled, "Pinchie Winchie? Harpo Marx!"

As soon as we got through telling each other how great we looked (he was lying, I wasn't) and what a lot of changes there'd been in the old world since we last spent an evening together, I asked Jaffe the question that had stuck in my mind for thirty years.

"Please tell me," I said, "why you gave me that dough back in Pittsburgh. Why no references? No security? No signature?"

"Harpo," he said, "I'll tell you. In my line of business, same then as now, the only security I have is my judgment of people. If I can't tell a good man from a dead beat with one look I don't belong in the business. If my instinct goes sour I go looking for another job. So what I've always done is practice on my judgment, same as you practice on your harp. Every once in a while I test myself on people. Always have. Still do.

"I tested myself on you that night on the boat. I said to myself if I wasn't right about you, I'd never be right about anybody else ever again. You want to know why? It wasn't because you had an honest face. To me there's no such thing as an honest face. I'll tell you what it was. You knew how to have a good time without spending money. A guy who has to blow his wad to have fun is a bad risk.

"Want to know another reason? You were a good risk from the life-insurance point of view. I could see you were one guy out of ten thousand, the kind that stays young forever. You weren't going to conk out on me before you paid me back."

Jaffe gave me a big grin. "Maybe I wasn't so cold-blooded about it as I make out," he said. "You know, I was pretty soft in the head by the time I handed you the dough. I don't think I ever

472

laughed so hard in my life." Remembering, he began to laugh hard all over again.

I knew what was coming. Jaffe said, "We've got to get a game going tonight, Harpo. Got to do it!"

"Oh, no," I said.

Jaffe didn't hear me. He was too steamed up. "We can use the main office," he said. "What do you need? Burnt cork? We'll get some from one of the dressing rooms."

"No," I said. This time he heard me. He looked at me like he was a kid and I was Santa Claus come to take back the toys I'd put under his Christmas tree. I let him down as gently as I could.

Pinchie Winchie, I told him, simply wasn't my speed any more. A lot of things weren't my speed any more. Leaping around onstage. Lugging a harp around. Whacking a golf ball. All behind me. The time comes, like it or not, when a man has to stop kidding himself that he's as young as he feels. That time had come for me. I felt fine, and there was nothing wrong with me. But I'd stopped kidding myself. I was retired.

Jaffe squinted at me as if a thick fog had rolled in between us. "Retired?" he said. "Retired from *what?*"

He didn't give me a chance to answer. I didn't have an answer ready anyway. "For God's sake, Harpo," he said, "don't you know how stiffs like me have always envied guys like you? Have you ever had to meet a payroll or sweat out the auditors or file for bankruptcy?"

I shook my head.

"You've been making a living," he said, "out of a life that all the rest of us dream about retiring to. How the hell can you retire *from* it?"

I had no answer for him.

Jaffe, embarrassed by his outburst, changed the subject and asked me how Zeppo was. I gave him the rundown on Zep's wheeling and dealing. He asked me how my other brothers were. I told him. Groucho never busier. Chico still in the thick of the action and planning a trip to Europe. Gummo still in business at the old stand, manager and den-mother to all the rest of us.

As I talked, Jaffe gave me a hard, close study. I knew what he was thinking. I said to him, "If you didn't know who I was, you wouldn't lend me two bits tonight, would you?"

"What the hell," he said, ducking a direct reply. "So we change. Time marches on. Like you say, you can't kid yourself. You're only young once."

We didn't have much left to say to each other. But I had an awful lot to think about, all of a sudden. The fight was over and the television set had been turned off. We were standing against the bar, where Jaffe could keep an eye on the casino, beyond the lounge. Having nothing better to do, I had picked up a book of matches from the bar and was lighting them, one by one, blowing them out, and dropping them into an ash tray.

Jaffe made a move like he had to go back to work. "Wonderful seeing you, Harpo," he said. He gave me his hand. Instead of shaking hands I gave him a squeeze on the cheek and said, "Pinchie Winchie!"

He laughed and did the same to me. The only difference was, I had planted a beaut on his kisser—having burnt enough matches to work up a good, black smudge. I wonder if he got the message when he finally discovered it.

An hour later I was on a plane to Los Angeles. I felt so terrific I could have flown without benefit of aircraft, except that I would have taken a short cut and sure as hell got lost. I had good reason to feel I had wings. I had just recovered from the longest and most serious illness I ever had: Retirement. But it was all over now, so Waltz Me Around Again, Willie!

I got my harp out of storage, aired out my costume, and ordered a new set of golf clubs.

My children stopped being pestiferous. My wife stopped making insinuations. I signed for a night-club date in Chicago and three TV appearances and told Bill he'd better hustle me up some new arrangements. I switched back to painting in oils. Everything I painted turned into a clown, but this was a rut I'd been in for quite some time and I didn't mind at all.

In those three television shows I succeeded in doing the three things I had been warned never to do again. In the first, I whanged away at the harp. In the second, I played a golf match with Sam Snead. In the third, I not only leaped around, but I leaped around for three days in the snow.

The other day Zeppo called up to say he was putting in a second crop on the ranch. So now I'm not only living on velvet and in the pink, but I'm in grapefruit and tomatoes too. I just reported this to Susan. Susan said, "For a guy who bills himself as a professional listener, you've been doing an awful lot of talking lately."

I get the message. Honk, honk!

I. *Susan*

Ode to the Silent Harp

I sing a song of joyous praise
Of one who labored in the garden of laughter.

A quiet man who sensed the absurd
In all he saw and all he heard;
Untutored by textbooks, he learned in the street;
Survival was foremost, to steal was to eat.

From whence came the gifts
Of musical taste,
The sense of beauty,
The gentle grace?
The gods safeguarded them through the years
Until he was ready.

I am glad we were there.

II. *Bill*

Imagine growing up in a house filled with music, hour after hour. Live music. Ravel. Debussy. Gershwin. Berlin. Silvery arpeggios and glissandos. Lush golden chords. All from the fingers of a magical little man sitting at a harp in the big bay window of the living room. This was my privilege for the first seventeen years of my life, thanks to fate, Susan and Harpo.

Until I started school, I took it all for granted. Didn't everybody's Dad fill his house with glorious music? The illusion was shattered when I entered the outside world, by way of Hawthorne Elementary School, and then had to start piano lessons. I hammered at my scales grimly. My heart was not in it. My heart was out on the baseball diamond. All this time Dad kept playing nonstop—strumming, plucking, rippling away— in the bay window. No fair! Dad *liked* practicing. No wonder—I never heard *him* playing any scales.

It was not long before I learned that Dad was not practicing. He played his harp three hours a day not for proficiency but for the sheer pleasure of it. I sat at my piano wishing mightily I were someplace else. When Dad sat at his harp, there was no someplace else. Gradually, watching my father—his eyes shut, a reverential grin on his face —and hearing the wondrous sounds that resonated from his instrument, I became a musician. I entered, at a very early age, the only profession I would ever know. No . . . I didn't really enter the profession. I absorbed it.

Dad's influence on all our lives was all-pervasive. It was never more apparent than at dinner time. Not to be outdone by the Algonquin or the Hillcrest, we had our own "Round Table"—which we moved into the den after our formal dining room became the neighborhood pool room. Dad would begin the nightly dinner ritual by raising a forefinger and intoning his favorite expression: "And in conclusion . . ." Then we would go around the table—Mom, Alex, Jimmy, Minnie and I—reviewing our triumphs and trials of the day. Dad fielded gripes and hang-ups with all the wit and wisdom of a second-grade dropout—which is to say, by reducing tragedy to absurdity. First thing you knew, he had you laughing at yourself and your problem faded away. He was a born healer.

When I was in the fourth grade, I agonized for days over a school assignment. I had to write a poem, and I was totally blocked. Dad sensed that I was suffering from some secret dilemma. He wormed it out of me. Now here was a challenge that delighted him. Write a poem! Before dinner was over he had it, raising the poetic art to new heights (well, at least to different heights). I still have a copy of it: "There they go! / I'm betting on Flo! / If she loses / I'll blow my dough! / Into the stretch / She's out in front! / But at the wire / Win—I dun't."

For the poem I got a B+. For being my ghostwriter, Dad got a big hug.

Whenever Uncle Groucho and Uncle Chico came to the house, they would wind up exchanging hilarious stories with my Dad about vaudeville. I got the impression, when I was little, that vaudeville was some marvelous, mythical kingdom where fathers and uncles came from. When I was twelve, Dad decided it was time to show me what his life had been like before Beverly Hills, before he was in the movies even, time to share the experience of vaudeville, the Harpo side of his life.

He and Uncle Chico had booked themselves into a three-month tour of the British circuit, culminating in a four-week stand at the London Palladium, and Mom and I went along. Dad knew I would not be content just watching from the wings. He assigned to me the grave responsibility of being his Personal Prop Man. I had to make sure the carrot was in the upper-left inside pocket of Dad's coat, the scissors in the middle right pocket, and the three-hundred knives properly lodged in his left coat sleeve. Soon he promoted me to doing "shtick" onstage. At the cue for his solo spot I would trundle his harp out to him, dressed as an angel. As I turned to exit the audience saw the sign on my back: EAT AT REVELLI'S CAFÉ. I got a laugh! My very own laugh! Dad was as tickled as I was.

Sometimes the combination of his innocence and his paternal mission to enrich my life caught me off guard. We were walking in London during a day off when we passed a certain theatre. "Let's go see this show," Dad said, and in we went. I was mortified at what we saw onstage: comics jabbering in cockney and cavorting with voluptuous showgirls clad only in what used to be called "scanties." The comics were not only making jokes about forbidden parts of the girls' anatomies, they were actually touching the parts! I shrank into my seat, over-whelmed with embarrassment. I didn't dare look at Dad. I knew that my poor father was suffering just as acutely, for having brought me to such a place. To my vast relief he nudged me and muttered, "Let's get out of here, Billy." I bolted to the street. When Dad caught up to me, he said, "Well, what'd you think?" I stammered that I didn't really much care for it.

"Same here," Dad said. "Big gyp, if you ask me. They didn't take all their clothes off."

What it was was burlesque. The theatre was the legendary, notorious Windmill. My father felt it should be part of my education.

Ten years later I came home from the Julliard School of Music, in New York City, with a head full of musical theory and composition. Dad, who could still not read a note, had to find a way to share all this erudition. He promoted me from student to Personal Arranger, and I subsequently produced two record albums of harp solos for him.

Funny thing about Harpo the natural musician. He was not a natural natural. Most people who play by ear pick up first on the melody, and next on the beat. The subtle colors and textures of harmony are usually way beyond them. With Harpo, just the opposite. He was virtually oblivious to melody. His sense of rhythm was, to put it kindly, unpredictable. But harmony! Ahhh! It was sheer sound that sent him

479

into raptures, swamping whatever sense of melody he had. When he discovered a complex new chord, he would play it over and over and over, hours on end, transforming the bay window into a corner of tonal heaven.

I realize now, on re-reading my Dad's life story, that he performed music the way his father, Frenchie, had performed tailoring: with an unerring feel for fabric and color (harmony) but very little for cutting and fitting (melody and tempo). This gave us a problem when we recorded the record albums. Harpo onstage could hoodwink an audience, getting away with murder in the tempo department. But Harpo on records had to obey the beat or risk sounding sloppy. "I've got an idea, Billy," Dad said. "You stand there and conduct me, O.K.?"

A solution that only Harpo could have thought of. But the idea of a solo conductor conducting a solo performer didn't work. When he leaned into the harp, concentrating on strings and fingering, he lost eye contact with me and wandered off the beat. "O.K.," he said. "I got a better idea." His better idea was that I should lie down on the floor, where he could see me through the strings. So I conducted him lying flat on my back, waving my flippers like a capsized turtle. We made it to the finish line together.

My father was a happy agglomeration of surprises and contradictions. He never got through *McGuffey's First Reader* but went on to read, and savor, Tolstoy and Dickens. His favorite words were "perspicacity" and "penultimate." When challenged he could reel off the correct spelling of "chrysanthemum" or "antidisestablishmentarianism." At the same time, his list of stage props included "sizzers," "karit," "dimund ring" and "telliscoap." He could recite word for word his bar mitzvah speech from fifty years before—but he never got any further than the line that always rendered him helpless with laughter: "And in conclusion . . ."

Fiendish competitor that he was on the golf course, the croquet court and the pool table, he was not out to humiliate the other players. His enemies were the pins, the wickets and the corner pockets. He took his pleasure from games wherever he could find it. Once at three o'clock in the morning Mom woke up to discover, with a sinking feeling, that Dad was not in bed. She searched through the house, upstairs and down, getting more apprehensive. No Dad. At last she found him—with four-year old Minnie, on Minnie's bathroom floor. They were in the midst of a rousing game of jacks. Why not? He couldn't sleep, and it was the only game in town at 3:00 A.M.

He was an unabashed fan, a worshipper of excellence in sports, the arts, literature. But his all-time favorite television star was Cecil, The Seasick Sea Serpent, a hand puppet on "Time for Beany." If any one of us dared break into the den while Dad was watching Beany and Cecil, we got grounded. Certain areas of our father's domain were unalterably sacred.

He was an inveterate radio listener. His favorite program was not, as one might think, "Information Please" (those pundits were, after all, descendants of the old Algonquin Round Table). His favorite radio show for many years was something that came on during the afternoon, when all the boys and girls were home from kindergarten: "Uncle Whoa Bill." The highlight of each hour was Birthday Time. Uncle Whoa Bill's assistant, one Piggy, would say: "And a Happy Birthday to Sally Green, who is five years old today. Sally—go look in the laundry hamper in your bathroom and you will find a big surprise!" Sally would scamper off to look and she would find, of course, her birthday present—all as prearranged by her mother's call to the radio station. Uncle and Piggy had worked their magic again!

My father was a true believer in that kind of magic. This led to the gravest family crisis I can remember from those years. One morning—the day after his birthday—Dad was ominously quiet at the breakfast table. Something was bothering him deeply. At length Mom got to the bottom of it. Dad had listened to "Uncle Whoa Bill" the day before with high hopes. But his name was never mentioned. He was genuinely, profoundly, hurt. Mom felt like crawling into a hole. From that year on, as long as the show was on the air, Uncle and Piggy never failed to wish "little Arthur Marx" a Happy Birthday and tell him where his present was hidden. Thus the peer of Dorothy Parker, F.P.A. and Oscar Levant.

Another contradiction: the way he dressed. Dad could harmonize music like an angel, but not the clothes he wore. I can still hear Mom gasp at the sight of Dad coming downstairs before they went out for an evening. His wardrobe was beautifully tailored, his accessories impeccable. But his selection was something else again: e.g., striped tie with checkered shirt under plaid suit. You knew he was in a room. Mom gave

481

up trying to change him; like all the rest of us she loved him for what he was—a free spirit.

I miss him. Harpo I can see on the "Late Show," along with my crazy uncles. It's Dad that I miss. Every time I laugh, every time I hear music, the vision of him comes back to me. I think what I miss most of all are the sounds of my father. Not just the music from the bay window, but also the sound of his voice. His voice was even softer than Groucho's, although he had the same Upper East Side accent, with the same lyrical, fractured vowels. "Turkey" became "takey," "hamburger" "hambaiger." "Oil" became "erl," but on the other hand, "early" became "aily." All of which made for a slight confusion when this ardent sun worshiper would announce at dinner that he would be "getting up aily tamarra mawning to erl up before going out on the golf cawss."

How did he pronounce his name? It came out "Hah-po."

I would call home on any pretext, just to hear Dad answer the phone. He did not say hello. He said, ever so gently, "Yeaaaaaaah? This is Haaaaah-po." He made you feel, before you spoke, that you were about to impart some glorious secret to him. There was balm in his voice. If something was troubling you, he wiped it out with those four sweet words.

My father's choice of title for his autobiography was *What's the Use Talking?* I can answer that question: There's plenty use talking when the subject is you, Dad. And in conclusion . . .

CPSIA information can be obtained
at www.ICGtesting.com
Printed in the USA
FSHW010920230221
78864FS